1,801
HOME
REMEDIES

1,801
HOME
REMEDIES

—⁓—

Trustworthy Treatments for
Everyday Health
Problems

Reader's
Digest

The Reader's Digest Association, Inc.
Pleasantville, New York/Montreal

Canadian Project Staff

Editor
Pamela Johnson

Designer
Andrée Payette

Copy Editor
Gilles Humbert

Reader's Digest Association (Canada) Ltd.

**Vice President,
Marketing and Books
and Home
Entertainment
Publishing**
Andrea Martin

U.S. Project Staff

Editor
Marianne Wait

Designer
Rich Kershner

Reader's Digest Health Publishing

**Editor in Chief and
Publishing Director**
Neil Wertheimer

Managing Editor
Suzanne G. Beason

Design Director
Michele Laseau

Reader's Digest Association, Inc.

**President,
North America
Global Editor-in-Chief**
Eric W. Schrier

Library and Archives Canada Cataloguing in Publication

1,801 home remedies: trustworthy treatments for everyday health problems / the editors of Reader's Digest; with a foreword by Carolyn Dean. -- 1st Canadian ed.

ISBN 0-88850-777-1

1. Therapeutics--Popular works. 2. Self-care, Health. I. Reader's Digest Association (Canada) II. Title: One thousand eight hundred and one home remedies.

RM122.5.A15 2005   616.02'4   C2004-905962-9

Address any comments about *1,801 Home Remedies* to:
The Reader's Digest Association (Canada) Ltd.
Book Editorial Department
1125 Stanley Street
Montreal, Quebec H3B 5H5

For information on this and other Reader's Digest products, visit our website at **www.rd.ca**

Printed in the United States of America

   3 5 7 9 10 8 6 4

Note to Readers
The information in this book should not be substituted for, or used to alter, any medical treatment or therapy without your doctor's advice. For a specific health problem, consult your physician for guidance.

Contributors

Bookside Press

Editors Edward B. Claflin, E. A. Tremblay
Writers Matthew Hoffman, Eric Metcalf
Researchers Janel Bogert, Elizabeth Shimer

Copy Editors Jeanette Gingold, Judy Yelon
Indexer Ellen Brennan
Illustrators Harry Bates, Inkgraved Illustration;
Cindy Jeftovic

Medical Advisors

Carolyn Dean, M.D., N.D. Consultant, Integrative Medicine,
City Island, New York
Mitchell A. Fleisher, M.D. Clinical Instructor, University of Virginia
Health Sciences Center and the Medical College of Virginia;
Family Physician, Private Practice, Nellysford, Virginia
Larrian Gillespie, M.D. Retired Assistant Clinical Professor
of Urology and Urogynecology, Beverly Hills, California
Chris Kammer, D.D.S. Center for Cosmetic Dentistry,
Madison, Wisconsin
Chris Meletis, N.D. Chief Medical Officer and Director
of Education Affairs, Pearl Clinic Professor of Natural
Pharmacology, National College of Naturopathic Medicine,
Portland, Oregon
Lylas G. Mogk, M.D. Henry Ford Visual Rehabilitation
& Research Center, Grosse Pointe and Livonia, Michigan
Zorba Paster, M.D. Professor of Family Medicine, Dean Medical
Center, University of Wisconsin-Madison
Ricki Pollycove, M.D., M.H.S. Clinical Faculty, University of
California School of Medicine; Private Practice of Gynecology,
San Francisco, California
David B. Posner, M.D. Chief of Gastroenterology,
Mercy Medical Center, Baltimore, Maryland; Assistant Professor
of Medicine, University of Maryland School of Medicine
Adrienne Rencic, M.D., Ph.D. Attending Dermatologist, Mercy
Medical Center, Baltimore, Maryland; Clinical Instructor,
University of Maryland Medical System
Kevin R. Stone, M.D. Orthopedic Surgeon and Founder and
Chairman of The Stone Foundation for Sports Medicine and
Arthritis Research and the Stone Clinic, San Francisco, California
Cathryn Tobin, M.D. Pediatrician, Private Practice, Markham,
Ontario

1,801 Home Remedies

Table of

Part One
Everyday Ailments

❧ SPECIAL FEATURE
Feel-Better
Baths
Page 54

❧ SPECIAL FEATURE
Remedies
from the Sea
Page 76

❧ SPECIAL FEATURE
A Gaggle
of Gargles
Page 108

❧ SPECIAL FEATURE
Healing Soups
from Around
the World
Page 118

❧ SPECIAL FEATURE
Healing
Your Home
Page 208

Contents

SPECIAL FEATURE

Putting the
Pressure On
Page 288

SPECIAL FEATURE

Teatime
Page 338

Part Two
20 Top Household Healers

Foreword

By Carolyn Dean, M.D., N.D.

When I was a young girl growing up in Dartmouth, Nova Scotia, my mother was known locally as "the Queen of Common Sense." A trained nurse, she was renowned throughout the neighborhood for her compassion and down-to-earth advice. And she was much called upon. There were no doctors around, and people tended to fend for themselves. Everybody knew they could come to my mother with their ills. Whenever anyone with a cut or wound would come in, my mum would patch him up. She always knew what to do.

I have my mother's medical genes and also some from my father's mother, who had a nurse's training and was, in addition, a homeopath and an herbalist. When my grandfather moved his family from Boston to the northern part of Newfoundland, Nanna immediately started an herb garden. And she kept vials of homeopathic preparations—which can be stored for decades—safely tucked away in her medicine cabinet. I grew up hearing incredible stories of her curing the most frightening conditions. Poultices were her particular favorites. She used them to remedy just about anything, from tonsillitis to badly infected wounds.

But if I came by my absolute love of home remedies through my family, that passion grew even stronger when I pursued medical training. An important part of medicine, I believe, is helping people take care of themselves. That has become even more evident in recent years. As medical doctors become busier, with many more patients and less time to spend with each one, the responsibility for taking care of our own small health problems falls increasingly on each one of us.

There's a great deal that we can do, as you'll quickly discover as you turn the pages of *1,801 Home Remedies*. This is the kind of practical knowledge that comes in handy all the time. Years ago my nephew Erik was rough-housing, and sure enough, he ended up with a black eye. With some ice and application of homeopathic arnica (for pain, swelling, and bruising), his mother was amazed that the black-and-blue was completely gone by the next morning. Being a kid of ten, Erik was actually annoyed because he wanted to show off his black eye at school. Or take another recent incident, when one of my family members got a 5.7-centimeter splinter in his back. It took a whole week of repeated poultice applications before the splinter came out, but with patience, it finally emerged nicely, without surgical probing and with no sign of infection.

I love the big benefits of using "little" home remedies. Not only do they work, they allow you to take control of your health. They save you money, if you can come up with the simplest, commonsense solution (like ice and arnica for a black eye). And even more important, they can often nip illness in the bud and sometimes prevent the grave consequences of dealing with a health condition that's allowed to get worse.

I am occasionally asked whether home remedies are really a collection of "old wives' tales." Well, some of them are. But, remember, some of those "old wives" were the healers and midwives of the past who held considerable clout in the community and were consulted by everyone. My own mother and grandmother were shining examples for me. It was their training in commonsense healing that inspired me and motivated me to get my degree as a medical doctor and my advanced training in naturopathic medicine.

Today I even tell people that it is their patriotic duty to learn about home remedies. If there is a time when we have to deal with an epidemic or other medical emergency in our community, those who study *1,801 Home Remedies* will be the ones who are able to deal with minor ailments at home and not overburden the health care system. It is up to us to learn these "cures" because doctors today are even less available and busier than ever.

We're at a turning point in medicine. At the same time that doctors are demanding "scientific" medicine, many are relying on research where only one drug is studied at a time, usually on a group of otherwise-healthy individuals. But there are no studies in which people take a handful of prescription medications together, which is unfortunately a much more common scenario for many people. That's just one of the reasons why so many people are looking for simpler alternatives, and why those alternatives are ever more readily available.

I hope that by using *1,801 Home Remedies* you may awaken your "inner healer" as you take charge of your own health and that of your family. The 100-plus health conditions that were selected for this book are absolutely appropriate for you and your family members to treat with home remedies, either by themselves or alongside conventional medical treatment. Much like my own practice, *1,801 Home Remedies* is not just about herbs or supplements—not just homeopathy, nutrition, or over-the-counter products—but a selection from all that we know about healing approaches from many different traditions. And all the tips have you, the reader, in mind. They focus, therefore, on things that are practical, convenient, and ultimately doable.

Carolyn Dean

About This Book

Y ou're about to discover more than 1,000 home remedies you can use whenever you need to treat an everyday health problem, from acne to yeast infection and just about everything in between.

Before you do, turn to Using Home Remedies, where you'll find some interesting background on home remedies as well as advice on using self-treatments safely and effectively. See page 19 for instructions for growing five useful medicinal herbs. And for cautions regarding specific herbs and supplements, turn to our four-page guide starting on page 434.

Part One, Everyday Ailments, is where you'll find home remedies for more than 100 common conditions, which are listed in alphabetical order. What's a home remedy? Mostly, anything you can use at home that doesn't require a doctor's prescription! Many of the healing agents you probably already have on hand, like aspirin (crush the tablets, mix with water and lemon juice, and dab on corns), vinegar (try it for swimmer's ear), and tea bags (hold a wet one against a canker sore for pain relief). Some of them, such as calendula cream, will require a trip to a natural foods store. A few of the remedies, such as the amino acid L-carnitine for angina, require a doctor's prescription, while zinc, for example for acne, should be used under a doctor's supervision because of potential side effects. We've noted these cases.

In Part Two you'll discover 20 Top Household Healers— herbs, foods, and other staples you'll want to have on hand in order to use many of the remedies in this book. Find out what vinegar, yogurt, Epsom salt, and ginger are good for, and discover omega-3 fatty acids, "good" fats found in fish (and supplements) that go beyond protecting your heart to help treat allergies, arthritis, asthma, and even depression.

This book was a labor of love for the people who worked on it. We hope you'll enjoy the book, too, and find lasting value in the treasury of remedies inside.

Using Home Remedies

At the age of 85, Adelia Liercke of Clarence, Iowa, still takes the same cough medicine that her mother and father used—a mixture of honey, onion, and lemon juice. When Betty W. Bishop of Hampton, Florida, gets a boil, she spreads the membrane of a boiled egg across it to "draw out the core"—a trick that her mom taught her. When Carol Bailey of Pointe-Claire, Quebec, detects the beginning of a cold, she mixes up a potent medicine brew using a recipe for "nature's penicillin" that includes lots of fresh cloves of garlic.

Nearly every family has some home remedies that have been passed along from one generation to the next. Their origins are lost in the mists of time. Who was the first grandmother to serve peppermint tea to a sick grandchild? Why did a woodsman decide to crush the leaves of a jewelweed plant and spread it on poison ivy? Who was the first cook to discover that chicken soup can help you recover from the common cold?

Considering how often favorite home remedies have been used to cure everyday ailments and relieve pain, it's a pity we don't know the names of the originators. They deserve Nobel Prizes in Practical Medicine. But maybe there's a better way to honor their contributions. We can *use* the home remedies that they so generously passed along to us.

More Than One Thousand Remedies—Right Here!

Home remedies begin at home—and often that's where the secrets remain.

But with this book, you're opening the doors to thousands of homes, discovering the cornucopia of remedies that have been passed along for hundreds of years.

Some of the remedies came to us by mail. We heard from Irving W. Kaarlela of Houghton, Michigan, who has a great way to cure hiccups. From Mrs. Asoph Haas of Venturia, North Dakota, we discovered a surefire remedy for insect bites. Faye

Edmunds of Hopkinsville, Kentucky, donated her sore-throat cure, while Doreen O'Brien of Vancouver, British Columbia, shared the secret recipe her mother concocted to help her recover from a deep chest cough. Their homegrown methods have been included in the chapters on hiccups, insect stings, sore throat, and colds and flu.

But that was only the beginning. We also uncovered folk cures used by early North American pioneers, acupressure treatments of Chinese doctors, and the healing methods of tribal shamans. We discovered the leading home remedies endorsed by naturopathic doctors and massage therapists, herbalists and homeopathic physicians, specialists in cardiovascular medicine and favorite family doctors. Our search for these remedies carried us through history, from the era of Hippocrates to the battlefields of World War I and the backyard gardens of twenty-first century herbal healers.

Selecting the Best

Though we cast a wide net, our final selection of the best home remedies was a selective process. To be honest, a number of traditional home remedies didn't make the cut because they were just too . . . well . . . strange. The asafetida bag, once a cherished cure for colds, has a smell so noxious that it's remembered with horror by those who used it. Other old remedies are so odd and complex that they aren't worth passing on, except for curiosity's sake. An Appalachian cure for warts, for instance, was to rub a potato on the wart, place the potato in a sack, and leave the sack at a fork in the road.

Of course, any remedy that does no harm might also do some good, especially when administered by someone who has a gentle, healing touch and cares deeply for the patient. But when we cast out the oddest, least-credible, most-complicated, and slightly risky, we were left with the wonderful (and sometimes wondrous) remedies that you'll find in this book—the more than 1,801 that have helped heal millions of people. Each of these remedies was then carefully reviewed by our board of advisors—including physicians, highly qualified specialists, and naturopathic doctors—to ensure that they are safe for you to use as recommended.

Every remedy in this book was carefully reviewed by our board of advisors to ensure that they are safe for you to use as recommended.

All Within Reach

As you read about the home remedies in this book—and start to use them yourself—you'll probably begin to recall tried-and-true healing techniques that come from your own family. But we've all gotten so used to blood tests, X rays, high-potency (and high-cost) prescription drugs, and all the other trappings of modern medicine that we tend to forget, or neglect, our amazing legacy of at-home cures. Time-tested remedies are just as useful today as they ever were. The tricks you learned from your parents and grandparents, like sprinkling meat tenderizer on a bee sting or putting a soothing tea bag on tired eyes, aren't replacements for high-tech treatments, of course. But you can count on them to feel better fast—and, in many cases, to prevent small problems from turning into bigger ones.

There's something almost magical about watching a burn heal when you follow your grandmother's advice and apply a dab of aloe vera gel.

There's something very satisfying about watching a burn heal almost like magic when you follow your grandmother's advice and apply a dab of aloe vera gel. Or when you inhale the scent of lavender and feel anxiety slip away. But nostalgia isn't the reason doctors continue to recommend home treatments. They recommend them because they work.

All those drugs in your medicine cabinet? At least 25 percent of them contain active ingredients that are similar or identical to those found in plants. The active substance in aspirin—one of the world's most popular medications—was originally derived from white willow bark. The decongestant ephedrine is based on chemicals in the ephedra plant. The heart drug digitalis is derived from the foxglove. The cancer drug taxol comes from the Pacific yew tree. In fact, big drug makers continually send teams of scientists to remote locations to scour the countryside for medically promising chemicals.

Finding What Works

In current medical practice, traditional healing techniques are sometimes neglected, but with luck they're never forgotten. Physical therapists use the same hot and cold treatments that were popular among Native North American tribes—treatments that often work better than aspirin, with none of the side effects. Kitchen cuts certainly heal better when you apply a dab of triple antibiotic. But guess what? A slathering of honey does the same thing, and may help the cut heal faster.

Molly Hopkins, a 60-year-old landscape designer in Albuquerque, New Mexico, discovered first-hand that traditional treatments are sometimes superior to their conventional counterparts. "I used to get sinus infections every time I got a cold, and then I had to take antibiotics," she says. Her friend, a family physician, told her to start taking echinacea at the first sign of sniffles. "I haven't had a serious cold since—and no sinus infections at all," she says.

Most of us use traditional cures for minor aches and pains, but doctors at top research institutions now realize that they also work for some of our most serious health threats. Take diabetes. Over two million Canadians need injections or oral drugs to keep blood sugar levels stable. Those who also eat a clove of garlic daily may naturally lower blood sugar and with it their doses of medicine. Depression is another condition that frequently requires medication, yet studies show that the herb St. John's wort may be just as effective as drugs for mild to moderate cases. And because the active ingredient (hypericin) enters the body gradually, it almost never causes the side effects common with prescription drugs, such as sexual dysfunction or low energy.

Many of the most popular at-home cures, such as yogurt for yeast infections or chamomile tea for insomnia, have been used for generations. Others—what you might call "future traditions" that will hopefully be passed along to your children and grandchildren—are being developed all the time.

- Researchers at Cincinnati Children's Hospital Medical Center recently found that duct tape, that all-purpose household fix-it, causes warts to disappear in just a few days.

- Creams laced with the herb arnica help bruises heal faster and with less pain because they contain natural painkilling and anti-inflammatory compounds.

- Zinc improves skin blemishes in about a third of people who take it—and this mighty mineral is just as effective as the drug tetracycline at healing severe acne.

"Why should I wait hours to see a doctor and run to the drugstore for a prescription when I know there are some problems I can treat myself?" asks Deborah Moroz, a special-education teacher in Kanata, Ontario. "You don't have to be a scientist to know that a cup of hot tea will help to thin nasal mucus and relieve the pain and discomfort of sinusitis."

The Commonsense Approach

While the remedies in this book comprise a veritable treasure-trove of health solutions, there's nothing like good judgment when it comes to using any home remedy. Sometimes you need to be on the lookout for signs of more serious problems.

Clara Boxer made the kind of mistake doctors always worry about. A 53-year-old Philadelphia accountant, she'd been suffering from occasional dizziness, usually in the morning when she got out of bed. She read on the Internet that ginger is a good remedy for the "whirls." She stocked up on ginger supplements at her local health-food store and took them for a few weeks. Then one morning she stood up in the bathtub, passed out, and fell and broke her wrist.

She was lucky in a way. The emergency room doctor who treated her took the time to find out why the accident happened in the first place. Ginger is in fact a traditional remedy for vertigo, a type of dizziness often associated with inner-ear disturbances. But Clara didn't have vertigo. What she had was orthostatic hypotension, a sudden drop in blood pressure sometimes caused by too-high doses of blood pressure medicine. Her doctor lowered her dose, and the dizziness went away.

Even though most home remedies are safe, people sometimes take them for the wrong reasons. Or they diagnose themselves when they really need a doctor. Some conditions are easy to recognize and treat at home. You don't need a battery of tests for gums that bleed for a couple of days, or for the occasional upset stomach. But it's not always easy to tell what's minor and what's not.

That's one reason it's important to check with your doctor before taking herbs or other supplements, or at least let your doctor know what you're already taking, especially if you're using other medicines at the same time. It's not uncommon for supplements to alter the effects of over-the-counter or prescription drugs—another good reason to be honest with your doctor about what supplements you take. For example, people who take high-dose vitamin E along with blood-thinning drugs have an increased risk of internal bleeding.

Even if a tea or an herb seems completely innocuous, if you're taking it regularly to treat a health problem—stinging nettle for arthritis, for example, or dandelion to lower blood pressure—let your doctor know. Some herbs aren't as effective as people claim, and you don't want to make a mistake and undertreat a potentially serious problem. Even if a supplement is safe and does what the manufacturer says it does, it won't do a bit of good if you take it for a condition you don't actually have—and you could wind up missing a health problem that's too serious to ignore.

Even though most home remedies are safe, people sometimes take them for the wrong reasons.

Proceeding with Some Cautions

If traditional cures have been used daily for thousands of years, they probably work or people wouldn't use them. But there are always risks—of side effects, interactions with drugs, or simply using the wrong remedy. The home remedies in this book are supported by anecdotal evidence of their effectiveness—and in many cases by scientific studies—and they have been carefully screened for safety by our board of medical advisors. But there are times when you'll want to exercise extra caution, such as:

If you are pregnant. Do not take any herbs, supplements, or over-the-counter (OTC) medications without first consulting your doctor. Many of these can affect the health of the fetus, particularly if they are taken in large doses.

If you are taking prescription medication. Talk to your doctor about possible interactions between your prescribed medication and any herbs, supplements, or over-the-counter drugs recommended in this book. The cautions on pages 434–437 provide some guidelines about drug, herb, and supplement interactions and some additional cautions. But you should also tell your doctor about any other supplements or medications that you take at the same time—particularly if you have a chronic condition such as diabetes or heart disease.

If you know you are allergic to a food or medication. Exercise caution or consult your doctor before you eat or drink any remedy that might contain the allergen.

If you have a serious health condition. Pay special attention to "Should I Call the Doctor?" at the beginning of each chapter. The purpose of these home remedies is to help you deal with everyday ailments and improve your overall health—not to mask serious conditions that require medical treatment.

If you are treating a child or infant. Some herbs, supplements, and home remedies just aren't appropriate for children or babies. Unless a remedy is specifically recommended for children, ask your pediatrician for advice before treating your kids. And choose over-the-counter products designed for children rather than adults (Children's Tylenol, for instance, instead of regular Tylenol).

Herbal Healing

When James A. Duke slipped a disk in his upper back in the early 1990s, he tried all the things his doctor recommended: rest, ultrasound, and stomach-gnawing doses of anti-inflammatory drugs. He didn't stop there. He took licorice to settle his stomach, milk thistle to protect his liver from the aspirin, and echinacea before surgery to protect against infection.

Duke, a former botanist at the U.S. Department of Agriculture, author of *The Green Pharmacy*, and a leading expert on medicinal herbs, is one of millions of people who appreciate the healing powers of nature's plants. In fact, according to the World Health Organization, about 80 percent of the world's population depends on herbs as their primary source of medical care. They're cheaper than drugs, and in many cases, they're just as effective. What's more, they're often safer than drugs.

> About 80 percent of the world's population depends on herbs as their primary source of medical care.

When you're used to snapping open a childproof cap and popping a convenient capsule, dealing with dried herbs can be a bit daunting. It shouldn't be. Nearly all herbs are available in capsule or liquid forms, with dosing instructions printed on the label. You can also buy bulk herbs—leaves, seeds, stems, or whatever part of the plant contains the active ingredients—at many health-food stores and brew them into tasty (or not so tasty!) teas.

Grow Your Own: Fresh Herbs Within Reach

You don't have to have a green thumb to grow medicinal herbs. Most thrive with a minimum of care as long as they're planted in good soil and get adequate amounts of sunshine. Here are a few versatile herbs to start with:

ALOE VERA leaves contain a clear gel that kills bacteria and helps cuts and burns heal more quickly. It's among the easiest herbs to grow because it requires little water and no daily care.

Planting tips: Buy a small plant and transfer it to a window planter filled with potting soil. Keep it warm; aloe vera doesn't like temperatures below about 4°C (40°F). As long as you keep it warm and watered, it will continue to put out new leaves.

How to use: Cut one of the fleshy leaves and squeeze the gel on minor cuts or burns. The gel dries and forms an invisible bandage, keeping bacteria out and moisture in.

CHAMOMILE is among the sweetest-flavored medicinal herbs. It has anti-inflammatory and intestine-soothing chemical compounds, but most people sip chamomile tea to ease anxiety and insomnia.

Planting tips: German chamomile, the most popular form, is an annual. Sow the seeds in the spring after the danger of frost has passed. Scatter the seeds in beds, tamp them down, and keep the soil moist. Chamomile prefers well-drained soil in areas that are partially shaded.

How to use: Snip the stems and hang to dry. Pluck off the dry leaves and store in dark, sealed containers to preserve the medicinal oils.

GARLIC grows in almost any soil, and it's among the most potent herbs in terms of flavor as well as healing. Eating a clove or two daily may help prevent colds, lower cholesterol, inhibit blood clots in the arteries, and reduce the risk of heart disease and stroke.

Planting tips: Break cloves from a head of garlic and plant them in full sun about 5 centimeters deep. Keep the soil slightly moist at first, but don't overwater. During summer, cut back the flower stalk so the plant puts all of its energy into producing fat, rich-tasting cloves. Harvest the bulbs in late summer.

How to use: Peel the cloves and add to recipes—or eat them whole if you like the extra-strong taste. Eat one to two cloves daily during the cold season for infection-fighting protection.

LICORICE ROOT has a deliciously sweet taste that's perfect for teas, especially when you're fighting a cold or cough. It contains a chemical compound, glycyrrhizinic acid, that suppresses coughs and soothes sore throats.

Planting tips: Licorice is grown from root cuttings that contain "eyes." Plant the cuttings vertically about 2.5 centimeters deep in rich, well-drained soil. The plants reach three to seven feet and have beautiful purple flowers. The roots can be harvested in the fall after the first year or two.

How to use: Dig up the roots, split them in half, and store them in a dark, shady place to dry; it takes about six months. Powder the root, add about half a teaspoon to a cup of boiling water, and steep for about 10 minutes.

ROSEMARY belongs in the spice cabinet as well as the medicine chest. It contains chemicals that aid digestion, fight bacteria, and act as a mental stimulant.

Planting tips: You can plant rosemary from seed, but cuttings are more likely to thrive. Place them in full sun in sandy soil, with about one-third of the twig showing.

How to use: Strip the leaves and store them in a dark, shady place until dry, then use to make a tasty tea.

You can easily grow your own herbs in your garden or in windowsill pots. The usual approach is to snip the stems, rinse the herbs with water to remove any dirt, then hang them upside down to dry. When the leaves feel brittle but aren't so dry that they crumble, pluck them and store them in a dark container. Packing jars to the lid keeps out oxygen and helps maintain freshness. If you're using herbs grown for their flowers, harvest the flowers just after the plant blooms.

Most herbal teas call for adding one rounded teaspoon of dried herb (or a tablespoon of fresh) to a cup of boiling water. Steep for about 10 minutes, let cool, then drink. (Teas made from bark, seeds, or roots need to steep longer.) Start with small amounts of tea—say, one to three cups daily. Only use larger amounts under the supervision of a professional herbalist or an herb-friendly doctor.

Other Supplements

"Supplements" used to mean garden-variety vitamins and minerals that people took to give their diets a boost. Today, pharmacy shelves practically sag under the weight of vitamin potions, natural hormones, and antioxidants, to name just a few.

Even tradition-bound doctors have come to realize that some supplements have earned their place alongside conventional drugs.

For a long time, doctors pooh-poohed the sometimes extravagant claims of supplement manufacturers. To be sure, there are a lot of questionable products, with claims ranging from instant weight loss to overnight improvements in virility. On the other hand, even tradition-bound doctors have come to realize that some supplements have earned their place alongside conventional drugs.

Glucosamine is a good example. It was initially dismissed by the medical community as snake-oil treatment, but studies in the last ten years have shown that it does in fact help the body repair damaged cartilage. Rheumatologists and orthopedists now routinely recommend it to people who need relief from arthritic joints. Maria Garcia, a Santa Fe homemaker, takes it every morning because it keeps her shoulders mobile and pain-free. Just to see what happened, she quit taking glucosamine for a few weeks—and her pain came right back.

Lycopene is another supplement that's received a lot of

scientific attention. An antioxidant found in tomatoes and sold in supplement form, it helps lower a man's risk of prostate cancer. Coenzyme Q_{10}, a chemical naturally produced by the body, improves the heart's pumping ability in people with congestive heart failure. Fish-oil capsules may lower levels of cholesterol along with inflammatory chemicals that increase the risk of heart attack. The list goes on and on.

Buying and Using Herbs and Supplements

Some manufacturers of vitamin and mineral supplements receive Drug Identification Numbers (DINs) for their products. Largely, the presence of a DIN number means that Health Canada has approved the product for sale based upon extensive reviews of effectiveness and safety and the manufacturer is restricted in the types of claims they can make for products. But the reality is that often not all health products are as carefully regulated as they should be.

Even if a herb or other supplement has been proven to be safe and effective, there's no guarantee that the particular product you're buying contains the active ingredients in the right amounts. Look to the following advice to help you choose a quality product.

Buy reputable brands. When independent laboratories analyze the contents of supplement bottles, they occasionally find—well, nothing very useful. Supplements may contain little or even none of the advertised active ingredient. And the amounts of those ingredients can vary unpredictably from pill to pill. How can you be sure the brand you're buying is a good one? One place to start is consumerlab.com. There you'll find the results of independent tests on many products. Or ask your doctor or pharmacist for their recommendations. Or call the manufacturer to find out how long the company has been in business and how the supplement's potency is assured.

Choose standardized supplements. Whenever possible, buy supplements with the word "standardized" on the label. This indicates that each pill or capsule contains a specified amount of the active ingredient.

Look for "DIN." This stands for Drug Identification Number (DIN). In the case of vitamins and minerals, the presence of a DIN means that the product has undergone safety testing, but with traditional herbal medicines, a DIN only means that there is reliable historical evidence of safety and efficacy. If a label doesn't say "DIN," it may be because the manufacturer chose not to supply the necessary evidence required. But if you have the choice between a product that's labeled DIN and one that isn't, choose the one that is.

Aromatherapy: The Scents of Healing

As you stroll through an herb garden, it's hard to resist the temptation to pluck a few leaves, crush them between your fingers, and enjoy the rich, pleasant fragrance. We now know those scents are not only pleasant but often therapeutic. Captured in essential oils, the fragrances pass directly to nerve centers of our brain, where they produce a wide range of responses. Essential oils can help relieve anxiety and depression, tame our physical reactions to stress, induce sleep, and enhance energy. Research shows that the scents of certain herbs—such as lavender, bergamot, marjoram, and sandalwood—actually alter brain waves, helping to induce relaxation and sleep.

Essential oils can help relieve anxiety and depression, banish stress, induce sleep, and enhance energy.

Today we can get these benefits from commercially prepared, highly concentrated essential oils. A plant may contain as little as one percent fragrant oil, but when that oil is extracted and distilled, the scent is intense. To make 30 grams of Bulgarian rose oil, for example, requires 270 kilograms of rose petals. One drop of herbal oil holds the equivalent of two cups of tea.

You can enjoy the healing benefits of essential oils in several different ways—inhaling the fragrance, soaking in water that contains an oil, or massaging it onto your skin. To inhale the fragrance, just put a drop or two of essential oil on a handkerchief or several drops on a lightbulb or lightbulb ring. Or, if you want to be surrounded by the scent, you can purchase a vaporizer or diffuser and follow the directions.

When you're using an oil for bathing or massage, you need to dilute it with a "carrier" oil. To create a massage oil, add 8 to 12 drops of essential oil to 8 teaspoons of a cold-pressed plant oil such as sweet-almond, grape-seed, or sunflower oil. For bathing, the usual mix is 10 to 30 drops of essential oil in 20 teaspoons of an unscented white lotion. Simply add this mix to the bathwater.

Because essential oils are so highly concentrated, they should not be taken internally. Some people have an allergic reaction to oils, so you'll want to take some care when trying out a new oil. Also, since essential oils can pass through the skin into the bloodstream, they should not be used by pregnant women. Talk to a qualified practitioner before applying essential oil if you have sensitive skin, epilepsy, high blood pressure, or if you've recently had an operation.

To make sure you purchase high-quality essential oils and store them properly, you may want to get some advice from an aromatherapist. Many of these oils can be stored for years without losing their fragrance, though some citrus oils—like orange and lemon—need to be refrigerated. Store them in dark bottles, tightly sealed, preferably in a cool place and always away from sunlight.

What Is Homeopathy?

If you haven't encountered homeopathy before, you might be wary of the strange little bottles marked with "C's" and "X's" on the shelves of many health-food stores. But there's no reason to fear these remedies. The homeopathic mixtures recommended in this book are extremely safe, and many of them have won widespread respect as healing agents—even if it's impossible to explain why they work.

Imagine taking a single drop of any drug—say, a liquid decongestant. Dilute that drop with 10 drops of water. Shake the mixture well, take out a single drop, and dilute it with another 10 drops of water. Repeat the process a few times, and what's left? According to the laws of science, not much. But according to homeopathy, the highly diluted mixture is among the most powerful drugs you can take.

You can see why homeopathy, a style of medicine developed by a German physician more than 200 years ago, hasn't won a lot of support in the mainstream medical community. But the experience of thousands of Canadians—and a handful of scientific studies—suggest there's something to it.

Here are the basics. Working from a list of more than 2,000 substances, homeopaths give sick patients a substance that in large doses would mimic the symptoms caused by their disease—but in very small amounts, theoretically relieves the symptoms. Most of the remedies used in homeopathy come from herbs or minerals. For example, St. John's wort for depression, comfrey for wounds or bruises, and eyebright for tired, burning eyes. But many are diluted with so much water that they contain little or even none of the active ingredient.

An analysis of 107 scientific studies of homeopathic medicines found that 77 percent of them showed positive effects.

Most experts say that homeopathy violates a basic principle of pharmaceutical science: The smaller the dose, the *smaller* the effects. Yet researchers who study homeopathy have come up with some intriguing results. A study of 478 flu patients, for example, found that 17 percent of those treated with homeopathy improved, compared to just 10 percent of those taking placebos. The prestigious *British Medical Journal*, in an analysis of 107 scientific studies of homeopathic medicines, found that 77 percent of them showed positive effects.

It's been suggested that the process of diluting and shaking the solutions somehow "potentizes" the remaining water and changes its chemical properties. But no one really knows how—or whether—homeopathy actually works. Since the doses of active ingredients are so small, however, there's no harm in trying it. That's what Gail Robinson of Kansas City, Missouri, thought when she took homeopathic doses of St. John's wort for depression. "I felt better than I had in years," she says.

You can buy homeopathic remedies in health-food stores, but you'll still want to work with an experienced homeopath. Different remedies are used for each symptom you're experiencing—and the remedies as well as the doses may change depending on your mental and emotional state at the time.

The strength of homeopathic medicines might be confusing at first. You'll usually see them listed as X or C on the label. A 1X remedy has been diluted one time, using one part of the active ingredient in 10 parts water. A 2X solution contains one part of the active ingredient in 100 parts water, and a 3X solution contains one part of the active ingredient in 1,000 parts water. The C solutions are even more dilute; they may only contain a trace amount of the original active ingredient.

Homeopathy isn't a substitute for regular medical care. Most homeopaths spend at least an hour with new patients. They take a complete health history, review your symptoms, and decide whether or not homeopathy is appropriate for you—and whether you need to see a conventional doctor.

Mind-Body Medicine

For many of the health conditions in this book, you'll find a number of remedies that involve meditation, progressive relaxation, yoga, or tai chi. Whatever form they take, relaxation and meditation techniques have proved their power. In recent years, the success of mind-body healing has been borne out by some remarkable evidence.

One of the most well-studied practices is transcendental meditation, or TM. In exploring the benefits of TM, Harvard researcher Herbert Benson, M.D., measured the physical responses of students who would sit quietly with their eyes closed and repeat a word or phrase (called a mantra) over and over again. The twenty-minute "exercises" were done once or twice a day. Dr. Benson discovered that the profound calm induced by TM could lower blood pressure as well as slow heart rate and breathing. Benson termed this the *relaxation response*. Many of the stress-relief benefits of meditation also help increase immunity and combat problems such as anxiety and depression.

Since all kinds of meditation and relaxation techniques can be done at home at any time and with minimal preparation, they are recommended for many health conditions, ranging from anxiety and high blood pressure to psoriasis and menstrual problems.

If you have no experience with meditation, start with a simple twenty-minute exercise that will give you some practice. Just sit in a comfortable, upright position, with your back straight, your head upright, and your body relaxed. With your eyes closed, concentrate completely on your breathing. Take deep, steady breaths, feeling the rise and fall of your abdomen, not your chest. Focus on a word or sound, such as "peace" or "om," and repeat it over and over again. Anytime your attention wanders, bring it back to your word or sound and your breathing again. After about twenty minutes, stop, open your eyes, and stretch. Go slowly at first as you stand up and begin to move around again.

If you find that you have difficulty meditating, you might want to get further guidance from an instructor who practices TM, yoga, or tai chi. Many classes are offered at health clubs, community centers, or adult-education centers.

You don't necessarily have to practice meditation or deep breathing to elicit the relaxation response. Many religions include practices of regular worship or reflection that can provide similar benefits, Dr. Benson has pointed out. Follow-up research has shown that daily prayer, for example, can help relieve various health problems and even help prolong life.

Teaming Up with Professionals

Even though North Americans see non-M.D. health professionals more often than we see primary care physicians and spend billions of dollars a year on herbs and supplements, we obviously haven't given up on conventional medicine. Nor are we interested in substituting one type of medicine for another. What most of us want is the best of both worlds—the cutting-edge tools of modern medicine combined with the natural, at-home treatments that earlier generations depend on.

This approach, known as complementary medicine, makes good sense. If you have heart disease or diabetes, for example, you'll obviously want the most advanced care you can get. Yet there's so much you can do yourself at the same time—not only to relieve symptoms and feel better, but also to give nature a hand and help your body reverse the condition or recover more quickly.

Don't hesitate to talk to your doctor about the remedies you use at home. You may even discover that your doctor has his or her own favorites, like flushing away ear pain with hydrogen peroxide, massaging away a headache, or soothing a rash with an oatmeal bath. After all, conventional medicine and at-home remedies aren't the adversaries they're sometimes made out to be. Each has strengths and weaknesses—and both work best when they're used hand in hand.

If you're especially interested in herbs, acupuncture, and other "natural" healing methods, consider seeing a naturopathic doctor (N.D.). These doctors specialize in treating health problems using a wide range of therapies.

The Remedies: A Final Word

This book contains a huge number of remedies from a wide variety of sources, including traditional folk remedies. Many of the traditional "recipes" we found for teas, elixirs, and tonics called for specific measurements. A grandmother may have specified, for instance, 2 teaspoons of honey, 24 cloves of garlic, or 3 handfuls of pokeberry root. But in many cases the exact amounts aren't critical to the success of the remedy. So the quantities that you find in this book may differ slightly from those in home remedies that you have heard about from your own family.

For each "recipe," however, we've included the ingredients that are most likely to provide some direct health benefits, while omitting those that are ineffective or might cause problems.

Whenever possible, we recommend ingredients available from common sources. In some cases, the ingredients in "regional" recipes have been excluded. Health cures used in India and Pakistan, for example, include herbs and spices such as Indian pennywort, butterfly pea, cardamom, cinnamon, cyperus, and turmeric. In this book, we have tried to include the ones that can be found in grocery stores. If you can't find a remedy in the grocery store, check your local health-food store, pharmacy, or medical supply store. If you still have a hard time finding a product, you may be able to order it online, so try searching the Internet.

Of course, many of the remedies in this book don't require any special supplies at all—just the right food, exercise, or hands-on healing. Temporary relief, or even a cure, may be as near as your kitchen shelf or medicine cabinet.

If one remedy doesn't work for you, try another. If it does work, be sure to tell a loved one or friend so that they might one day benefit from it too. Happy healing!

> Complementary medicine is what most of us are looking for. It's the best of both worlds—the cutting-edge advances of modern medicine combined with natural, at-home treatments.

1,801 Home Remedies

Part

One
Everyday Ailments

When you itch, ache, or sting, when you're coughing, sneezing, swelling, or otherwise suffering, it's **deeply comforting** to know that there are thousands of **effective remedies** that can help. And you don't need a doctor's prescription for any of them. Just stock your cabinets with a few **healing essentials** (see The Top 20 Household Healers, page 384), then raid your **refrigerator**, plunder your **pantry**, harvest your **garden**, and rob your **garage** to find what else you need. Some of the remedies, like simple acupressure techniques, are literally **at your fingertips**. Something ailing you? Find out how to **soothe** it with oatmeal, **pamper** it with peppermint, **banish** it with baking soda, or **tame** it with tea bags. From bad breath to bug bites, head lice to heartburn, shingles to splinters, here are treatments for more than a **hundred health complaints**.

Acne

If scientists can decipher the human genome, you'd think they could find a way to eradicate acne. No such luck. It's up to you to deal with the outbreaks that can damage your pride of appearance long after teenage angst is past. When a pimple rears its ugly black, white, or red head, over-the-counter products can help. But so can simple remedies from Mother Nature's medicine chest.

What's **wrong**

Your skin is producing too much sebum—the thick, oily substance that acts as a natural lubricant—and the excess is blocking your pores. There are two kinds of acne. The most common form, acne vulgaris, shows up on your face, chest, shoulders, or back as blackheads, whiteheads, or red blemishes. Cystic acne appears as painful cysts or firm, painless lumps. Fluctuating hormones caused by puberty, menstruation, pregnancy, perimenopause, or birth-control pills often increase the production of sebum, which can trigger an outbreak of either type. Other culprits include emotional stress, clothing that rubs against the skin, and some drugs, such as steroids. Genetics may also play a role.

Zap Zits Now

➤ The first avenue of assault is an over-the-counter cream or gel formulated with **benzoyl peroxide**. It works by mildly irritating the skin, which encourages dying skin cells to flake off. This helps reopen clogged pores. Benzoyl peroxide also kills the bacteria that infect clogged pores.

➤ **Alpha-hydroxy acids** (AHAs), such as glycolic acid, slough off the outermost layer of skin, which helps keep pores clear and unclogged. Opt for a cream, lotion, or gel that contains 8% glycolic acid.

➤ At the first hint of a pimple, wrap an **ice cube** in a piece of plastic wrap and hold it to the area at least twice a day—every hour, if you can, but for no longer than five minutes each time. The cold will reduce the redness and ease the inflammation.

➤ Pop an **aspirin** or two. Taking one or two 325-milligram tablets four times a day can help calm an acne outbreak by reducing inflammation. (Check with your doctor before taking aspirin regularly.)

Try Alternative Acne Treatments

➤ Three times a day, dab a drop of **tea-tree oil** on blemishes to discourage infection and speed healing. Research has found that 5% tea-tree oil is as effective against acne as a 5% benzoyl peroxide solution.

➤ For acne that flares at that time of the month, drink one to two cups of **chasteberry tea** a day. Some studies show that this herb helps regulate female hormones. Give the herb two or three months to work. And don't drink copious amounts of the tea to hasten the results—it may make your skin look worse.

- Dab **vinegar** or **lemon juice** on pimples. All vinegars contain acids that can help flush out pores—so does lemon juice.
- An old folk remedy for healing pimples is to use a mixture of **spice and honey** on them. Combine 1 teaspoon powdered nutmeg and 1 teaspoon honey, and apply it to the pimple. Leave on for 20 minutes, then wash off. There's no proof that this helps, but honey does have antiseptic properties.
- Apply **aloe vera.** One study found that 90 percent of skin sores were completely healed with aloe vera within five days.
- Think **zinc.** People with acne tend to have lower than normal zinc levels. Zinc supplements produce visible improvement in about a third of people who take them. You'll need high doses, though—between 200 and 600 milligrams daily—so take it only under your doctor's supervision.

Should I call **the doctor?**

Getting a pimple now and then is no big deal. But a visit to a dermatologist is in order if your blemishes don't respond to over-the-counter treatments within three months or your skin becomes severely inflamed, with painful, fluid-filled lumps and a reddish or purplish cast. You'll want a doctor to take a look at your skin if it's always red and flushed, even if acne isn't present; you may have the beginnings of rosacea, a skin condition characterized by persistent redness, pimples, and enlarged blood vessels.

The Power of Prevention

- If you keep skin free of dirt and excess oil—the thinking goes—perhaps your pores will never get clogged. But over-cleansing can cause acne by making your sebaceous glands produce more oil. **Forgo granulated cleansers.** And **avoid washcloths**; they are abrasive and can accumulate bacteria if you reuse them. Instead, use a disposable cleansing cloth.
- Make a skin-cleansing solution to help clear up blackheads. Add one teaspoon of **Epsom salt** and three drops of **iodine** to one-half cup of water and bring to a boil. Let cool. Dip in a clean cotton pad and use it to clean the pores.
- Men: **Rinse your razor** in alcohol after you use it so any bacteria it harbors won't transfer itself to your face.

To Squeeze or Not to Squeeze

If you absolutely, positively must squeeze your blemishes, here's the dermatologist-approved method—and it's only valid for whiteheads. Clean the area well. Light a match and hold the tip of a needle in the flame for three seconds. Then gently nick the surface of the pimple. Use a cotton swab to drain it, then clean it with hydrogen peroxide, if you wish. But don't squeeze or pick—you'll make it worse. To "squeeze" a blackhead, use a blackhead extractor, available in drugstores. Soften the blemish with a hot-water compress for 10 minutes before you use it, and wash your hands beforehand to reduce the chances of infection.

Age Spots

Let them count your birthday candles, not your age spots! The best way to block the spots—and skin cancer too—is by slathering on the sunscreen. But if past lapses have shown up on your skin, shop for an over-the-counter fade cream, or raid your kitchen for a simple spot remover. Keep in mind that it may take weeks or months to see improvement. And from this day forward, vow never to leave the house without proper protection.

What's **wrong**

Despite their name, these flat or rounded brown spots that dot the backs of your hands or face aren't caused by age. They're simply areas of excess pigment, which result from years of unprotected sun exposure. Because it takes decades to see the sun damage, many people won't notice the splotches until later in life, but people who have had significant sun exposure can develop them in their 20s and 30s. Some drugs can make you more vulnerable to sun damage and related age spots, including tetracycline, diuretics (water pills), and drugs for diabetes and blood pressure.

Lighten Up

~ A fade cream called **Porcelana** contains a 2% solution of the bleaching agent hydroquinone. (Darker spots may need a 3% solution, but for that you will need a prescription from a dermatologist.) Before you use Porcelana, read the package directions.

~ Dab the juice of a fresh **lemon** on the spots at least twice a day. Lemon juice is mildly acidic, and may be strong enough to slough off the skin's outer layer and remove or lighten age spots.

~ Blend **honey and yogurt** to create a natural bleach that can lighten age spots. Mix 1 teaspoon of plain yogurt and 1 teaspoon of honey. Apply, let dry for 30 minutes, then rinse. Do this once a day.

~ Spread your spots with **aloe vera gel**, straight from the leaves of a living plant, if possible. The plant contains chemicals that slough away dead cells and encourages the growth of new, healthy ones. Apply the gel once or twice a day.

~ Try **buttermilk**. An old folk remedy for age spots, it contains lactic acid, which gently exfoliates sun-damaged skin and pigmented areas.

Go Undercover

~ Camouflage age spots with a cosmetic concealer like **Dermablend**, a heavy foundation sold at major department stores. Ask a salesperson to help you pick the right shade for your skin and show you how to apply it.

The Power of Prevention

🐾 **Avoid the sun** as much as possible during peak hours— 10 A.M. to 4 P.M. during summer, and 10 A.M. to 2 P.M. in the winter.

🐾 Every day, 30 minutes before you set foot outside, slather your skin—including your face and the backs of your hands— with **sunscreen**. Make sure it has a sun protection factor (SPF) of at least 15. The most effective sunscreens for guarding against age spots contain zinc oxide or titanium dioxide. If you will be outdoors for long periods of time, reapply every two hours.

🐾 After you've been out in the sun, slather on some **vitamin E** oil. An antioxidant, vitamin E may help prevent age spots by neutralizing skin-damaging free radical molecules. Because vitamin E produces free radicals when it's exposed to sunlight, smooth it on only *after* sun exposure.

Should I call
the doctor?

Age spots, which usually look like dark, smooth freckles, are generally harmless. However, if a spot starts to tingle, itch, change size or color, or bleed, it's time to call the doctor. Some skin cancers, like melanoma, can look like age spots. If home remedies don't work on your age spots, your dermatologist can most likely get rid of them through laser treatment or by applying liquid nitrogen.

Allergies

Itchy, scratchy, sneezy—they might sound like three of the Seven Dwarfs, but in fact they're allergy symptoms that can leave you, well, grumpy. Reach for an allergy pill if you wish—take it *before* an allergy attack sets in for better results—or try one of the natural antihistamines listed below. You'll also want to wage war on pollen, mites, dander, and other microscopic menaces that send your immune system into overdrive.

What's **wrong**

Allergies? Your symptoms are signs that your immune system is on a rampage, reacting to normally harmless substances like pollen, ragweed, dust, pet dander, or mold. Usually, the immune system ignores these "triggers" and concentrates on protecting you from real threats, such as viruses or bacteria. But when you have allergies, your immune system can't tell certain benign substances from dangerous ones. Triggers can include substances you eat (such as wheat and peanuts), absorb through the skin (such as poison ivy or insect venom), inhale (such as mold or dander), or receive by injection (such as a shot of penicillin).

Nature's Antihistamines

🌿 **Nettle** contains a substance that works as a natural antihistamine. In fact, the famous naturopathic doctor Andrew Weil reportedly takes it for his allergies. You'll find capsules of the freeze-dried leaf in health-food stores. Take 500 milligrams three times a day.

🌿 **Ginkgo biloba** has become renowned for its memory-boosting properties, but it can also be an effective allergy fighter. Gingko contains substances called ginkgolides, which can stop certain allergy-triggering chemicals (platelet activating factor, or PAF) in their tracks. Take 60 to 240 milligrams a day.

🌿 **Quercetin**, the pigment that gives grapes their purple hue and puts the green in green tea, inhibits the release of histamine. Take one 500-milligram capsule twice a day. (*Off-limits*... if you're already taking nettle, which contains quercetin.)

Try Something Fishy

🌿 **Omega-3 fatty acids** help counter inflammatory responses in the body, such as those triggered by allergies. Salmon and mackerel are good sources of these fats. If you prefer the idea of fish-oil capsules, try taking 3,000 milligrams a day.

🌿 **Flaxseeds** are another excellent source of omega-3 fatty acids. Take one tablespoon of flaxseed oil a day. You can add it to a glass of juice or blend it into a smoothie, but avoid heating it.

Use a Simple Soother

🌿 To soothe red, itchy, swollen eyes, dampen a washcloth with **cool water** and place it over your eyes. Repeat as often as necessary.

🌿 **Saline nasal sprays** are time-tested mucus-busters and can also help to keep your nasal passages moisturized. However, a recent study shows that some commercially made sprays contain a preservative that can actually damage the cells of your sinuses, so it may be safer to make your own. Dissolve a half-teaspoon salt in one cup of warm water. Load a bulb syringe, lean over the sink, and spritz the saline into your nose.

Repel Pollen Attacks

🌿 **Stay indoors** with the windows closed and the air conditioner turned on to filter out pollen, especially in the early evening, when pollen counts hit their peak.

🌿 **Take shelter** inside before a **thunderstorm**—and up to three hours afterward. Storms are preceded by high humidity, which makes pollen grains swell, burst, and release their irritating starch.

🌿 When you have to go out, wear **wraparound sunglasses** to keep the pollen away from your eyes. And if you don't mind resembling Michael Jackson, a face mask works well too.

🌿 You can also protect yourself outdoors with a "pollen trap." Dab a little **petroleum jelly** under your nose—trap spores that are wafting around before they land in your nostrils.

🌿 When you're in a car, keep the **windows closed**. Turn on the air conditioner to filter out the pollen, and choose the "recirculate" setting so you don't pull in pollinated air.

🌿 **Wash your hair** prior to going to bed so you don't transmit a headful of dust and pollen to your pillow.

Should I call **the doctor?**

Allergic symptoms run the gamut from the merely miserable to the downright dangerous. If drugstore remedies don't do the trick or no longer work, or you can't figure out what you're allergic to, it's time to call the doctor. Wheezing or difficulty breathing requires an immediate call: It can be a sign of an asthma attack or other serious allergic reaction. Ditto if you develop hives or welts. Hives may signal the onset of a potentially fatal allergic reaction—for example, to a bee sting.

Love to Garden? Don't Throw In the Trowel

Most ornamental flowering plants don't release pollen—they rely on insects to pollinate them. Generally speaking, the plants that release the most pollen are trees, grasses, and ragweed. So put on your gardening gloves, and continue to prune those prizewinning roses. Daisies and chrysanthemums are fine too.

Skip it!

Though air purifiers may seem like a good idea, research has shown that most of them have little effect on allergens. Small machines simply don't have enough power to rid the air of dust and pollen. Electrostatic precipitators, which give particles an electrical charge and use polarized metal plates to pull them out of the air, can actually aggravate allergy symptoms by polluting the indoor air with ozone. There is one type of purifier that is effective, however: those that use HEPA filters.

Solve a Mighty Problem

🌿 **Dust mites**, nasty little flesh-eating monsters too small to be seen by the naked eye, live in your carpets, curtains, and bedding. Their feces can be a significant cause of allergies. To starve mites of the dust they eat—which is made of your skin—**cover your mattress, box spring, and pillows** with covers made specifically to repel allergens. These covers are sold in drugstores and department stores.

🌿 **Vacuum your carpets** regularly. If you can afford one, purchase a vacuum cleaner that uses a double bag and a HEPA (high-efficiency particulate-arresting) filter. These machines can filter out allergens that are microscopic in size. If you have attractive flooring underneath your carpets, think about getting rid of the carpets altogether.

🌿 **Change your sheets** once a week and wash them in very hot water to kill the mites.

🌿 **Clear away clutter**, which can house mites.

🌿 If you don't have **a dehumidifier**, it's a good idea to get one. Keeping the air in your home dry will significantly reduce the population of dust mites, which perish at humidity levels below 45 percent.

Reduce Reactions to Rover and Fluffy

🌿 **Keep your pet out of the bedroom.** Animals' dander, hair, and saliva—all of which linger even when the animal leaves the room—can contribute to allergic reactions.

🌿 Some dogs are perfectly happy in the traditional outdoor

A Kiss Is Just a Kiss?

Avoiding known food or drug allergens would seem to be easy, but sometimes you can be exposed in not-so-obvious ways. A recent report from the Mayo Clinic describes a woman who had a life-threatening allergic reaction to shellfish when she kissed her boyfriend. He had eaten a few shrimp with dinner an hour before he kissed her good night. Almost immediately, her lips swelled, her throat began to close, she started wheezing, hives appeared, her stomach cramped, and her blood pressure plummeted. Fortunately, she survived. The lesson, however, is clear: If your love partner is allergic to some food, you'll have to give it up as well. No one knows whether simply brushing your teeth or rinsing your mouth out would do much good, so it's better not to take the chance at all.

doghouse. If you're allergic to yours, that **outdoor lodging** might be the best solution for both of you.

➤ **Give your pet a bath once a week.** Bathing can remove up to 85 percent of pet dander. You can use a pet shampoo, grooming solution, or even plain water.

Clear the Air

➤ The single best thing you can do to keep allergens out of the air is **air-condition** your house. It keeps humidity low, which discourages mold and dust mites, and it filters the air while it cools it. Keep all windows closed when you're running the AC. And be sure to clean the filters at least once a month.

➤ If you can afford to **install an air filter**, it can bring dramatic relief from allergies to mold, pollen, and pet dander. HEPA filters are best. When you use a HEPA filter in your bedroom, keep the door closed, so it will effectively filter just the air in that room.

➤ Studies show that vigorous household cleaning significantly reduces dust, mold, dander, and other common allergens. So **do a serious cleaning job** in your home twice a year—once in the spring, and again in the fall. Wash—with bleach—every scrubbable surface, from the insides of cupboards to the baseboards. Clean furniture with a damp cloth. If your allergies are bad, you may want to hire someone to do the cleaning.

➤ A basement is prime breeding ground for molds, mildew, and dust mites, especially if it gets wet after rainstorms. In any damp basement, **run a dehumidifier** all the time.

➤ A clothes dryer can spew out all kinds of fine particles of lint and dust. **Make sure the dryer hose is completely sealed,** so that you don't have those allergy-inducers floating through the house.

Anal Itching

Just the words "anal itching" are enough to make you stir in your seat. Fortunately, the solutions are simple—creams and soaks to ease the irritation, plus one rather surprising compress and some new ways to cleanse and wipe. Take note of what you eat too. Though it's just passing through, food can influence how pretty you're sitting a few hours later.

What's wrong

This indelicate problem has a wide variety of causes. Itching can start because of disregard for personal hygiene—or because you're overzealous about it. But it can also arise from food sensitivities, allergic reactions to soaps or toilet paper, sweating caused by tight clothing or pantyhose, or hemorrhoids. Fungal infections may also be a cause, particularly among people with diabetes. If you have children in the house, don't discount the notion that they—and you—may have picked up a case of pinworms, especially if the itch worsens at night.

Try Instant Itch Busters

‹ If anal fissures (a tear or cut in the skin lining the anus) or hemorrhoids are the problem, pick up a tube of **hydrocortisone cream.** It can stop the swelling—the main source of discomfort—as well as the itching. (*Off-limits*... petroleum-based products like Vaseline on the anal area. Petroleum holds in moisture, which can encourage the growth of fungus or bacteria.)

‹ **Benzocaine cream,** a local anesthetic that numbs the skin, also works for anal itching, as do many other over-the-counter anti-itch medications.

‹ In the bathtub, dissolve 3 or 4 tablespoons of **baking soda** in 8 centimeters of warm water. Have a seat for about 15 minutes. Baking soda can help soothe skin irritation.

‹ **Witch hazel** is a skin cleanser and can remove irritants that cause an itchy bottom. More important, its astringent action can help reduce swelling responsible for the itching. Soak a cotton pad, and apply it to the irritated area. This may sting for a few minutes after application.

‹ Use a warm **tea bag** as an astringent compress to ease itching and swelling. Just boil the tea bag as you would to make a cup of tea to release the chemicals in the leaves, let it cool down to a comfortable temperature, then hold it against the problem area for several minutes.

The Power of Prevention

‹ **Wipe more than once** to remove all traces of stool. To avoid irritating your skin, choose the softest, least scratchy

When the Itch Turns to Pain...

...you may have anal fissures, which are tears in the delicate lining of the anal canal. Fissures are usually caused by a rock-hard stool that rips and tears at the anal canal. To help prevent new fissures, aim to get at least 30 grams of fiber a day from fruits, vegetables, beans, and whole grains. Also, drink six to eight glasses of water each day. Water bulks up and softens the stool. If your fissures don't clear up within 4 to 8 weeks or if there's any bleeding, call your doctor.

toilet paper (white, unscented) you can afford. Wet it beforehand if that helps, and dry the area afterward.

☙ If overzealous wiping has irritated your bottom, toss the toilet paper and rely instead on a baby's best friend: **moisturizing wipes.**

☙ Keep your nether regions dry and sweat-free. Use a **hair dryer** set on low for 30 seconds to dry your bottom. Then sprinkle the area generously with **baby powder** or **cornstarch**. If you use baby powder, look for a brand that doesn't contain perfume, which causes skin irritation in some people.

☙ Choose **roomy cotton underwear,** which will keep your rectal area drier than synthetic fabrics, and avoid tightfitting pantyhose.

☙ **Pass up acidic foods,** like citrus fruits. And stay away from **spicy foods,** like hot sauce and hot peppers. Both can set you to scratching.

☙ The oils in coffee beans are irritants too. Limit yourself to one or two small cups of **coffee** a day, or forgo the java altogether, and see if the itch subsides.

☙ Use **fragrance-free** laundry detergent, fabric softeners, and soaps. Avoid fragranced bath products too.

Should I call **the doctor?**

If you notice blood or discharge, or feel a lump, your doctor will want to know. Call, too, if you have diabetes or take prescription steroids, or if your children are also complaining that their rectums itch.

Angina

As soon as you describe an angina episode to the doctor, he or she is likely to hand you a prescription for a very convenient medication, nitroglycerin. Far from causing an explosion, when used as directed, the pills will help you deal with the onset of attacks, easing the pain and tightness in your chest by getting more blood and oxygen to the heart. As with traveler's cheques, you should never leave home without them. But there are plenty of other things you can do to deal with these episodes and even prevent them from happening.

What's wrong

That crushing, squeezing chest pain is telling you—loudly—that your heart isn't getting enough oxygen-rich blood. Most likely, that's because a buildup of a fatty substance called plaque is blocking the arteries that serve the heart. Angina pain often begins below the breastbone and radiates to the shoulder, arm, or jaw. It may be accompanied by shortness of breath, lightheadedness, irregular heartbeat, and anxiety.

Immediate Measures

 If you're standing, walking around, or exercising when an attack occurs, **sit down and rest** for a few minutes.

 If you're lying down or resting when the telltale pressure presents itself, **change your body position** by sitting or standing up. That takes pressure off the nerve in your heart that is signaling pain. Angina that occurs at rest is a sign that you may be at much higher risk for a heart attack, so call your doctor immediately.

 If the attack comes on when you're emotionally excited or anxious, try to **calm yourself.** Like physical stress, mental stress can increase your heart's demand for oxygen. Do your heart a favor by learning yoga, tai chi, meditation, or some other stress-relieving technique you can practice regularly.

Help Your Heart with Supplements

Coenzyme Q_{10} (CoQ_{10}) is a substance that is present in every cell of the body, where it aids in the production of energy. However, 75 percent of people who have angina also have a CoQ_{10} deficiency, so taking supplements may be helpful. In one study, CoQ_{10} supplements cut the frequency of angina attacks in half. People who took it were also able to exercise longer and harder. The usual dose is 150 milligrams twice a day.

Unstop Those Bottled-Up Feelings

Many doctors believe that suppressing your emotions can damage your heart. In studies, men and women who kept their feelings to themselves secreted more of the stress hormone cortisol. Researchers concluded that people who tended to keep their feelings "bottled up" were putting extra stress on the heart. If you can talk to a partner, friend, or counselor about your feelings, instead of trying to keep a stiff upper lip, you may literally help relieve some "heartache."

 L-carnitine, an amino acid available by prescription only, helps the heart muscle use its limited oxygen supply more efficiently. In studies, people with angina who took the supplement showed significant improvement in their ability to exercise after 45 weeks. The usual dose is 500 to 1,000 milligrams three times a day.

 Try taking 500 milligrams a day of hawthorn, an herb that's been used for heart trouble for more than a century. Hawthorn increases the flow of blood—and thus oxygen—to the heart by dilating blood vessels. It may also increase the force of heart contractions.

The Power of Prevention

 With your doctor's help, develop a program of moderate physical exercise, which can help ward off angina pain.

 If you smoke, quit. The nicotine in cigarettes constricts the arteries, triggering angina or making it worse.

 If you're a java junkie, keep your habit in check. Research shows that drinking five or more cups of coffee a day can increase your risk for angina attacks.

 After eating a large or heavy meal, rest or engage in some quiet activity like reading. When you have a big meal, the body diverts extra blood flow to the digestive tract to aid digestion, meaning the heart receives less oxygen and is more vulnerable to an attack.

 Don't stay out in cold weather. Cold air stimulates muscular reflexes that can cause angina.

 Avoid sudden physical exertion, such as running to catch a bus or lifting a heavy object.

Should I call the doctor?

Many people who experience angina for the first time think they're having a heart attack. While angina does not completely block the flow of blood to the heart, as a heart attack does, it's a warning that should not be ignored. If you think you might have angina, get to the doctor as soon as possible. If you have chest pain, as opposed to chest pressure, that lasts for 15 minutes or is accompanied by shortness of breath and nausea, go to the ER immediately.

Anxiety

If it seems like the causes of your anxiety are all around you, take heart: so are the cures. Herbs and oils to boost the soothing powers of a warm bath, worry-taming teas, and even some classic comfort foods... For those times you're feeling anxious, here are some forms of kindness you owe yourself.

What's wrong

Anxiety is a reaction to a threat or danger that is vague or even unknown. You feel worried, but you're not quite sure why. It can manifest any number of symptoms: poor concentration, sweating, trembling, irritability, rapid heart rate, shallow breathing, or unwanted thoughts or behaviors.

Soak Away Your Cares

A **warm bath** is one of the most pleasant and reliable ways to soothe your senses. For an even better balm, add some **lavender oil** (or dried flowers if you have them) to the tub and soak to your heart's content. Although no one knows what gives this wonderfully scented herb its calming effect, lavender has a 2,000-year-old reputation as a calmative that soothes the nerves. No time for a bath? Dab a bit of lavender oil on your temples and forehead and sit quietly for a few minutes.

Suck It In...Deeply

Regulating your breath can help bring your anxiety under quick control. To slow and deepen your breathing, sit down, put one hand over your abdomen, and slowly inhale so that your belly expands under your hand but your shoulders do not rise. Hold your breath for four or five seconds, then very slowly exhale. Repeat until you feel calmer.

Sip Your Way to Serenity

An old-time remedy for insomnia, drinking a glass of **warm milk**, can tame tension any time of day. Milk contains tryptophan, an amino acid that is needed for the production of the brain chemical serotonin, which enhances feelings of well-being.

Catnip, the dried herb that makes cats bizarrely hyperactive, has the opposite effect on humans. It contains chemicals that act as a mild sedative. Simply purchase catnip tea bags and enjoy a cup as often as you like.

Hops, which give beer its distinctive bitter flavor, have a long history as a sedative. In fact, workers who picked hops in the fields were known to suffer from unexplained sleepiness known as hop-picker fatigue. Place 2 teaspoons of the dried herb in a cup of very hot water. Drink up to three cups of this "anti-anxiety tea" a day.

Don't Fuel the Jitter Bug

Limit yourself to a single cup of **coffee, tea, or cola drink** per day. Studies suggest that people with anxiety symptoms may be more sensitive to caffeine than most people.

Watch your intake of wine, beer, and other alcoholic drinks. While they seem to subdue anxiety at first, when the alcohol wears off, anxiety can actually heighten.

Speed Up and Slow Down

Aerobic exercise is a great anxiety reliever. Taking a brisk 30-minute walk spurs the release of endorphins, chemicals that block pain and improve your mood.

Whether it's meditating, praying, tending your flowers, or watching your goldfish, do some sort of **meditative activity** for 15 minutes several times a day. Deeply focusing your attention on the moment at hand steers your mind away from anxious thoughts.

Try a Tablet of Tension Tamer

A pleasant smell *isn't* something you can expect from the herb **valerian**, but if you want relief from anxiety, you might forgive the odor. Research suggests that the active ingredients

Should I call **the doctor?**

Prolonged, severe anxiety can take a serious toll on your physical health. Seek help if you're anxious most of the time, can't sleep or concentrate, turn to alcohol, drugs, or food to quell your anxiety, or feel you might harm yourself or others. It's worth noting that anxiety symptoms can mimic those of serious conditions, such as hyperthyroidism, hypoglycemia, and heart attack, or occur as a side effect of some medications. So it's wise to discuss your symptoms with a doctor.

Anxiety Attacks

Unlike generalized anxiety, anxiety attacks come on suddenly and with overwhelming force. Your heart begins to race, your blood pressure rises, you struggle to breathe, and you feel as if you're about to faint. You may even think you're having a heart attack. Anxiety attacks are most likely to appear after a period of unusual stress, such as a death or divorce. The best way to handle them is to see them for what they are: harmless, if frightening, emotional states. Just tell yourself that you're not in any danger; you're having a panic attack, and it will soon end. Stay calm, try to take a few deep breaths and let the attack run its course.

Repeat these gut-steeling statements to yourself when facing a situation that threatens to send your anxiety level soaring.

Meeting strangers: "This will be a great opportunity to get to know someone I've never met before."

Beginning a new job: "I am well prepared to begin this job, and I know I will be able to master the skills that will allow me to excel."

Making a public speech or presentation: "I have something important to say that will touch the lives and influence the decisions of everyone in this room."

Initiating a new project: "I will succeed by helping others to be successful and by making my best personal contribution."

Dealing with setbacks and insecurity: "Because I have overcome obstacles like this in the past, I know I will be able to do it again."

When challenged: "It does not matter whether others see me as right or wrong as long as I make the best judgment I can and express my views honestly."

When faced with rejection: "I have been given a terrific opportunity to try new alternatives and take a different path, and I am prepared for new challenges."

in valerian attach to the same receptors in the brain that are affected by the anti-anxiety drug diazepam. Take 250 milligrams twice a day and 250 to 500 milligrams before bedtime.

⮞ **5-hydroxytryptophan (5-HTP)** can replenish your supply of serotonin, an anxiety-calming brain chemical. The 5-HTP in your body comes from the amino acid tryptophan, but small quantities are also found in the seeds of griffonia, a tree grown mostly in Ghana and the Ivory Coast. Supplements of 5-HTP are made from extract of the Griffonia or produced synthetically. In Canada, 5-HTP is a drug and it has not been approved for sale, though Canadians may import it into the country for personal use (defined as a three-month supply). Take 50 milligrams three times daily with meals. But consult your doctor if you're also taking an antidepressant such as Prozac, Paxil, or Zoloft. These drugs also affect serotonin receptors, and the combined effect could be dangerous.

⮞ Swallow a **B-complex multivitamin** each day. Studies show that the B's are natural stress-reducers—the body requires vitamin B_6 to make serotonin, for example—and not getting enough of them can contribute to anxiety.

Arthritis

Join the club. So many people have osteoarthritis, you'll soon be getting advice not only from your doctor and friends but also from Mom, the plumber, and the next-door neighbor. Yes, anti-inflammatory drugs—prescription and over-the-counter—can ease your pain, and most people will want to take them. But relief doesn't end there. A host of other feel-good, stay-well measures can move you further down the field toward your goal of easy-moving, pain-free days.

Pain Removers

↳ Supplement with **glucosamine and chondroitin** to reduce pain and slow cartilage loss. There's evidence that this combination can be effective for people with mild to moderate arthritis. Follow the dosage directions on the label. And keep at it: You might have to use it for a month or more before you begin to see benefits.

↳ Take a half-teaspoon of **powdered ginger** or up to 30 grams (about 6 teaspoons) of fresh ginger once a day. Research shows that ginger helps relieve arthritis pain, probably because of its ability to increase blood circulation, which ferries inflammatory chemicals away from painful joints.

↳ Take two 400-milligram doses of **SAM-e** every day. SAM-e has been shown to help relieve arthritis pain by increasing blood levels of proteoglycans—molecules that seem to play a key role in preserving cartilage by helping to keep it "plumped up" and well oxygenated. In a review of SAM-e studies sponsored by the U.S. government, the supplement proved comparable to anti–inflammatory drugs (such as ibuprofen) in fighting arthritis pain. If you get good results with 800 milligrams a day, reduce the dose to 400 milligrams a day after two weeks. If not, you can raise the dose, but don't take more than 1,600 milligrams a day. SAM-e has no known side effects, and it seems to be safe in combination with all prescription and OTC drugs.

What's **wrong**

Of the more than 100 types of arthritis, the most common is osteoarthritis. Symptoms include painfully stiff, swollen joints in any part of the body. The pain is the result of wear and tear on cartilage, the gel-like shock-absorbing material between joints. When cartilage wears away, bone grinds against bone. Although you can develop osteoarthritis at any age, it usually occurs in people over 45, and it's more common among women. Other forms of the disease are rheumatoid arthritis and fibromyalgia.

Should I call **the doctor?**

Since you can't be sure what kind of arthritis you have, or whether your symptoms suggest another condition entirely, report any joint stiffness, swelling, redness, or pain. If you've already been diagnosed with arthritis, call your doctor if you notice a new or different type of swelling in your joints.

Seek Heat Relief and Cold Comfort

✒ **Applying heat** to a painful joint can provide significant relief. For heat sources, you can use electric blankets and mitts, heating pads, or hot packs. Heat things up for 20 minutes. Simply taking a hot bath or shower can also be soothing.

✒ **Cold treatments** may work equally well when joints are inflamed. Wrap an ice cube in a towel or washcloth, and press it to the sore joint. Alternatively, you can use a bag of frozen peas or corn.

Go Hand in Glove to Bed

✒ If you frequently have stiff, swollen hands in the morning, **wear a snug-fitting pair of gloves**, like Isotoners, to bed. They'll keep the swelling in check.

Oil Aching Joints

✒ Eat more **cold-water fish.** Many people who supplement their diets with omega-3 fatty acids—found in cold-water fish like salmon—discover that pain and stiffness are lessened. These substances seem to discourage inflammation in the body.

✒ If you dislike fish, get the healing oils in capsule form. The recommended dose is 2,000 milligrams of an omega-3 supplement three times daily. If you take blood-thinning drugs, check with your doctor before taking **fish-oil capsules.**

✒ As an alternative to fish-oil capsules, take one tablespoon of **flaxseed oil** a day. It's loaded with the same type of omega-3's. Take the oil straight, or add it to your salad dressing.

✒ If you like **nuts**, indulge in them a bit. They also contain beneficial oil.

Rub On Relief

✒ **Capsaicin** is a substance that gives hot peppers their "heat." Rub on a store-bought capsaicin cream (brand names include Zostrix and Menthacin) and let it go to work. It irritates nerve endings, diverting your brain's attention from arthritis pain. Capsaicin may also take away pain by depleting the nerves of substance P, a chemical that transmits pain impulses to the brain. You'll need to use it for at least a week or two for full effect.

Rheumatoid Arthritis

A more serious form of arthritis, rheumatoid arthritis, results when the immune system attacks rather than defends the body. Along with joint pain and swelling, rheumatoid arthritis can cause fatigue, poor circulation, anemia, and eye problems. Here are some strategies to cope with the condition:

🍂 Start a food diary to track what you were eating when your symptoms flared. You may find that your body's inflammatory response goes into overdrive when you eat wheat, dairy foods, citrus, corn, eggs, or tomatoes.

🍂 Try going vegetarian. In a year-long study, people with rheumatoid arthritis who followed a vegetarian diet that was also free of eggs, gluten (a protein in wheat), caffeine, alcohol, salt, refined sugar, and milk products had less pain and swelling in their joints after just one month. And they were able to start eating dairy products again after the first three months or so without any adverse effects.

🍂 One study found that people with rheumatoid arthritis who took capsules of gamma-linolenic acid (GLA), the active compound in evening primrose oil, had less pain and inflammation at six months than people who took a placebo. Take 1,000 milligrams of evening primrose oil three times a day.

🍂 Some doctors believe that people with rheumatoid arthritis can ease their pain with a brief fast of one or two days. The theory behind fasting is that it gives the overworked immune system a much-needed rest. But check with your doctor before you fast, especially if you take prescription medications.

🍂 **Oil of wintergreen** and **eucalyptus oil** are also effective. Put a few drops on the skin and rub it in. Be cautious with wintergreen, however, since some people develop a skin reaction. Also, don't use either of these oils under a heating pad or hot compress, as the additional heat can cause them to burn or irritate the skin.

Keep Those Joints in Motion

🍂 Whether it's walking, swimming, biking, or yoga, commit to a gentle **exercise regimen**. The better your physical condition, the less pain and stiffness you'll have. If you have arthritis in your ankle, knee, or hip, you might need to walk with a cane—at least at first—to help stabilize those joints. If your joints are swollen and inflamed, don't work through the pain. Instead, take a day off.

🍂 Talk to your doctor about how to start a **weight-training** program. Strong muscles will help to support your joints and absorb shock.

continued on page 50

Do-It-Yourself Healing: Arthritis

Exercise is probably the most important thing you can do to keep joints from becoming overly stiff. Each of these gentle exercises can be repeated at least 3 to 5 times, but be sure to stop if you feel intense or sudden pain.

Shoulder Stretch

The following stretches will help increase shoulder mobility while relaxing the neck and shoulder muscles.

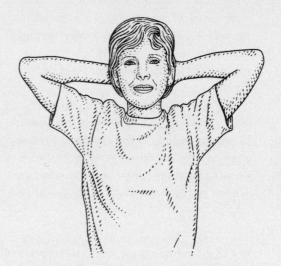

A. Stand upright with your fingers interlocked behind your neck and your elbows pointing straight ahead.

B. Slowly bring your elbows back, breathing in deeply as you do so. Hold for about 5 seconds, then expel your breath and bring the elbows forward again until they touch.

Knee Exercise

Strengthening the quadriceps muscles at the front of your leg will give your knees the support they need.

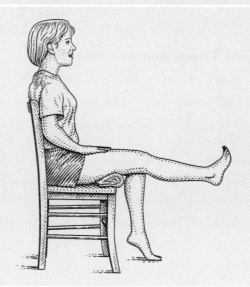

Sit in a hard-backed chair with a towel under your knees. Straighten one leg, without locking the knee, and hold for 3 to 5 seconds. Lower the leg back down and repeat with the other leg.

Finger Exercise

If you have arthritis in your hands, the following exercises will help improve finger flexibility so you can grip and hold objects more easily.

Hold one hand upright with palm open and fingers relaxed, as if you were stopping traffic.

Bring your thumb across the palm as far as you can, reaching for the base of your little finger. Hold for 3 seconds, then bring the thumb back to normal position and spread your fingers as much as possible.

Make a loose fist, with your thumb outside the curl of your fingers.

Hold for 3 seconds, then open the fist. Straighten and spread your fingers.

Ankle Exercise

To maintain flexibility in swollen ankles, do the following exercises when you're seated comfortably in a straight-backed chair with your feet flat on the floor.

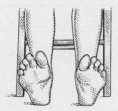 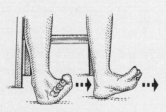

A. With heels resting on the floor, lift the balls of your feet.

B. Pivot your toes back and forth slowly, using your heels as fulcrums.

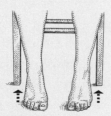 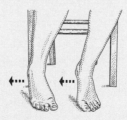

C. Now put the balls of your feet on the floor and lift the heels.

D. Gently pivot your heels left and right.

Try to Measure Up

If you have hip or knee arthritis, ask your doctor to **measure the length of your legs.** One out of five people with arthritis in these joints have one leg that is slightly longer than the other. Your doctor may be able to suggest corrective shoes for you.

Check the Weather Report

Many people with arthritis find that their pain is triggered by **changes in the weather.** If you're one of them, it's not all in your head: A sudden increase in humidity and rapid drop in air pressure affect blood flow to arthritic joints. When a storm is brewing, turn on your air conditioner or dehumidifier to dry out the air.

The Power of Prevention

Maintain a healthy weight to help prevent osteoarthritis of the knees and other weight-bearing joints. If you lose just 4.5 kilograms (10 pounds) and keep it off for 10 years, you can slash your risk of arthritis in your knees by half, no matter what your current weight.

If walking is part of your exercise program, make sure you **don't cover the same terrain every day.** Varying the kind of ground you walk on will prevent you from repeatedly stressing the same joints in the same way.

Invest in a pair of **walking shoes.** The softer heels will lessen the impact of walking on your foot, ankle, leg, and hip joints. Needless to say, high heels are out.

Recent clinical studies have shown that **vitamin C** and other antioxidants can help reduce the risk of osteoarthritis and its progression. Antioxidants prevent bone breakdown by destroying free radicals—harmful oxygen molecules that cause tissue damage. Take 500 milligrams of vitamin C every day.

Take **zinc** supplements. One long-term study of nearly 30,000 women found that those who took zinc supplements lowered their risk of rheumatoid arthritis. Taking too much zinc may cause other health risks, however, so limit your intake to one daily 15-milligram dose, and take it with food.

Asthma

For severe asthma attacks—the kind of tightness, wheezing, and shortness of breath that can be really frightening—most people do just what the doctor recommends. Often, that means quick action with an inhaler containing a drug such as albuterol. If that's what you use, and it works, don't give it up. And always have your doctor's telephone number near at hand in case of severe attacks. But for non-emergencies, you'll want to figure out ways to help yourself breathe easy.

Breathe Easier Right Now

When an asthma attack comes on, **stay calm.** Panic can make your symptoms worse. Help yourself along with this visualization trick: Close your eyes. As you inhale, see your lungs expand and fill with white light, and feel your breathing become easier. Repeat this exercise twice more, then open your eyes.

In a pinch, have a strong cup of **coffee** or two 355-milliliter cans of caffeinated cola or Mountain Dew (which is also high in caffeine). Caffeine is chemically related to theophylline, a standard medication for asthma. It helps open airways.

Cancel Your Constriction

Practitioners of traditional Chinese medicine have been using the herb **ginkgo** to treat asthma for centuries. If you want to try it, take 60 to 250 milligrams of standardized ginkgo extract once a day. One recent study suggests that this herb interferes with a protein in the blood that contributes to airway spasms.

Magnesium may make you feel better. Much research suggests that magnesium relaxes the smooth muscles of the upper respiratory tract. The recommended dose is 600 milligrams a day.

Trump Inflammation

Omega-3 fatty acids, found in fatty fish such as tuna, salmon, and mackerel, work much like a class of asthma drugs

What's **wrong**

An asthma attack can occur when an irritant—usually a common substance like smoke, cold or dry air, pollen, mold, or dust mites—meets a set of temperamental lungs. Hormonal fluctuations, stress, and anger can also trigger an attack. Sometimes there's no apparent cause. Your difficulty in breathing occurs because the bronchi, the tubes that allow oxygen into your lungs, go into spasms. Accompanying them may be coughing and tightness in the chest. The spasms trigger the release of histamine and other chemicals that cause inflammation and the production of airway-clogging mucus.

Should I call **the doctor?**

Yes, if you develop asthma symptoms for the first time. If you're already being treated for asthma, you probably have medication that you take at the onset of an episode. Even so, call your doctor if you notice you're using your medication more often, or if your symptoms worsen even after you take it. Get someone to take you to the emergency room if you can't speak without gasping for breath, develop a bluish cast to your face or lips, find it extremely difficult to breathe, or become confused or exhausted.

called leukotriene inhibitors. These drugs stop the actions of body compounds that cause inflammation in the airways. Take six 1,000-milligram capsules a day in divided doses.

 Evening primrose oil is rich in an essential fatty acid called GLA, which is converted by the body into anti-inflammatory substances. Take two 500-milligram capsules three times a day. Take them with meals to avoid stomach upset.

 Bioflavonoids, the compounds that give fruits and vegetables their Technicolor hues, have powerful anti-inflammatory and anti-allergenic properties. One of the best-known bioflavonoids, **quercetin**, inhibits the release of histamine. Take 500 milligrams of quercetin three times a day, 20 minutes before meals.

 Turmeric, that yellow cooking spice used to flavor Indian curry dishes, is a first-rate anti-inflammatory. The compounds it contains inhibit the release of COX-2 prostaglandins, hormone-like substances involved in inflammation. Mix one teaspoon of turmeric powder in a cup of warm milk and drink this up to three times a day. Turmeric capsules and tinctures are also available.

Keep a Record

 In a date book, **make a note of everything you eat** for a month. Also record your asthma symptoms. While food allergies are rarely associated with asthma, occasionally there is a connection. Check your diary against your symptoms to see if anything you're eating increases the frequency or severity of your attacks.

 If you take asthma medication, **get a peak-flow meter**, available at drugstores. This gadget measures the speed at which air leaves your lungs—an indication of how well you're breathing. By reading your "peak flow" at certain times, you can tell how well a medication or remedy is working. You can also use it during an attack to determine its severity and decide whether you need emergency care.

The Power of Prevention

 Don't smoke, and stay away from people who do. Cigarette smoke irritates the airways.

 Don't huddle around a **fireplace** or wood-burning stove.

Breathe by the Book

This simple deep-breathing trick can help reduce the severity and frequency of your asthma attacks. When an attack starts, you naturally become more anxious as it gets harder to breathe. This produces a "clenching" response that can further restrict your airways. But if you've practiced this breathing technique ahead of time, you can use it to help yourself breathe more freely.

~ Lie on your back on a carpet or mat and place a book on your stomach.

~ Inhale gently and deeply, but not by expanding your chest. Instead, expand your abdomen. Keep an eye on the book. If it rises up, you're breathing the right way.

~ Just when you think you've reached full capacity, take in a little more air. See if you can raise the book a little higher.

~ Exhale gradually, slowly counting to five. The more you exhale, the more relaxed you'll feel.

~ Repeat at least five times.

~ In cold weather, **wrap a scarf** around your nose and mouth to help warm frigid air before you inhale it.

~ **Be alert** for unusual asthma triggers, such as **strong-scented foods** or the **intensely perfumed sample strips** bound into magazines, and do what you can to avoid them.

~ **Try eating smaller, more frequent meals**, and don't eat before you go to bed. The upward migration of stomach acids that cause heartburn can also trigger asthma attacks.

~ About 5 percent of people with asthma are allergic to nonsteroidal anti-inflammatory drugs (NSAIDs) like aspirin and ibuprofen. For these people, taking the drugs can trigger an attack. If you are one of them, use an **aspirin-free pain reliever** like acetaminophen (Tylenol) instead.

Feel-Better Baths

In ancient times, and in cultures around the world, baths were used to treat everything from kidney stones to scorpion stings. Today we have more reliable means of treating serious conditions such as these. But for a host of minor ailments—including itchy skin, sore muscles, achy joints, sleeplessness, and anxiety—it's hard to beat a long soak in the tub. But baths do much more than feel good, especially when you add healing substances to them.

The warmth of the water subtly massages tired muscles and stimulates blood circulation, speeding delivery of healing nutrients to the tissues while helping remove lactic acid and other waste products that contribute to soreness. A hot bath can even help you burn a few extra calories by temporarily boosting your metabolism just a bit. Just avoid prolonged soaks in very hot baths (such as whirlpools). While the heat feels good, it can promote inflammation.

A technique that's been practiced around the world for eons is contrast hydrotherapy. Alternating between hot and cold water causes blood vessels to alternately dilate and constrict. This translates into a sort of pumping action that increases circulation and is said to reduce congestion and inflammation, enhance digestion, and stimulate activity of the organs. Natural healers believe it also boosts immune function. To try this technique at home, you'll need a large basin to act as the second bath, or you can simply sit in a warm tub and use a handheld shower nozzle to douse yourself now and then with cold water. Always start with hot water and finish with cold.

End the Itching

If itching is your problem, a bath—with certain ingredients added—may be just what the doctor ordered. Here are some soothers to put in the tub.

 Baking soda. Baking soda is a wonderful remedy for itchy skin, as you may well know. If your child has the chicken pox, add a half-cup of baking soda to a shallow bath or one full cup to a deep bath to soothe the itch.

 Oatmeal. For relief from poison ivy, skin rashes, or an itchy sunburn, take a lukewarm bath to which you've added a few tablespoons of colloidal oatmeal (like Aveeno), sold in drugstores. If you don't have colloidal oatmeal on hand, simply place a cup or so of plain old oatmeal in a discarded nylon stocking, tie the top, and float it in the bathwater while you soak. Be extra careful when getting out of your oatmeal bath—oatmeal makes the tub very slippery.

 Vinegar. Vinegar is another substance that can tame itching. It works by acidifying the skin. To relieve an itchy sunburn or psoriasis, take a cool bath, adding about 2 cups of vinegar to the bathwater before you get in.

Basin Baths

You don't have to immerse your whole body in the tub to reap the benefits of a bath. A footbath or sitz bath can provide a fast, simple solution to everything from headaches to hemorrhoids.

🍂 For fever, congestion, or headache, add a bit of mustard powder along with warm water to a basin and soak your feet. This draws blood to the feet, which boosts circulation and also eases pressure on the blood vessels in your head.

🍂 For hemorrhoid pain and itching, fill a basin with warm water and a handful of Epsom salt and have a seat.

🍂 For a soothing foot soak, add two drops of peppermint oil along with four drops of rosemary oil.

Aches and Sprains

For minor sprains, an Epsom-salt bath can provide rapid relief. Epsom salt draws fluid out of the body and helps shrink swollen tissues. Add 2 cups Epsom salt to a warm bath, and soak.

As it draws fluid through the skin, Epsom salt also draws out lactic acid, the buildup of which can contribute to muscle aches. After a vigorous exercise session, add a cup or two of the salt to a hot bath and enjoy a relaxing soak.

Adding Essential Oils

A wonderful way to enhance a bath's medicinal value is to add essential oils, available at natural food stores. Each oil has its own healing profile. And after a long, hard day, a few drops of pine oil added to the water can be wonderfully invigorating. Eucalyptus oil promotes alertness and breaks up congestion. Geranium oil reduces anxiety. Lavender fights depression. Rosemary is said to stimulate memory. Combinations of essential oils can be especially beneficial.

🍂 **Arthritis-away bath.** Try a combination of four drops of juniper oil and two drops each of lavender oil, cypress oil, and rosemary oil, along with a half-cup of Epsom salt. For a simpler soak, use three drops of lavender oil and three drops of cypress oil.

🍂 **Deep-sleep soak.** Use two to four tablespoons of sea salt, four drops of lavender oil, three drops marjoram oil, and three drops lemon oil. Other oils that help promote sleep include lime-tree flower, Roman chamomile, frankincense, neroli, and rose.

🍂 **Tension-taming bath.** Add five drops of lavender oil, three drops of ylang-ylang oil, two drops of bergamot oil, and a half-cup of Epsom salt.

If you're prone to allergies, test your reaction to essential oils before using them. Dab a small amount of diluted essential oil on the inside of your arm. If you don't have a reaction within 12 hours, you're good to go.

If you have dried herbs on hand instead of essential oils, you can use those. Add chamomile—along with other calming herbs such lavender and valerian—to bathwater for a nerve-soothing soak. To disperse dried herbs in the water, wrap them in a piece of cheesecloth and hold it under the faucet while you fill the tub.

Athlete's Foot

It's not fair that a locker-room problem should follow you home, but once it does, you have to get tough with it. Consistency counts. Think marathon training, and go the extra distance. The more you can treat your feet and dry your toes, the better. Use these remedies to soothe the itch and fight the fungus that causes it. And follow our prevention tips so athlete's foot doesn't gain a foothold again.

What's wrong

Your feet have been attacked by tinea pedis. This stealthy intruder, which targets the nails, skin, and hair, causes skin to redden, crack, burn, scale, and itch. When the fungus invades the area between your toes, the classic symptom is itchy, flaking skin. Sometimes tinea stays between the toes. But it may also appear on the soles and sides of the feet and even spread to your toenails. Severe cases of athlete's foot can be accompanied by oozing blisters. The locker-room floor is one place where tinea hangs out, but it also loves warm, moist places. Your feet, often confined in sweaty shoes and socks, are an ideal breeding ground.

Bring Itchy Dogs to Heal

⬤ When you scan the pharmacy shelves for an OTC remedy, look for creams and ointments that contain **miconazole nitrate** or **tolnaftate,** such as Micatin 2% Miconazole Nitrate Cream. Massage a small amount into the affected area two or three times a day. And don't make the mistake of stopping the cream when your symptoms subside. Use it for six weeks or more to permanently eradicate the fungus.

⬤ The box of **baking soda** you keep in the fridge to absorb odors can relieve the itch and burn between your toes or on your feet. Add enough water to one tablespoon of baking soda to make a paste. Rub in the paste, then rinse and thoroughly dry your feet. Finish up with a dusting of **cornstarch** or **powder**.

⬤ For a soothing foot soak, add two teaspoons of **salt** to two cups of warm water. Soak your feet for 5 to 10 minutes. Repeat this soak at frequent intervals until your feet are completely healed.

⬤ **Tea** contains tannic acid, a natural astringent that works wonderfully to dry out sweaty feet. Steep five tea bags in a liter of boiling water for five minutes. Let cool to lukewarm, then soak your feet in this "tea bath" for 30 minutes.

⬤ A soothing compress containing a mild astringent can ease itching and burning and help dry up blisters. Use a solution containing liquid proviodine detergent or try mixing one tablespoon of **bleach** with one liter of cold water. Soak a white cotton cloth in the solution and apply it three or four times a day for 15 to 20 minutes at a time.

Don't Give Fungus a New Home

The tinea fungus that causes athlete's foot is also the cause of notorious jock itch. That's why, when you have athlete's foot, you need to be careful not to infect your groin area. Make certain you thoroughly clean your hands after touching your feet. And don't pull your undies on over your bare feet. Put on your socks first. If you wear pantyhose, put on socks, don your drawers, remove the socks, and put on the hose.

Fight Fungus with Food

🖝 Plain **yogurt** containing live acidophilus bacteria is an instant remedy for athlete's foot. These friendly microorganisms keep the fungus in check. Simply dab the yogurt on the infected areas, let dry, and rinse off. (But don't use the flavored kind!)

🖝 Add a few drops of **mustard** oil or a bit of mustard powder to a footbath. Mustard will help to kill the fungus. Soak your feet in the bath for up to half an hour.

Seek Herbal Relief

🖝 The oil of the Australian tea tree is a potent antiseptic. It alters the environment of the skin, making it harder for tinea to do its nasty work. For a soothing, healing treatment, mix **tea-tree oil** with the same amount of **olive oil** and rub the combination into the affected area twice a day. The olive oil helps to tenderize skin toughened by athlete's foot so the tea-tree oil is better absorbed.

🖝 Alternatively, mix **tea-tree oil** with **aloe gel**, another skin softener. Mix three parts tea-tree oil to one part aloe gel and rub this salve into the infected area twice a day. Give this treatment six to eight weeks to work.

🖝 The heavenly scented herb **lavender** also has antifungal properties. Make a massage oil by adding three drops of lavender oil to one teaspoon of carrier oil (any vegetable oil or skin lotion will do). Rub into the infected skin daily.

🖝 **Calendula** has been valued for centuries as a topical treatment for wounds and skin conditions. This herbal healer is said to have both antifungal and anti-inflammatory powers. Rub calendula ointment, sold at health-food stores, on the affected areas, especially between your toes.

Should I call **the doctor?**

Give home treatments at least three weeks to work. If your symptoms are severe, however, get to a dermatologist or podiatrist. Left untreated, a fungal infection can cause the skin to crack, which allows infection-causing bacteria to gain entry. You should also get to the doctor as soon as possible if you see signs of a more serious infection such as skin that is angry red and tender to the touch or oozing. Other warning signals are swelling of the foot or leg accompanied by a fever, or red streaks radiating from the infected area.

Tried...

Some people claim
that they've used their
own saliva to cure
athlete's foot.

**...and
true**

Studies in
animals suggest that saliva
does appear to have
antibacterial and
antifungal powers. For
example, when the
salivary glands of rats are
removed, their wounds
heal more slowly, and a
dog's saliva kills bacteria
that can cause infections
in newborn puppies.
Human saliva contains
substances called
histatins, shown to have
antifungal activity.

The Power of Prevention

- After a bath or shower, **dry your feet thoroughly.** You might try using a blow-dryer, particularly between your toes.

- Wear clean white socks made of natural fiber—they absorb moisture best—or synthetics designed to **draw moisture away from the foot.** If you can, change your socks during the day to keep your feet sweat-free.

- Wear shoes made of canvas or leather, which **allow your feet to breathe.** Forgo rubber and plastic, which hold moisture in and can cause feet to sweat.

- Don't wear the same shoes two days in a row. It takes at least a day for shoes to dry out. If your feet sweat heavily, **change your shoes** twice a day.

- Dust the insides of your shoes with **antifungal powder** or spray. To kill fungus spores, spray some **disinfectant,** like Lysol, on a cloth and wipe out the insides of your shoes after you take them off.

- **Wear slippers or shower shoes** in places where others go barefoot, like gyms, health clubs, locker rooms, and around swimming pools.

- If your toenails are thick, yellow, crumbly, and brittle, you may have a fungal nail infection, which can lead to athlete's foot. **Kick the toenail fungus**—with either an over-the-counter antifungal medication or a visit to your podiatrist or dermatologist—and you'll reduce your chances of getting athlete's foot.

Back Pain

"Oh, my aching back!" Wish you never had to utter those words again? Take it easy for a couple of days while taking some ibuprofen to ease swelling and relieve the pain. Also try the fast-acting solutions below—especially ice and heat—for immediate relief. Then, as soon as possible, slowly get moving again. When your back is feeling moderately better, do the stretching and strengthening exercises starting on page 62—every day, religiously—and in four to six weeks your back should be back in action.

Ice First, Heat Later

⌐ As a pain reliever, **ice** works great. It temporarily blocks pain signals and helps reduce swelling. Several times a day, lay an ice pack wrapped in a towel on the painful area for up to 20 minutes. Alternatively, you can use a bag of **frozen peas** or **corn**. During the first few days of home treatment, apply the ice pack as frequently as necessary. Later you may still want to use ice after exercise or physical activities.

⌐ After about 48 hours, switch to **moist heat** to stimulate blood flow and reduce painful spasms. Dip a towel in very warm water, wring it out, then flatten and fold it. Lie on your stomach with pillows under your hips and ankles. Place the towel across the painful area, cover the towel with plastic wrap, then put a heating pad—set on medium—atop the plastic. Leave it on for up to twenty minutes. You can repeat this three or four times a day for several days.

Rub In Some Relief

⌐ Ask a partner to **massage** the aching area. If you want to use a "back rub" cream or ointment, go ahead, but use caution, as most topical creams produce skin irritation after a few applications. For a simple back-massage aid, stuff several tennis balls into a long sock, tie the end of the sock, and have your partner roll it over your back.

What's **wrong**

Something's amiss with the delicate column of bones, muscles, ligaments, and joints that holds you up. You might have strained a muscle, pulled a ligament, or maybe you have a herniated disk. These disks, which separate the vertebrae, are fibrous rings surrounding a pulpy core. If a disk is herniated, some of that pulpy material is pushing against a nerve root. You have sciatica if a herniated disk presses on the sciatic nerve, causing sharp pain to shoot down the leg. But there are numerous other causes of back pain: strains, arthritis, hairline spine fractures, even kidney infections.

Should I call the doctor?

 Rub on creams containing **methyl salicylate.** Derived from the wintergreen shrub, it's a natural pain reliever related to aspirin. Often combined with menthol or camphor, it's a common ingredient in many liniments such as Ben-Gay, Deep Cold, Rub-A535, and Myoflex cream. The creams, called counterirritants, stimulate nerve endings in the skin, distracting you from deeper pain. When you use them, you're also giving yourself a massage—and that hands-on pressure combined with the surface action packs a one-two punch. (*Off-limits* . . . if you're also using heating pads or hot compresses on the area.)

 Pick a pepper product. Your drugstore carries liniments like Heet Liniment or creams such as Zostrix or Menthacin that contain **capsaicin,** the heat-producing substance in hot peppers. Applied to your skin, capsaicin depletes nerve endings of a neurochemical called substance P. Researchers have found that substance P is essential for transmitting pain sensations to the brain, so when there's less substance P in circulation, the pain meter is turned down a bit. Look for a cream or ointment containing 0.075% or 0.025% capsaicin. And be patient: You may have to use it for several weeks to feel the full effect. Stop using it if you begin to feel any skin irritation.

Swallow These Soothers

 Three or four times a day, take 500 milligrams of **bromelain.** Derived from pineapples, this enzyme promotes circulation, reduces swelling, and helps your body reabsorb the by-products of inflammation. Look for a strength between 1,200 and 2,400 MCU (milk-clotting units) or 720 and 1,440 GDU (gelatin-dissolving units). Wait for at least an hour after each meal before taking the bromelain, or it will work mainly in your gut instead of your muscles.

 Try taking one 250-milligram capsule of **valerian** four times a day. Some scientists claim that this herb's active ingredient interacts with receptors in the brain to cause a sedating effect. Although sedatives are not generally recommended, valerian is much milder than any pharmaceutical product. (Valerian can also be made into a tea, but the smell is so strong—resembling overused gym socks—that capsules are vastly preferable.)

Fast Relief from the Doc

Doctors used to prescribe muscle relaxers for quick relief, but the drugs are rarely prescribed anymore. They tend to make people tired and contribute to poor muscle tone and coordination—just the opposite of what you really need for back-pain relief. If you visit your doctor or hospital to be treated for intense pain, you're more likely to be given a drug called Toradol. This powerful, prescription anti-inflammatory and pain reliever stops the muscle spasms and relieves pain.

Perfect Your Posture

↝ Look for the **posture that places the least stress** on your back. To do it, stand straight with your weight evenly balanced on both feet. Tilt your pelvis forward, then back, exaggerating the movement. Then settle into the position that feels most comfortable. Now "work your way up" your back, focusing on one area at a time. First concentrate on the area near your waist, then your chest area, and finally your neck and shoulders. Try to feel which position is least stressful and most comfortable. This is the position to maintain when you're standing, walking, and beginning or ending any exercise.

↝ **When you're sleeping**, lie on your back or your side (*unless* you have sciatica). If you're more comfortable on your back, place a pillow under your knees as well as under your head to relieve pressure on your lower back. Prefer to sleep on your side? Place a pillow between your legs. For anyone who has sciatica, the recommended sleeping position is on your stomach.

↝ If you like to sit up in bed to read or watch TV, get a **large foam wedge** that couches your upper body in a comfortable position. For added comfort—and to keep your neck in the proper position—use a foam or inflatable neck support when you're sitting up.

↝ When you're seated in a chair at the office or home, keep your feet flat on the floor, with your hips slightly higher than your knees. Use a **lumbar support** behind your lower back. The lumbar roll is a chair-width foam cylinder about 15 centimeters in diameter. You can improvise with a rolled-up towel, but the foam product is lighter, easier to position, and usually has straps that attach to the back of the chair.

Tried...

In frontier days, a mustard plaster was a favorite remedy for sore backs and aching joints.

...and true

Like capsaicin and other counter-irritants, mustard delivers a warm, tingling sensation that can distract you from deeper pain. To make a plaster, mix one part powdered mustard with two parts flour, adding water until you have a paste. Spread it on a dishcloth, then fold the cloth and apply it like a compress to your skin. It can burn if left on too long, so remove it if you feel skin discomfort. Don't use a mustard plaster more than three times a day.

continued on page 64

Do-It-Yourself Healing: Back Pain

The following exercises, from Kevin R. Stone, M.D., orthopedic surgeon and founder of the Stone Clinic in San Francisco, California, are designed to improve flexibility and strengthen the muscles that play a role in supporting your spine—in your abdomen, along your back, and around your trunk.

A. Lie with your hands palm-down on the mat, directly under your shoulders, in a push-up position, with your lower body completely relaxed.

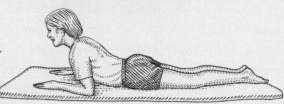

B. Keeping your hips in place and legs relaxed, slowly raise your upper body until you can feel the stretch in your back. Return to starting position. Repeat 10 times.

A. Kneel on all fours with your knees hip-width apart.

B. Keeping your stomach muscles tensed, arch your back, stretching as a cat does. Hold for 5 seconds, then release. Repeat.

C. Now hollow your spine slightly, hold for 5 seconds, then release. Repeat.

D. Finally, sit back on your heels and reach your arms in front of you for a nice stretch.

Lie on your back with your knees bent. Slowly pull your right knee toward your chest until you can feel a stretch in your lower back. Count to five, then slowly lower the leg. Switch legs. Repeat 10 times, alternating right and left.

Lying on your back with knees bent, raise your right leg and grasp the thigh near your knee with both hands. Holding firmly, slowly extend that leg to raise it as high as possible. You'll feel the stretch in the back of the thigh. Hold for the count of 15. Repeat 5 times with each leg.

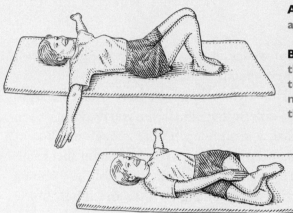

A. Lie on your back with your knees bent and your arms out to the side.

B. Keeping your knees bent, slowly drop them to the right, using your right hand to gently pull the top knee toward the mat. Hold for the count of 5. You'll feel the stretch in your back and hips. Return your knees to the starting position, then repeat on the other side. Alternating, repeat 10 times.

A. Lie on your stomach with a rolled-up towel under your forehead. Without moving the rest of your body, contract the muscles in your buttocks as if you were pressing your pelvis down into the mat. Slowly count to five, then relax. Repeat 10 times.

B. Keeping your hips pressed into the mat, raise your right arm and, at the same time, your left leg. Keep balance by tensing your stomach muscles. Lower the arm and leg to the mat, then lift the left arm and the right leg. Alternating lifts, repeat 20 times.

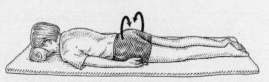

NOTE: Do these on an exercise mat. Alternatively, you can use a well-padded carpet or rug. Perform the recommended number of repetitions, but be sure to stop if you feel unusual discomfort or sharp pain.

Sciatica: What's the Connection?

The roots of the sciatic nerve lie near the base of your spine. They pass through a tunnel in your pelvis called the sciatic notch, then come together like separate lanes merging into superhighways—the two large sciatic nerves that lead all the way down your legs. When the sciatic roots are pinched—by pressure from a herniated disk, for instance—sensations of pain, tingling, or numbness may extend all the way from your buttocks to your legs, feet, and toes.

About half the people who have sciatica get good results from most of the treatments recommended for lower back pain. If you have sciatica and don't get relief with these treatments, however, you should keep your doctor informed. And tell your doctor at once if you start to have trouble controlling your bladder or bowels. In a small percentage of cases (5 to 10 percent), doctors may recommend other procedures, such as surgery.

➤ Keep a **foam wedge** in the car and place it behind your lower back whenever you're seated.

➤ If you're accustomed to walking around with **a wallet** in your hip pocket, **take it out** whenever you're sitting. Even though it feels like a small lump, it's big enough to tilt your backside, throwing your spine ever so slightly out of alignment.

➤ When you're standing at the sink doing dishes, or waiting in a long line, **raise one foot higher than the other.** In the kitchen, keep a low sturdy box or a couple of old books by the sink, and put up a foot while you're standing there. Waiting in line, use a step or curb. (Think of the traditional brass rail in a bar, which serves the same purpose.) Periodically change position by putting up the opposite foot. This shifting of weight gives alternating back muscles a chance to relax.

Rise and Shine

➤ Each morning before **you get out of bed**, lie on your back and slowly stretch your arms overhead. Gently pull your knees to your chest, one at a time. To rise, roll to the edge of your bed, turn on your side, put your knees over the edge, and use one arm to push yourself up as you let your feet swing to the floor. Once you're on your feet, put your hands on your buttocks and lean back very slowly to stretch out your spine.

Bad Breath

Suppose you conduct a "breath test" as you head to an important encounter, and you flunk. Don't worry—the following fast fixes can help tame your wild-and-woolly breath. If odor-causing bacteria seem to be fond of your gums, tongue, and teeth, you'll want to adopt some daily habits to inhibit these inhabitants. That's when special rinses, attention to toothpaste, and faithful brushing and flossing can begin making bad breath good.

Take Emergency Measures

🔊 Dry mouth is a haven for the bacteria that cause bad breath. So find a tap, and swish the **water** around in your mouth. Water will temporarily dislodge bacteria and make your breath a bit more palatable.

🔊 At the end of your power lunch or romantic dinner, munch the sprig of **parsley** that's left on your plate. Parsley is rich in chlorophyll, a known breath deodorizer with germ-fighting qualities.

🔊 If you can get your hands on an **orange**, peel and eat it. The citric acid it contains will stimulate your salivary glands and encourage the flow of breath-freshening saliva.

🔊 If there are no oranges in sight, **eat whatever is available**, except known breath-foulers like garlic, onions, or a stinky cheese. Eating encourages the flow of saliva, which helps remove the unpleasant, odor-causing material on the back of your tongue.

🔊 Vigorously **scrape your tongue** over your teeth. Your tongue can become coated with bacteria that ferment proteins, producing gases that smell bad. Scraping your tongue can dislodge these bacteria so you can rinse them away.

🔊 If you have a metal or plastic spoon, use it as a **tongue scraper**. To scrape safely, place the spoon on the back of your tongue and drag it forward. Repeat four or five times. Scrape the sides of the tongue as well, with the same back-to-front

What's **wrong**

People are backing away from you whenever you stop to talk with them. Or someone has told you frankly that you have bad breath. The most obvious cause: You've eaten a dish laced with onions, garlic, or blue cheese. But there are other reasons galore. Perhaps you're a smoker or could it be that you don't brush your teeth or floss often enough? Gum disease is another common cause of bad breath. If you have an abscessed tooth or a sinus infection, your unpleasant breath is most certainly a side effect. Rounding out the list of suspects: certain medications, a chronically dry mouth, or too many cups of coffee.

Should I call **the doctor?**

While all of us have malodorous breath from time to time, good oral hygiene should keep it to a minimum. But bad breath that hangs on can also be a sign of intestinal problems, cancer, or lung or kidney problems. If you brush and floss diligently, yet can't banish bad breath on your own, place a call to your doctor or dentist. And see a doctor if your breath smells sweet or fruity, since that's one sign of diabetes.

motion. Don't push the spoon too far back, however; you may activate your gag reflex.

Raid the Spice Shelf

🔸 **Cloves** are rich in eugenol, a potent antibacterial. Simply pop one into your mouth and dent it with your teeth. The pungent aromatic oil may burn slightly, so keep that spicy nub moving. Continue to bite until the essence permeates your mouth, then spit it out. Don't use clove oil or powdered cloves; they're too strong and can cause burns.

🔸 Chew on **fennel, dill, cardamom,** or **anise seeds.** Anise, which tastes like black licorice, can kill the bacteria that grow on the tongue. The others can help mask the odor of halitosis.

🔸 Suck on a stick of **cinnamon.** Like cloves, cinnamon is effective as an antiseptic.

Choose Your Fresheners

🔸 The most obvious brand-name products advertised as breath-fresheners are rarely, if ever, effective in the long run. But with a therapeutic oral rinse, you can rid yourself of the compounds that are responsible for breath odor. These products are available both at your local drugstore and over the Internet. One brand, Steri/Sol, is available at pharmacies. Another, ProFresh, can be purchased at www.profresh.com.

🔸 Use a toothpaste that contains **tea-tree oil,** a natural disinfectant. If you can't find it in the pharmacy, look for it in health-food stores.

The Power of Prevention

🔸 Use an **oral irrigator,** which is a handheld device that rapidly pulses a small jet of water into your mouth, to flush out

How to Sniff Out Bad Breath

Just how bad is your breath? To find out, cup your hands over your mouth, exhale heartily, and take a whiff. If your breath smells bad to you, it smells bad to others too. You can also perform the "sniff test" on dental floss after you pull it gently between your teeth. But if you think you might have become desensitized to your own bad breath, you can ask your dentist to test you with a halimeter. This device measures the sulfur content of your breath—which is what makes it smell bad.

the bad bacteria, which can go deeper than a brush or floss string can reach.

 Carry a **toothbrush** with you and brush immediately after every meal. With prompt brushing you thwart the development of plaque, the soft, sticky film that coats the teeth and gums.

 To keep your toothbrush free of stink-triggering bacteria, store it, head down, in a lidded plastic tumbler of **hydrogen peroxide.** Rinse the brush well before you use it.

 If you wear **dentures**, it's possible that they are absorbing the bad odors in your mouth. Always soak them overnight in an **antiseptic solution**, unless your dentist has advised you otherwise.

 Don't skip meals. When you don't eat for a long period of time, your mouth can get very dry. It becomes a perfect breeding ground for bacteria.

 Some things can sour your breath even if there are no bacteria in the neighborhood. These include cigarettes, alcohol, onions, garlic, and especially strong cheeses like Camembert, Roquefort, and blue cheese. In situations where sweet breath is a must, use the commonsense approach—just say no.

 Ask your doctor if a **medication** could be fouling the air you expel. Any drug that dries out your mouth, thereby depriving it of saliva, is suspect. These include over-the-counter antihistamines, decongestants, diet pills, and prescription medications for depression and high blood pressure.

Skip it!

It's a common misconception that minty mouthwash or breath mints will turn your breath fresh. Not so. Most mouthwashes contain alcohol, which dries up saliva. When you use them, you actually make your breath worse afterward. And mint candy is just a cover-up; it actually feeds the odor-causing bacteria more sugar! For a natural mouthwash that won't dry out your mouth, mix 1 tablespoon baking soda with 1 cup of a 2%–3% solution of hydrogen peroxide. The foam it kicks up has a powerful oxidizing effect that kills odoriferous bacteria.

Bedwetting

Kids may not be able to help wetting the bed, and that's important for you to remember, especially on those mornings when you're faced with sopping sheets. And the problem certainly can't be "solved" by punishment. It does help to keep a "dry" sense of humor about the situation, which will undoubtedly pass. And try these techniques in the meantime.

What's wrong?

Nothing, usually: When you're raising a child, bedwetting comes with the territory. In fact, as many as seven million children over the age of six don't heed nature's call during the night. Most likely, your child is not waking up when his bladder is full—and this is only a problem because the child is producing a lot of urine in the night or has a bladder that's somewhat low on capacity.

Keep Those "Wee Hours" Drier

~ Restrict your child's fluid intake before bedtime. In particular, cut out sodas or other beverages that contain **caffeine**, which irritates the bladder.

~ If your child usually drinks a glass of **milk** at bedtime, try discontinuing that practice and see if it helps. Some children are allergic to the proteins in milk, primarily casein and whey, and the allergy can cause bedwetting. This problem is usually present from infancy, and can also cause bloating and diarrhea, among other symptoms.

~ Make sure your child **voids** before he or she goes to bed. It won't stop the bedwetting, but there will be less stored urine, which means less urine to wet the bed.

~ Make her pre-bedtime routine **calm and quiet**. Rough, active play or even an exciting TV program increases the risk of bedwetting. Read her a story, or suggest that she read to herself.

~ Buy a **bedwetting alarm**, which emits a loud sound or vibrates silently when it detects moisture. It conditions kids to recognize the need to urinate and wake up before they have to go. The alarms are battery-operated and cost around $60. Ask your pediatrician to recommend a brand or type. And don't give up if the alarm hasn't solved the problem after a week or two; it may take several weeks or even a month or two.

Limit the Damage

~ Put a zippered **plastic mattress cover** on your child's bed. Not only does it protect the mattress, it also ensures that

Medical Help

Some studies show that children who wet their beds may have an abnormally low level of antidiuretic hormone (ADH). This hormone helps the kidneys retain water, and if there's a deficiency of it, more urine gets into the bladder. A doctor can prescribe a nasal spray containing a synthetic version of the hormone, to be used before bed. But behavior modification (with the help of a bedwetting alarm) may be more effective.

you can treat the accident as just that—an accident, not a tragedy. Both you and your child will sleep better knowing that there's not a major cleanup job to worry about.

Enlist Your Tot's Support

Have your child assist you with the **tasks that go along with bedwetting**, like laundering the sheets, making the bed, or putting out a fresh pair of PJs before she hops into bed. Make it clear that her participation isn't a punishment, just a responsibility.

Did you **know?**

Research suggests that if both parents wet the bed as kids, their child has a 70 percent chance of having the same problem.

Belching

Admittedly, most burps are no big deal. But sometimes manners matter. So when there's too much gas in your gastrointestinal system, try the following bubble-busters. Some remedies right in your kitchen will take the wind out of your sails. Also, your mother may have urged you to eat politely for social reasons, but good table habits are key to squelching belching. And, since a surprising amount of air and gas enters your digestive system as passengers inside your food and drink, you'll want to choose your comestibles carefully.

What's wrong

A belch simply means you have accumulated a buildup of air in your stomach, and your body wants to get rid of it to reduce this pressure. The air comes out with the distinctive sound that's usually called a "belch" or a "burp." (Not many people tangle with the multisyllabic scientific term *eructation*.) The human digestive tract takes in about 10 cups of air and other gases during an average day. Most of the swallowing occurs unconsciously, when we're doing things like eating, drinking, and gulping nervously when under stress. But what goes in must come out. Hence, the belching.

Bust Those Bubbles

Belches start with air bubbles and end with breaking those bubbles down or else preventing them from forming. **Simethicone** is an ingredient common to many over-the-counter antacids such as Mylanta, Diovol Plus, Maalox, and Ovol. It breaks large bubbles in the stomach down to smaller bubbles, easing belching.

Supplements labeled **"digestive enzymes"** assist your body in breaking down food. (Often, the gas that goes into burping is a by-product of incomplete digestion.) These formulations contain a variety of ingredients. Look for **protease** and **pancreatin**, which help digest protein, and **lipase**, for the digestion of fat. Other beneficial ingredients are **cellulase**, for the digestion of vegetable fiber, and **lactase**, which can help your gastrointestinal system deal with milk sugar. Check the label to make sure you're purchasing a product with all or most of these enzymes.

Follow the Spice Route

Ginger can provide quick relief. It's available in various forms; experiment to find out which works best. Take two 550-milligram capsules of powdered ginger or 30 drops of tincture before your meals. Or eat a bit of fresh gingerroot (though you may find that's a challenge!). Alternatively, you can make a very tasty tea. Finely grate a teaspoon of fresh ginger-root, pour a cup of boiling water over it, and steep for five minutes. Strain and let it cool a bit before you begin sipping.

~ **Fennel, anise,** or **celery seeds** can relieve belching. (Fennel are the tiny seeds that you often find in bowls at Indian restaurants.) All these seeds are available in the spice section of most supermarkets, and you just need to chew a pinch of them to help prevent after-dinner belching. These seeds have carminative agents, which help expel gas from the intestinal tract.

~ **Chamomile tea** is a folk treatment for stomachaches that may also help relieve burping. Store-bought chamomile tea bags will work just fine.

~ **Cardamom tea** helps you digest your food better so the food you eat will be less likely to produce gas. Place 1 teaspoon cardamom in 1 cup of water and boil for 10 minutes. Drink the hot tea with your meals.

Choose an Airless Menu

~ **Avoid carbonated drinks.** Ever open a fizzy soda after it's been shaken? A similarly explosive situation will build in your stomach if you gulp down bubbly drinks.

~ **Sparkling wine and beer,** like soda, have the same power to remind you of their presence. If you don't want to burp, steer clear.

~ Some foods contain more air than others. **Avoid** them. The aeration club includes **whipped cream, soufflés,** and **fluffy omelets.**

~ Give your hot drinks a few moments to **cool.** Sipping a blistering drink like hot coffee may cause you to gulp lots of air.

Should I call **the doctor?**

Just because you've unleashed a belch or two after a satisfying meal? No. However, belching *can* be a sign of many serious problems, including stomach ulcer, gallbladder disease, gastroesophageal reflux disease, hiatal hernia, and even colorectal and esophageal cancer. So see your doctor If your belching is accompanied by another troublesome symptom, such as bloating, or a bit of uncontrollable vomiting. You should also check in with your doctor if you get a burning sensation in the chest when you burp, or if frequent belching is accompanied by unexplained weight loss or changes in bowel habits.

The Remedy That Isn't

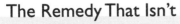

Do you deliberately swallow air to trigger a burp, hoping that will dispense with the issue once and for all? It won't. In fact, it will probably cause you to swallow more air than you expel, starting a vicious cycle of swallowing and burping. Sometimes this turns into an unconscious habit. Observe yourself to see if you're doing it—if so, work at stopping.

Go for Closure

Certain foods can weaken an important valve that's designed to keep food and gas in your stomach. That valve, called the lower esophageal sphincter, controls the intersection of your esophagus (the tube that carries food from your mouth) and the top entrance of the stomach. Foods known to weaken the valve include chocolate, high-fat meats, fried foods, and caffeine. Avoid them, and you'll be less likely to burp.

Skip it!

An old remedy for heartburn—and burping—was to down a mixture of baking soda and water. Unfortunately, this actually *makes* people belch. The bicarbonate interacts with the hydrochloric acid in your stomach to produce carbon dioxide, the same stuff that makes soda bubble.

🌱 **Set the straw aside.** Drinking through straws causes you to—you guessed it—swallow air.

🌱 Ditch the **after-dinner smokes.** When you inhale air through a cigarette, you're also *swallowing* some.

Take a Mannerly Approach

🌱 If you wolf down your food, you're gulping air that will eventually want to re-emerge. **Eat slowly.** Tough to do? Try setting down your fork between bites. If you're clearing your plate before everyone else at the table, you're probably eating too fast.

🌱 Chew with your **mouth closed** so you're less likely to swallow air. For the same reason, don't try to talk and chew at the same time. Finish what you're eating before you begin sharing your opinion on the nation's political future.

Search for Other Suspects

🌱 Poorly fitting dentures may cause you to chew abnormally and swallow air. If you wear **dentures**, make sure they are **properly adjusted.**

🌱 Postnasal drip from a cold or allergy can make you swallow excessive air. An over-the-counter **nasal decongestant** can sometimes reduce belching as well as relieving the nasal symptoms.

🌱 In some people, calcium supplements that contain calcium carbonate can release carbon dioxide in the stomach. If you take calcium, choose another form, like **calcium citrate.**

🌱 Pressure around your midsection can squeeze out burps. Are you trying to squeeze into pants that are too small? You might want to **loosen up** a bit. A tight girdle or skirt can have the same effect.

Blisters

The eternal dilemma: Should I drain this thing or leave it alone? In general, don't bother blisters that are small or those that probably won't pop on their own. They are less likely to become infected if you leave the natural covering intact, and under the sheltering cushion of fluid, the area has time to form new skin. Meanwhile, follow these tips to relieve the pain and itching and speed healing. If your blister is large, or in a spot where you can't avoid putting pressure on it, drain it the proper way. Never pop a burn blister, though. There's a serious risk of infection if you do.

Let It Be

ᐧ Keep the blister clean with soap and water. You can dab on **petroleum jelly** or some other emollient to minimize further friction.

ᐧ Cover the blister with a clean **bandage** that you change at least once a day.

ᐧ Protect the blister with a piece of **moleskin**—a soft, adhesive cushion that's sold in pharmacies. (Don't worry—no real moles have been sacrificed to make this product.) Leave it on for two days, and remove it carefully so it doesn't tear the fragile skin beneath.

ᐧ Apply **calendula ointment**, a product made from marigold. It's traditionally used as a soothing wound healer. To keep the ointment clean, cover it with an adhesive bandage or a gauze pad. At night, remove the bandage so the blistered area is exposed to air.

ᐧ No calendula? Smear some **aloe vera gel** on the blister and cover it with a bandage to help it heal. But be sure you use the pure gel of the plant. Some processed products contain ingredients, like alcohol, which have a drying effect.

ᐧ Another option for blister treatment is **Preparation H.** While this isn't the normal use for the hemorrhoid reliever, the cream has ingredients that relieve itching and burning, and it provides a coating that protects the skin.

What's wrong?

You've most likely rubbed your skin the wrong way... literally. The most frequent cause of blisters is excessive friction on moist skin. As a blister forms, clear fluid accumulates in a pocket between the layers of the skin. Sometimes a small blood vessel in the area is damaged, and the fluid in the blister becomes tinged with blood. These types of blisters are generally found on the hands and feet, but can occur elsewhere too. Other potential blister causes include poison ivy and oak, sunburn and other burns, and eczema and other skin conditions.

Should I call **the doctor?**

If your blister is extremely large—more than 5 centimeters across—you should seek medical care. Symptoms of infection should also send you to the doctor. These include prolonged pain that isn't fading, fever, redness that extends beyond the borders of the blister, yellow crusting, and oozing pus. Some disorders that cause blisters, such as chicken pox, eczema, and impetigo, also may require a doctor's care.

🖐 Relieve pain and itching with a **wet washcloth.** Soak the cloth in cold water, wring it out, and lay it over the blister.

If It Pops by Accident...

🖐 Wash it with soap and water. Apply a healing cream or gel like **Neosporin.** Cover it with a bandage. Four times a day, remove the bandage and treat the raw spot with a mixture of one part **tea-tree oil** and three parts **vegetable oil.** The tea-tree oil will help kill bacteria and prevent an infection.

Practice the Art of Careful Draining

🖐 If your blister is large, or in a spot where you can't avoid putting pressure on it, you may be better off **draining** it rather than trying to protect it. To drain a blister properly, first sterilize a needle. Use a pair of pliers or tweezers to hold the needle over a flame for a few seconds until it glows red. Let it cool.

🖐 Clean the blister with **rubbing alcohol** or a disinfecting product like **hydrogen peroxide.**

🖐 Open a **sterile gauze pad** and lay it gently on top of the blister. Pierce the edge of the blister, sliding the needle in sideways, and gently squeeze out the liquid by pressing down on the gauze pad. Make sure you don't tear or remove that top layer of skin—it's protecting an extremely sensitive circle of skin beneath.

🖐 Smear on an antibiotic ointment like **Neosporin** and cover it with a clean bandage. You can also cover it with a **2nd Skin Blister Pad,** made by Spenco. This is a moist, jellylike covering that can be cut to size and taped in place. Change it twice a day.

🖐 If the blister refills again later, **drain it again** the same way.

🖐 Apply a mixture of **vitamin E** and **calendula ointment** to help your skin heal faster. Vitamin E comes in gel capsules. Slice open a capsule, mix equal amounts of the vitamin and calendula oil, and smear the mixture on your blister. Reapply as needed for up to a week.

The Power of Prevention

🖐 Don't assume you know your proper shoe size or that your feet haven't changed since you last bought shoes. **Have**

Felled by a Blister

your feet measured every time you buy. And when you try on shoes, be sure you're wearing the same kind of socks you normally wear.

➤ Shop for shoes in the **afternoon.** Your feet swell during the day, and if you buy a pair in the morning, you might be getting a half-size too small.

➤ Be sure new shoes are **roomy in the toe area.** When you're standing up, you should have a thumb-width of space between your longest toe and the end of your shoe.

➤ For long walks or hikes, try wearing **two pairs of socks** to reduce friction. The inner pair should be a thin, sweat-wicking fabric like acrylic, with an outer sock made of cotton.

➤ You may also want to **use an antiperspirant** on your feet to keep them dry. Dry feet are less likely to develop blisters.

➤ Cover blister-prone spots with a lubricant, such as **Lube-Stick for Runners,** before you go for a run.

➤ If you're going to be doing yard work, you can prevent blisters on your hands by wearing **work gloves.** If you always get blisters when you weed the garden, even if you wear gloves, shop for a weeder with a larger handle or a cushioned grip.

➤ Anyone who plays racket sports will probably have to contend with hand blisters. But if they keep recurring, talk to a pro about **changing the grip** on your racket or wrapping it with an absorbent, soft covering.

Remedies from the Sea

If you're looking for a respite from stress, few things can match a lazy day at the beach. Blue skies, warm sand, and lapping water have a way of melting away tension. But did you know that the world's oceans are balm for the body as well as the mind? Marine plants and animals are the source of various drugs, and many more marine-based pharmaceuticals are now in development, including cancer drugs from starfish eggs, the world's most powerful sunscreen from a certain species of jellyfish, and an osteoporosis drug derived from coral.

Fish Oil for Your Health

You've probably heard that a diet rich in cold-water fish like mackerel and tuna can help protect you against the blood clots that cause heart attack. That's been demonstrated again and again in clinical trials initiated after researchers noticed a curiously low incidence of coronary artery disease in Greenland's indigenous people, for whom fish is a dietary staple.

Now it appears that the same omega-3 fatty acids in fish that protect against blood clotting also seem to be effective against a host of other health problems, including depression and inflammatory conditions such as psoriasis, rheumatoid arthritis, and Crohn's disease, as well as lupus, eczema. They may even ease menstrual cramps. If you don't like the taste of fish, ask your doctor about taking fish-oil capsules. For more information on fish-oil capsules, see page 414.

Seaweed Superfoods

Seaweed is more than a great wrap for sushi and spa-goers. Nori, kelp, dulse, and other seaweeds—there are more than 2,500 varieties—are good sources of protein and dietary fiber. What's more, they contain up to 20 times the vitamin and mineral content of vegetables that grow on land.

Unlike terrestrial plants, seaweed contains vitamin B_{12}. That's significant because as more people reduce their consumption of meat and dairy—the usual sources of B_{12} in the diet—more people are becoming deficient in the vitamin. Deficiencies can cause fatigue, depression, and numbness and tingling.

Seaweed is also a rich source of alginic acid, which helps rid the body of toxic heavy metals such as lead. What's more, it contains compounds that may help prevent cancer.

Nori, for example, is rich in the antioxidant beta-carotene. Like all antioxidants, it neutralizes harmful molecules known as free radicals before they cause the DNA damage that leads to malignancies. Sea vegetables are just as popular in Asian cuisine as potatoes are in the United States and Canada. That popularity may help explain why cancer rates in Asia are just a fraction of what they are in North America.

Seaweeds to Savor

"What do I do with this stuff?" That's what many people say the first time they encounter dried sheets of seaweed. Don't be daunted. Seaweed is easy to cook with, though each type does have to be handled a bit differently.

Alaria. It's traditionally used to flavor miso soup, although its salty flavor works well in many dishes. Soak it in water for two minutes, then use scissors to cut it into thin strips. Add them to stews, stir-fries, pasta, or salads.

Dulse. The dried red leaves have a pleasant crunch and can be eaten straight from the package.

Kelp. It's usually cut into pieces and added to soups and stews as a salt substitute.

Nori. Milder in flavor than most seaweeds, it's great for wrapping rice or sushi. Or you can cut it into strips and use it as a flavorful, decorative condiment for soup.

As you'd expect from plants harvested from the ocean, seaweed is full of salt. If high blood pressure has you limiting your intake of sodium, you'll want to soak the leaves before adding them to recipes.

Help for an Underactive Thyroid

As with cancer, obesity is much rarer in Japan than in most Western countries. But why? According to one theory, the abundance of iodine-rich seaweed in the traditional Japanese diet helps boost metabolism. Metabolic processes are governed in part by thyroid hormones. And an underactive thyroid gland can be caused by an iodine deficiency. If that's the case, get more iodine and you'll boost your thyroid hormone production and, along with it, your metabolism. Signs of an underactive thyroid gland include fatigue, lethargy, and dry skin. Consult with your doctor if you think your thyroid isn't performing up to par.

Most people in developed nations get plenty of iodine from iodized salt. But if your doctor has advised you to consume more iodine—to help an underactive thyroid, for instance—inquire about adding sea vegetables to your diet.

Sea Salt for Healthy Skin

For millennia, people have been bathing in the super-salty waters of the Dead Sea to cure what ailed them. While the waters of the Dead Sea may not work miracles, there is no doubt that bathing in salt water is a great way to moisturize dry, damaged skin.

Even severe cases of psoriasis can sometimes be cleared up by bathing repeatedly in water to which sea salt has been added. Whether it's the minerals in the sea salt or the salt itself isn't clear, though there is no doubt that the salt makes a great natural exfoliant.

When simple dry skin is the problem, a salt scrub is often the answer. Make a paste with about a cup of sea salt and enough glycerin (sold in drugstores) to get the salt to stick together. After a shower, while your skin is still wet, rub this mixture over your body using your hands or a loofah sponge. Once you rinse away the salt and dry off, you'll be amazed at how soft your skin feels.

Body Odor

All's swell that ends smell. If antiperspirants (which plug up sweat glands) and deodorants (which mask odors) don't do the trick, or you prefer a natural approach, there are myriad paths to an agreeable essence. BO battles begin in the shower and continue throughout the day, with a simple goal: Stop the odor at its source.

What's wrong

Long ago, nature provided us with strong smells to entice the opposite sex. But BO won't get you far today. The problem starts with certain types of sweat. *Eccrine glands* pour out clear, neutral-smelling sweat, which cools your body as it evaporates. *Apocrine glands,* concentrated in your underarms and genitals, secrete a substance that bacteria feast upon, causing strong odors. Stress, ovulation, sexual excitement, and anger can cause apocrine glands to kick into high gear. Some diseases cause the body to produce particular odors, and so do drugs such as venlafaxine (Effexor) and bupropion (Wellbutrin).

Watch the Daily Soaps

➣ Pick an **antibacterial soap**, such as Lever 2000, Zest, Dial, or Irish Spring. These leave ingredients on your skin that kill bacteria even after you're finished bathing. If the soap doesn't irritate your skin, use it daily. If you find that these soaps are too drying, use them only on your underarms and groin, where you need their antibacterial power the most.

➣ If BO is still bothering you, bring out the big guns. **pHisoHex**, an antibacterial cleanser, is so effective that some formulations are used to clean patients before surgery. Since it can dry your skin, however, you should use it in the shower, where it will rinse off quickly, and only on high-smell areas such as the armpits and groin. Squeeze out a small amount of cleanser, wash the target areas first, then rinse off the pHisoHex and finish your shower with regular soap.

➣ Another, milder antibacterial formulation is **proviodine**. It's gentler on the skin than pHisoHex.

Beyond Deodorant

➣ Wipe **rubbing alcohol, vinegar,** or **hydrogen peroxide** onto your underarms during the day to cut down the numbers of odor-causing bacteria.

➣ Dab on **witch hazel.** You can splash it directly on your skin or apply it as often as necessary with a cotton pad. The clear, clean-smelling liquid has drying and deodorizing properties.

➣ Dust **baking soda** or **cornstarch** on any odor-troubled part of your body. Both of these powders absorb moisture, and baking soda also kills odor-causing bacteria.

~ **Shave regularly** under your arms. Underarm hair can increase body odor because it traps sweat and bacteria.

Help from the Garden

~ Apply **tea-tree oil** to problem areas, as long as it doesn't irritate your skin. This oil, from an Australian tree, kills bacteria and also has a pleasant scent.

~ Essential oils of **lavender, pine,** and **peppermint** fight bacteria. They also smell nice. Since some people have a skin reaction to certain oils, test the underarm area or a small patch of skin before using.

~ Delightfully fragrant, **sage** can fight bacteria and reduce perspiration. You can purchase a solution of sage tincture or diluted sage oil, or brew some sage tea that you cool and store in a bottle. Any of these liquids can be used in the underarm area, but not around the genitals. And after using sage, wash your hands before touching your face.

~ A citrus fruit like **lemon** changes the pH level of your skin, making it more acidic. All bacteria, including the odor-causing kinds, have a hard time surviving in a highly acidic environment. Just rub on some lemon and pat dry.

Eat Green, Smell Clean

~ Eat plenty of **spinach, chard,** and **kale.** Green, leafy vegetables are rich in chlorophyll, which has a powerful deodorizing effect in your body.

~ Have a few sprigs of **parsley**, credited with anti-odor properties. Or make parsley tea by steeping a teaspoon of chopped fresh parsley in a cup of boiling water for five minutes. Let it cool a bit before you drink it.

~ Try **wheatgrass juice**, sold in health-food stores. Warning: It has a very strong taste, and some people feel nauseated the first time they try it. You might want to start with just 30 milliliters of wheatgrass juice in 200 milliliters of water, then increase the proportion of juice in subsequent tastings. On first tasting, it's wise to try this drink on an empty stomach just in case your stomach overreacts.

~ Buy tablets containing **chlorophyll.** Many brands are available, made from plants like kelp, barley grass, and blue-green algae. Check the label for the dosage recommendation.

Should I call **the doctor?**

If you're sweating frequently or heavily, you could have an overactive thyroid gland, low blood sugar, or a problem with the part of the nervous system that controls sweating. If you think you're sweating too much or you may have a medical condition causing your body odor, see your doctor. And if you're taking a prescription medication that might be contributing to excessive odor, ask your doctor about switching to another drug.

Did you **know?**

Hunters often use special soaps to mask all traces of human odor so their keen-smelling quarry won't smell them. You can try this approach so *human* noses won't notice you. Look for the products in hunting stores or catalogs.

Boils

There's only one thing to do with a boil: Get rid of it ASAP. And you can, but not by putting on the squeeze. Instead, use heat and moisture to hustle it to a head, then safe and sterile methods to induce draining and provide pain relief. Or try drying treatments to shrink the offender out of existence.

What's wrong

Sometimes called an abscess or a furuncle, a boil by any other name is still a boil. Highly infectious bacteria—usually staphylococci—work their way down a hair follicle into your skin. The boil fills with pus, swells, and forms a white or yellow "head" as the fluid forces its way upward. Most often, boils arise where clothing rubs against your skin or where moist body parts are in constant contact: on the neck, under the arms, near the buttocks, or around the inner thighs. Typically, a boil bursts on its own within about two weeks, and that starts the healing process. If you can bring the boil to a head and help pus escape, you can often safely accelerate this process.

Put Heat on the Boil

🍂 **Moist heat** will help bring a boil to a head. Among folk remedies, there is a grocery list of items that seem to work when heated—including warm bread, milk, cabbage, and even figs. But a simple washcloth works too. Soak a clean washcloth or towel in very hot water—as hot as you can stand without burning yourself. Wring out the cloth and apply it to the boil for 10 to 15 minutes. Repeat this several times a day.

🍂 You can also use warm **thyme** or **chamomile tea** instead of plain water when you prepare the compress. Thyme has an antiseptic compound called thymol that may help prevent infection. And chamomile tea contains a chemical, called chamazulene, that has anti-inflammatory properties.

🍂 Also beneficial is a compress of the homeopathic tinctures of **calendula (marigold) and hypericum (St. John's wort)**. Put one teaspoon of each tincture in a cup of hot water and saturate three layers of cotton gauze. Apply this compress several times daily to decrease pain and inflammation.

🍂 A warm, moist **tea bag** will serve as a compress all by itself. Tea contains tannins, astringent compounds with antibacterial properties.

🍂 If you favor old folk remedies and have a **green cabbage** on hand, use a well-cooked cabbage leaf to pull the pus out of a boil. First, boil a cabbage leaf for a minute or so. Let it cool slightly, then wrap it with gauze. Fasten the gauze-covered leaf over the boil with a bandage and leave it for an hour. Use a fresh leaf and gauze each day.

👈 If the boil is in a hard-to-reach area, simply soak in a **hot bath.** While you're in the tub, keep the water as hot as possible without burning your skin.

A Draining Experience

👈 To drain a boil after it comes to a head, **sterilize a needle** by holding it over an open flame, using tongs or an oven glove so you don't burn your fingers. Then gently prick the thin layer of skin on top of the boil. (*Off-limits*... if you detect any signs of infection such as redness or inflamed-looking streaks.)

👈 Once the head is popped or has ruptured on its own, place a clean, **warm washcloth** on top. First soak the washcloth in a solution of **salt water** and **hydrogen peroxide.** (Mix one teaspoon each of 3% hydrogen peroxide and salt in a cup of hot water.) During the next three days, as the boil drains, replace the compress as frequently as possible.

👈 Each time you take off the washcloth, use **liquid antibacterial soap** and water to clean the boil and the surrounding skin area. Then apply an **antibacterial ointment** on and around the boil with a cotton-tip applicator to guard against infection. Or try **Silver Liquid 400 PPM**, a natural homeopathic antimicrobial agent, instead.

All Dried Up

👈 Sometimes a boil will go away if it just dries out. To help kill the bacteria causing the boil—as well as dry it out—apply an acne medication containing **benzoyl peroxide** twice a day.

👈 Another way to make a boil clear out is by applying **tea-tree oil.** This natural antiseptic kills germs and helps your skin heal faster.

The Power of Prevention

👈 If you've had problems with boils in the past, consider switching to an **antibacterial soap**, such as Dial, or an alcohol-water-based cleansing gel.

👈 With heat and pressure, bacteria can get trapped in body hair. Avoid wearing tight pants, a sweatband, or any other clothing that rubs against your skin and captures perspiration. Instead, opt for **loose, comfortable clothing.**

Should I call the doctor?

Boils on the face pose a special risk because they might allow bacteria to get into your sinuses (leading to sinusitis), blood (septicemia), or even brain (cerebral abscess). So seek a doctor's treatment for these. And if you frequently get boils of any size, you should have a medical examination to make sure you don't have diabetes or an immune-system problem. Also check with your doctor if you develop boils in the armpits, in the groin, or (if you're a nursing mother) on your breasts. Otherwise, a boil needs attention if it's larger than 1.5 centimeters in size or if you detect signs of infection—intense redness, chills, a fever, or swelling anywhere on your body.

✎ **Don't share clothing** with anyone who has a problem with boils. The infectious material can spread on contact. For the same reason, you shouldn't use anyone else's washcloths and towels. If someone in your household has boils, their laundry should be washed separately.

✎ If you're overweight, you're at greater risk of boils because they tend to crop up where moist skin is rubbing against itself. **Shedding some weight** can help.

✎ In areas where skin friction leads to boils, **dust on some talc** to reduce moisture and chafing. (*Off-limits* . . . for women's use in the genital area. Talcum powder has been linked to ovarian cancer.)

✎ Pressure on the skin can also lead to boils, which is why they so often crop up on the part of your body you sit upon. If you sit in a car a lot, consider getting a **beaded seat pad**, which allows air to circulate behind you.

Breast Tenderness

As sure as the moon has phases, breast discomfort waxes and wanes. Here are some approaches to ease the unpleasantness hatched by your hormones. Vitamins, herbs, and oils keep fluid retention in check and coax your hormones into a breast-friendly balance (more progesterone, less estrogen). And a few dietary changes will help you get some bothers off your chest.

A Soap-orific

🍂 When you're in the shower, soap your breasts and gently **massage** them from the center of your chest out to your armpits. This improves blood circulation and the drainage of lymph, the clear fluid that carries infection-fighting agents through your body.

Take Cold Comfort

🍂 Wrap a towel around a bag of **ice cubes** or frozen vegetables and apply it to each breast for about 10 minutes. The cold-pack treatment reduces swelling and dulls the pain.

Schedule Some Supplements

🍂 **Dandelion** is a natural diuretic. Take the herb in capsule form, or make a tea using powdered dandelion root, available at health-food stores or from Web sites that market dried herbs. Simmer two to three teaspoons of the powder in a cup of water for 15 minutes. Drink three cups a day.

🍂 Try **evening primrose oil**, a traditional herbal remedy for premenstrual symptoms. It contains an essential fatty acid called gamma-linolenic acid (GLA) that may help balance a woman's hormones and seems to ease cyclical breast tenderness. Take 1,000 milligrams of the oil in liquid or capsule form three times a day. Take it with meals to enhance absorption.

🍂 **Vitamins E and B$_6$** may also work together to help prevent breast pain. The effective dose is 800 IU of vitamin E

What's **wrong**

Just as the uterus cycles through changes each month, so do the breasts. Shifting levels of hormones—mainly estrogen and progesterone—trigger tissue growth and fluid retention in the breasts as the milk glands get ready for potential pregnancy. This can lead to pain and may also cause lumps to form. Cyclical breast tenderness was once called fibrocystic breast disease, but is now recognized to be just a side effect of menstruation. Almost half of women under 50 experience it. Breast tenderness tends to be most noticeable just before menstruation. However, it can also be related to the taking of certain drugs, such as cimetidine.

Should I call **the doctor?**

daily, along with 50 milligrams of B_6, though you should discuss supplementation of this level with your doctor. While you won't be able to meet these goals with food alone, you can boost the vitamins in your diet by eating nuts, barley, and wheat germ for more vitamin E, and avocados, lean meats, and spinach for plenty of B_6.

Get a New Lift

🍂 Consider wearing **support bras** instead of underwire bras when your breasts are tender. You may want to wear your bra to bed to reduce nighttime jostling. When you try on a new bra, make sure it cups your breasts without pinching. Once you have new, more comfortable bras, throw away the stretched-out old ones that just don't provide the right support anymore.

Look to Food Solutions

🍂 Eat more **soybeans** and other soy foods. Population studies have shown that in traditional Asian cultures where people consume a lot of soy, women have fewer estrogen-related problems like breast pain and menopause symptoms. Soy contains hormonelike compounds called phytoestrogens that can influence hormonal fluctuations related to menstruation and menopause. Try some soy-based meat substitutes, or add tofu or soy nuts to your meals. Soy milk is another excellent source; try it in fruit smoothies.

🍂 Consume plenty of **fiber**, such as fruits, vegetables, legumes (like lentils and black beans), and whole grains. A study at Tufts University School of Medicine found that women on a higher-fiber diet excreted more estrogen.

🍂 Aim to get less than 30 percent of your calories from **fat.** Women who live in cultures where low-fat diets are the norm generally have a lower incidence of breast pain.

🍂 Cut back your intake of **hydrogenated oils**, found in margarine, packaged baked goods, and snack products. When you eat these oils, your body loses some of its ability to convert the fatty acids in your diet (essential to your health) into GLA—a necessary link in a chain reaction that prevents breast tissue from becoming painful.

🍂 Reduce your consumption of **methylxanthine**. Methyl ... *what?* As unfamiliar as this sounds, it's a component of many common foods, including coffee, cola, tea, wine, beer, bananas, chocolate, cheese, peanut butter, mushrooms, and pickles. Most women who endure painful lumps on a cyclical basis will improve if they cut way back, or eliminate, foods that are high in this compound.

🙠 Go easy on the salt shaker, and **watch your intake of sodium** from canned soups and packaged foods. Sodium increases water retention, which causes your breasts to swell. Be especially careful to keep a cap on your salt consumption starting about two weeks before your period.

More Ways to Improve Hormone Harmony

🙠 To help get your hormones into a more breast-friendly balance, try a natural **progesterone cream.** Ask your doctor for a prescription. Rub the cream into your skin every day, following the label directions.

🙠 If you're on birth-control pills or hormone-replacement therapy, talk to your doctor about **altering your drug regimen.** Some relatively minor adjustments in dosages might help.

🙠 **Exercise** vigorously 30 minutes at least three times a week, especially during the week before your period. Exercise decreases the stress hormones in your body. And that's significant, because those hormones play a role in causing breast pain. Exercise also helps reduce fluids in your body while increasing levels of feel-good chemicals in your brain.

🙠 Regularly engage in **meditation, breathing exercises,** or other **relaxation techniques** that can reduce stress hormones.

Breast-Feeding Problems

Now you know why Victorian wet nurses were so highly prized. For many new mothers, it's a shock to discover that this most basic of all bonding experiences is not necessarily a breeze. You'll probably learn a thing or two from a hospital nurse or friends, but every newborn gives birth to an all-new nursing experience. When your breasts start producing their regular milk supply a few days after your baby's birth, they may feel painfully tight, and your baby may have trouble latching on. Many other factors affect your baby's refuelings—and your own comfort. When problems arise, like nipple soreness or a clogged duct, it helps to know a few tricks of the trade.

What's wrong?

A number of problems can arise during breast-feeding that leave the mother sore and the baby fussy. Common issues include cracked or sore nipples, blocked milk ducts, and breasts that are painfully engorged with milk (or, conversely, don't seem to be providing enough milk). Also, especially in the first few weeks, breast-feeding can be a physically tiring process, and it may take a while for the mother and child to learn how to work smoothly together.

Take the Pressure Off

❧ Before nursing, **release a bit of milk by hand.** This will take away some of the pressure and allow your baby to attach more easily. To do it, press repeatedly with your fingers above and below the areola (the dark area around the nipple).

❧ If your breasts are so full that no milk comes out, **apply a hot compress** for several minutes. A wet washcloth will work, or try a sopping-wet diaper, which holds a lot of water and retains heat. Just soak a diaper in hot water and apply it when you're in the tub or shower.

❧ **Use a breast pump** to get the milk flowing, or to finish the feeding. With a breast pump you can apply steady, constant suction. This encourages the milk to "let down" and makes suckling easier for the baby. Also, if your baby is full or falls asleep before you finish nursing, use the breast pump to finish.

❧ **Nurse frequently**, day and night. In fact, you should nurse about 8 to 12 times during every 24-hour period. This will keep your breasts from filling up with too much milk. Feed the baby every time he seems interested in eating.

Position Yourself (and Your Baby) for Success

❧ **Use a nursing pillow**, a horseshoe-shaped cushion specially designed for nursing mothers. It fits around your midriff, providing a convenient armrest when you're cradling your baby. Two popular brands are the Boppy and My Brest Friend.

~ Make sure your baby is **not too warm.** If an infant is all wrapped up while nursing, she's more likely to drowse off in the middle of feeding.

~ Feed your baby in a **quiet, dimly lit** environment. Relaxation makes the process easier for everyone.

~ When you feed the baby, make sure **her entire body is facing yours.** Hold her buttocks in one hand, supporting her head in the crook of that elbow. Slide your other hand under your breast, fully supporting it. **Tickle your baby's lower lip.** This will prompt her to open her mouth. Pull her straight in, quickly, so her mouth attaches to your areola. Be sure she **takes the whole areola** into her mouth, or as much of it as possible.

~ When the baby is full, gently insert your pinkie between the corner of her mouth and the skin of your nipple to **break the suction.** Babies have a natural survival reflex: They hold on tighter if they're suddenly interrupted while sucking. If you can gradually break the seal between your nipple and her mouth before you pull her away, you'll reduce needless tugging.

Left, Right, Left

~ To make sure each breast is doing its share, start each feeding with the breast you ended with at the previous feeding. Too tired to remember which breast that was? **Fasten a safety pin** to your bra on the side where you should begin next time. By switching the breast you offer first, you give each one a chance to get completely emptied.

Become More Productive

~ If you feel you aren't producing enough milk, drink one glass of **nonalcoholic beer** a day. There's a yeast derivative in the beer that increases levels of prolactin, a hormone that influences milk production. Just make sure it's nonalcoholic, and drink the beer thirty minutes before a feeding.

~ Apply **pressure** to your chest to stimulate milk flow. According to doctors who specialize in acupressure techniques, the best pressure points are directly above your breasts. Place your thumbs between the third and fourth ribs directly

Should I call **the doctor?**

If you're concerned that your baby isn't getting enough milk, immediately talk to your doctor or lactation educator. Definitely contact the doctor if your baby hasn't eaten in 24 hours. You also need to consult with your doctor if you have a red, tender area on a breast, as well as flulike symptoms and a fever. These are symptoms of a breast infection known as mastitis, which is caused by bacteria slipping into your breast through cracks in the nipple. It's treatable with antibiotics, and you can continue breast-feeding your baby while you're being treated.

down from your collarbone and in line with your nipples. Press steadily for a minute or so. If this helps, you can repeat as often as you like.

☙ Drink **fennel tea** each morning. Herbalists have long recommended fennel to first-time mothers to help increase milk production. No one is certain why—or even if—it works, but some research indicates that fennel may have a mild estrogen-like effect, which could encourage the production of breast milk. Or perhaps babies just like fennel's licorice-like taste. Simmer one teaspoon of fennel seeds in one cup of hot water for about five minutes, strain out the seeds, and drink the tea.

☙ Another herb said to promote lactation is chaste tree, also known as **chasteberry**. It's been shown to affect hormone production (it's also used to help regulate a woman's menstrual cycle). Drink a cup or two each day, or take 225 milligrams of a chasteberry supplement.

☙ Try a daily dose of **fenugreek**. In the past, nursing mothers used to eat a teaspoon or so of fenugreek seeds every day. Now you can purchase fenugreek in capsule form. The recommended dose is 600 to 700 milligrams.

Munch Some Strong Encouragement

☙ **Eat garlicky foods.** Apparently garlic affects the flavor of mother's milk in a way that's appealing to babies. A study at the Monell Chemical Senses Center in Philadelphia showed that babies suckled more milk, and stayed at the breast longer, if their mothers ate some garlic a few hours before breast-feeding.

Nip Soreness in the Bud

☙ If one nipple is particularly sore, **offer the other one** first to your baby. Even if that's the same nipple you offered first during the previous feeding, you'll want to favor the "good" nipple until the painful one feels better.

~ Between feedings, place a **cold washcloth** on each breast to relieve soreness.

~ If your nipples are cracked or tender, try vitamin-E oil. Pierce a vitamin E capsule, squeeze out some of the liquid, and rub it in. Be sure to clean off any remaining liquid before the next feeding. No vitamin E capsules on hand? Try olive oil, sweet almond oil, lanolin cream, or a product called Bag Balm.

Conduct Some Duct Maintenance

~ For a clogged milk duct (which may present itself as a red, tender lump in your breast), soap the affected area while you're in the bath or shower and then gently run a **wide-toothed comb** over it to stimulate milk flow and help clear the blockage. (In general, however, avoid using soap on your nipples, as it can dry them out.)

~ **Empty your breasts** as completely as possible during each feeding. Offer your baby the affected breast first.

~ Try to gently **press the lump** toward your nipple during feeding.

~ Increase blood flow to the area by placing **a warm washcloth** on your breast, then gently massaging the breast.

~ Make sure your **bra is loose enough** that it's not pressing into the breast and causing the blockage.

Old **wives' tale**

For a long time, it was believed to be "common knowledge" that a mother's breasts would become too full of milk if she fed her baby very frequently. Actually, frequent nursing keeps them better drained.

Bronchitis

Your goal: Thin the phlegm in your chest and get it moving, so you can cough it up and out. The most direct approach to your lungs is the air you breathe, so inhalation treatments are a first resort. Think of them as a steam cleaning for your airways. The right food and drink can also help to keep mucus on the move. At the same time, you'll want to get some germ-fighters into your body's ecosystem so the bugs that cling to that mucus are mightily discouraged. Here's how to proceed:

What's wrong

Short-lived cases of bronchitis are usually caused by a viral or bacterial infection, though they can also be brought on by allergies. The bronchial tubes swell up, and the cilia—tiny hairs lining the respiratory tract—become paralyzed. Mucus accumulates, forcing you to cough heavily. You may also experience achiness, shortness of breath, wheezing, sweating, chills, fatigue, and fever. These symptoms generally go away after 10 days. Chronic bronchitis, on the other hand, can last a lifetime. Most chronic bronchitis is caused by cigarette smoking, though some cases originate from exposure to fumes and dust.

Have Good Self-Steam

◦ **Breathe steam.** You can do that just by taking a hot shower, of course. Or pour steaming-hot water into a bowl and lean over it, draping a towel over your head. Inhaling the steam will help loosen the secretions in your lungs.

◦ To make the steam treatment even more effective, add a few drops of **eucalyptus** or **pine oil** to the water. Eucalyptus helps to soften mucus in obstructed airways and has some antibacterial properties. (If you want to use eucalyptus leaves, simply boil them in a pot of water, then remove from the heat and inhale the steam.) Pine oil acts as an expectorant, so it will help you "bring up" phlegm from the bronchial tubes.

◦ Run a **humidifier** in your bedroom when you're sleeping to moisten the air you breathe. But be sure to follow the manufacturer's directions for cleaning the humidifier. Otherwise, bacteria and mold can accumulate in the works.

◦ If you have an ultrasound, cool-mist humidifier, add the contents of a one-pint bottle of **3% hydrogen peroxide** and a quarter-cup of water. The hydrogen peroxide works to thin mucus and may even help get the infection under control. You can leave the humidifier running day and night so you're constantly breathing in the vapors.

Make a Run for It

◦ To thin mucus and help you cough it up more easily, **drink lots of water**—at least eight 250-milliliter glasses each day. And **avoid alcohol** and caffeinated drinks, which dehydrate your system and make the mucus tougher to dislodge.

⌢ Eat **chile peppers, hot spicy salsa,** or dishes prepared with **cayenne pepper.** Fiery foods don't just make your nose run—they also thin the mucus in your lungs, helping you cough more productively.

⌢ Drink **mullein tea.** Mullein, a traditional folk remedy for respiratory ailments, offers another way to clear mucus from your lungs. It contains saponins, which help loosen phlegm, along with a gelatinous mucilage that soothes raw mucous membranes. Boil a cup of water, remove from the heat, and drop in two teaspoons dried mullein leaves. Let the tea steep for 10 minutes, then strain out the wet leaves and drink the tea. You can drink up to three cups a day.

⌢ **Avoid milk products.** Cow's milk contains lactalbumin, which stimulates the production of mucus in the upper and lower respiratory tract and in the intestines. (Young calves, with four stomachs, need this extra mucus to help protect their intestinal tracts from strong stomach acids . . . but you don't!) When humans drink cow's milk, the result is excessive mucus production.

Supplement Your Efforts

⌢ **N-acetyl cysteine (NAC),** a form of the amino acid cysteine, helps thin and loosen mucus. Take one 600-milligram dose three times daily, between meals, until the bronchitis has cleared up. If you're treating short-lived bronchitis, continue taking NAC for another few weeks after the cough goes away.

⌢ **Echinacea** and **astragalus** are herbs that strengthen the immune system and help you fight off bacteria and viruses. Take 500 milligrams of either herb four times a day for acute bronchitis or twice daily for chronic bronchitis.

⌢ **R-lipoic acid** is a powerful antioxidant nutrient that is vital in the repair of inflamed airways. Like other antioxidants such as vitamins E and C, R-lipoic acid contributes to your health by counteracting the effects of harmful molecules called free radicals, which damage cells. Usually your body produces enough lipoic acid on its own, but when there's inflammation, cells are under stress and need all the help they can get. Take 100 milligrams of R-lipoic acid three times daily with meals.

Should I call
the doctor?

See your doctor if your cough is interfering with your sleep or your normal routine, or if breathing is difficult. You should also call the doctor if you have a fever above 37.8°C (100°F) or you're coughing up blood. Bronchitis can lead to pneumonia.

Skip it!

When you're coughing, it might seem like the most obvious treatment is a cough suppressant. But if you have a wet, productive cough, you shouldn't try to suppress it. Instead, use an expectorant cough syrup that helps loosen mucus, so the coughing clears out your bronchial passages. To make sure you're getting an expectorant, look for products containing the ingredient guaifenesin.

A medicinal formula called **Arcozon** has potent antibacterial and immune-stimulating properties. It contains four herbs that have been traditionally used by healers in the Amazon rainforest: *uña de gato* (cat's claw), pau d'arco, suma, and jatoba. You can use it to prevent or treat bronchial infections. Take one teaspoon or four capsules four times daily for short-lived bronchitis or twice daily for chronic bronchitis.

The Power of Prevention

To prevent chronic bronchitis, the most essential advice is: **Don't smoke.** If you're a smoker, find out about programs that will help you give it up.

If your job exposes you to lots of dust, fumes, or pollutants—any of which can contribute to chronic bronchitis—be sure you're wearing the proper **mask** or **respirator** to filter the impurities from the air you breathe.

To slash your risk of getting viral bronchitis, **wash your hands** frequently and keep them away from your face, especially when you've been around someone who has a cold. **Clean your nose and sinuses** with saline nasal spray. Or use a sinus-clearing over-the-counter medication recommended by your pharmacist. It should help prevent allergens and infectious agents from getting into your lungs.

Vitamin C helps you fight off respiratory viruses. It works well in conjunction with supplemental flavonoids, also called bioflavonoids. As a preventive measure, take up to 2,000 milligrams daily of vitamin C with flavonoids in divided doses. (With higher doses of vitamin C, some people get diarrhea.)

Bruises

Bang! That's going to leave a bruise. Though bruises eventually go away on their own, you can take steps to reduce the pain and encourage faster fading. First, reduce blood flow to the area with ice and compression to minimize discoloration. Next, use heat to boost circulation and help clear away the pooled blood. At the same time, as long as the skin isn't broken, a number of herbal ointments and compresses can help erase the evidence of a klutzy moment that left its mark.

Speed the Paling Process

➤ Apply **ice** as soon as possible. If you cool the blood vessels around the bruised area, less blood will leak out into the surrounding tissue. Many flexible ice packs are available, specifically designed for injuries, and most rough-and-tumble athletes have the foresight to keep a couple of them in the freezer. If you're not so equipped, soak a cloth in ice-cold water and lay it over the bruise for 10 minutes. Or use a bag of **frozen vegetables** wrapped in a towel. Take it off after 10 minutes, and wait 20 minutes or so before you reapply the ice pack so you don't overchill the skin underneath.

➤ If you've bruised your arm or leg, immediately wrap an **elastic bandage** around the bruised part. By squeezing the tissues underneath, the bandage helps prevent blood vessels from leaking. The bruise won't be quite as severe.

➤ **Reduce blood flow** to the bruise to minimize discoloration. If you bruise your leg, for instance, and you can take a time-out, settle into a couch or lounge chair with your leg up on a pillow, above heart level. If it's your arm that's bruised, try to keep it propped up above heart level whenever you're sitting.

Have a Heat Exchange

➤ After cooling the bruise for 24 hours, start applying heat to bring more circulation to the area and help clear away the pooled blood. Use an **electric heating pad** for 20 minutes several times a day. Be sure to follow the instructions on the

What's **wrong**

You've had a bump, blow, or knock to your body that was hard enough to damage small blood vessels under your skin. Blood leaks out of these blood vessels, called capillaries, and seeps into the surrounding tissue. For a while you see the traditional black-and-blue colors, which are the trademark of most bruises. As the pooled blood gradually breaks down, the colors take on a full palette of hues, from purple to green and yellow. Normally, bruises will fade away in 10 to 14 days without any treatment.

Should I call
the doctor?

If your bruises appear mysteriously—that is, in places that you haven't even injured—be sure to see your doctor. Sometimes bruises are the mark of serious conditions like hemophilia, leukemia, and aplastic anemia. Consult your doctor if you have a bruise at a joint and it leads to swelling, if a bruise doesn't fade after a week, if it's accompanied by severe pain or fever, or if you get a bruise on the side of your head over your ear (this area fractures easily).

heating pad: To avoid burns, it should go on top of—not under—the bruised limb.

🌱 Alternatively, you can apply a **warm compress** either under or over the bruised area. A hot-water bottle will work. Or use a compress that can be heated in a microwave, such as **Thera-Temp Microwavable Moist Heat Pack**, available at medical supply stores and on Internet sites.

🌱 A warm compress of **comfrey** can also offer comfort. Comfrey contains compounds that reduce swelling and promote the rapid growth of new cells. Make a warm herbal solution by pouring 2 cups of boiling water over 30 grams of dried comfrey leaves or 60 grams of fresh leaves. Steep for 10 minutes, then strain. This is for an external use only—it's *not* for drinking. Soak a gauze pad or a washcloth in the solution and apply it to the bruise for an hour. (*Off-limits . . .* if the skin is broken or you have an open wound.)

🌱 **Vinegar** mixed with warm water will help the healing process. Vinegar increases blood flow near the skin's surface, so it may help dissipate the blood that has pooled in the bruise area. **Witch hazel** will also do the trick.

Here's the Rub

🌱 **Arnica** is an herb that has long been recommended for bruises. It contains a compound that reduces inflammation and swelling. Apply arnica ointment or gel to the bruise daily.

🌱 Take a handful of fresh **parsley** leaves, crush them, and spread them over the bruise. Wrap the area with an elastic bandage. Some experts claim that parsley decreases inflammation, reduces pain, and can make the bruise fade more quickly.

🌱 Gently rub **St. John's wort** oil into the bruise. Though St. John's wort is often taken as a capsule or tea for mild

The Do-It-Yourselfer's Flexible Ice Pack

If you tend to like bumptious sports—or you clobber your shins at regular intervals—it helps to have an ice pack handy. To prepare one in advance, fill a resealable plastic bag with two cups water and one-third cup rubbing alcohol. Zip it shut and stick it in the freezer. Overnight it forms a slushy ice that will conform to any body part that gets damaged in the course of daily activities.

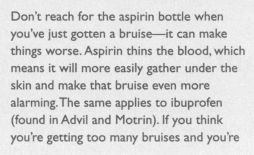

Be Selective About Pain Relievers

Don't reach for the aspirin bottle when you've just gotten a bruise—it can make things worse. Aspirin thins the blood, which means it will more easily gather under the skin and make that bruise even more alarming. The same applies to ibuprofen (found in Advil and Motrin). If you think you're getting too many bruises and you're also taking aspirin regularly (to reduce your risk of heart attack, for example) talk to your doctor about the problem but don't stop taking the aspirin on your own. For pain relief when you have a bruise, use acetaminophen, the ingredient found in Tylenol.

depression, the oil has long been known as a wound healer. It's rich in tannins, astringents that help shrink tissue and control capillary bleeding. For the best effect, start this treatment soon after the bruise occurs, and repeat it three times a day.

↜ Look for **vitamin K cream** in the drugstore. Your body needs vitamin K to help with blood clotting. Rub it into the bruise twice a day to prevent further bleeding.

Swallow, Please

↜ **Bromelain**, an enzyme found in pineapples, actually "digests" proteins involved in causing inflammation and inducing pain. Take 250 to 500 milligrams of bromelain daily between meals until the bruise has faded.

↜ Use a **homeopathic version of arnica**. As soon as you get the bruise, start taking one dose every four hours. Take four doses the first day, then reduce your dosages to two or three pills daily as the bruise fades.

The Power of Prevention

↜ If you feel like you bruise too easily, you may be deficient in **vitamin C**. It strengthens capillary walls so they're less likely to leak blood and make a bruise. Get additional vitamin C by eating more peppers and citrus fruit, and take a multivitamin.

↜ Increase your intake of **flavonoids** by eating more **carrots, apricots, and citrus fruits**. These help vitamin C work better in the body. Grape-seed extract is also a rich supplier of flavonoids. Take 20 to 50 milligrams daily.

↜ People who are susceptible to bruising may be deficient in **vitamin K**, which you can get from broccoli, Brussels sprouts, and leafy green vegetables, as well as from supplements.

Bursitis and Tendinitis

There's nothing worse than having a much-valued limb go on strike, particularly if it's the one you rely on for gardening or golf, whittling or Wiffle Ball. The first lesson most athletes and weekend warriors need to learn is respect: Healing begins when you acknowledge the need for some time off from your usual activities. While you're on the mend, the name of the game is reducing the inflammation that's causing your soreness. Then you'll want to give your joint some TLC to ease it back into action and recover a full range of motion.

What's wrong

These somewhat related conditions are often the price you pay for too much repeated motion, whether something fun like playing tennis, or not so fun, like shoveling snow. Tendinitis is inflammation of the tendons, the tough cords that attach muscles to bones. Bursitis is inflammation of the bursae—tiny, fluid-filled sacs that provide cushioning where muscle touches bone or rubs up against another muscle. Where bursitis often feels like a dull ache at a joint, tendinitis tends to produce sharp pain. These conditions crop up most often in the shoulders, hips, elbows, knees, and ankles.

Make a Rest Stop

⤙ **Take a break** before you repeat the activity that triggered the pain. Be patient, since the problem may take a few weeks to resolve.

⤙ To hold down swelling, wrap an **elastic bandage** around the joint—but not too snugly. Then elevate the joint above the level of your heart. If it's your elbow that hurts, keep it on a high armrest, or sit in a low chair with your elbow propped up on the table. If you're treating your knee, lie on your back with the knee propped up on pillows.

Run Cold and Hot

⤙ **Ice your sore joint** to ease pain and inflammation. Wrap up an ice pack in a towel and apply it for 10 to 20 minutes every four hours. Or freeze a paper cup full of ice, tear off the top edge, and rub the ice where it hurts. Repeat three or four times a day, allowing two to five minutes for each treatment.

⤙ After about three days of giving joints the cold treatment—or until the joint is no longer warm to the touch—start **alternating cold with heat.** Heat increases blood flow to the injury, helping it to heal faster. Use a microwavable heat pack or an electric heating pad. Or, for form-fitting warmth, place two to three cups of rice in a large sock, tie off the sock, and microwave for 60 to 90 seconds. The rice will conform nicely to a knee, elbow, or ankle.

Reach for Pain Relievers

⌁ **Ibuprofen (Advil or Motrin)** will help relieve the swelling and is very effective for short-term pain relief of this kind of pain.

⌁ Try **boswellia.** Your body produces certain chemicals that actually increase pain. But this extract, from the frankincense tree, reduces your production of those chemicals. Take 400 to 500 milligrams three times a day. As your pain fades, cut down on the dosage.

⌁ If you favor alternative approaches, consider a **homeopathic remedy.** If your joint is stiff and painful when you move it but feels better with more use, take a dose of *Rhus toxicodendron* at the 6C or 12C dilution every three to four hours until you feel relief. If the joint pain gets worse as you keep moving, take **bryonia** at the 6C or 12C dilution every three to four hours until the pain diminishes. For pain that comes on suddenly and acutely, homeopathic physicians recommend **ruta** and **arnica.** The recommended dose is a 6C or 12C dilution every three to four hours.

Take a Topical Vacation

⌁ To soothe the aching area, rub on **arnica cream** or ointment—a remedy derived from the mountain daisy—two or three times a day. Also popular for treating bruises and sprains, arnica reduces swelling and inflammation. For even greater relief, press a hot-water bottle or heating pad against the joint after you've applied the arnica.

⌁ **Tiger Balm,** a menthol-laced cream imported from China, can melt away pain. Rub it on the sore spot once or twice a day. But test a small patch of skin first. This is hot stuff, and some people develop a rash or redness if they use it too often.

⌁ Use a soothing **ginger compress** to help stop the hurt from the outside in. Chop two tablespoons of fresh ginger, drop it in three cups of hot water, and let it steep for 20 minutes. Immerse a folded piece of cloth in the warm tea and wring it out. Lay the cloth over your sore joint for five minutes. Repeat three or four times a day.

continued on page 100

Should I call **the doctor?**

If the problem gets worse after three or four days, or interferes with your daily activities, see your doctor. Also seek treatment if your joint is warm, red, and tender. These are signs of septic bursitis, a type of infection that can spread from one joint throughout your body.

Do-It-Yourself Healing: TLC for an Aching Shoulder

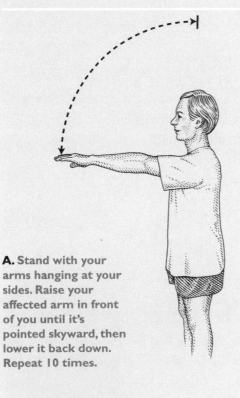

If you have shoulder pain, you might be tempted to stop using one arm because it hurts so much. But don't wait too long before putting it into action again. You might develop a condition called "frozen shoulder." Once you've treated the shoulder to the point where it's not severely hurting anymore, do some daily exercises to make sure your shoulder remains flexible.

Lie on a bed or firm sofa facedown, with your sore shoulder just slightly over the side of the bed and your arm hanging down. Swing your arm gently back and forth. Do this for 15 to 30 minutes, three to five times a week. (That's a long time to swing your arm, but fortunately, it's easy to watch TV from that position.)

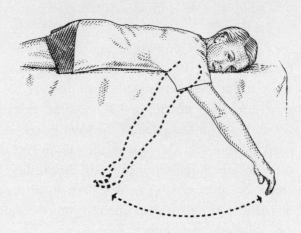

A. Stand with your arms hanging at your sides. Raise your affected arm in front of you until it's pointed skyward, then lower it back down. Repeat 10 times.

B. Now lift it out to your side, then lower. Repeat 10 times.

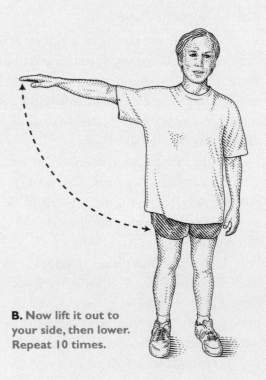

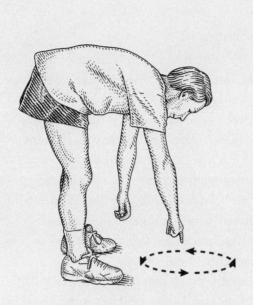

Bend over with your arms hanging loosely in front of you and swing one hand around as if you were drawing circles on the floor. After you've "drawn" 10 circles with one hand, repeat with the other.

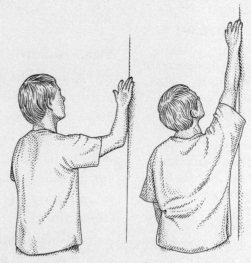

A. Stand facing a corner and place the fingertips of one hand against the wall. Use your fingertips to "crawl" up the corner, stepping closer as your hand moves higher.

B. When your arm is fully extended, hold the position for a few seconds, then lower your arm. Repeat 3 times, then do the same exercise with the other arm.

A. Get down on your hands and knees with your arms straight and your hands planted slightly forward of your shoulders.

B. Gradually sit back on your heels until you can feel the stretch in your shoulders. Then return to the crouch position. Do 5 repetitions.

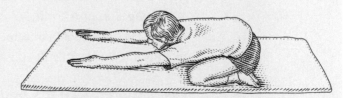

🍃 **Vinegar**, applied topically, also eases aches. Soak a cloth or dishtowel in equal parts hot water and vinegar. Wring it out and apply.

Swallow Some Soothers

🍃 **Ginger** isn't just for compresses. Supplements of this natural anti-inflammatory can also help. For acute pain, take six 500-milligram capsules a day.

🍃 Give the "curry cure" a go. **Curcumin** is the active ingredient in turmeric, an Indian spice that's a key ingredient in curry. While turmeric has a venerable reputation as an anti-inflammatory and pain-relieving agent, it seems to be curcumin that does the real work—inhibiting the synthesis of prostaglandins, which are hormonelike compounds in the body involved in transmission of pain signals. Take 400 to 500 milligrams of the extract three times a day.

🍃 **Bromelain**, an enzyme from pineapple, reduces inflammation. The strength of the standardized extract is measured in milk-clotting units (MCU) or gelatin-dissolving units (GDU). Look for a product that contains between 1,200 and 2,400 MCU or between 720 and 1,440 GDU. Take 500 milligrams one hour after meals three or four times a day.

🍃 Consider **black cherry juice**, an old-time folk remedy. It contains an antioxidant plant pigment called quercetin, which works as an anti-inflammatory. Quaff 475 milliliters a day, and there's a good chance your pain will dissipate.

🍃 Supplemental antioxidants will help strengthen and repair connective tissue in your joints. **Grape-seed** and **pine bark extract** are sources of powerful antioxidants called proanthocyanidins. Take 30 to 60 milligrams daily of both extracts.

🍃 **Manganese** helps the body clear away the waste products from inflammation related to bursitis or tendinitis. Take 50 to 100 milligrams of the mineral daily in divided doses for one or two weeks. If the pain continues, you can keep taking it for up to a month, but reduce the dose to 15 to 30 milligrams per day.

Favor the Fats That Coddle Your Joints

🍃 **Omega-3 fatty acids** help reduce inflammation. Increase the amounts in your diet by eating more cold-water fish, such as salmon, bluefin tuna, and mackerel. And consider taking supplemental flaxseed oil, which is rich in these "good" fats.

⤳ **Avoid** chips and other packaged foods that contain **hydrogenated oils**, and pass up fried foods, which are often cooked in those oils. These oils increase the inflammation in your body.

Ease into Sporting Life

⤳ As you resume sports or other normal activities, the joint that's been giving you pain will need some extra attention. Give the muscles near the joint a good **massage**—either on your own or with the help of a massage therapist—for additional pain relief and relaxation.

⤳ Always **stretch** properly before and after you exercise.

⤳ If you've had knee pain, make sure that you're using proper **shoes** for your sport. That's especially important before you resume a sport like tennis or running, where it's critical to have shoes that are well-fitting and in excellent condition. Get rid of those worn-out pairs that just have too many kilometers on them.

The Power of Prevention

⤳ Start a **strength-training** program using light weights to improve the muscles around the injured joint.

⤳ Avoid going to sleep with **your arm bent over your head**—that's a recipe for bursitis.

⤳ Be sure to interrupt long, repetitive chores with regular **stretch** breaks.

⤳ If you're a tennis player, avoid tennis elbow by making sure your racket has a large-handled grip and decreased string tension. Also, tennis elbow can develop if the racket head is too big or too small. Have the **grip, tension,** and **racket size** checked by a tennis instructor.

⤳ If you're going to be on your knees scrubbing the floor or pulling weeds, kneel on a **foam-rubber pad** designed for this purpose.

Calluses and Corns

In every pharmacy you'll find a section devoted to tender care of corns and calluses. This is a good aisle in which to start your search for relief. But the quest for treatment ingredients can take you much farther afield. If your feet are afflicted, you'll need the right oil to soften hard skin, customized patches for all-day protection, along with the socks, shoes, and insoles that protect you from pain. For hands, the right gloves count for a lot. Here's how to make corns and calluses take their lumps.

What's wrong

When your body tries to defend itself from injury, it sometimes creates strange armor. The outermost layer of skin piles up a thick fortress of dead cells whenever it's rubbed too much or too often. That's what happens when an ill-fitting shoe keeps rubbing the same toe, or a metal-handled rake puts friction on the inside of your thumb. The epidermis gradually builds up a callus. That, in turn, can evolve into a corn, which is simply a callus with a hard core. Calluses on the hands and feet can be painless and protective. But if a callus or corn presses on a bone or nerve underneath your three layers of skin, it can be as painful as a pebble between your toes.

Wield a Stone and Board

If a callus is causing you pain or aggravation, you need to scrape away some of those dead cells so the callus won't put so much pressure on your nerves. Immediately after a warm shower or bath, when your skin is wet and softened, rub a **pumice stone** on the callus to remove dead cells. A pumice stone, available at pharmacies, is simply a rough piece of volcanic mineral. Don't try to grind the whole callus away in one sitting, as you'll rub your skin raw. Instead, sand it down a little every day, and be patient. If the callus is very thick or hard, the sanding project might take a few weeks.

For what are called "soft corns," use an **emery board.** Soft corns occur between your toes. They arise when the bones in adjacent toes rub until the skin thickens. A pumice stone won't fit in that tight space between toes. Instead, purchase the same kind of emery board that's designed to pare down fingernails and file away a little bit after every bath.

Soften Up the Opposition

Instead of filing corns and calluses, you can soak and moisturize them until they grow soft. For corns on your toes, use **castor oil** as a softener with a **corn pad** as protector. To protect the corn, you want nonmedicated, doughnut-shaped pads, sold at pharmacies. Place one of these pads around the corn, dab a few drops of castor oil onto the corn with a cotton swab, then put adhesive tape over the top of the pad to hold it in place. The little padded doughnut encircles the corn and shields it from pressure while also holding in the moisturizing castor oil. (Since the castor oil can leak out through the bandage, causing stains, wear some old socks when you're using this treatment.)

❧ Another good way to soften calluses and corns is to soak them in water containing **Epsom salt.** Follow the directions on the package.

Stalk the Corn with Acid

❧ Look for medicated corn-removing patches that contain **salicylic acid.** Apply the patch after you've taken a shower. You might be able to leave on the patch until you shower again. But be sure to examine the area around the corn when you change the pad. The salicylic acid can cause sores on normal skin, and these can become infected.

❧ Another source of salicylic acid is plain old **aspirin.** To create your own corn-softening compound, crush five aspirin until they turn into a fine powder. Mix the powder thoroughly with one-half teaspoon of lemon juice and one-half teaspoon water. Dab the paste onto the thickened skin, circle it with a piece of plastic wrap, then cover the plastic with a heated towel. Remove everything after 10 minutes and gently scrub away the loosened skin with a pumice stone.

Create Some Non-Friction

❧ To help protect a callus or corn on your foot from pressure, custom-design a protective "doughnut" using a piece of adhesive **moleskin.** Cut a circle larger than your callus or corn, fold it in half, and cut a half-circle in the center. When you open it up, you'll have a padded ring. Apply it over your corn or callus.

❧ If you have a soft corn between two toes, stick a **foam toe separator** between them to keep them from rubbing each other. Look for these in the foot-care section at the pharmacy.

❧ Try socks that have very **thick, cushioned soles.** They could keep your calluses from getting worse.

❧ Sometimes, adding an over-the-counter **insole** to your shoes—such as a Dr. Scholl's product—can decrease the pressure on the area with the callus, and help to resolve it more quickly.

Should I call **the doctor?**

For anyone with diabetes, calluses and corns on the feet are particularly hazardous. Poor circulation puts you at high risk of foot infections, and it's dangerous to attempt self-treatment with nonsterile instruments that could introduce bacteria. So if you have diabetes, be sure to call your doctor whenever you have a callus or corn that needs attention. Others can probably try home treatments first, with the proviso that you need to get in touch with your doctor at once if the corn or callus becomes inflamed-looking. That's a sure sign of infection.

Skip it!

Some people may advise you to trim corns and calluses yourself, using a razor blade, scissors, or tweezers. Don't believe it! No matter how awesome your surgical skills, you have better things to do than practice on your own flesh. There's real danger of infection from mishandling sharp instruments.

The Power of Prevention

Apply a lotion containing **urea** to rough spots before they turn into troublesome calluses. **Dermal Therapy** is one brand. Start with a small amount, as urea-based lotions can sting.

Another way to prevent skin from toughening up is by soaking your feet in a tub of **warm water** once a week. Afterward, apply a **moisturizing lotion.**

Choose shoes that fit well. You should have a thumb's width of distance between your longest toe and the end of the shoe. Shoes should be wide enough so that your toes and the balls of your feet aren't cramped from side to side. If shoes are too roomy, your feet slide around and rub against the sides.

Since feet naturally swell during the day, **shop for shoes late in the afternoon** when your feet are plumpest. If you shop in the early morning, you might get stuck with a pair of shoes that are too small.

For women, it's advisable to **save the high heels for special occasions.** Even for the grand soiree, however, you should choose high heels that have a lot of cushioning in the front to reduce pressure on your toes.

Don't play tennis in your running shoes. For each sport, select the **appropriate type of shoe.** A lot of research and engineering has gone into the development of shoes that are perfect for particular foot motions.

To prevent calluses on your hands, wear thickly cushioned **gloves** when you're doing work such as raking, painting, or pruning.

Canker Sores

That little crater in your mouth causes more pain than anything so small deserves to. Rest assured that in a week or two, your canker sore will most likely be history, and you can chomp a chip, drink a cup of joe, or smooch your spouse without regretting it. Meanwhile, here are ways to blunt the pain and become a sore loser faster.

Seal the Sore

🔅 Over-the-counter topical analgesics such as **Zilactin-L** and **Xylocaine** (or ask your pharmacist for a generic version) form a long-lasting protective coating over the sore to speed healing and provide fast pain relief.

🔅 A form of licorice known as **deglycyrrhizinated licorice, or DGL,** also coats canker sores. It's available in health-food stores. Chew one or two 200-milligram tablets two or three times a day.

🔅 The sap of **aloe vera**—the ubiquitous "first aid plant"—can bring welcome relief. Squeeze a bit of gel from an aloe vera leaf. Dry the sore with a cotton swab, then dab on the gel. Repeat as often as you like.

🔅 Cut open a **vitamin E** capsule and squeeze a bit of the liquid onto the sore.

Put It in Neutral

🔅 Munch a chewable antacid **Tums** or **Rolaids** tablet or put it on the sore and allow it to dissolve. The pain you feel from a canker sore is caused by acids and digestive enzymes eating into the tissue in the sore. The tablets will neutralize the acids and may also speed healing. Check the label for dosage directions.

🔅 Use a small amount of **milk of magnesia** as a mouth rinse, or apply it to the canker sore three to four times a day.

🔅 Apply a damp **tea bag** to the sore for five minutes. Tea is alkaline, so it neutralizes acids. It also contains astringent compounds, which may help relieve the pain.

What's wrong

A mysterious condition known medically as recurrent aphthous stomatitis, canker sores typically appear inside the lips or cheeks, around the gums, or on the tongue. They are white or yellowish, with a halo of red, ranging from the size of a pinhead to the dimensions of a quarter. Experts aren't sure what causes them, but an immune-system malfunction is thought to play a role. A stressful episode or a mouth injury often precedes a breakout. Recurrent sores can also be brought on by eating certain foods.

Should I call the doctor?

If the pain is too distracting or it's keeping you from eating or drinking, call your dentist. Definitely call the dentist if you have more than four sores at a time or if the sores last longer than two weeks. Also, if you find that you're getting canker sores frequently, tell your dentist at your next visit so he or she can recommend evaluation and treatment, such as an antibiotic mouth rinse, a steroid ointment, a prescription oral paste, or chemical cautery of the sores.

Get That Numb Feeling

🖎 Dab on a **topical anesthetic** such as **Anbesol** or **Orajel**.

🖎 Let a **pain-relieving lozenge**, such as **Chloraseptic**, dissolve in your mouth.

Battle Bacteria

🖎 Mix one-quarter cup of **hydrogen peroxide** with one-quarter cup of water. Add one teaspoon of **baking soda** and one teaspoon of **salt**, and stir until they dissolve. Swish the solution around in your mouth and spit it out. Hydrogen peroxide is a strong disinfectant. That's a plus, since a canker sore is an open wound that's vulnerable to infection, which increases the pain. And since baking soda is alkaline, it provides extra relief by neutralizing acids.

🖎 To speed healing, apply a liquid form of herbal **goldenseal** on the sore three times a day, at least an hour before eating. Goldenseal has modest antibacterial properties.

🖎 Put a single drop of **tea-tree oil**, an antiseptic, directly on the sore.

🖎 Make a tea from **calendula**, better known as pot marigold, valued for centuries in the treatment of minor sores. Pour a cup of boiling water over a teaspoon or two of dried petals. Let it steep for 10 minutes, strain out the leaves, and let the tea cool down until it's barely warm. You can gargle and rinse several times a day, or drink the tea.

🖎 Eat **yogurt** that contains live acidophilus cultures (check the label). Have a few teaspoonfuls daily for prevention—more when you're having a breakout.

Take Extra Measures

🖎 Many experts think **lysine**, an amino acid available by prescription, may be needed to fix a deficiency associated with canker sores. Take 500 milligrams of L-lysine three times a day on an empty stomach until your sore is healed.

🖎 **Echinacea** is an herb that strengthens your immune system. Take 200 milligrams two or three times a day when you first notice a sore starting to appear.

🖎 **Vitamin C** helps heal your mouth's mucous membranes. Normally, we would turn to citrus fruits for vitamin C, but these may actually cause canker sores in some people. Instead, take vitamin C supplements. Try 1,000 milligrams three times a day. If you develop diarrhea with dosages this high, switch to 500-milligram supplements instead.

⁓ **Zinc** may help mouth injuries like canker sores heal faster. As soon as you detect a sore developing, take 30 milligrams of zinc lozenges each day until it's gone.

The Power of Prevention

⁓ **Stay away from foods that trigger canker sores.** Potential troublemakers include whole wheat, rye, barley, shellfish, pineapple or citrus fruits, figs, chocolate, tomatoes, green peppers, and strawberries. To find out which, if any, cause your cankers, cut all of them out of your diet. Then slowly reintroduce them, one at a time, and see which one makes the problem recur.

⁓ Check the label of your favorite toothpaste for an ingredient called sodium lauryl sulfate, or SLS. This foaming agent, found in many brands of toothpaste, contributes to canker sores in some people. And it really isn't necessary for teeth cleaning. If you get frequent sores, **look for brands that are free of SLS** such as Biotene and Arm & Hammer Dental Care Tooth Powder.

⁓ Tiny cuts and scrapes inside your mouth can cause canker sores. **Take care when eating jagged foods** like chips and pretzels. When you brush your teeth, **use a soft-bristled brush** to avoid scraping your gums.

⁓ See your dentist if you have any kind of tooth problem that could irritate the inside of your mouth. **Ill-fitting dentures**, especially, can be a problem.

⁓ People plagued with frequent canker sores may have a deficiency in certain B vitamins or iron. Try taking a **daily B-vitamin complex** and a **daily multivitamin/multimineral** for iron. To get more B vitamins into your diet, look to beans, wheat germ, and fortified cereal. Lean beef is a good source of iron.

⁓ Stressful episodes trigger many cases of canker sores. If you tend to get a little wired, try some of the classic methods of keeping your cool—**meditation, yoga,** and **aerobic exercise.**

A Gaggle of Gargles

Gargling isn't just for freshening bad breath—though a quick swish or two with clove tea does that quite well. (To make the tea, pour a cup of just-boiled water over 1 or 2 teaspoons of bruised cloves, steep, strain, then let cool. Or add 2 tablespoons of bruised cloves to 2 cups of vodka, sherry, or light wine, let sit for a week, then strain and bottle. To use as a mouthwash, add 1 to 3 teaspoons to water.) Depending on what you gargle with, gargling is also a wonderfully simple and remarkably effective way to kill germs, soothe a scratchy throat—even stop heartburn.

Like most other home healing techniques, gargling has a long tradition. If you believe the practitioners of the ancient Indian healing system known as Ayurveda, gargling with vegetable oil (or at least swishing it around the mouth) improves sleep and boosts brainpower while whitening the teeth and rejuvenating the gums. Closer to home, mainstream doctors are increasingly convinced that germ-killing gargles may help prevent cardiovascular disease. It seems the same germs that cause bad gums can enter the bloodstream and trigger blood clots that cause heart attack and stroke.

Just how do gargles work? The glug-glug-glugging action helps rinse away mucus and cellular debris that irritate the mouth and throat. And the ingredient or ingredients you add to the water act directly on raw, inflamed tissues, helping soothe areas roughed up by dry or polluted air—or by an afternoon of enthusiastic cheering at the local soccer field.

No need to get fancy with your gargles. All you really need is hot water and a few simple ingredients that you may already have on hand.

Soothe a Sore Throat

For a sore throat, it's hard to beat a lemon-juice-in-water gargle. The astringent juice helps shrink swollen throat tissue and creates a hostile (acidic) environment for viruses and bacteria. Just mix **1 teaspoon lemon juice in 1 cup water.** Of course, there's also plain old salt water. Use ¼ **teaspoon salt in 1 cup warm water**. Add **1 tablespoon of Listerine** for germ-killing power.

But plenty of other sore throat gargles abound. One popular concoction calls for 1 teaspoon sage, ½ teaspoon alum, ¼ cup brown sugar, ⅜ cup vinegar, and ⅛ cup water. And this down-home remedy makes short work of a sore throat: Mix 1 teaspoon each of powdered ginger and honey, ½ cup of hot water, and the juice of ½ squeezed lemon. Pour the water over the ginger, then add the lemon juice and honey. Honey coats the throat and also has mild antibacterial properties.

Gargling with the herbal germ-killer

Gargling Basics

- Mix a fresh batch of gargle for every use. Better to waste a bit pouring it out than to leave it in your glass, where it might become contaminated with bacteria.
- Use the hottest water you can comfortably tolerate. Cold gargles are ineffective.
- Don't swallow the gargle. Spit it out.

goldenseal (1½ teaspoons goldenseal tincture in 1 cup of water) kills viruses and bacteria as it soothes inflamed throat tissue.

Another good bet: Wheatgrass juice. A quick rinse and spit with this chlorophyll-rich liquid is said to ease throat pain. Held in the mouth for five minutes or so, wheatgrass juice is said to help revitalize weakened gums and stop toothache pain.

Head Off Heartburn

For occasional heartburn, try a saltwater gargle (¼ teaspoon salt in 1 cup warm water). The briny solution helps rinse away and neutralize acids in the throat, relieving the burning sensation and promoting fast healing of irritated mucous membranes.

If you have chronic heartburn, see a doctor. You may have gastroesophageal reflux disease (GERD), a potentially dangerous condition in which highly acidic gastric juices seep upward into the esophagus.

Battle Mouth Bugs

Even the healthiest mouth is home to millions of bacteria. These microscopic bad guys excrete chemicals that spur the growth of dental plaque. That's the sticky coating that rots teeth and irritates gums. For some people, brushing and flossing simply aren't good enough to keep these bugs in check. If that seems to be the case for you, ask your doctor about gargling each day with a 50/50 solution of water and 3% hydrogen peroxide. For even greater germ-killing punch, chlorhexidine mouthwash may be a better option. Both hydrogen peroxide and chlorhexidine are sold over the counter in drugstores.

Clobber the Cold Virus

Next time you feel the sniffles coming on, you might try gargling with a dash of Tabasco sauce in water. Hot-sauce aficionados swear it's the quickest way to open up clogged airways. Not hot for hot sauce? Use echinacea, the herbal virus-killer. Add 2 teaspoons tincture of echinacea to 1 cup water and gargle three times daily. In addition to easing throat pain, an echinacea gargle will give your immune system the boost it needs to fight the infection.

Lay Into Laryngitis

There's no substitute for simply giving your voice a rest and boosting your intake of fluids. But you may be able to speed the healing process by gargling with myrrh (a few drops of tincture of myrrh in a cup of water). Highly astringent, myrrh is superb at combating inflammation. It's an antiseptic too. Gargle six times a day—a bit of an effort, true, but well worth it.

Carpal Tunnel Syndrome

The last time you needed a signed note from your doctor might have been senior year of high school. But if you now suffer from CTS, it may be time to ask your family physician for another one, because you need to play hooky from the activity that inflamed the tendons inside your carpal tunnel. Once you've got license to give wrists a respite, you can use splints, supplements, and exercises to help them recover. But even as you renew normal wrist action, take some preventive steps and keep up the strengthening exercises.

What's wrong

Inside each wrist is a narrow passageway called the carpal tunnel. Running through this tunnel are nine tendons that move your fingers, along with the median nerve. These tendons can become inflamed and swell, compressing the nerve. Repetitive hand motion is one well-known cause of carpal tunnel syndrome, but other factors include pregnancy, birth-control pills, rheumatoid arthritis, and being overweight. Among the symptoms are numbness or tingling in your thumb and first three fingers, pains that shoot up your wrist and forearm, soreness in the neck and shoulders, and hand weakness.

Get a Grip on the Pain

🔹 To quickly ease the pain and inflammation, cool your wrists with an **ice pack** wrapped in a thin towel. Leave it on for about ten minutes. You can repeat the treatment every hour or so.

🔹 **Heat** can also ease pain by relaxing muscles. Soak your hands and wrists in warm to hot water for 12 to 15 minutes before you go to bed each night.

🔹 Twice a day, rub your wrists with an ointment containing **arnica.** This herbal treatment, renowned for its anti-inflammatory properties, helps ease aches and pains. Dab the inside of each wrist with about one-quarter teaspoon of the ointment, then massage that area with the thumb of the other hand, all the way to the base of your palm. Repeat every morning and night until your symptoms ease.

🔹 **Wear a splint at night.** While sleeping, you may be bending your hand and wrist under your pillow, and this puts pressure on your wrist. In fact, people with CTS are often awakened by the pain. A splint will hold your fingers in a neutral position and relieve pressure on the median nerve. You can purchase the splint in a medical supply store or pharmacy. But check with your doctor or physical therapist to make sure it fits properly.

🔹 You may also want to **wear a splint during the day**, especially if you're doing jobs that require a lot of hand motion.

Look for Supplemental Relief

☙ **Bromelain**, an enzyme derived from pineapples, digests inflammatory proteins, so it can reduce inflammation in your sore wrists. Along with reducing the pain, it may help you heal faster. Bromelain's potency is measured in MCU (milk-clotting units) or GDU (gelatin-dissolving units). Look for supplements rated between 1,800 and 2,400 MCU or 1,080 and 1,440 GDU, and take 1,000 milligrams twice a day when you're having a CTS flare-up. You can cut down to 500 milligrams twice a day once your symptoms start resolving. Just be sure you take these supplements between meals. If you take them near mealtimes, much of their potency will be misspent digesting your food.

☙ The herb **St. John's wort**, best known as an antidepressant, can also help repair nerve damage and reduce pain and inflammation. Take 150 to 250 milligrams of extract standardized to contain 0.3% hypericin three times a day. If that's not working after two weeks, take 300 to 400 milligrams three times a day.

☙ Take a tablespoon of **flaxseed oil** every day, and give it at least two weeks to have an effect. Flaxseed oil is extremely rich in omega-3 fatty acids, which reduce inflammation. Take it with food for better absorption. If you like, you can mix it into your orange juice or add it to your salad dressing.

Should I call **the doctor?**

Seek a doctor's care if symptoms interfere with your daily activities. If CTS goes untreated, you could be left with weakened grip in your hands and significant pain in your forearms or shoulders. Also, the condition is associated with arthritis, diabetes, and underactive thyroid gland; a doctor needs to evaluate you to make sure you don't have one of those other conditions in addition to CTS.

B for Benefit?

Vitamin B_6 is probably the most well-known supplement when it comes to treating carpal tunnel syndrome, but it's also controversial. Many experts claim it works, and many claim it doesn't. On top of that, excessive vitamin B_6 in the range of 1,000 to 2,000 milligrams a day can even *cause* nerve problems.

Supplementation with B_6 might be helpful, since the vitamin is important in maintaining healthy nerves, and it may speed up nerve impulses to your hands. Some people claim CTS is actually caused by vitamin B_6 deficiency. What we know for sure is that some people require more of the vitamin than others, and stress can increase your need for it.

To err on the side of caution, eat plenty of foods rich in the vitamin, including chicken breast, whole-grain cereals, brown rice, salmon, green vegetables, and egg yolks. If you want to try a supplement, take 50 milligrams of B_6 one to three times a day until your symptoms resolve, but do it under a doctor's supervision, especially if you take more than 100 milligrams a day.

~ **Curcumin** is an anti-inflammatory component found in the spice turmeric. In Ayurvedic medicine—which originated in India—turmeric has a long history of use as a medicine for pain and inflammation. But the spice doesn't pack the punch of curcumin supplements. Take 300 milligrams three times a day of a supplement standardized to contain 95% curcumin.

~ Try taking 300 milligrams of elemental **magnesium** two or three times a day. This trace mineral is involved in nerve function and muscle relaxation. A supplement may help, especially if you don't eat a lot of magnesium-rich whole grains, legumes, or green vegetables. The most absorbable forms are magnesium lactate, magnesium orotate, magnesium glycinate, and magnesium gluconate. The only side effect might be loose bowel movements. If you have that problem, just reduce the dose.

Take Precautions at the Keyboard

~ If you spend a lot of time in front of the computer, **adjust your chair and keyboard.** Your arms should be bent at a 90-degree angle when you type so that your wrists are parallel with the ground. Knees, too, should obey the "90-degree rule." And sit up straight, making sure your shoulders aren't slumped forward.

~ If the keyboard can be lowered, bring it down to a position where the **keys are slightly lower than your wrists** so that your fingertips drop down to rest lightly on the keys.

~ **Tap the computer keys**, don't pound them. The less pressure you apply, the better.

~ Use ergonomic, hand-friendly products whenever possible. Especially helpful is **a wrist rest**, sold at most office supply stores.

~ Get a **contoured keyboard** or **split keyboard.** They are specially designed so your hands can rest in a natural position while your fingers tap lightly on the keys. (The pressure required to depress a key is much lighter than on regular keyboards.) In contour models, two sets of keys are held in a single, molded frame, with comfortable areas to support each of your wrists. Split keyboards have separate frames that can be angled in different ways for maximum wrist comfort.

Do-It-Yourself Healing: Carpal Tunnel Syndrome

When doing computer work or any other job that involves repetitive hand motion, it's essential to take regular breaks and do some stretching exercises. Try to take a fifteen-minute break every couple of hours. Stand up, relax your shoulders, and shake your arms to relax your wrists and restore circulation. Make a fist with each hand, hold for a few seconds, then open it, separating your fingers and spreading them as wide as possible. Repeat four times. When you have time during the day, do the following exercises.

Extend your left arm straight in front of you and bend the wrist upward. Place the fingers of your right hand against the palm of your left and pull back gently. Hold for a count of ten. Switch hands.

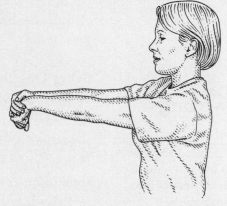

Extend your left arm and make a fist. Fold your right hand over the top of the fist and pull gently, holding for a count of ten. Switch hands.

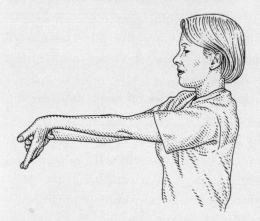

Extend the left arm in front of you, palm up, then bend your wrist downward. With your right hand on the knuckles of your left, pull the hand gently toward you. Hold for a count of ten. Switch hands.

Place a rubber band around your slightly separated fingertips. Slowly spread your fingers, then close them, keeping steady resistance against the rubber band. Repeat ten times.

Chapped Lips

It's one of the few flaws in our otherwise almost-perfect design: Our lips, so exposed to sun, wind, and other irritants, don't have oil glands to keep them soft and moist. Nor do they contain much melanin, the pigment in our skin that turns us tan and offers some protection from the sun. It's no wonder that lips can get as parched and cracked as old shoe leather. If you want to keep them kissable, give them some protection.

What's wrong

Your lips are dry, irritated, and cracked. They may be painful or they may itch. Dry spells can be triggered by sunburn, winter weather, allergic reactions, fever, or simply licking your lips too often.

Bring Out the Balms

🔸 Dairy farmers use **Bag Balm** to keep their cows' udders soft and comfortable. Humans have found that this product, formulated with lanolin and petrolatum, (the stuff in petroleum jelly) soothes a chapped kisser. You can find it in drugstores or order it on the Internet.

🔸 Another all-natural salve is **Burt's Beeswax Lip Balm**, which contains beeswax, coconut oil, sweet almond oil, lanolin, vitamin E, peppermint oil, and comfrey extract.

🔸 Some people swear by **Cloverine salve** to relieve chapped lips. (It also works on chapped hands.) You can order it from GA Labs at www.galabs.com.

🔸 When you're alone in the house, **olive oil** or **Crisco** will help to soften and moisturize chapped lips quite nicely. In fact, any vegetable shortening will do.

🔸 If you have **vitamin E** capsules on hand, puncture one and apply the oil to your lips.

🔸 **Petroleum jelly** is a tried-and-true chapped-lips remedy. For the healing power of petroleum jelly with more staying power, try **Aquaphor**, a heavy cream available in the drugstore's skin-care section. It tends to stay on longer than petroleum jelly. Like Bag Balm, it contains lanolin.

Moisturize from the Inside Out

🔸 If your lips are continually chapped, drink eight 250-milliliter glasses of **water** a day—more, if you can. While this won't prevent dryness, it will keep it from getting worse.

Go After the Yeast

If the corners of your mouth are painfully cracked and chapped, you may have a yeast overgrowth. To help clear the yeast, use over-the-counter antifungal cream, such as clotrimazole, which can be found in supermarkets. It's usually sold with feminine-hygiene or foot-care products. Apply it twice a day. If you wear dentures and have this condition, be sure you clean your dentures thoroughly and frequently. Yeast can grow on them and spread by contact to your lips.

The Power of Prevention

～ Apply a balm with a **sun protection factor (SPF) of at least 15** before you go out into the sun. Lips need just as much sun protection as the rest of your skin. (*Off-limits*... if your lips turn red and itchy. Some people have an allergic reaction to lip balms that contain sunscreen.)

～ A dark, creamy **lipstick** helps protect lips from the sun and keep moisture in.

～ When indoor air is very dry, prevent chapped lips by running a **humidifier** in your bedroom while you sleep.

～ Try eating more foods that are rich in **vitamin B**, such as whole grains, nuts, and green vegetables. Lack of B vitamins contributes to chapped lips in some people.

～ **Avoid licking your lips.** Your saliva may momentarily provide a coating of moisture, but it evaporates quickly, leaving lips drier than before. And the saliva contains digestive enzymes that dry out tissue.

～ Stay away from balms that contain **phenol** or **camphor**. They're very strong antiseptics that induce a major lip drought.

～ **Don't give a child lip balms with exotic flavors.** Kids tend to eat the flavored varieties right off their lips, which further aggravates the chapping.

Should I call **the doctor?**

Usually, a little TLC takes care of chapped lips. But if they remain chapped after you've babied them for two or three weeks, it's time to make a call to the dermatologist. Don't panic, but lips that are persistently red, dry, or scaly can suggest a precancerous condition. Also make a call if your lips are often cracked; you may have a yeast infection. An allergic sensitivity to ingredients in toothpaste, lipstick, or lip balms can also cause dry lips.

Chicken Pox

Chicken pox lasts only a week or two, but generally the end can't come soon enough. If pain is the problem, ease it with acetaminophen—never aspirin. If the itching is too much of a bear to bear, try cool baths and an antihistamine such as liquid Benadryl. And have a few other tricks to keep up your sleeve to minimize the misery.

What's wrong

Your child has a common childhood illness, caused by the varicella zoster virus. The virus debuts with the eruption of a rash and/or red spots on his back, chest, and belly, which spread to other areas within a few days. He may have a few spots or hundreds of them. Over a period of about a week, many of the spots turn into small blisters, which break and scab over. Your child may also have a fever and develop itching, which can be mild or intense. After the blisters heal, the virus goes into a latent stage and lives in sensory nerves in the body. It may surface years later in the form of the painful ailment shingles.

Stay Cool

🍂 If it's winter, **turn down the heat** to the lowest comfortable temperature. In summer, use **air conditioning**. Heat brings more blood to the skin, which exacerbates the itch.

🍂 Soak your child in a tub of slightly cool water for 15 to 20 minutes every few hours. Don't use soap. Instead, add one-half cup of **baking soda** to a shallow bath or one full cup to a deep bath to provide extra relief. **Colloidal oatmeal** (such as Aveeno) added to a bath also counteracts itching. If you don't have colloidal oatmeal, place regular oats in a nylon stocking, tie the end, and place the stocking in the water.

🍂 Offer your child a **cool, wet washcloth** to press against her skin when she feels like scratching. Scratching can lead to infection and scarring. By using the washcloth, she'll satisfy the scratching urge without doing any damage. For insurance against scratching, keep her nails trimmed, and put her to bed with cotton gloves on her hands.

Attack the Itch

🍂 Swab on some **calamine.** This over-the-counter lotion, made mostly of zinc oxide, helps by drying up the blisters.

🍂 Try **bergamot oil.** Bergamot, which is derived from a citrus fruit closely related to the orange, is often used to flavor tea. But it has also been used for centuries in Italy to dry chicken pox blisters and relieve the itching. Bergamot is composed of 11% to 22% alcohols, which have a soothing, drying effect. Add 10 to 20 drops of bergamot essential oil to a carrier

Shun the Blistering Sun

If your child has recently been exposed to someone who has the chicken pox virus, keep her out of the sun. A dose of sunshine may make the blisters worse when they finally appear. After the chicken pox is over, your child's skin will remain sensitive to the sun for as long as a year. You don't have to barricade her in the house, but do apply sunscreen every day.

oil (such as olive oil, sweet almond oil, etc.) and mix well. Then apply to blisters.

- If the itching is bad, give your child an **oral antihistamine** such as **Benadryl.** Just be aware that it might make her drowsy.

Calm with Cotton

- Keep him in fresh **cotton PJs.** Cotton is less irritating than other fabrics. Make sure they have long sleeves and pants to discourage scratching.

Mind the Mouth

- If your child has chicken pox in his mouth (yes, it can happen), have him gargle with **salt water.**
- Give him **ice pops.** They can be soothing.
- Feed him **bland food** like Jell-O, soups, and bananas as long as the blisters are painful.

The Power of Prevention

- You can protect your child from chicken pox with a vaccine called **Varivax,** recommended for children one year and older who are in good health. The same vaccine is effective in adults who have never had chicken pox.
- If your child has not been vaccinated, you can prevent infection by keeping him away from other children who have chicken pox—but that may not be advisable. It is **far better to get chicken pox as a child.** The virus is much more serious in adults.

Should I call **the doctor?**

Chicken pox is usually more of an annoyance than a danger; most cases clear up in 10 to 14 days without problems. However, approximately 50 deaths related to chicken pox occur among children every year. Call your pediatrician if your child has a high fever accompanied by severe headache, has a fever that lasts more than a few days, feels severe pain in his limbs, repeatedly vomits, develops a cough, or has a large area of redness surrounding one or more blisters—a sign of infection. Also call your doctor if your child has convulsions, becomes disoriented, or complains that his neck hurts when he stretches it.

Healing Soups from Around the World

Just about every grandmother has her own special soup recipe for times of sickness. Soups have a lot to recommend them. They're easy on the stomach and easy to digest—good news when you're feeling too sick to eat. And they provide nutrients that your body needs in order to recover.

Chicken soup, also known as Jewish penicillin, is the ultimate home remedy for colds. But it's not the only healing soup. In China, hot-and-sour soup is used to break up congestion. Its rice vinegar, ginger, and garlic will get your nose running for sure. Cabbage soup, popular in Eastern Europe, is now being touted as a home remedy for ulcers. Elsewhere in the world, other soup recipes are revered for their health benefits. Here is just a sampling:

India: Horse-Gram Soup for High Blood Pressure

In the farming communities of central India, an indigenous crop called horse gram is often prescribed to control high blood pressure. Horse gram is a small oval seed resembling lentils, with the aroma of freshly cut hay. When the seed-bearing pods of horse gram mature, they are picked, dried, and beaten with wooden poles. The seeds are cleaned and sorted.

Kuluth saar, or horse-gram soup, is a light dish with a slightly musty taste. It's often mixed with yogurt and served with rice. Horse-gram seeds are soaked for eight hours, then left to sprout for another eight hours before they're simmered in water. Other ingredients include kokum (a small, dark-purple fruit from an evergreen tree) and many cloves of crushed garlic. A tablespoonful of pomegranate seeds, ground into a fine paste, is sometimes added to a cupful of horse-gram soup to help dissolve kidney and bladder stones.

Horse gram can be purchased in most Indian food stores. Of course, if you can't find horse gram, a plain old bag of lentils will make a fine high-fiber soup.

China: Ginkgo Nut Porridge for Jet Lag

Grace Young is a Chinese cook who logs thousands of frequent-flier miles every year. But whenever she returns to her family in San Francisco, there's a big pot of ginkgo nut porridge on the stove. It's a late-night snack *(siu ye)* that helps heal the body from the damaging effects of flying. The ginkgo nuts in this recipe, according to traditional Chinese medicine, are beneficial for relieving coughs and reducing phlegm.

Key ingredients in the soup are dried bean curd *(foo jook)*, unshelled ginkgo nuts *(bock guo)*, and Chinese dried scallops *(gawn yu chee)*, along with a generous helping of finely shredded ginger. Some cooks like to include flank steak as well.

Philippines: Ginger Chicken Soup for Joint Pain

Drugs such as aspirin and ibuprofen can ease painful arthritis flare-ups, but why not try this flavorful alternative: ginger soup. Ginger contains gingerol, a compound that blocks the action of prostaglandins, hormone-like chemicals that contribute to inflammation. It's also active against the virus that causes the flu. In the Philippines, ginger chicken soup (chicken tinola) is usually made with green papaya, but you can substitute fresh spinach instead.

Chicken Tinola

The following classic recipe comes from the Maya Culinary Arts Center in Manila.

- 6 tablespoons vegetable oil
- 3 cloves chopped garlic
- 2 tablespoons minced fresh ginger
- 1 large onion
- 1.5 kilograms boneless chicken, sliced for sautéing
- 1.5 liters water
- 1 cup fresh spinach
  Fish sauce to taste
  Pepper to taste

In a heavy casserole, heat half the oil, sauté the garlic, ginger, and onion. When the onions turn clear (not brown), remove all the ingredients and set aside. In the same casserole, add the remaining oil, and stir-fry the chicken until it's cooked through. Return the garlic, ginger, and onion to the casserole, add water, and bring to a boil. Reduce heat and simmer, partly covered, for 30 minutes. Add spinach and stir. Just before serving, add the fish sauce and pepper.

Makes 8 servings

United States: Mom's Favorite Chicken Soup

This could very well be the most popular home remedy ever invented. Recent research shows there's science behind the folklore: Chicken soup can help prevent white blood cells from triggering inflammation and congestion in the upper airways.

There are many reasons to keep a pot simmering when you have a cold or flu. The rich, steamy broth breaks up congestion, and spicy ingredients such as garlic and onion have mild antiviral properties. To give the soup an extra cold-beating boost, slice a few cloves of garlic and add them to the pot when the soup is almost done.

Mom's Favorite Chicken Soup

For extra congestion-busting power, add a few dashes of cayenne pepper and a tablespoon of chopped fresh ginger to this recipe.

- 1 whole chicken, cut into 8 pieces
- 1 kilogram chopped carrots
- 1 kilogram onions
- 4 cloves minced garlic
  Salt, pepper, parsley, and dill to taste

Place the chicken pieces in a large pot, cover with water, and bring to a full boil. Reduce the heat to a simmer and skim off any foam that develops. Add the chopped carrots and onions, and simmer for 2 to 3 hours, adding water as necessary. Mince the garlic and add, then season to taste with salt, pepper, parsley, and dill. For a thicker soup, remove a cup of the vegetables, puree in a mixer or food processor, then add them back into the soup.

Makes 10 servings

Cold Sores

Since the blisters come and go, the goal of every cold-sore veteran is to make sure they're absent a lot more than they're present. Once the virus is with you, you have to mount a constant campaign to keep it discouraged. However, you'll learn to recognize the telltale tingling or burning sensation that notifies you of a sore's imminent arrival, and if you're prepped ahead of time, you can pepper it with your defensive home remedies.

What's wrong

Cold sores are usually caused by the herpes simplex type I virus. The painful, fluid-filled blisters might appear on your lip, or you may have painful ulcers in your mouth and throat. If you get a sore once, you'll likely have a recurrence. A tingling sensation around your mouth heralds the sore's imminent arrival, usually within a day or two. The blister swells, bursts, oozes fluid, crusts over, and departs, often in 7 to 10 days. Painful sores on your tongue and inside your lips and cheeks may accompany an initial outbreak. Common triggers of a new outbreak include sunlight, stress, menstruation, and fatigue.

First Aid for Cold Sores

▪ Apply **ice** directly to the sore. It will bring down the swelling and ease the pain temporarily. If you use this tactic early enough in the game—at the first sign of tingling—you may end up with a smaller sore than you otherwise would have.

▪ You can also use **aspirin** for pain relief, and it may have an added benefit. The results of one study published in the *Annals of Internal Medicine* suggested that taking 125 milligrams of aspirin a day can cut the time a herpes infection remains active by 50 percent.

Vanquish the Virus

▪ Time and again, the amino acid **lysine** (available by prescription from your doctor) emerges as the hands-down healer for cold sores. When you're having an outbreak, take 3,000 milligrams daily until the sore goes away. Research has shown that it thwarts the replication (copying) of the herpes virus.

▪ Herbal healers commonly recommend **lemon balm** (also called melissa), which is used throughout Europe to treat herpes simplex 1. Its essential oils contain substances that have been shown to inhibit the virus. In German studies, people with recurrent cold sores who used a lemon balm ointment regularly had less frequent outbreaks, or stopped developing the sores altogether. Look for a lemon balm ointment in health-food stores, and use it as needed.

Dab the sore with a tincture of **myrrh** on a cotton swab up to 10 times a day. Myrrh directly attacks the virus that causes herpes. You'll find myrrh in health-food stores.

 Blend **tea-tree oil** with an equal amount of **olive oil**, and apply it to the sore two or three times a day. Tea-tree oil is a powerful natural antiseptic. Research conducted in the 1920s showed it had up to 13 times the antiseptic power of carbolic acid, which was then a common germicide.

 Eat **yogurt** that contains live acidophilus bacteria. Some studies have shown that the acidophilus bacteria found in some brands of yogurt actually hinder the growth of the virus.

 Use an over-the-counter medication like **Abreva.** OTCs like this are most effective if you take them as soon as you feel the telltale tingle of an oncoming cold sore. The medication contains **docosanol**, which works by shielding healthy cells from those that have been infected by the virus. If taken immediately, the medication can shorten healing time by a day or so.

Bolster Your Defenses

 During an outbreak, take one 300-milligram capsule of **echinacea** four times daily. Studies have shown that the herb can boost your immune system's ability to fight off the virus.

 Take 1,000 milligrams of the immune-boosting flavonoid (plant pigment) **quercetin** each day in divided doses. Research published in the *Journal of Medical Virology* has shown that this supplement can speed the healing of cold-sore blisters. It's available in drugstores or health-food stores.

Don't Crack Up

 After the sore has crusted over, coat it with some **petroleum jelly** to prevent it from cracking and bleeding. When you do this, however, make sure you don't transmit the virus to the stuff in the jar. Instead of using your finger, apply the petroleum jelly with a cotton swab. Use a fresh swab every time.

The Power of Prevention

 If you get more than three cold sores a year, you might benefit from taking a daily **lysine** supplement as a preventive. The recommended dose is 500 milligrams a day.

Should I call **the doctor?**

Yes, if this is your first outbreak, if your sores last longer than two weeks, or if you get four or more cold sores a year. You may need the prescription antiviral drug acyclovir (Zovirax). Your doctor will also want to see you if your sore is accompanied by fever, swollen glands, or flulike symptoms, or if it's so painful that you avoid eating or brushing your teeth. Finally, if you develop eye pain or become sensitive to light, it may mean the virus has spread to your eyes. Get to a doctor quickly: Your vision may be in jeopardy.

Did you **know?**

Nearly all of us carry the cold-sore virus, even when it's not causing symptoms. An estimated 90 percent of adults age 40 and over carry herpes simplex I virus, the cause of most cold sores.

Since the virus that causes herpes is carried through saliva, some extra dental hygiene may be *de rigueur* to avoid recontaminating yourself after an outbreak.

🌿 Keep your toothbrush in a dry spot, preferably on an open shelf where it's exposed to circulating air and sunlight. If that means keeping it outside the bathroom, so be it. A damp toothbrush in a moist bathroom is an invitation for viral breeding.

🌿 Buy a small tube of toothpaste, use it during the outbreak, then throw it away.

🌿 Replace your toothbrush after an outbreak.

Tried...

When nothing else was handy, folks used a dab of vinegar to head off a cold sore.

...and true

Vinegar is acidic, and viruses don't do well in an acidic environment. Use a cotton swab dipped in any kind of vinegar and apply to the affected area, repeating several times a day at the first suggestion of the telltale tingle. Throw the swab away after each use.

🌿 **Stay away from** foods rich in **arginine**, an essential amino acid that the herpes virus needs in order to thrive. If you want to take maximum precautions to avoid an outbreak, **avoid chocolate, cola, beer, peas, nuts** (peanuts, cashews, almonds, and walnuts), **gelatin**, and **whole-grain cereals.**

🌿 Take 15 milligrams of **zinc** each day. In test-tube studies, this nutrient has been shown to block the replication of the virus. Zinc also boosts the immune system and fortifies the surface tissue on your lips and on the inside of your mouth, making it difficult for the virus to take hold.

🌿 Try to **avoid whatever seems to trigger outbreaks.** Do they appear after you've spent time in the sun, or during times of stress? Once you can pinpoint a likely cause, you can take measures to avoid setting the stage for new episodes.

🌿 Use a **lip balm** that contains a sun protection factor (SPF) of at least 15. In one study of people with recurrent sores, those who didn't shield their lips were much more likely to develop blisters during extended exposure to sunlight.

🌿 Like laughter and yawns, the sores are contagious. **Don't kiss your partner** if either of you has a cold sore. Direct contact with an infected person's saliva is usually necessary to pass the bug along, but if anyone in your house has cold sores, **don't mix up washcloths**, towels, drinking glasses, or toothbrushes.

🌿 When you have a cold sore, **avoid touching your eyes.** Transmitting the virus to your eyes could cause a nasty infection that could potentially damage your eyesight.

Colds and Flu

It may be "just a cold," but it's nothing to sneeze at. And the flu can make you feel downright flattened. Fortunately, fast action on your part can mitigate the misery. Herbs, chicken soup, zinc—and even your blow-dryer—are part of the healing arsenal. At the first sign of a sniffle, turn to these remedies, which can unstuff your head, boost your immune engines, and speed your illness on its way—unlike typical cold medicines, which can dry you out, put you to sleep, keep you up at night, do nothing at all to make you better faster, and may even prolong your illness.

Think Zinc

At the first hint of a cold, suck on a **zinc gluconate** lozenge every few hours. In one study, people who sucked on one lozenge that contained about 13 milligrams of zinc every two hours while awake shook off their symptoms three to four days sooner than people who didn't. Don't take zinc gluconate longer than a week, though, because excessive zinc can actually weaken immunity. And avoid zinc lozenges that contain citric acid or are sweetened with sorbitol or mannitol; these ingredients seem to weaken the mineral's effectiveness.

Zicam (available only in the U.S. at present), a nasal gel spray that contains zinc, may be even more effective. In a study at the Cleveland Clinic, people who used the gel saw their colds resolve in fewer than three days. Subjects who used a placebo had to wait nine days for their symptoms to go away.

Head Off a Head Cold

As soon as you notice cold or flu symptoms, start taking 500 milligrams of **vitamin C** four to six times a day. Buy a brand with added bioflavonoids, which have been shown to enhance the effectiveness of vitamin C by as much as 35 percent. If you develop diarrhea, cut down on the dose.

Take one 250-milligram **astragalus** capsule twice a day until you're better. This ancient Chinese herb stimulates the immune system and seems to be highly effective at fighting

What's wrong

If your symptoms are above the neck—congestion, sore throat, sneezing, coughing—you probably have a cold, caused by any one of 200 viruses that other people's sneezes or coughs have placed in the air or on something you've touched. If you have all those symptoms *plus* a fever of 38.8°C (102°F) or more, headache, muscle aches, extreme fatigue, diarrhea, nausea, or vomiting, you're more likely to have the flu. The flu arises from one of three viruses, imaginatively named influenza A, B, and C. The flu can last from three to seven days.

colds and flu. To prevent a relapse, take one capsule twice a day for an additional week after your symptoms are gone.

➤ **Goldenseal** stimulates the immune system and has germ-fighting compounds that can kill viruses. As soon as you begin to feel sick, take 125 milligrams five times a day for five days.

Bring On the Flu Fighters

➤ At the first sign of the flu, take 20 to 30 drops of **elderberry** tincture three or four times daily for three days. Elderberry has been used in Europe for centuries to fight viruses, and research appears to bear out its effectiveness. In one study, people who took elderberry recovered faster from the flu than those who didn't. Ninety-three percent of the elderberry group saw their symptoms subside within two days, compared to six days in a group that didn't get the herb.

➤ The homeopathic medicine Oscillococcinum, commonly called **Oscillo**, is widely recommended by naturopaths, doctors, and herbalists to reduce the severity of flu symptoms. Be sure to use it within 12 to 48 hours of the first appearance of your symptoms. It comes in packages of three to six vials. Buy the three-vial pack and take one vial every six hours.

➤ Try **N-acetyl cysteine (NAC),** a form of the amino acid cysteine. It helps thin and loosen mucus and reduce flu symptoms. It can be dispensed by a pharmacist without a prescription. Take one 600-milligram dose three times daily.

Soothe a Sore Throat

➤ For a sore throat, fill a 250-milliliter glass with warm water, mix in 1 teaspoon of **salt**, and gargle away. The salt really does soothe the pain.

➤ The traditional sore-throat gargle—a squeeze of **lemon juice** in a glass of warm water—is ideal because it creates an acidic environment that's hostile to bacteria and viruses.

Soup Up Your Cold-Fighting Engine

➤ "Jewish penicillin," otherwise known as **chicken soup**, that time-honored remedy of remedies, offers more than comfort for colds and flu. Modern scientists have confirmed that chicken soup stops certain white blood cells, called neutrophils, from congregating and causing inflammation, which in turn causes the body to produce copious amounts of mucus. It also thins mucus better than plain old hot water. Homemade soup is the best bet, especially if it's made by someone you love.

⌒ Add fresh chopped **garlic** to your chicken soup. The Egyptian pharaohs used garlic to fight infection, and its healing powers are legendary. Among its dozens of active compounds are allicin and allin, shown in test-tube studies to kill germs outright. The "stinking rose" also appears to stimulate the release of natural killer cells, part of the immune system's arsenal of germ-fighters.

Wet Your Whistle—and Everything Else

⌒ Fighting off colds and flu can rob your body of moisture. Drink as much **water** as you can—eight or more 250-milliliter glasses—to keep your mucous membranes moist and to help relieve dry eyes and other common flu symptoms. Fluids also help thin mucus so that it's easier to blow it out.

⌒ To help keep mucus loose, stay in a **moist, warm, well-ventilated room.** To keep the air in your bedroom moist, place bowls of water near the radiator (in the winter) or run a humidifier.

A Reeking Remedy

⌒ A dose of **garlic**—a natural antiseptic—will do a job on those viruses. If you're feeling very brave, hold a small clove or a half-clove of garlic in your mouth and breathe the fumes into your throat and lungs. If it gets too strong as the clove softens, just chew it up quickly into smaller pieces and swallow with water.

Get a Shot at Staying Flu-Free

Consider getting a yearly flu shot (now also available as a nasal spray). Health authorities recommend it, especially for people with chronic heart or kidney disease, chronic lung diseases like asthma, bronchitis, emphysema, diabetes, or those with depressed immunity. It's also recommended for people over the age of 65. It takes 6 to 8 weeks for the shot to build up your immunity, so get vaccinated in the late fall, before the start of flu season.

You can also get a therapeutic dose of **garlic in capsule form.** Buy enteric-coated capsules, the kind that are easiest for the body to absorb. The typical dose is 400 to 600 milligrams four times a day, taken with food. Look for pills standardized to 4,000 micrograms of allicin potential.

Blow Away That Virus

You can cut short a cold with your…**blow-dryer?** As outlandish as it sounds, inhaling heated air may help kill a virus working its way up your nose. In one study conducted at Harvard Hospital in England, people who breathed heated air had half the cold symptoms of people who inhaled air at room temperature. Set your hair dryer on warm (not hot), hold it at least 45 centimeters (18 inches) from your face, and breathe in the air through your nose for as long as you can—at least 2 or 3 minutes, and preferably 20 minutes.

Clear Out Congestion

For a serious congestion-busting blast, buy fresh **horseradish** or **gingerroot**, grate it, and eat a small amount. (Alternatively, you can get the bottled forms of grated horseradish or ginger and eat as much as one-quarter to one-half tablespoon.) To guard against stomach upset, wait until after a meal to try this.

Drink a cup of **ginger tea.** Make it with a ginger tea bag or with one-half teaspoon of grated gingerroot. Ginger helps block the production of substances that cause bronchial congestion and stuffiness, and it contains compounds called gingerols, which are natural cough suppressants.

Spike broth or soup with a dash of **Tabasco sauce, red pepper flakes,** or **wasabi,** the condiment (usually made from horseradish) that's eaten with sushi. All of these red-hot add-ins can increase the broth's decongestant power. In fact, adding any of them to any food can help you breathe more freely.

Wear **wet socks** to bed. Believe it or not, this soggy strategy can help ease a fever and clear congestion by drawing blood to the feet, which dramatically increases blood circulation. (Blood stagnates in the areas of greatest congestion.) Best method: First warm your feet in hot water. Then soak a thin pair of cotton socks in cold water, wring them out, and slip them on just before going to bed. Put a pair of dry wool socks over the wet ones. The wet socks should be warm and dry in the morning, and you should feel markedly better.

~ Try soaking your feet in a **mustard footbath.** In a basin, mix 1 tablespoon of mustard powder in 1 liter of hot water. The mustard draws blood to your feet, which helps to relieve congestion.

~ An old-as-the-hills remedy for chest congestion involves a **mustard plaster** made from mustard seeds and flour or corn-meal. Grind up three tablespoons of mustard seeds and add the powder to a cup of flour or cornmeal. Stir in just enough water to make a paste, then slather it on your chest. The pun-gent aroma helps to unclog stuffy sinuses, and the heat improves blood circulation and eases congestion. Don't leave the plaster on for more than 15 minutes, however, or your skin may burn. You may want to smear on a bit of petroleum jelly before you apply the plaster to protect the skin.

Steam Clean Your Nasal Passages

~ Pour just-boiled water into a large bowl. Drape a towel over your head to trap the steam, and breathe in through your nose for 5 to 10 minutes. Don't lower your face too close to the water or you risk scalding your skin or inhaling vapors that are too hot.

~ To make steam inhalations even more effective, add 5 to 10 drops **thyme oil** or **eucalyptus oil** to the water. Keep your eyes closed as you breathe the steam, since both the essential oil and steam can be irritating to your peepers.

~ When you're on the go, dab some tissues with a few drops of **eucalyptus oil** and bring them with you. Whenever you feel congested, hold a tissue to your nose and inhale.

Ring a Stiff Neck

~ The flu can give you one doozy of a stiff neck. To take the ache away, wet a hand towel, wring it out, place it in a plastic bag, and **microwave it for 60 seconds.** Or simply **boil a towel in hot water.** The towel should steam when you remove it from the bag or the pot of water. When it's cool enough, wring it out. Then wrap the towel around your shoul-ders and neck and lie down. (Put a beach or bath towel under

Did you **know?**

When you blow your nose, do it gently. Otherwise you might create reverse pressure that can lead to the virus or bacteria going up into your sinuses. To keep the reverse pressure to an absolute minimum, blow one nostril at a time.

you to keep the bed or couch dry.) To lock in the heat, wrap a dry towel around the wet one.

The Power of Prevention

~ During cold and flu season, take 20 to 30 drops of **echinacea** tincture in a half-cup of water three times a day. A tincture made with pure echinacea should cause a slight numbing sensation on your tongue. Take it for a few weeks, then wait a week before resuming.

~ **Wash your hands often** with soap and warm water, especially after you use a public restroom or if you're around people who are sick. Don't touch your face with unwashed hands either. In 1998 the Naval Health Research Center conducted a study of 40,000 recruits who were ordered to wash their hands five times a day. The recruits cut their incidence of respiratory disease by 45 percent.

~ Use a **humidifier** or **cool-mist vaporizer** during the winter months to keep indoor air moist.

~ Practice **stress-control techniques** year-round, but especially during cold and flu season. Research suggests that the more stress you're under, the more likely you are to get sick.

~ **Make love** at least once a week. In one study, men and women who were sexually active at least that often had higher levels of immune-system molecules called immunoglobulin A—which play an important role in shielding the mucous membranes from invaders—than people who weren't.

~ **Get some rest.** Most people get colds and flus when they're run down. So call in sick and sleep. Research shows that even if you are marginally sleep-deprived, your resistance to viruses can decline dramatically. In one study, certain immune cells that stalk viral infections dropped by 30 percent in people who got just slightly less sleep than usual in a single night.

~ **Widen your circle of friends.** In a study of over 200 men and women, people who had strong social ties developed fewer colds. Researchers gave the subjects nasal drops containing rhinovirus, the bug that causes most colds, and they found that those with only one to three social relationships were four times more likely to come down with a cold than those who had six or more friends.

Colic

The plaintive cries of a colicky child can stress parents to the max and even put them into a panic if they can't find a way to assuage their little darling. So the first order on the agenda: Relax. Take a break. If there are two of you, spell each other. If not, get a friend to stand in for you now and then. To calm the crying, first check the most obvious causes of distress—hunger, wet diaper, excessive heat or cold, or simply wanting to be held. Then try the time-tested strategies below.

Belly-Down Is Best

‿ Hold her in a **tummy-down** position. For some reason, a colicky baby seems to be more comfortable when she's lying on her stomach. If you're in a rocking chair, hold her along your forearm, facedown, as you gently rock back and forth. Her head will be cradled in one hand. (An infant at this age always needs head support.)

‿ When you want to **walk around**, continue holding her on your forearm, with her head in your hand. But bring her close to your chest, supporting her with your other hand.

‿ Put her in a **chest carrier** like a **Snugli**. Just being nestled against your warm chest is comforting, and so is your heartbeat. With your hands free, you can take a nice, long stroll. That, too, may help console your child (and give you some much-needed mobility).

‿ Your baby might settle down in his crib if he's **tightly wrapped** and lying on his stomach. But stay nearby and keep watch. If he falls asleep on his stomach, he's at an increased risk of SIDS (sudden infant death syndrome).

Swaddle Snugly

‿ Babies sometimes stop crying if they're snugly swaddled. If you find it's difficult to keep your baby well wrapped in a regular blanket, buy a **swaddling blanket** designed for this purpose. It has curved edges, with an ample "pocket" for the

What's
wrong

Your baby is crying...and crying...and crying, and nothing you do seems to help. She may clench her hands into fists and draw her legs against her belly, which can be as tight as a drum. She may also pass gas or have a bowel movement right before or after her screaming bout. A baby who cries for more than three hours a day, three days a week, for at least three weeks is said to have colic. Colic is a term for a baby who cries a lot even though there's no underlying health problem.

Colic   **129**

Should I call the doctor?

baby's feet. The short flap on one side folds over her torso and the long flap, on the other, wraps all the way around her body.

≈ For extra comforting, put your baby's blanket in the dryer and **warm it up.** When you take it out, test it with your hand to make sure it's not too hot, then wrap it around her. Alternatively, you can heat the blanket in a microwave. Just be sure to unfold it completely and check that the inside folds are not too hot.

Do the Swing Thing

≈ Place your infant in her **baby swing.** For some reason, the back-and-forth motion has calmed many a squalling child. Continual, steady movement is the key.

Let Appliances Lull

≈ Run the **vacuum cleaner.** The sound is music to the ears of some colicky infants. As an added bonus, you'll get a clean rug. If the vacuum cleaner doesn't work, try the hair dryer.

≈ Find a **radio station that's all static**, and leave the radio on with the volume turned low. The steady "white noise" helps some babies settle down.

≈ If you want to go high-tech, **purchase CDs** on the Internet with titles like *Baby's Answer for Colic* or *For Crying Out Loud!* They feature sounds—like a distant lawn mower, a whirring fan, or monotonous white noise—that babies find comforting.

≈ Some colicky babies respond to the sound and vibrations of a **clothes dryer.** If you're in sight of the laundry room, put the baby in a seat that touches the side of the dryer.

Proffer a Pinkie

≈ Even when he's not ready to nurse, a baby draws comfort from **oral stimulation.** Let your baby suck on your little finger. As long as the nail is well-trimmed and you're not wearing nail polish, it's just as good as a pacifier—even better, in fact, since it doesn't keep falling out.

Cut Out the Cheese

≈ Some experts have surmised that crying is caused by the mother-to-baby transmission of **cow's milk.** If you nurse your baby and you've been drinking milk or eating milk products (such as cheese), try going without. If this doesn't solve the problem after a week, you can go back to your usual diet.

⤳ **Avoid** foods and drinks that contain **caffeine**, like tea, coffee, colas, and chocolate. Try this for a few days to see if it helps.

⤳ **Monitor other "trigger foods"** that could be affecting your baby through the breast milk. Common ones are beans, eggs, onions, garlic, tomatoes, bananas, oranges, strawberries, and anything spicy. Of course, if you find that eliminating these foods for a week makes little or no difference, go ahead and eat them again.

De-Stimulate Your Darling

⤳ Sometimes the more you try to calm a colicky baby, the more he seems to squall. That's because his nervous system may be too immature to handle any noise or even gentle movement like rocking or swinging. Even the sound of your singing voice, softly crooning, may be too much noise. To **minimize stimulation**, try letting him cry for 10 to 15 minutes. Put him down or hold him passively in your arms. Avoid direct eye contact, which is a form of stimulation.

Feed with Care

⤳ When you feed your baby, **keep him upright**, not horizontal, and **burp him frequently.** When you bottle-feed, burp him after every 30 milliliters.

⤳ **Don't let a baby suck on an empty bottle**; it can cause him to swallow air, leading to trapped gas. For the same reason, don't let him suck on a bottle nipple that has a hole that's too large. While trapped gas is not the cause of colic, it can sometimes cause just as much crying.

Skip it!

The annals of mothering include many "colic relief formulas" like freshly squeezed onion juice. To this day, some formulas for curing colic, or "gripe," are advertised in magazines and on Web sites. Some may help relieve gas, but if your infant has colic, the problem is not gas. So neither the old folk remedies nor the "newly created" formulas will do much good.

Conjunctivitis

Conjunctivitis can itch. It can hurt. It can make you look like a beet-eyed alien. It can also injure your eyes, and if caused by bacteria or a virus, can spread like the plague. So what are you supposed to do? Start by seeking the help of a doctor. If you have an infection, he'll give you medicated eye drops that will speed healing and shorten contagion time. Meanwhile, you can take steps to ease the itch and control the crusting.

What's wrong

When eyes are red, irritated, and glued shut with gummy secretions, you've probably got conjunctivitis. It's an inflammation of the conjunctiva, the transparent membrane that lines the inner eyelids and sheathes the globe of the eye. Commonly known as pinkeye, conjunctivitis is usually caused by a bacterial or viral infection or an allergic reaction to pollen, cosmetics, contact lens cleaning solution, or other substances. Depending on the type, conjunctivitis can cause your eyes to burn, itch, tear profusely, and become intensely sensitive to light. A sticky discharge glues your eyelashes and eyelids together while you sleep.

Get an Eyeful of Relief

🍃 **Hot or cold compresses** can help. If you have a lot of discharge from your eyes, run a washcloth under warm water and use it as a compress to prevent the sticky secretions from drying on the lashes. Use a cold compress (soak a washcloth in ice water) to shrink swelling and reduce itchiness, especially if your conjunctivitis is caused by allergies. Do either one—or both—for five minutes three or four times a day. Use a fresh washcloth each time.

🍃 Wipe away the secretions and crusty material with a cotton ball soaked in 1 part **baby shampoo** to 10 parts warm water. The warm water loosens the crust, and the shampoo cleans the area where your eyelid and eyelashes meet.

🍃 Use an eyewash made of lightly **salted water.** Bring 2 cups of water to a boil, add 1 teaspoon of salt, and let it simmer for at least 15 minutes. Let the solution cool down. Use a sterile eyedropper or eyecup to apply the wash. After each treatment, sterilize the eyedropper or eyecup again in boiling water.

🍃 A **goldenseal** eyewash will help fight infection. Goldenseal contains a compound called berberine that has antibacterial properties. To make the wash, steep one teaspoon of dried goldenseal in boiling water for ten minutes, strain, and let it cool. Apply with a sterile eyedropper three times daily.

Brace Yourself for Bed

🍃 If your doctor has prescribed antibiotic or steroid **eye drops** or ointments, use them each night before you go to bed to ensure that your eyelids don't get "glued shut" while you sleep. Make sure the tip of the eye-drop bottle or tube does not touch your eyes. Otherwise, you might contaminate the medicine and potentially re-infect your eyes the next time you use it.

Soothers for Sore Eyes

➤ Soothe your eyes with a **chamomile** compress. Place a chamomile tea bag in warm (not hot) water for 2 to 3 minutes, squeeze out the excess liquid, then place the tea bag over your sore eye or eyes for 10 minutes. Repeat three or four times a day with a fresh tea bag. Keep your eyes closed so the wash doesn't come into direct contact with your eye.

➤ Practitioners of Ayurveda, the traditional medicine of India, treat conjunctivitis with the pulp of fresh **cilantro** leaves. In a blender or chopper, blend a handful of cilantro leaves with one-quarter to one-third cup water. Strain out the juice, and apply the pulp to your closed eyelids. Leave it on for a few minutes, then wipe away the mixture before you open your eyes.

➤ Another Ayurvedic treatment is to steep 1 teaspoon of **coriander** seeds in 1 cup of boiling water for at least 15 minutes. Strain thoroughly, cool, and use the water to bathe your closed eyes. Wipe away the excess before you open your eyes.

Contain the Contagion

➤ To avoid re-infection of one or both eyes, **don't wear eye makeup or contact lenses** until the infection is com-

Should I call **the doctor?**

Mild cases of pinkeye, especially those caused by viruses, should go away on their own within a week. Still, some forms of the condition can lead to potentially serious eye damage, so call your doctor if your symptoms are severe. You will want to get your doctor's advice as soon as possible if your vision is blurred, if conjunctivitis doesn't go away on its own in a week, or if you don't see any improvement after 3 to 4 days of steady treatment. If you have bacterial conjunctivitis, quick treatment will prevent complications.

Three Types of Pinkeye

The three most common types of conjunctivitis are viral, bacterial, and allergic. Because there is some overlap of symptoms, you will need a doctor's diagnosis to distinguish one from the other. However, here are the characteristic signs of each kind:

VIRAL
➤ Infection usually begins with one eye, but may spread to the other
➤ Watery discharge
➤ Irritation/redness

BACTERIAL
➤ Usually affects only one eye, but may spread to the other
➤ Irritation, redness, and/or a gritty feeling
➤ Copious discharge

ALLERGIC
➤ Usually affects both eyes
➤ Itching and tearing
➤ Swollen eyelids

Skip it!

Some herbal healers recommend eyebright to treat conjunctivitis, based on its traditional use among North American Indians for relieving eye problems. However, recent studies have shown that eyebright can actually cause tearing, itching, and redness if it comes in contact with the eye. Its therapeutic value has never been proved.

pletely gone. Throw away any eye makeup you were using when the infection developed.

☙ **Try not to touch your eyes.** If you touch them accidentally, wash your hands with soap and water, then dry with a paper towel or hot-air dryer instead of a hand towel.

☙ If you have to dab your eyes, use a **separate tissue** for each eye. Immediately throw both tissues in a plastic bag and wash your hands. When it's time to throw out the plastic bag, do it yourself and wash your hands thoroughly afterward.

☙ Carry a small bottle of **antibacterial hand gel** with you and use it often.

☙ If you wear **contact lenses, clean and sterilize them** exactly according to the manufacturer's directions, whether or not you or anyone around you shows signs of conjunctivitis. Wash your hands before you put in or take out your lenses. And never, ever clean a contact with saliva.

☙ At home, after you eat, **put your dishes and utensils in the dishwasher yourself.** Don't let anyone else handle them.

☙ Throw your towel, washcloth, and pillowcase **into the laundry** every day. This helps prevent you from re-introducing the bacteria or virus to the same eye or spreading it to the other eye. (Also, other people can pick up infectious conjunctivitis by using the same washcloth or towels that you've been using.)

☙ **Let someone else make the bed.** Conjunctivitis can be spread from your hands to the sheets.

☙ If you have young children with conjunctivitis who are too young to follow the rules about not touching their eyes and washing their hands, they should **stay home from school.**

For Allergic Conjunctivitis

☙ If your eye itches and produces a stringy discharge, your conjunctivitis may be the result of allergies. Try taking an **oral antihistamine** to relieve the itching and swelling.

☙ To help combat inflammation caused by allergies, try a combination of **vitamin C** and **quercetin.** Take 1,000 milligrams a day of vitamin C in divided doses, together with 1,500 milligrams of quercetin. Quercetin is one of a class of nutrients called bioflavonoids—derived from a wide range of fruits and vegetables—that have anti-inflammatory properties.

Constipation

Your first instinct when you're in this predicament might be to reach for a laxative. But chances are you don't need one. The best way to get "regular" again is simply to eat more fiber—20 to 35 grams a day. Fiber absorbs water and makes your stool softer and larger, which speeds it through your system. To cope with all that fiber, you'll need more fluids too. And don't forget about exercise, which can also help keep things moving. Do all three things and you'll certainly put a smile back on your face instead of that, well, constipated look.

Fix It with Fiber

Start your day with a **high-fiber bran cereal.** Some brands contain as much as 14 grams of insoluble fiber, the kind that adds bulk to stool, which spurs the body to move it through the digestive tract more quickly. A word to the wise: If you're not used to eating this much fiber, start with a smaller serving—say, one-quarter cup, served with skim milk or low-fat yogurt—then work your way up. Otherwise you may experience gas, bloating, and cramps.

Fill up on cooked **dried beans, prunes, figs, and oatmeal.** All are rich in soluble fiber, the kind that turns to gel in the intestines and helps to soften stool. Pears are also good sources of soluble fiber.

Mix one to two teaspoons **psyllium** seeds into a cup of hot water. Let it sit for two hours, add lemon and honey to taste, then drink. Psyllium adds bulk to stool and is the main ingredient in many OTC bulk-forming laxatives. You'll find the seeds in most drugstores and health-food stores. You can also try this remedy with flaxseeds.

Flaxseeds are high in fiber and also contain heart-healthy omega-3 fats. Take 1 tablespoon of the ground seeds, which are sold in health-food stores, two or three times a day. Some people like the taste of flaxseed (it faintly resembles walnuts). If you don't, you can hide it in your morning cereal, stir it into applesauce, or add it to a fruit smoothie. Or grind the seeds in a

What's **wrong**

You hear nature's call, and you want to answer, desperately. But your body won't respond—or when it does, your stools are hard, dry, and difficult or painful to pass. The most common reason bowels go on strike is because you lack fiber or water in your diet. But there are other possible causes, such as lack of exercise, using laxatives or enemas too often, and health conditions such as diabetes, hypothyroidism, severe depression, or irritable bowel syndrome. Certain prescription or nonprescription medications may be culprits as well.

Should I call the doctor?

Although bothersome, constipation is usually not grave. However, it can sometimes signal a serious condition such as colorectal cancer or bowel obstruction. Tell your doctor if it lasts two weeks or more even when you're following the recommendations in this chapter. And call your doctor immediately if you see blood in your stool or if constipation is accompanied by fever, severe abdominal pain, or cramps. Also, if you've recently started a new medication that seems to cause constipation, you'll want to talk to your doctor. Possible drug culprits include antihistamines, diuretics, blood-pressure drugs, sedatives, calcium supplements, certain antidepressants, and antacids that contain calcium or aluminum.

spice grinder or coffee grinder, keep the ground-up seeds in the fridge, and sprinkle a half-teaspoon into your orange juice.

꙯ As you increase your intake of fiber, also be sure to drink **lots of water**—at least eight 250-milliliter glasses a day. Fiber is extremely absorbent, and when you don't drink enough, your stools may become small, hard, and painful to pass.

Have a Hot Cup to Loosen Up

꙯ Have a morning cup of joe. If you're a java drinker, you may have already discovered that the **caffeine** in coffee has a bowel-loosening effect. It induces a bowel movement by stimulating the colon. Just don't drink too much of it—caffeine is a diuretic and will eliminate fluid from your body.

꙯ If you don't like coffee, try any other **hot beverage** first thing in the morning. Herbal or decaffeinated tea or a cup of hot water with a little lemon juice or honey may stimulate the colon as well. (Lemon juice is a natural laxative.)

꙯ **Dandelion tea**, which has a mild laxative effect, may help to get you regular again. Steep 1 teaspoon dried root in 1 cup boiling water and drink one cup three times a day. You'll find the dried dandelion root in health-food stores.

Wrinkle Your Nose—but It Works

꙯ One of Mom's favorite remedies, **castor oil**, really does help relieve constipation. A component in the oil breaks down into a substance that stimulates the small and large intestines. Take 1 to 2 teaspoons on an empty stomach, and give it 8 hours to do its work.

Wrinkled Fruit Works Too

꙯ The humble **prune** is one of the oldest home remedies for constipation. It's high in fiber (three prunes contain 3 grams

Constipation—Reality or Illusion?

The advertising world would have us believe that daily elimination is the pinnacle of perfect health. Untrue, say doctors. Many of us fall prey to what they call "perceived constipation"—that is, we think we're constipated, but our bodies don't. People have varying body rhythms, and it's just as healthy (for some people) to go once every three days as it is (for others) to go three times a day.

Fiber All-Stars

If you're wondering how to get more fiber in your diet for better regularity, look to these foods, all excellent sources of soluble and insoluble fiber.

Food	Portion Size	Grams of Fiber	Food	Portion Size	Grams of Fiber
Bran cereal	½ cup	10–14	Pinto beans, canned	½ cup	5.5
Raspberries	1 cup	8.4	Lima beans,		
Red kidney beans, canned	½ cup	8.2	frozen, cooked	½ cup	5.4
Shredded Wheat			Oatmeal, cooked	1 cup	5.0
'N Bran cereal	1¼ cups	7.9	Green split-pea soup	1 cup	5.0
Lentils, boiled	1½ cups	7.8	Pears, raw	1	4.0
Blackberries	1 cup	7.6	Almonds	30 grams	3.3
Black beans, boiled	½ cup	7.5	Prunes, canned	5	3.3
Figs, dried	3	6.9	Pearl barley, cooked	½ cup	3.0
Navy beans, canned	½ cup	6.7	Dates	5	3.0
Whole-wheat spaghetti,			Prunes, dried	5	3.0
cooked	1 cup	6.3			

of fiber). Also, prunes contain a compound called dihydrox-yphenyl isatin, which stimulates the intestinal contractions that make you want to go.

‣ Don't like prunes? Open a box of **raisins.** They, too, are high in fiber and contain tartaric acid, which has a laxative effect. In one study in which people ate 130 grams (one small box) of raisins a day, doctors determined that it took half the time for digested food to make it through the digestive tract.

Get Up and Go

‣ Get regular **exercise.** There's a reason a daily walk is called a daily constitutional. When you move your body, you also help move food through your bowel more quickly. Aim for a daily walk at the very least.

Put the Pressure On

‣ One of the more unusual remedies for constipation is **acupressure.** Practitioners of this technique say that it helps stimulate your digestion—and, therefore, your bowels. Apply pressure with your thumb to the point four finger-widths above your wrist on the back of the forearm. Do this for two minutes every day while the problem persists.

Last Resorts

🍂 The herb **cascara sagrada** is so effective it's even added to several over-the-counter laxatives. It's known as a stimulant laxative because it stimulates the intestinal tract. The herb comes in a variety of forms; follow the dosage directions on the package. But don't take it for more than two weeks; it can make your body lose too much fluid and salt—and with habitual use, you can become dependent on it.

🍂 If other remedies fail to bring relief, try the mother of all natural laxatives: **senna.** It should work in about 8 hours, so most people take it before bedtime. Take 20 to 40 drops of the tincture at night, but don't plan on making it a long-term cure. With repeated use, it can cause cramps and diarrhea. As with cascara sagrada, long-term use can cause dependency.

Final Pointers

🍂 **Never** try to **force a bowel movement.** You may give yourself hemorrhoids or anal fissures. These not only hurt, they aggravate constipation because they narrow the anal opening.

🍂 **Never ignore nature's call.** If you do, you're asking for a case of constipation.

Coughs

Coughing not only annoys you but also makes you persona non grata at the movies, the symphony, and any other place where people congregate. But if you have a "wet" cough, you don't want to suppress it; that's because it's the body's way of clearing out mucus. Rather, you actually want to encourage it so you can get rid of the phlegm faster and get the coughing over with. If you have a "dry" cough, on the other hand, the trick is to coat the throat and tame the tickle.

Take the Candy Cure

For "wet" coughs, suck on **horehound candy**, available in drugstores. A bittersweet herb, horehound acts as an expectorant, triggering the coughing reflex and helping bring up phlegm.

For "dry" coughs, rely on **slippery elm lozenges.** Made from the bark of the slippery elm tree, these were once medicine-chest staples. Slippery elm is loaded with a gel-like substance that coats the throat and keeps coughing to a minimum.

No slippery elm lozenges? For a dry cough, any hard candy will do because it increases saliva and causes you to swallow more, suppressing coughs. **Lemon drops** work especially well for "wet" coughs.

Another remedy calls for combining **peppermint candy, lemon juice,** and **honey.** Heat the candy in lemon juice until the latter is dissolved. Then add honey and stir. Take 1 to 2 tablespoons as needed.

Dose a Cough with Down-Home Syrups

Blend **lemon juice** with a little **honey,** then add a pinch of **cayenne pepper** and swallow. The honey coats your throat, soothing irritated tissues, while the lemon reduces inflammation and delivers a dose of infection-fighting vitamin C. The red pepper increases circulation to the area, which hastens the healing process.

A very simple cough syrup calls for 2 tablespoons **lemon juice** and 1 tablespoon **honey.** Heat until warm and take as

What's **wrong**

Most likely, a cold or the flu is the cause of your hacking. An infection of the upper respiratory tract can cause swelling and irritation of the upper airways and, at times, mucus, which you cough up as phlegm. There are two kinds of coughs. A wet, or productive, cough, which yields mucus, is usually caused by allergies, colds, or other respiratory infections. A dry, or unproductive, cough may also be caused by a cold but is more often caused by cigarette smoke, dust, fumes, or some other form of irritation. This cough does nothing but irritate your throat, making you hack more.

Should I call **the doctor?**

Most coughs clear up on their own within a week to 10 days. But if yours lasts more than 2 weeks, or you cough up blood, make the call. Coughing can be a symptom of a more serious illness, such as chronic obstructive pulmonary disease (COPD) and asthma. It can even indicate congestive heart failure, especially if it's accompanied by wheezing, shortness of breath, or swelling of the legs. If you have sharp chest pains, chills, or a fever higher than 38.3°C (101°F) as well as a cough, you may have pneumonia.

many teaspoons as you need, Add a bit of grated onion for a stronger kick. Onions contain irritating compounds that trigger the cough reflex and bring up phlegm.

 Peel and finely chop 6 medium **onions**. Put them, along with a half-cup **honey**, into the top of a double boiler or in a pan over a pot of boiling water. Cover and let simmer for 2 hours. Strain and pour the mixture into a covered jar. Take 1 tablespoon every 2 to 3 hours.

 For a throat-soothing syrup, mix 5 or 6 **cloves** with 1 cup **honey** and leave the mixture in the refrigerator overnight. In the morning, remove the cloves and take 1 teaspoon or 1 tablespoon of the honey as needed. Cloves dull the pain of a sore throat, while honey soothes inflamed throat tissues.

 Rock candy, made from crystallized sugar, and one of the oldest forms of candy, is the basis of several old-time cough syrups. One recipe combines 1 box rock candy, 450 grams raisins, the juice of 3 lemons, one half-cup sugar, and enough whiskey to form a syrup. Another calls for 450 grams rock candy, 4 jiggers brandy, a half-jar honey, and the juice of 3 lemons. You'll have to make either recipe ahead of time, as it takes a few weeks for the rock candy to dissolve.

 For a tasty old-time cough syrup, slice 3 **lemons** and place them in a pan with **honey** and a bit of **horehound** leaves and flowers. Horehound, a bitter herb once popular in cough "candies," acts as an irritant to trigger the cough reflex and bring up phlegm. Simmer the concoction until the syrup thickens. Strain the syrup and let it cool.

Brew Up a Cough-Taming Tea

 Thyme is an expectorant and also contains substances that relax the respiratory tract. To make thyme tea, place

Steam Away the Croup

A child with croup has a barking cough that often worsens at night. Caused by a viral or bacterial infection, croup is not usually dangerous, but it can be extremely frightening to parents. To treat it, take your child into the bathroom and run a hot, steamy shower. Keep him in the steam until the croup subsides. If it doesn't improve—or if the child is struggling to breathe—call your doctor or take him to the emergency room.

If your cough kicks up mainly after meals, at night, or while lying down, your problem might not be in your chest but in your stomach. Heartburn results when stomach acids back up into your lower esophagus, irritating the delicate tissue—which can lead to coughing. If you deal with heartburn symptoms (see page 205), you may find that you take care of the cough as well.

2 tablespoons fresh thyme (1 tablespoon dried) in a cup of hot water. Allow it to steep, then drain out the herb, add honey if you like, and drink.

🍃 Sip a cup of **marshmallow tea.** When combined with water, marshmallow yields a gooey mucilage that coats the throat and also thins mucus in the lungs, making it easier to cough up. To make the tea, steep 2 teaspoons of the dried herb in one cup hot water. Have a total of three cups a day.

🍃 Add 45 drops of **licorice** tincture to a cup of hot water and sip. Licorice loosens phlegm and relaxes bronchial spasms. A caution: Don't take licorice for more than a few weeks, as it can raise blood pressure.

🍃 Steep 2 teaspoons **horehound leaves or flowers** in 1 cup boiling water, strain, and drink.

🍃 Practitioners of Ayurveda, the traditional medicine of India, recommend a spice tea that you can drink several times a day. To make the tea, add a half-teaspoon powdered **ginger** and a pinch each of **clove** and **cinnamon** powder to a cupful of just-boiled water and drink.

Rub On Relief

🍃 Buy a **chest rub**, such as Mentholatum Ointment Aromatic Cold Care, that contains **camphor** or **menthol** and apply it to your throat and chest. They should not be taken internally.

🍃 If you don't have any store-bought chest rub, try making a **mustard plaster** to loosen up chest congestion. Mix one part mustard powder and two parts flour in a bowl. Add just enough water to make a paste. Spread the paste on a dishtowel, fold the towel in half, and press it against the skin. (Never put the mustard mixture directly on your skin.) Check your skin often and remove the plaster if your skin becomes too red or

Choosing a Cough Syrup

When you're staring at a drugstore shelf jammed with cough elixirs, which one do you choose? If you're bringing up phlegm, buy an expectorant cough syrup (one that contains guaifenesin) to take during the day. It will loosen up the mucus and help you expel it. Only take a cough suppressant (look for codeine or dextromethorphan on the label) if you have a dry cough. Don't buy any cough syrup that contains both an expectorant and a cough suppressant— believe it or not, some do! As an alternative to these cough syrups, try Chestal syrup by Boiron. It's a cough preparation recommended by homeopathic doctors, and has no unwanted side effects.

irritated. Some people suggest using an egg white instead of water to make a plaster that's less likely to burn.

Learn a New Coughing Technique

~ If your throat is strained and irritated from nonstop coughing, try this technique to head off a coughing fit. The next time you feel a cough coming on, **force yourself to take a series of small, gentle coughs**, finally ending with a large one. The tiny coughs help move mucus toward the upper part of your air passage so you can expel more of it with that last, big cough.

Put Some Rhythm in Your Remedy

~ If you're at home and you have a partner who can help, use a chest-percussion technique to help clear chest congestion. Lie on your stomach on a firm bed or mat. Ask your partner to **slap cupped hands rhythmically** over the back, progressing from the lower back up toward the neck. Repeat several times until your congestion starts to loosen up.

Lights Out, Vapor On

~ To help prevent nocturnal coughing, use a **humidifier** in your room to moisten the air, particularly in winter.

Cuts and Scrapes

If you can stop the bleeding and keep the wound clean to prevent infection, you've done your part; nature will take over from there. Required: some bandages and antibiotic ointment (doctors recommend any triple antibiotic variety). Other wound remedies that work in a pinch are within easy reach—from honey to garlic to your own saliva.

Clean, Cover, and Disinfect

~ To stanch bleeding, apply **pressure** to the wound with a clean cloth or piece of gauze. In a pinch, use your hand.

~ Once bleeding has stopped, gently clean the area around the wound with soap and water. Then apply a bandage.

~ You can also cleanse a cut with a tincture of **calendula**, a bacteria-slaying herb known for its wound-healing powers. Look for calendula succus, which is a low-alcohol formula. If you can't find it, use the regular tincture and dilute it with a little water. To heal scrapes faster, try a calendula cream, sold in some health-food stores.

~ Twice a day, you can clean your cut with **myrrh**, which stimulates the production of white blood cells. These are the infection-fighting cells that gather at the wound site. Mix 1 teaspoon myrrh tincture (available at health-food stores) with 120 milliliters water. Dribble it over the cut or scrape, and allow the wound to remain exposed to the air until it dries.

~ Try **tea-tree oil**. It contains a strong antiseptic compound and is popular the world over for treating wounds. Stir 1½ teaspoons of the oil into a cup of warm water and use this to rinse cuts and scrapes.

Cures from Your Kitchen

~ No antibiotic cream handy? In a pinch, dab on a little **honey** and then cover with a bandage. Honey has antibacterial properties, and studies have shown that it can speed wound

What's **wrong**

You have just sliced yourself with a sharp object—a kitchen knife, your razor, a broken drinking glass, even a piece of paper. Or you've had a sudden encounter with a section of concrete and lost a bit of skin on your elbow or knee. There may be visible bleeding—and perhaps an invisible invasion of bacteria into the wound, bringing a risk of infection.

healing. In certain cases some doctors believe that honey might even be superior to triple-antibiotic creams as a wound dressing. Don't have a Band-Aid? Don't worry—honey dries to form a natural one.

⮞ **Garlic** is another of nature's antibiotics. Try taping a crushed clove over the cut. If it irritates your skin, take it off right away.

Scraped Knee? Bag It

⮞ It seems like kids manage to scrape their knees every day. Solution: **Bag Balm.** Originally designed for use on cows' udders, it protects scraped skin and keeps scabs soft so that they're less tempting to pick at. Vaseline, or any other kind of **petroleum jelly**, is also effective.

Take a Lesson from Rover

⮞ If you can't wash a wound—say you're smack in the middle of the woods—**lick it.** Researchers at the National Institute of Dental and Craniofacial Research demonstrated that a protein in saliva not only helps to heal wounds, it also acts as an anti-inflammatory, antiviral, antifungal, and antibacterial agent.

Glue It Together

⮞ Read the warning label on **Instant Krazy Glue**, and you'll learn that it "bonds skin instantly." But if you've got a very small slice in your finger (like a paper cut), maybe an instant skin-sealer is just what you want. In fact, Krazy Glue contains the same ingredients as a new "liquid Band-Aid," and just a drop on a cut will seal it closed for quicker healing. Just make sure you don't touch that drop while it's drying, or you'll end up with a very awkward case of Siamese fingers.

Dandruff

Do your shoulders look as if you just walked in from a snowstorm? Are you blinded by a blizzard every time you comb your hair? Dandruff isn't a serious health problem, but it sure can be embarrassing. To factor out those flakes, use the right shampoo. You can also whip up a homemade scalp rinse that will beat the yeast behind many cases of dandruff and give the dreaded itch the axe.

Wash Dandruff Away

🪶 Look for shampoos with **selenium sulfide, tar,** or **zinc pyrithione,** such as Denorex Enriched Formula Dandruff Shampoo. Anti-dandruff shampoos with these ingredients retard the rate at which scalp cells multiply. They are more effective than products formulated with sulfur or salicylic acid, such as Neutrogena T/Sal Therapeutic Shampoo, which loosen flakes so they can be washed away.

🪶 If your dandruff doesn't respond to a shampoo like Denorex, try one that contains **ketoconazole,** such as Nizoral. Ketoconazole is an antifungal medication that will kill the yeast that may be causing your dandruff.

🪶 If your dandruff shampoo stops working after a few months, your scalp probably got "used to" the active ingredient and started to "ignore" it. Just switch to a shampoo made with a **different active ingredient.** You may need to switch back in another few months.

🪶 Leave on dandruff shampoo for **at least 10 minutes** before you rinse to let it do its best work. For a serious case of flakes, lather up, plunk a shower cap on your head, and leave the shampoo on for an hour. You might want to extract a promise from your spouse or significant other not to laugh.

Rely on Rinses

🪶 Make a dandruff rinse using the herb **goldenseal**. It contains berberine, which has strong antibacterial and antifungal properties. Pour 1 cup of boiling water over 2 teaspoons

What's **wrong**

Like snakes, we humans continually shed outer layers of dead skin. When those skin cells slough off the scalp at turbo speed, you have yourself a case of dandruff. The condition has many possible causes. Stress is one. Others include overactive oil glands and seborrheic dermatitis—an itchy, scaly rash that can affect the face and chest as well as the scalp. There's evidence to suggest that dandruff is often caused by an overgrowth of a common yeast, called *Pityrosporum orbiculare*. The yeast feeds on skin oils—which may explain why people who have oily scalps are more susceptible to dandruff.

of chopped root. Steep, strain, and let it cool. Use it as a rinse after you've shampooed, or any time during the day. If you can't find goldenseal root, add a few drops of goldenseal tincture to a little bit of shampoo.

Brew up a fragrant **rosemary** rinse. Like goldenseal, rosemary fights bacteria and fungi. And rosemary is a lot easier to find. To make the rinse, pour 1 cup of boiling water over 1 teaspoon of chopped rosemary. Let it sit for a few minutes, then strain. Use the liquid as a rinse once a day. If the rinse irritates your skin, move on to a different remedy.

Another herbal anti-dandruff rinse is made with **bay leaves**. Add a handful of crushed bay leaves to one liter of very hot (just boiled) water. Cover and let steep for 20 minutes. Strain, allow to cool, and apply. You might want to leave it in your hair for an hour or so before rinsing.

Apple cider vinegar, which kills a variety of fungi and bacteria, is frequently recommended as a home remedy for dandruff. Mix one part water with one part apple cider vinegar. Apply as a rinse after you shampoo.

Try Tea Tree

Tea-tree oil has strong antifungal properties. Dilute the oil in a little bit of a carrier oil (such as olive or grape-seed oil) and apply to your scalp. Leave it overnight. Or add a few drops to your shampoo. In health-food stores you may find shampoos with tea-tree oil already in them.

A Cultured Cure

It's not pretty, but it may work: Spread **yogurt** on your scalp and leave it there for half an hour, then rinse. Yogurt contains "friendly" bacteria that keep yeast in check. That's why it's also a traditional remedy for yeast infections.

Get the Flax

Take 1 to 2 teaspoons of **flaxseed oil** a day. It contains essential fatty acids, which seem to help itchy skin conditions such as psoriasis and eczema—and possibly dandruff. Be patient; you may need to take it for up to 3 months to see a difference. A side benefit: Flaxseed oil also helps guard against heart disease.

Depression

What did Ludwig van Beethoven, Winston Churchill, and Vincent van Gogh have in common? They all, at one time or another, suffered from depression. In fact, depression is so widespread that some psychologists call it the common cold of emotional disorders. If you're depressed, you're not alone. Neither do you have to let depression control your life. For severe, chronic depression, there are effective prescription medications as well as various forms of therapy. For mild to moderate depression that comes and goes, there are plenty of depression-busting strategies you can implement on your own.

Work It Out

🍃 Get out there and move your body. Numerous studies have confirmed that **frequent exercise** can be a powerful mood enhancer. For mild or moderate depression it may even work as well as antidepressants. All you need is at least 20 minutes' worth of aerobic exercise three times a week. Walk, lift weights, jump rope, cycle—any form will do. Work up a sweat to get the best effect.

Look to Food to Change Your Mood

🍃 If you're on a high-protein diet for weight loss, **lack of carbohydrates** could be contributing to your blue mood. Foods like fruits and vegetables, beans, and whole grains help your brain make the mood-regulating brain chemical serotonin.

🍃 Aim to **eat fish** three times a week or more. Researchers in Finland found that people who ate fish less than once a week had a 31 percent higher incidence of mild to moderate depression than people who ate fish more often. Albacore tuna, salmon, sardines, and mackerel are top choices; they're rich in omega-3 fatty acids, essential to normal brain function. There's preliminary evidence that they influence serotonin production.

🍃 If you drink **coffee** or **cola**, cut back or even **give it up**. Research links caffeine, which suppresses serotonin production, to depression.

What's **wrong**

Maybe you've experienced a traumatic event. Or maybe, for no reason you can put your finger on, you just feel sad and empty. Depression is usually linked to a combination of medical, genetic, and environmental factors. There are four types: major depression, in which the emotional low is severe and lasts for more than two weeks; mild depression, or dysthymia, which has milder or fewer symptoms; bipolar disorder, which causes extreme mood swings; and postpartum depression, which sometimes happens to a mother after giving birth.

Should I call the doctor?

A divorce, a death, a move, or a career change can give you temporary feelings of sadness, as you experience a loss or confront new challenges. Almost everyone experiences a mild depression at some point in life. But if your sadness lasts more than two weeks, or is accompanied by sleep and appetite changes (eating and sleeping too much or not at all), loss of interest in sex, and a reduced ability to concentrate, chances are you need treatment. Your doctor will be able to advise you whether you need psychotherapy, medication, or both.

✎ **Nix alcohol.** While wine, beer, or hard liquor may initially raise spirits, alcohol is actually a depressant.

Put It in Writing

✎ **Record your feelings** on paper—especially painful feelings. Research shows that people who write about their most painful emotions for 20 minutes a day dramatically improved their psychological well-being after just four days. Sit with a blank piece of paper in front of you and write nonstop about the most distressing event in your life right now. Don't think; just write.

Lift Your Spirit

✎ **Attend services** at your church or temple. In a study of 4,000 older people, researchers found that those who frequently attended worship services were half as likely to be depressed as those who didn't.

Down a Mood Lifter

✎ Take 1,600 milligrams daily of **SAM-e**, pronounced "Sammy." In many European countries, the effectiveness of SAM-e against depression is so well accepted that the supplement is often prescribed by doctors for it. SAM-e is a naturally occurring substance found in every living cell. Low levels have been linked with depression. Dozens of studies have shown that SAM-e produced significant improvement after three weeks. In animal studies, SAM-e was found to boost the levels of three neurotransmitters—serotonin, dopamine, and norepinephrine—involved in mood changes. Some doctors point out that the form most often available—tosylate disulfate—is highly unstable, and is only effective if it's taken in enteric-coated capsules. The preferred form is butanedisulfonate, which can be ordered from Nature Made and GNC on their U.S. websites and imported into Canada. Look for enteric-coated capsules. The recommended dosages range from 400 to 600 milligrams for mild depression, up to 1,600 milligrams daily.

✎ Three times a day, take 300 milligrams of **St. John's wort**. In folk medicine, it was originally said to ward off witches.

Now that witches are more or less a thing of the past, more than 20 scientific studies have shown that St. John's wort can help ease mild depression, possibly by allowing certain brain chemicals to build up between nerve cells, as some antidepressants do. Opt for a brand standardized to 0.3% hypericin. Because this herb can cause sensitivity to sunlight, try to stay out of the sun as much as possible while you're taking it.

➤ **5-HTP**, which is one form of the amino acid tryptophan, is thought to work the same way Prozac does, by increasing serotonin levels. 5-HTP can be ordered from reputable sources on the Internet and imported into Canada. Take 100 micrograms 3 times a day of 5-HTP. But don't take this supplement for more than 3 months unless you have your doctor's consent.

➤ Take 1,000 milligrams, three times a day, of the amino acid **acetyl-L-carnitine** (also available on the Internet). It's chemically similar to acetylcholine, a neurotransmitter that acts in the muscles as well as the central nervous system. Acetyl-L-carnitine helps increase energy production in brain cells, protect

Five Steps to Positive Thinking

Is your inner monologue bringing you down? Here's how to turn your thinking around:

1. Take a just-the-facts approach. Challenge irrational beliefs that chip away at your confidence. If you think everyone is laughing at you, demand evidence. Are they actually laughing? Could they be laughing at something else?

2. Don't be perfect. It isn't possible—but you knew that. So why worry if someone doesn't like you or you're not masterful and competent in every situation?

3. When something bad happens, don't automatically think the worst ("I failed the test because I'm stupid"). There are usually many reasons things go sour. Look at all of them objectively and focus on those you can change ("Next time, I'll do better if I study harder").

4. If self-examination does reveal a personal weakness, keep the implications from spiraling ("I can't do anything well"). And remember: Recognizing that you're weak in one area doesn't make you a weak person. Instead, it can help you identify where to invest more effort and guide you to your strengths.

5. Loosen your grip on the controls. Inevitably, things don't always go your way. Accept that the world isn't under your control and strive to be calm in the face of adversity. That way, two problems—the upsetting situation and your reaction to it—are whittled to just one.

nerve cell membranes, and improve both mood and memory.

⌘ The mineral **chelated magnesium** is very important for restoring and maintaining healthy nerve function. Magnesium is a key component in the production and function of serotonin. Supplements may help alleviate anxiety and depression. Follow the dosage recommendations on the label.

⌘ Take one **vitamin B-complex** supplement each morning with food. Low levels of vitamin B have been linked with depression. Look for a brand with 50 micrograms of vitamin B_{12}, 400 milligrams of folic acid, and 50 milligrams of the other B vitamins.

The Power of Prevention

⌘ **Get enough sleep.** Studies have shown that people who get less than eight hours of sleep, night after night, tend to have lower serotonin levels than those who get full nights of rest. To help ensure a good night's rest, try to go to bed at the same time every evening and rise at the same time every morning— even on weekends.

⌘ **Shut off the TV.** Research suggests that the longer you watch television, the more your mood suffers. Watching hours of reruns, movie marathons, or game shows may seem like a way to relieve stress and fill up on entertainment. But studies have shown that, to the contrary, people who watch a lot of television usually have intensified feelings of isolation.

Diaper Rash

The sight of a child's raw, red bottom can fill a parent with unrelenting guilt, especially if the baby is wailing in discomfort. Obviously, the treatment for diaper rash is to change your baby's diaper frequently. But sometimes even that doesn't seem to help. What to do? Try a new cleansing technique, give baby's bottom some air, and use the right ointment to provide protection.

Clean with Care

🔹 When you remove stool from a baby's bottom, do it as gently as possible. Fill a spray bottle with **warm water** and a few drops of **baby oil**, spritz on the mixture, and then gently wipe the area with a clean cloth.

🔹 If you use baby wipes, look for a brand that **does not contain alcohol** or **fragrances**.

🔹 If wiping seems too painful, rinse the baby's bottom with water, then pat dry. **Do not use soap**, which is irritating.

Bring Out the Blow-Dryer

🔹 If your baby's bottom is too sore to towel-dry after a bath or a change, use your **blow-dryer**. Set the dryer on the coolest setting. (Keep checking the air to make sure it's not too hot.) Hold the dryer at least 25 centimeters (10 inches) from your baby's skin, and keep it moving back and forth.

Give Him Some Air

🔹 When the diaper is off and your baby is all cleaned up, give him an **air bath** for 10 to 15 minutes, letting the diapered area stay exposed to air. As long as he's happy, he can remain chest down, on a towel placed on top of a waterproof sheet. The longer he remains diaper-free, the better.

Opt for the Right Ointment

🔹 Use an ointment made with **zinc oxide**, which has weak antiseptic properties and provides a barrier between your

What's **wrong**

Every parent knows that the red, bumpy, painful-looking rash on a baby's most tender parts is caused by a wet or dirty diaper. Much of what is typically called diaper rash is actually a burn from ammonia, which is produced when urine comes in contact with bacteria from feces. Stool itself is also an irritant.

If your baby's rash is a beefy red with round pink spots inside the reddened area, she may not have diaper rash at all—she may have a yeast infection. Damp diapers are a breeding ground for yeast. Yeast infections aren't serious and are easily treated with an over-the-counter antifungal cream such as Canesten or Myclo. See your pediatrician if the rash persists.

Should I call the doctor?

Chances are, your baby's diaper rash will clear up quickly if you take some of the measures recommended in this chapter. If it doesn't clear up completely in three or four days, call the pediatrician. The doctor will want to know if the rash has spread to other areas, if the creases between your baby's legs are red and raw, or if blisters have developed. A pimple or blister in the diaper area could be a staphylococcus infection that will require antibiotic treatment. If your baby has a rash that is ulcerated and bleeding, and creams aren't working, the child should be seen by her doctor as soon as possible.

baby's skin and the moisture that irritates it. There are many excellent brands of diaper rash ointment on the market that contain this ingredient.

☙ For a rash that is deep red, has an irregular border and tiny dots around the edges, use a combination of the **antifungal cream Canesten** and **hydrocortisone creams**. Mix together equal parts of Canesten and 0.05% hydrocortisone and apply the mixture to the genital area, the buttocks, groin, and creases that look inflamed. Then, on top of that, apply a **barrier cream,** such as **Penaten,** that protects the baby's skin from irritating substances. (Don't use petroleum jelly as a barrier cream. It prevents the diaper from absorbing urine.) You can use these creams three to four times a day.

☙ For an all-purpose cream that clears up diaper rash caused by yeast and ammonia, mix together equal parts of **Nivea cream, Canesten cream, cornstarch,** and **Penaten.** Apply this mixture with each diaper change.

Puttin' On the Sitz

☙ A **sitz bath** may also ease your baby's discomfort. Several times a day, fill the tub with a shallow bath of warm water and let your child sit and play with his toys for five or ten minutes. Stay right there with him, of course.

The Power of Prevention

☙ If you use disposable diapers, get the **superabsorbent** type. They draw more urine toward the center of the diaper and therefore away from the skin. You should still change the diaper just as often.

☙ If you use cloth diapers and wash them yourself, add one-quarter cup of **white vinegar** to the final rinse. The acid in the vinegar will discourage the growth of bacteria and bring the pH of the diaper closer to the neutral pH of your baby's skin.

 Unless you absolutely have to, **don't cover cloth diapers with plastic pants**. The plastic holds in moisture, which encourages the onset of diaper rash.

 Whether you use disposable or cloth diapers, **fit them more loosely** than you see on the TV ads. Supertight diapers prevent the circulation of air and contribute to skin irritation.

 Moms and grandparents alike love the fresh, clean "baby" smell of baby powder. But some baby powders contain additives that can actually cause a rash, rather than prevent it. And the powder contains fine granules that babies should not inhale. If you want to use a powder, use **cornstarch** (which has no irritating additives). Mix it with a gentle cream like Nivea and apply it to the baby's bottom.

Did you **know?**

Babies who are breast-fed have half the risk of bottle-fed infants for developing diaper rash. Doctors speculate that the urine and feces of a breast-fed baby contain fewer irritants. If you nurse your baby and he develops diaper rash, examine your diet for potential irritants, such as spicy foods or caffeine.

Diarrhea

When a case of the runs has you running to the bathroom, your aims are two: stave off dehydration, and avoid anything that will make the diarrhea worse. If you can stay close to home, simply let the problem "run" its course (and don't forget to drink plenty of fluids). If you can't, try astringent teas, eat more soluble fiber (which soaks up excess fluids in the intestine), or try an ancient Chinese "cure."

What's wrong

Normally, as food goes through your digestive tract, the large intestine soaks up extra water. Sometimes, though, it doesn't, and you get rid of the fluid in your stool—a bothersome problem we call diarrhea. Common causes include viral infections, like flu; exposure to parasites or foreign versions of the bacterium *E. coli* while traveling; bacterial food poisoning; and intolerance to an ingredient in dairy foods. Diarrhea that lasts for days or weeks, however, can point to irritable bowel syndrome. And diarrhea that's not quickly resolved can cause dehydration, which is especially dangerous in infants and the elderly.

Tame Diarrhea with Tannins

～ Drink **black tea** sweetened with **sugar**. The hot water helps with rehydration, and tea contains astringent tannins that help reduce intestinal inflammation and block the absorption of toxins by your intestines. The sugar improves sodium absorption.

～ Tannin-rich **blackberries** have long been used as folk treatments for diarrhea. Make blackberry tea by boiling one or two tablespoons of blackberries or dried blackberry leaves in 1½ cups water for 10 minutes, then strain. Drink a cup several times a day. You can also purchase store-bought blackberry tea bags, but check that they contain blackberry leaves and not just blackberry flavoring. **Raspberry tea** is also said to be effective.

Root Out the Problem

～ Capsules of dried **goldenseal**, made from the bright-yellow root of a perennial herb, appear to kill many of the bacteria, such as *E. coli*, that cause diarrhea. The key compound in the herb is berberine, which is so effective that goldenseal is sometimes called an "herbal antibiotic." Take two or three 125-milligram capsules daily until the diarrhea improves.

Infuse Your Body with Fluids

～ When your diarrhea is considerable, you need to replace your body's supply of water and electrolytes, which include sodium, potassium, and chloride. These keep your heart beating properly and play many other crucial roles as well. Mix up the perfect **electrolyte drink** by stirring a half-teaspoon of salt and four teaspoons of sugar into a liter of water. Add a little bit of orange juice, lemon juice, or salt substitute for potassium. During the day, drink the full quart. Don't use more than this amount of sugar or salt; much more, and you're likely to become dehydrated.

↪ Brand-name sports drinks like **Gatorade** can also replace lost electrolytes.

↪ When you're caring for a child with diarrhea, use an oral rehydration solution such as **Pedialyte**, which is designed specifically to replace kids' electrolytes.

↪ If your diarrhea is mild and you're not dehydrated, just drink **flat sodas** (you don't want the carbonation to give you gas) to keep your fluid levels normal. Leave one soda open in the refrigerator for a few hours so it de-fizzes. Take sips for a few hours, then start drinking as much as you comfortably can until you're getting two cups of fluid each hour.

Rebuild Your Diet

↪ Start by eating only foods that are see-through, like **chicken broth** and **Jell-O**. Broth is an especially good choice, since it supplies your body with water as well as electrolytes from the salt. Stick with these "clear" foods for a day or two. But **avoid fruit juices**. They can contain large amounts of a kind of sugar called fructose, which many people have trouble digesting even when they're feeling well.

↪ Spoil yourself with the **BRAT diet**. BRAT stands for bananas, rice, applesauce, and toast. All are bland and soothing, and the bananas and applesauce contain pectin, a type of soluble fiber that soaks up excess fluid in your intestine and slows down the passage of stool. (Avoid apple juice, however, which can make diarrhea worse.)

↪ **Carrots** are another soothing source of pectin. Cook some carrots until they're soft, then drop them in a blender with a little water and puree into a baby-food consistency. Eat a quarter to a half-cup each hour.

↪ **Avoid** foods that are rich in **roughage**, which can be hard to digest. That means no beans, cabbage, or Brussels sprouts.

Should I call **the doctor?**

If your diarrhea lasts longer than two days, recurs frequently, or is accompanied by lightheadedness, a fever, intense cramping, or blood or pus in the stool, call your doctor. A particularly serious form of diarrhea is related to *Clostridium difficile,* a bacterium that occurs normally in many children under the age of two and in some adults as well. When antibiotics are overused, *C. difficile* alters the flora in the intestine in such a way that it causes a particularly foul-smelling form of diarrhea. It requires immediate treatment.

Traveler's diarrhea, also known as Montezuma's revenge or turista, is the bane of international travelers, usually caused by exposure to foreign strains of bacteria in the food or water. Before you board the plane for points remote, learn how to avoid spending the bulk of your trip in the bathroom.

🍂 Take Pepto-Bismol before, during, and after the trip. A number of studies have shown that this can help prevent traveler's diarrhea. And even if the diarrhea has started, Pepto-Bismol can help reduce the severity of the symptoms. Following the directions on the package, chew two pills four times a day or (if you're taking the liquid) one tablespoon four times a day.

🍂 Before you leave, start taking acidophilus capsules twice a day to boost the number of beneficial bacteria in your intestine. Continue taking them while you're abroad. Follow the dosage instructions on the bottle. But make sure you're getting live bacteria. One brand is Westcoast Naturals Super Acidophilus, produced by Westcoast Naturals.

🍂 Drink only water or drinks that are in sealed bottles or cans, or water that has been boiled for three to five minutes. Use bottled water to brush your teeth and cook, and never have ice cubes in your drinks (you don't know what water was used to make them).

🍂 Acidic drinks like orange juice and sodas are also good for diarrhea prevention because they help keep the bacterium *E. coli* in check.

🍂 Eat only cooked foods and fruits that you can peel yourself.

🍂 Have a glass of wine with meals. In the lab, wine has been shown to kill the bacteria that cause traveler's diarrhea. There's no research to say whether drinking wine actually helps, but if you enjoy wine (in moderation) anyway, why not? You're on vacation!

🍂 Eat **yogurt** containing **"live cultures"** as specified on the label. "Cultures" refers to beneficial bacteria like *Lactobacillus acidophilus* and *Bifidobacterium*. Eating yogurt with live cultures helps restore healthy levels of these bacteria to your intestine and may speed recovery from diarrhea. If your diarrhea is related to taking antibiotics, which kill good and bad bacteria indiscriminately, it's especially important to replenish the "good guys." If you don't like yogurt, buy **acidophilus pills** and follow the dosage instructions on the label.

Solve It with Psyllium

🍂 One good treatment for diarrhea is also a remedy for the opposite problem—constipation. Ground-up **psyllium seeds** soak up excess fluid in the intestine, making the stool bulkier. They are the key ingredient in Metamucil and in many other natural-fiber products. Take one to three tablespoons mixed in water each day.

Ancient Chinese Treatment

✎ Here's an old Chinese remedy for diarrhea. We have no idea if it works, but it can't hurt. Peel and crush 2 cloves **garlic**, add 2 teaspoons **brown sugar**, boil in ¾ cup water, and drink 2 to 3 times a day. Because garlic has potent antibacterial properties, it may kill the bacteria behind many cases of diarrhea.

The Power of Prevention

✎ If you find that you frequently get diarrhea after consuming milk and other dairy products, delete those foods from your diet. They contain a sugar called lactose, and some people are **lactose intolerant**. If you do eat dairy, take supplements (such as Lactaid) that contain the enzyme lactase. Or only eat low-lactose dairy, such as yogurt, aged cheddar, and Lactaid-brand milk.

✎ **Steer clear** of any products containing the sweeteners **xylitol, sorbitol**, and **mannitol**. These are often found in diet candies and sugar-free gum, but also in strawberries, prunes, cherries, and peaches. Our bodies cannot easily digest the sweeteners.

✎ **Wash your hands** with soap and warm water before you prepare foods and after you handle raw meats. And be sure to wash all plates and cooking implements that have come in contact with raw meat.

✎ To prevent food poisoning, **defrost foods in your microwave or the refrigerator**, not on the counter.

✎ **Avoid** taking large doses of **vitamin C**, which may give you diarrhea.

✎ If you customarily take antacids that contain **magnesium hydroxide**—like Maalox or Mylanta—consider **switching to another brand**. This ingredient can cause diarrhea.

Skip it!

As soon as diarrhea hits, you might be tempted to swallow an over-the-counter anti-diarrhea medication. Don't—particularly during the first few hours. Diarrhea is a natural way for your body to quickly rid itself of bacteria and irritants, so you don't want to slow down this process.

Dry Hair

Believe what you see on TV and you might get the idea that only brand-name shampoos and conditioners can give you the buoyant and swirling strands that make life such fun. What those ads don't tell you is that something as simple as mayonnaise can add just as much luster to too-dry locks, giving you the bounce and flounce that those models flaunt.

What's wrong

Your hair can become dry, rough, brittle, and frizzy for many reasons. It's a non-living material, similar in composition to your fingernails, but each strand has an outer layer of cells that protect the inner hair shaft. If this coating becomes damaged, hair loses moisture and luster, and the ends become frayed. Chlorine, excessive sunlight, and heat from blow-dryers and curling irons can all damage it. Also, some people tend to have dry hair just because they don't have an abundance of oil-producing glands on their scalps.

Start in the Shower

✎ Only wash your hair **every other day**. Your hair will stay clean enough, and you'll leave in more of its natural oils.

✎ Use **baby shampoo**, which is less drying than some other shampoos.

✎ Wash and rinse your hair with **warm** rather than hot **water**. Hot water strips protective oils from your hair. The best temperature for your hair is just a bit warmer than your body temperature.

✎ Thoroughly **rinse** your hair after you shampoo it. Shampoo can leave a residue in hair, which dries out the strands.

Salad Solutions

✎ **Avocado** moisturizes hair shafts and loads them with protein, making them stronger. Thoroughly mix a ripe, peeled avocado with a teaspoon of wheat-germ oil and a teaspoon of jojoba oil. Apply it to freshly washed hair, and spread it all the way to the ends. Cover your scalp with a shampoo cap or a plastic bag, wait 15 to 30 minutes, then rinse thoroughly.

✎ **Mayonnaise** is an excellent alternative to avocado; the egg it contains is a good source of protein for your hair. Rub the mayo into your hair and leave in for anywhere up to an hour, then wash it out.

Stay in Condition

✎ If you use a store-bought conditioner, pick one with a "thermal protector" ingredient like **dimethicone** or **phenyl** trimethicone. These protect your hair from heat, which is especially important if you blow-dry.

⁓ Make your own conditioner by mixing 60 milliliters of a good-quality **olive oil** and 60 milliliters **aloe vera gel** with six drops each of **rosemary** and **sandalwood** essential oils. Olive oil is a natural emollient, aloe vera hydrates, while rosemary adds body and softness to hair. (The sandalwood, which is optional, just adds fragrance.) Leave the mixture on for an hour or two, then rinse it out.

⁓ When you use a conditioner, first apply it liberally to the **ends**, where hair is the driest. Then work your way toward your scalp.

⁓ In a frizz emergency, simply use a little bit of **hand lotion** and smooth it through dry hair.

Deft Drying

⁓ Let your hair **air-dry** whenever possible. If you must use a blow-dryer, use it sparingly. The same goes for curling irons or hot rollers. When you apply heat, it's like drying out a leaf in sunlight: You're inviting brittleness.

⁓ When you do use the hair dryer, make sure you use a **warm**, not hot, setting.

Brush Up on Your Brushing Technique

⁓ Use a brush that has **natural rather than plastic bristles**. Plastic generates static electricity, which will make your hair more brittle.

⁓ First **brush the ends** to remove tangles. That way, you won't pull and break your hair when you take full strokes with the brush.

Should I call **the doctor?**

If your hair's appearance suddenly changes on its own—and you start feeling fatigued, chilled, irritable, and constipated—talk to your doctor. These could be signs of hypothyroidism. It's also worth calling your doctor if you have dry hair and also a crusty or itchy scalp, which could be a sign of psoriasis.

◆ After you brush the ends, take long, full strokes all the way from the roots of your hair to the ends to **spread hair's natural oils**.

Strengthen Your Strands

◆ **B vitamins** may make hair stronger. Take one 50-milligram B-complex supplement twice a day with food.

◆ The mineral **selenium** is also helpful for maintaining healthy hair. Take 200 micrograms twice a day.

◆ A beneficial oil that may help keep hair lustrous from inside your body is **evening primrose**. Try taking 1,000 milligrams of evening primrose supplements three times a day. The oil is high in gamma-linolenic acid, an essential fatty acid.

The Power of Prevention

◆ When you swim in a chlorinated pool, wear a **swimming cap** to keep the chlorine away from your hair. As soon as possible after getting out of the pool, wash your hair.

◆ Use a **humidifier** in your bedroom. In cold weather, your home heating probably keeps the air very dry, which in turn dries out your hair.

◆ Get your hair **trimmed** at least every six weeks to eliminate dry, split ends.

Dry Mouth

If a lack of saliva makes it hard for you to lick envelopes or even talk, you'll definitely want to wet your whistle. First, talk with your doctor about what might be causing your kisser to be parched. Consider an over-the-counter saliva substitute such as Salivart. Drinking plenty of plain old H_2O will keep your mouth moist, as will the other tricks in this chapter.

Check Your Medicine Cabinet

🔹 Dozens of common medications can cause dry mouth. **Check the label** or package insert of any drug you're taking to see whether dry mouth is listed as a side effect. If it is, ask your doctor if you can switch to a different drug. Frequently implicated drugs include many antihistamines and decongestants as well as Prozac (fluoxetine), Norvasc (amlodipine), Paxil (paroxetine), and Vasotec (enalapril).

Just Add Water

🔹 Carry a **water bottle** with you and sip water frequently. Swirl each sip around in your mouth before you swallow. You should be going through two liters each day.

🔹 To stimulate saliva flow, squeeze in some **lime** or **lemon juice** or add one-half teaspoon **apple cider vinegar**.

Make Your Mouth Water

🔹 Chew **sugarless gum** or suck on **sugarless hard candy** to stimulate the flow of saliva. Sugar-free gums with the ingredient xylitol can help reduce cavity-causing bacteria.

🔹 Keep a **red-pepper** shaker handy at the table. The same "hot stuff" that makes your eyes water and your nose run can make your saliva pour forth. Add just a touch to spice up your meals.

🔹 The herb **echinacea**, taken in tincture form, has been shown to help stimulate saliva production. Drink 10 to 15 drops of tincture in a glass of juice. This remedy is safe to use every hour, if needed, for up to eight weeks.

What's **wrong**

The mucous membranes in the mouth have become abnormally dry due to a lack of saliva. Dry mouth can be caused by medications or by the radiation, chemotherapy, and surgery that are used to treat oral cancer. And sometimes it's the result of an autoimmune condition called Sjögren's syndrome, in which the immune system attacks moisture-producing glands in the body. Dry mouth is also related to aging: About 40 percent of people over age 65 have it. Because saliva protects us from oral infections and tooth decay, having dry mouth can lead to bad breath, mouth sores, cavities, and fungal and bacterial infections in the mouth.

Should I call the doctor?

If you notice that your mouth is unusually dry for more than a few days, talk to your doctor or dentist. A consultation is especially important if the condition prevents you from eating or speaking normally or your mouth is red and irritated. When you discuss it with your doctor, be sure to mention any medications you're taking, since they may be contributing to the problem.

Avoid These Drought-Inducers

❧ **Limit** your intake of **coffee** and other **caffeinated drinks**, as well as **alcohol**. These cause you to urinate more frequently, which makes your body lose more fluids.

❧ **Eschew sodas**, even those without caffeine. If your mouth is dry, you don't have enough saliva to break down the acid they contain.

❧ **Shun salty foods** or **highly acidic drinks** like orange juice and lemonade. These can cause pain if your mouth is too dry.

❧ Keep **sugary snacks** to a minimum.

❧ **Tobacco** dries up saliva. If you smoke, try to stop.

Add a Little Night Moisture

❧ To avoid getting dried out at night, use a **humidifier** or **vaporizer** in your bedroom.

Swishing Well

❧ If you use a store-bought mouthwash, pick one that **doesn't contain alcohol**, which dries your mouth and can irritate already-sensitive gum tissues.

❧ For a homemade mouthwash, mix one-eighth teaspoon **salt** and one-quarter teaspoon **baking soda** in a cup of warm water. Rinse your mouth and spit. This solution will counteract acids in your mouth and rinse away infectious agents.

Teeth Treatments

❧ Choose a toothpaste that **doesn't contain sodium lauryl sulfate (SLS),** which can irritate mouth tissues. A brand without SLS is Biotene's Dry Mouth Toothpaste.

❧ Make sure you **brush** and **floss** thoroughly. Saliva is important for clearing away food debris in your mouth, and when your mouth is dry, this food can stick around.

Keep Your Mouth Shut

❧ When you inhale through your nose, you moisturize the air going into your body. But when your sinuses are clogged, you naturally do a lot of mouth breathing, and that means you're taking in a lot of dry air. Take steps to treat a **sinus condition or allergies**, and you will also help prevent dry mouth.

Dry Skin

The outer layer of your skin works like a self-oiled machine, but sometimes oil production can't keep up with demand. Trouble occurs when you shower a lot, use skin-drying soap, or live in a house where the air is Saharan. What's the best refreshment for parched skin? Most moisturizers (which don't actually *add* moisture to the skin but serve to lock in moisture that's already there) will do the trick. Or try one of the home remedies below.

Exfoliate for Softer Skin

🍂 Give your skin a **milk bath.** The lactic acid in milk exfoliates dead skin cells and may also increase skin's ability to hold in moisture. Soak a washcloth in cold milk. Lay the cloth on any area of skin that is particularly dry or irritated. Leave the cloth there for five minutes, and when you rinse off the milk, do it gently, so some of the lactic acid stays on your skin.

🍂 To soften rough patches of skin, fill your tub with warm water and add two cups of **Epsom salt**, then climb in and soak for a few minutes. While your skin is still wet, you can also rub handfuls of Epsom salt on the rough areas to exfoliate the skin. You'll be amazed at just how good your skin feels when you get out. If you have some, you can also add a few strips of **dried seaweed** to your bath to boost the softening effect.

🍂 Apply **aloe vera gel** to help your dry skin heal more quickly. It contains acids that eat away dead skin cells. To obtain the gel, cut off a leaf at the base and split it open with a knife. Scrape out the gel with a spoon.

🍂 Use a moisturizer that contains **alpha-hydroxy acids.** These remove loose, flaky skin cells, leaving the skin softer. Lotions that contain **urea** have a similar effect.

Add More Moisture

🍂 Pit an **avocado,** puree the pulp, and pat it on your face as a moisturizing mask. The oil acts as an emollient. It also contains beneficial vitamin E.

What's **wrong**

When all is well with your skin, its glands are constantly producing an oil called sebum that keeps skin moist and supple. During winter, however, dry air (both outdoors and in) can cause your skin to become flaky, itchy, cracked, and rough. Hands and face suffer the worst because they are the most exposed. And hands produce the least amount of protective sebum.

Should I call the doctor?

If your skin is so dry that you're still intensely uncomfortable after two weeks of self-care techniques, call your doctor. Dry skin can be a sign of a medical condition such as hypothyroidism. Also seek medical care if you develop a severe, itchy rash or if your skin shows signs of infection, such as redness, crustiness, or oozing. If you experience a fever, chills, streaks of redness, and pain, these could be signs of a deeper infection called cellulitis, or the spread of an infection through your lymph system known as lymphangitis: Both are medical emergencies.

⌒ Turn to any of these inexpensive products to trap in skin's own moisture: **lanolin** (obtained from wool), **petroleum jelly, mineral oil, peanut oil**, or even **vegetable shortening** (such as Crisco). Just use them sparingly to avoid feeling greasy.

⌒ For seriously chapped hands, try a product called **Bag Balm**, used by farmers to soften the udders of cows.

Switch Soaps

⌒ If you use a **deodorant** soap, **stop.** These soaps dry the skin. And they contain perfumes, which are irritants.

⌒ Use a **superfatted** soap like Dove, Oil of Olay, or Neutrogena. These have extra oil or fat added late in the soap-making process. They leave a beneficial oily film on the skin.

⌒ Try gentle cleansers like **Cetaphil** and **Alpha-Keri.** The milder soaps in general have a pH (a measure of acidity) which is closer to that of your skin. They remove dirt without stripping away too much natural oil.

⌒ **Liquid soaps** also tend to be gentler on your skin. Put a squirt bottle next to your sink for washing your hands.

Shower Sparingly

⌒ Never stay in the bath or shower for more than 15 minutes. When you take long soaks, you're washing away your skin's protective oils. And use **lukewarm water**, not hot. Hot water tends to strip the oil from your skin.

⌒ During winter months, when your skin is extra dry, just bathe **two or three times a week.** On the "days off," you can get by with sponge-bathing sweaty areas.

⌒ Take a **bath or shower in the evening**, so your skin can replace protective oils overnight while you're sleeping.

Dampen Your Domestic Life

⌒ In the winter, make sure the humidity in your house is between 30 and 40 percent. If your house has forced-air heating or steam radiators, the actual humidity may be far less—often, as little as 10 percent. Buy a plug-in **humidity gauge** at a home-supply or hardware store to keep tabs on the humidity. When it gets below 30 percent, turn on a **humidifier.**

⌒ In summer, turn on the **air conditioner only when you absolutely need it.** It dehumidifies the air as well as chilling it.

Homemade Moisturizer

To make your own moisturizer, melt 1 teaspoon white beeswax and 2 tablespoons lanolin in a double boiler. Stir in one-third cup olive oil, 1 tablespoon fresh aloe vera gel, and 2 tablespoons rose water (sold in pharmacies). Let cool.

⁘ If you have a **fireplace or wood-burning stove**, use it sparingly. The heat that's generated from these sources is extremely drying.

Eat, Drink, and Be Moister

⁘ Be sure to drink at least eight 250-milliliter glasses of **water** each day. **Herbal teas** and **juices** also count, but not caffeinated beverages like black tea, coffee, and sodas containing caffeine, or any drinks that include alcohol. All of those have a diuretic effect, which means you'll lose body fluids because you'll have to urinate more frequently.

⁘ At least twice a week, eat some oily, cold-water fish like **herring** or **salmon**. These are rich in **omega-3 fatty acids**, which help keep your skin-cell membranes healthy. Other good sources of these fatty acids are **walnuts, avocados**, and **flaxseed oil**. Mix up to two tablespoons of flaxseed oil each day into your salad dressing or your morning oatmeal. (If you add it to hot cereal, do so only after the cereal is cooked. Flaxseed oil breaks down into less-useful compounds if you cook with it.)

Get Your Fill of Vitamins and Minerals

⁘ Certain vitamins and minerals help support healthy skin. Every day, take 100 milligrams of a B-complex vitamin supplement containing **thiamin, riboflavin, and pantothenic acid**; 15 milligrams of **beta-carotene** in divided doses, with meals; and 15 milligrams of **zinc**.

⁘ Look for products that offer an array of skin-enhancing nutrients in one pill. Look for a pill formula containing vitamin A, vitamin C, vitamin E, riboflavin, vitamin B_6, folate, zinc, selenium, and other minerals.

Did you **know?**

Having a lot of houseplants can help prevent dry skin. Plants add moisture to the air in two ways: through photosynthesis (their leaves produce water), and also evaporation from their well-watered soil.

Earache

There's nothing like an earache to take you back to the less pleasant aspects of childhood. Put simply, earaches are no fun. You can approach the problem from the outside in, using carefully chosen eardrops or even a bit of garlic juice, or from the inside out, with soups and gargles that help drain mucus and expand the Eustachian tubes. Warm and cold treatments can also help you weather the pain.

What's wrong

Something has probably gone awry in the middle ear, which is the tiny space located behind your eardrum. A thin tunnel called the Eustachian tube runs from the middle ear to the back of the throat. That tube allows fluid to drain away, and it's also a passage where the pressure inside your ear adjusts to meet outside air pressure. The common cold virus can cause fluid to accumulate in the Eustachian tube, triggering significant pain. Bacteria thrive in the fluid, leading to middle-ear infections. These are all too common in children, but can strike adults as well. If you get an earache from flying, the cause is probably excessive air pressure rather than infection.

Just Drop In

🔊 Place 3 to 5 drops of 3% commercial grade **hydrogen peroxide** into the painful ear canal every 3 to 4 hours. This will help quell infection, inflammation, and pain.

🔊 Warm a bottle of **baby oil** or **mineral oil** under hot water for a minute, then drip a few drops of the warm oil into your ear to help ease discomfort.

Drain It, Dry It

🔊 Try a **spicy chicken-noodle soup** or fiery bowl of **chili**. The spiciness gets your mucus flowing and can help your ears drain, relieving painful pressure.

🔊 Gulp down plenty of **water** every day. The muscles that work when you swallow help your Eustachian tubes open up, allowing your ears to drain.

🔊 Gargle with warm **salt water**. It helps increase blood circulation to the Eustachian tubes and decreases swelling that may be blocking them.

🔊 Make a healing remedy of **echinacea** and **goldenseal**. Echinacea helps your body fight off the infection, and goldenseal helps dry out the fluid in the ear. Put a dropperful each of tincture in a quarter-cup of water, then drink the mixture every two to three hours. Or buy a tincture containing both herbs.

🔊 Use an **extra pillow** to prop your head up slightly more than normal while you're sleeping. This will help your ears drain, easing pressure.

Warm and Chill

↪ Lie on your side and place a comfortably warm **hot-water bottle** or **heating pad** over your ear. Or use a towel dampened with hot water. The soothing warmth increases circulation to the ear and also helps relieve pressure.

↪ Use a **hair dryer** as another source of warmth. Set the dryer on the lowest warm temperature, hold it at least 15 centimeters from your ear, and direct the airstream down your ear.

↪ To draw inflammation away from the affected ear, wear **ice-cold socks** on your feet and apply a **warm compress** to your ear. Saturate cotton socks in ice water, wring them out, and place them against the soles of your feet. Then pull wool socks over the cold socks to hold them in place. Simultaneously, place a hot moist compress over the painful ear.

Ease the Ache with Garlic

↪ Eat one or two raw cloves of **garlic** every day. The pungent bulb helps fight viruses and bacteria. Some brave souls just chew on the cloves. A more palatable alternative: Chop up the fresh garlic, mix it with olive oil, and spread it on your favorite bread.

↪ If you find that raw garlic tends to upset your stomach, take a capsule of **garlic supplement** with each meal.

↪ Squeeze a clove of garlic and put a few drops of the juice in your ear. Because garlic has antibacterial properties, this direct approach fights infection.

Turn on the A and C

↪ Take 50,000 IU of **vitamin A** twice a day until your symptoms improve. Vitamin A is an antioxidant that helps fight infection, promote healing, and maintain mucous membranes. If you still need to take it after a week, drop the dosage to 25,000 IU a day, and continue taking it for another week—but not longer unless you consult with your doctor.

↪ Take 1,000 milligrams of **vitamin C** and 500 milligrams of **flavonoids** three times a day until the infection is gone. Vitamin C is an antioxidant that promotes healing. When it's combined with flavonoids—anti-inflammatory components extracted from plants—the vitamin works even better.

Should I call **the doctor?**

See your doctor if your ear is extremely painful, if it hurts for more than a week, or is accompanied by 37.8°C (100°F) fever or higher. You should also tell the doctor about any fluid discharge from your ear, feelings of dizziness, or painful sensations when you chew. Sudden, intense pain, followed by some relief, could indicate a ruptured eardrum. Other common signs of ruptured eardrum are discharge (sometimes with blood), muffled hearing, a ringing in the ears, and a feeling of dizziness or vertigo. If you have these symptoms, see your doctor before trying any of the remedies in this chapter.

The Power of Prevention

A few simple steps can keep you from having to worry about aching ears:

 ❧ When you have a cold, **blow your nose gently.** If you honk too forcefully, you can push bacteria back into your middle ear from your sinuses and trigger an infection.

 ❧ Frequent ear infections can be a sign of **food allergy.** Most often, the troublesome foods are dairy products, wheat, corn, peanuts, or oranges. Try removing these foods from your diet for a several weeks to see if you feel any better. Then add them back one at a time. If your ears start aching, delete the food from your diet for good.

 ❧ Chew **sugarless gum** that contains the sweetener xylitol, which comes from birch trees and is also found in strawberries and plums. In one study, children who chewed two pieces of the gum five times a day for two months had 40 percent fewer ear infections. The xylitol may cut down the growth of bacteria that cause middle-ear infections. One brand of gum is VitaDent.

Earwax

Just the annoyingly resonant rumble of your own voice is probably enough to tell you that earwax buildup is out of hand. Easy-does-it earwax removal is usually a two-part project—first the insertion of something to soften up the wax, then an ear wash to flood the gunk and carry it out. Easier said than done? Here are some tips to help the wax wane.

Try an Ayurvedic Approach

~ Gently **massage** the area directly behind your earlobe to help loosen the wax. Then **tug the earlobe** while opening and closing your mouth.

Soften and Rinse

~ Fill an eyedropper with warm **hydrogen peroxide** that is body temperature or a little warmer. Lie down or tilt your head so that your blocked ear is pointing up. Drip the hydrogen peroxide into the ear until it feels full. Wait three minutes before tilting your head the other way over a wash-basin or hand towel to let the peroxide drain out. Now tilt your head back once more and gently squirt warm water from a bulb syringe into your ear. Let it settle, and then tilt your head to the other side and let it run out again. Clean away the water and softened wax from your outer ear with a washcloth or cotton balls.

~ An alternative to the hydrogen peroxide treatment is using oil to soften the wax. Tilt your head and place a few drops of warm **baby oil** or **mineral oil** into the affected ear with an eyedropper. Let the oil work its way down into your ear. You can leave it in for up to one hour. Then, with a bulb syringe, squirt in some warm water to flush the oil out of your ear. Turn your head from side to side as long as the water continues to drain out.

What's **wrong**

Earwax, known medically as cerumen, is normally a useful substance. Secreted by glands in the outer portion of the ear canal, that wax traps dirt before it gets deep into your ears. When your ears produce too much wax, however, or you inadvertently push it into the canal by trying to clean it out, cerumen can form a hard plug deep in the ear. This can cause earaches, ringing in the ears, hearing loss, and balance problems.

Should I call the doctor?

You should contact your physician if you develop itching, pain, swelling, tenderness, ringing in the ears, feelings of dizziness or vertigo, or any kind of discharge from the ear (either milky or bloody). These may be signs of a severe ear infection or ruptured eardrum. Also, consult your doctor if your ear remains blocked because of impacted wax. If you have the symptoms of a ruptured eardrum, or you've had one in the past, do not put oil or any other liquid in your ear without first consulting your doctor.

Air Your Ear

 After you finish washing the wax out of your ears, use a **hair dryer** to air-dry them. Set the hair dryer on its coolest setting and hold it about 30 centimeters (12 inches) away.

The Power of Prevention

 Whenever you're washing up, rub a damp washcloth around the loops and whorls of your outer ear. **Never stick a cotton swab** or any other type of probe into your ear, however. You'll ram the wax deeper, and since there are no oil glands deep in the ear canal to keep the wax soft, it will harden like a rock. The other risk is that you could puncture your eardrum or scratch your ear canal.

 Cut down on consumption of **saturated fats** found in animal foods like meat and dairy, and minimize your consumption of the hydrogenated fats found in commercially baked snacks and other processed foods. Some experts believe these types of fats prompt your body to produce greater amounts of earwax and also make the wax stickier. Replace these dietary fats with healthier ones, such as those found in cold-water fish, nuts, and seeds.

 If you wear a **hearing aid**, wipe it with a tissue every night at bedtime when you remove it. This gets rid of wax residue before it has time to accumulate.

 For people who have a lot of ear hair—particularly some older men—it helps to trim the hair with small scissors or a battery-operated **ear-hair trimmer**. The trimming will help prevent earwax from getting enmeshed in hair around the opening of the ear canal.

Eczema

Like so many skin problems, eczema can itch worse than a bad conscience. Your avenues of attack: Keep out of the water (that means no dishwashing, frequent hand washing, or long showers) as much as possible. Guard your skin with a thick, heavy-duty cream—not a watery lotion. Stay away from eczema aggravators, such as harsh soaps and anything you discover you're sensitive to. And, hard as it may be, avoid scratching.

Rash Relief

 To cool your itch, soak a washcloth in ice-cold **milk** and lay the cloth onto the itchy area. Repeat several times daily as needed.

 For an oozing rash, apply **calamine lotion.** It can help with the itching and also dry out the rash.

Soak and Seal

 Add **colloidal oatmeal** to your bath. This ground oatmeal floats suspended in the water and is soothing to itchy skin. A well-known brand is Aveeno.

 Keep your baths and showers under 10 minutes. In fact, **don't bathe every day** if you don't have to. Eczema tends to get worse when skin is dry, and excessive bathing washes away the protective oils that keep your skin moist.

 Use **lukewarm water** in the tub or shower instead of piping hot water.

 After you bathe, use a **heavy cream-based moisturizer** to guard the skin against irritants. Even petroleum jelly or solid vegetable shortening, such as Crisco, works well. Avoid water-based lotions, as well as lotions that contain fragrance.

Get Some Internal Revenue

 Eat more foods rich in essential fatty acids like omega-3s, which help reduce inflammation and allergic reactions. You'll find these in rich amounts in **walnuts, avocados, salmon, mackerel, and tuna.**

What's wrong

There are several types of eczema. Atopic eczema, the most common, usually occurs in people with a family history of allergies or asthma. Symptoms— red, itchy skin—generally begin before the age of five, then reappear periodically during adulthood. During acute flare-ups, the skin may be marked with small, fluid-filled blisters. Over time, excessive scratching causes patches of skin to look thick and scaly. Skin damaged by eczema and scratching is prone to bacterial infections. Another type of eczema, called contact dermatitis, stems from contact with an irritating substance such as detergent, soap, and cosmetics.

Should I call the doctor?

If your eczema is widespread or keeps recurring despite your self-care treatments, contact your doctor. And you'll need a doctor's attention as soon as possible if an itchy patch of skin begins to show signs of infection. These include crusting sores, pus, red streaks on the skin, excessive pain, swelling, or fever.

⁓ Another good source of omega-3s is **flaxseed oil.** Take up to one tablespoon each day; it won't hold up in high cooking temperatures, so drizzle it on salad, mix with yogurt, or hide it in other foods.

⁓ Take 400 IU of **vitamin E** each day to help counteract itchy, dry skin. (*Off-limits*... if you're taking blood-thinning drugs unless you have your doctor's approval.)

⁓ Take 25,000 IU of **vitamin A** each day for up to 10 days when you're having an eczema flare-up, then reduce the dose to 10,000 IU daily. But check with your doctor first. Long-term use of vitamin A can result in osteoporosis, and an overdose of this vitamin can cause thickening and peeling of skin and hair loss.

⁓ **Zinc** helps your skin heal, and it also helps your body make use of essential fatty acids. Take 30 milligrams of zinc daily. Because zinc can interfere with copper absorption, also take 2 milligrams of copper each day if you continue to take zinc for more than a month.

Go to Gotu

⁓ The herb **gotu kola**, used externally, can help ease itchy skin conditions. Look for a commercial cream or extract. If you use the extract, dilute it first (5 parts water to 1 part extract). Alternatively, you can make a cup of the tea, soak a cloth in it, and use the cloth as a compress. To make the tea, steep 1 teaspoon of the dried herb in 1 cup of hot water. Steep for 10 minutes, then strain.

⁓ As an alternative to gotu kola, look for a cream containing **chamomile, licorice**, or **witch hazel.** All of them reduce skin inflammation.

Stop the Scratching

⁓ If the itchy spot is somewhere way too accessible, such as your wrist or the back of your hand, **cover it with a small bandage** to remind yourself not to scratch.

⁓ Some people scratch in their sleep. If you're waking up with scratched skin, **wear thin cotton gloves** (or, in a pinch, a pair of socks) over your hands at night.

⁓ **Keep your fingernails cut short** to minimize skin damage if you do scratch.

Strong Medicine

In December 2000, more than 40 years after the last new drug was developed to treat eczema, a prescription ointment called tacrolimus (brand name Protopic) was approved for sale. In studies, more than two-thirds of the people who used the ointment showed improvement, many after using the ointment for only one week. If you have eczema that isn't helped by home remedies, see a dermatologist about a prescription for this new medicine.

The Power of Prevention

Many experts feel that **food allergies** play a significant role in eczema, particularly in children under the age of two. In kids, the problems most often come from eggs, dairy, peanuts, soy, wheat, and tree nuts. In adults, the troublesome foods are usually dairy, wheat, eggs, yeast, and citrus products. Eliminate all these foods from the diet for about a month, then bring back one at a time for three days to see if the skin reacts. In children, this food-elimination diet may produce a visible change in a short time. Dramatic change is rarer in adults, but still, you might note some improvement.

During winter months, use a **humidifier** in your bedroom to help keep your skin moist.

To minimize sweating in the summer, which can aggravate eczema, run the **air conditioner.**

Rely on your **dishwasher** as much as possible to avoid contact with detergents and water.

When you do wash dishes, wear a pair of **lined rubber gloves** or wear rubber gloves over a pair of thin cotton gloves. **Avoid direct contact with latex**, since it can cause allergic reactions—and make eczema worse—in some people.

Keep your use of laundry chemicals to a minimum. Use a **fragrance-free** and **dye-free** detergent. **Avoid bleach, fabric softeners**, and **dryer sheets.**

Give your clothes an **extra rinse** in the washing machine to remove all traces of detergent.

Consider whether something you've touched has caused a breakout, and steer clear of these substances in the future. **Contact dermatitis** can be caused by nickel used in earrings and other jewelry, as well as latex, cosmetics, perfumes, and cleaning agents.

Skip it!

Over-the-counter corticosteroid creams, like hydrocortisone, can help tame eczema. But if you use them too often—say, every day for more than three weeks—they can thin and damage the skin.

Eye Irritation

Jeepers, creepers. When your peepers are unhappy, they let you know it. A speck of dust no bigger than the period at the end of this sentence can feel like a jagged-edged boulder if it lodges beneath your eyelid. And if your eyes dry out in the wind or cry out against chlorine, it's hard to focus on anything else. Fortunately, you can often fix the problem in the blink of an eye.

What's wrong

The world can be a dusty, gritty place, and when one of those specks lands on your eyeball, the discomfort is nothing to blink at. Fortunately, tears come to the rescue, cleaning the surface of your eyes, nourishing their cells, and countering the desiccating effects of dry air. Without them, your eyes become irritated and red. As we age, we produce fewer tears, which is one reason older people tend to have more eye irritation. Allergies can cause red, itchy eyes, as can exposure to dry air and cigarette smoke.

Dust Begone

➤ If there's a particle in your eye, gently pull the upper lashes to lift the lid away from your eyeball. Roll your eye around. If you don't produce enough tears to wash out the particle, use **sterile eyewash** or **artificial tears.**

➤ Some people take that technique one step further and flip an **upper eyelid inside out.** Sometimes that's all it takes to flick out the particle.

➤ If that maneuver doesn't work, or you don't want to attempt it, try a simple **eyewash.** Wash and rinse your hands at the sink, cup some warm water in your palms, and then put your closed eye into your cupped hands. Open your eye underwater to flush away the particle.

Get Out of Contact with Your Contacts

➤ If you wear contacts and you get something in your eye, **remove the lens** and clean it, using normal cleaning techniques. Before you put the lens back in, examine it closely to see whether a particle is stuck to it. If you do have to remove a speck, clean the lens one more time before putting it back into your eye.

Soothe Itchy Eyes

➤ Soak a washcloth in **cool water** and lay it over your closed eyes for as long as needed. This is particularly effective if your eyes are red and itchy from allergies. The cold constricts blood vessels, while the moist cloth keeps your eyes damp.

Soak **tea bags** in cool water and place one over each closed eye for 15 minutes. Any kind of tea bag will do: it's the cool dampness that soothes the eye—not what's inside the bag.

Moist-your-eyes

Run a **humidifier** in your home, particularly in the TV room, living room, kitchen, or bedroom—wherever you spend a lot of time.

For eyes that are dry and irritated, use **artificial tears.** Buy a product that doesn't contain preservatives, such as Tears Natura Sol Free OP or Refresh Endura eye drops. Read the label for directions.

The Power of Prevention

Get more sleep. Lack of sleep can cause eyes to become dry and red because the blood vessels are swollen.

Eat a **banana** every day to help relieve dry eyes. Bananas are rich in potassium, which helps to control the balance of sodium and the release of fluid in your cells.

Add a tablespoon of **flaxseed oil** to juice or cereal. It's a good source of omega-3 fatty acids, which are essential for keeping your eyes well lubricated. (Teardrops contain not only water but fat and mucus. To have a healthy tear film, you need to eat plenty of omega-3 fatty acids, also found in nuts and certain cold-water fish.)

If your eyes are frequently dry, review the **drugs** you take. Common troublemakers include antihistamines, antidepressants, blood pressure medications, and tranquilizers.

Wear **goggles** when you're doing chores that raise debris.

Wear watertight **swim goggles** whenever you're swimming in a chlorinated pool.

In the sun, wear **sunglasses** to protect your eyes from ultraviolet radiation. Sunglasses can also keep them from drying out on windy days.

If you use a **skin cream** or **ointment** on your upper eyelids, make sure it won't irritate your eyes. Some of that ointment may ooze into your eyes, making them dry and raw.

Stay away from **tobacco smoke.** If you're a smoker yourself, you'll probably find that your eyes feel a lot better as soon as you give it up.

Should I call **the doctor?**

If you get a speck on your pupil or a foreign body embedded in your eye, call your doctor. He may want you to come to the office or head to the emergency room. Also call the doctor if you remove a particle from your eye but still feel something there, if your eye is red, or if you have trouble seeing. You may have scratched your cornea. Treatment with drops is often required to avoid infection and control pain. If the scratch was inflicted by a dirty object, have it checked promptly.

Skip it!

Avoid eye drops that clear the "red" out of your eyes. These constrict your blood vessels, but don't provide the moisture your eyes really need. They can wind up making your eyes drier. Instead, use artificial tears.

Eyestrain

Your eyes may be the windows to your soul, but when overworked, they become doorways to pain, headaches, and blurred vision. Unfortunately, eyestrain is all too common when people spend countless hours staring into the glare of computer monitors and televisions. What to do about it? Give the eyes as much rest as possible. And make some adjustments to your computer and your work habits to make life easier on the eyes.

What's wrong

Hold a dumbbell in your outstretched hand, and your muscles soon grow tired. The same happens to eyes when you overtax them. If the eye muscles that focus your vision don't have a chance to relax, you'll soon feel the strain. You may even have trouble focusing. And if you're squinting in bright sunlight, a case of eye ache comes on very quickly.

Rest 'Em, Blink 'Em, Close 'Em

🕊 Whenever you're working on a task that requires close concentration, **take a break** every 20 minutes or so. Look at a faraway object—a picture on the opposite wall, or a view out the window—for at least 30 seconds. By allowing your eyes to shift focus, you give them a rest.

🕊 Try to **blink often**—every few seconds or so—when you're paying close attention to your television or computer screen. Blinking moistens your eyeballs and relaxes your eye muscles.

🕊 If you have a long task that involves prolonged staring, **close your eyes** periodically. Even if you just shut your eyelids for a few seconds, you'll get some immediate relief.

Warm and Cool Relief

🕊 Another way to **relax your eye muscles**: Briskly rub your hands together until they grow warm, and gently place the heels of your palms over your closed eyes. Hold them there for a few seconds.

🕊 If you soak a washcloth or hand towel in **cool water**, wring it out, and lay it over your eyes for five minutes, it will relieve strain.

🕊 Cool your eyes with sliced **cucumber.** Lie on your back and place one slice over each closed eye. Leave on the slices for two or three minutes, or replace the first pair with another, cooler set of slices.

Glasses for Your Neck

If you wear bifocals, you can get neck strain from working at a computer. That's because with bifocals, the "reading" lens is at the bottom of the glasses, so you have to tilt back your head to see the computer screen. Ask your eye doctor to prescribe another pair of glasses that will give you clear vision at a distance of 50 centimeters, so you can read what's on the monitor without awkward head tilting.

Tear Up

🌱 For eyestrain that is related to dry eyes, use **artificial tears**, available at pharmacies. Two common brands are Tears Natura and Refresh Endura.

Adjust Your Monitor

🌱 **Turn the contrast** on your computer monitor to high. Letters and images become crisper.

🌱 Adjust your **chair height** so you're looking slightly downward at the screen. Tilt the screen to meet your gaze.

🌱 Make sure that your eyes are at least **50 centimeters** from the screen.

🌱 Adjust your computer screen or close the shades near your work area so that you **don't have window-glare** on the screen.

🌱 If glare still bothers you, attach a special **antiglare filter** to the screen.

🌱 **Clean the dust** off the screen regularly to improve clarity.

🌱 If you're mildly nearsighted, try reading or viewing the computer screen **without your "distance" glasses.** Your eyes might be more comfortable that way.

🌱 Choose a **bigger font** so your eyes don't have to work as hard to focus, or use the **zoom feature** to enlarge what you're viewing.

Use Shades

🌱 In any bright sun—even in the winter—**wear sunglasses.** They will reduce eyestrain that comes from squinting. Choose sunglasses with yellow, amber, orange, or brown lenses. Light in the blue part of the spectrum is what makes us squint, and these lenses block it.

Should I call the doctor?

If your eyes frequently feel strained and home remedies don't work, if your vision grows increasingly worse, or you're very sensitive to light, consult an eye doctor. Also, if dizziness or double vision occur suddenly and don't go away when you rest your eyes, be sure to talk to your doctor promptly.

Light Up Your Life

When you're reading, be sure the light is adequate so you don't have to strain to see the print. The best results are with a **gooseneck lamp** directed so that the light falls on the page. Generally, a lower-watt bulb in a gooseneck lamp is more effective than a higher-watt bulb in a shade lamp. A 45- to 65-watt indoor floodlight bulb should give plenty of illumination.

Don't settle for one reading lamp in an otherwise dark room. Be sure that **other lights are also turned on.** If there's too much contrast between the light where you're reading and the rest of the room, your pupils will constantly have to narrow and widen to adjust for the difference.

Avoid reading or working under **fluorescent lights.** They may flicker, contributing to eyestrain. The incandescent light from ordinary light bulbs is your best bet.

Check Out Cheap Specs

After age 40 or so, many people have trouble focusing on nearby objects—a condition called presbyopia. If your distance vision is still fine and both eyes are focusing equally, try purchasing an inexpensive pair of **reading glasses** from your local drugstore to resolve the problem.

Fatigue

Feeling bone-tired, as so many people do, is disheartening, demoralizing, and frustrating. You want to race like a Thoroughbred, but you feel stuck in the mud. Half the time you're struggling just to stay awake. Life is passing by, and you can't keep up with it. Willpower doesn't work, so what does? Sometimes your best bet is a total energy makeover—changes in the way you eat, drink, and exercise. Certain supplements can also help. Or maybe your solution is simple: sleep, beautiful sleep. Of course, it wouldn't hurt to have your doctor test your blood for hypothyroidism, anemia, vitamin B_{12} deficiency, and other conditions that can cause fatigue.

Quick Fixes

 For a quick pick-me-up, put two drops of **peppermint oil** on a tissue or handkerchief, hold it to your nose, and breathe deeply. If you have more time, try adding two drops of the oil to bathwater along with four drops of **rosemary oil** for an invigorating soak.

 Lie on your back and use pillows to prop your feet at a level higher than your head or, better yet, lie on an adjustable exercise bench or other surface that slants. In India, yogis fight fatigue through such practices by encouraging **blood flow to the brain**, which is thought to boost alertness.

High-Octane Eating

 Eat a good breakfast along with several small meals and healthy snacks throughout the day. That's better than eating two or three large meals. Try to limit the size of your meals to 300 calories. This will keep your blood sugar levels steady and help prevent your energy from plunging.

 Go easy on foods high in **refined carbohydrates**—that is, lots of white sugar or white flour. These foods make your blood sugar rise rapidly, then crash quickly. French bread, spaghetti, and cake are not your best choices. You'll end up feeling weak and tired.

What's **wrong**

People complain of feeling drained and exhausted so often that doctors call fatigue the number one health complaint. Often fatigue is accompanied by lack of motivation and low sex drive. A long list of medical conditions and lifestyle issues can contribute to fatigue, including lack of sleep, inadequate nutrition, flu, obesity, allergies, infections, anemia, alcohol abuse, hypothyroidism, heart disease, cancer, diabetes, and AIDS.

Should I call the doctor?

If you feel tired "all the time" even after you've taken steps to treat fatigue, make an appointment to see your doctor. If you have fatigue along with sudden onset of abdominal pain, shortness of breath, or severe headache, seek immediate medical attention. Other chronic symptoms that might require a doctor's attention are muscle aches, nausea, depression, fever, or difficulty seeing.

☙ Eat more high-fiber foods that are rich in **complex carbohydrates**, such as whole-grain cereals, whole-wheat bread, and vegetables. These help stabilize blood sugar.

☙ **Cut down on** your intake of **fatty foods.** To improve the function of your adrenal glands—which influence the way you metabolize nutrients—you should have no more than 10 percent saturated fat in your diet.

☙ Cut an **unpeeled potato** into slices and let the pieces soak in water overnight. In the morning, drink the juice for a natural tonic brimming with potassium. Your body needs this mineral for transmitting nerve impulses and making muscles move, along with other vital functions, and some natural healers say deficiencies are common in people with fatigue.

Supplement Your Energy Stores

☙ Ginseng is an age-old cure for that run-down feeling. Look for a supplement containing at least 4% ginsenosides, and take two 100-milligram capsules daily. This herbal remedy stimulates your nervous system and will help to protect your body from the ravages of stress. (*Off-limits* . . . if you have high blood pressure.)

☙ Try taking 400 milligrams of **magnesium** every day. This mineral is involved in hundreds of chemical reactions in the body. It plays a role in changing protein, fat, and carbohydrates into energy sources. A mild deficiency may be the cause of fatigue in some people.

☙ **Ginkgo** improves blood flow to the brain, which can make you feel more alert and less fatigued. Take 15 drops of ginkgo tincture in the mornings.

☙ Consider supplements of the amino acid **carnitine** (available for sale on the Internet). This amino acid helps fuel the activity of mitochondria, cell components that produce energy. It's found in some foods, but most people don't get enough in their diets. Follow the dosage directions on the label.

☙ **Coenzyme Q$_{10}$**, a substance produced by the body, also helps your mitochondria make energy. Take 30 milligrams twice a day, at breakfast and lunch. (It's best absorbed when taken with food.) Coenzyme Q$_{10}$ is also found in certain foods, including nuts and oils.

What to Drink

🌢 Sip **water** all day long, at least eight glasses. Don't wait until you're thirsty, because your "thirst alarm" isn't always accurate. Even a little dehydration can make you fatigued.

🌢 **Keep caffeinated drinks to a minimum.** The caffeine in coffee and some sodas can give you a short-term burst of energy, but following that "rush," there's typically a "crash."

🌢 **Limit alcohol consumption.** Alcohol depresses your central nervous system. It also reduces your blood sugar level.

Get Your Engine Moving

🌢 Most days of the week, try to get at least 30 minutes of **aerobic exercise.** Not only does exercise help you shed pounds (carrying extra weight is tiring), it gives you an energy boost. People who exercise regularly also tend to sleep better.

🌢 Consider taking up **yoga** or **tai chi.** These ancient forms of exercise allow you to get physical activity, but they also include relaxation components that can be reinvigorating.

🌢 Slip in 10 minutes of **low-level exercise** when you feel sluggish. Usually people with fatigue have a decreased supply of adenosine diphosphate (ADP), an intracellular "messenger" involved in energy metabolism. Translation: There's not enough "spark" in the engine. Almost any kind of activity will help— singing, taking deep breaths, walking, or stretching.

Nod Off to Switch On

🌢 Always **get up at the same time**, even on weekends. Your body will eventually get the hang of the steady sleep schedule.

🌢 **Go to bed earlier** than normal if you need extra sleep. As long as you're getting up at the same time every morning, it's fine to have a flexible getting-to-bed schedule.

🌢 **Keep naps short.** If you snooze more than half an hour during the day, your body will want more, and you'll be groggy when you wake up.

Complete the Picture

🌢 Take a daily **multivitamin** to ensure you're getting the minimum amount of nutrients your body needs. Deficiencies can pull the plug on your energy stores.

Tried...

Eating spinach once a day is an old-time remedy for relieving fatigue, and we all know what it did for Popeye.

...and true

You can't go wrong. Spinach contains potassium as well as many B vitamins, all of which are important to energy metabolism.

Fever

If your forehead is fiery with fever, you could reach for acetaminophen (Tylenol) or ibuprofen (Advil) to lower your temperature. (Don't treat fevers with aspirin in anyone under the age of 19; doing so can trigger a potentially fatal disease called Reye's syndrome.) But if your fever is 38.3°C (101°F) or below, don't be afraid to let it run its course; Mother Nature has raised your temperature for a reason. If you're uncomfortable, though, and you want to take action, try these tips to tame the fires within.

What's wrong

A fever is often a sign that your body is fighting off infection. As your white blood cells battle with microscopic invaders, they release chemicals that raise your body temperature, making the environment less friendly to viruses and bacteria. A fever in adults is generally regarded as a temperature higher than 37.7°C (100°F). In infants and young children, any fever should be treated. But in older children and adults, a fever below 38.9°C (102°F) doesn't necessarily need to be treated unless the person has intense discomfort because of sweating, chills, or both.

Be Cool

Take a **bath in lukewarm water.** This temperature will feel plenty cool when you have a fever, and the bath should help bring your body temperature down. Don't try to bring a fever down rapidly by plunging yourself into cold water; that tactic sends blood rushing to internal organs, which is how your body defends itself from cold. Your interior actually warms up instead of cooling down.

Give yourself a **sponge bath.** Sponging high-heat areas like your armpits and groin with cool water can help reduce your temperature as the water evaporates.

When you're not bathing, place **cold, damp washcloths** on your forehead and the back of your neck.

Sweat It Out

Brew a cup of **yarrow tea.** This herb opens your pores and triggers the sweating that is said to move a fever toward its end. Steep a tablespoon of herb in a cup of freshly boiled water for 10 minutes. Let cool. Drink a cup or two until you start to sweat.

Another herb, **elderflower**, also helps you sweat. And it happens to be good for other problems associated with flu and colds, like overproduction of mucus. To make elderflower tea, mix two teaspoons of the herb in a cup of boiled water and let it steep for 15 minutes. Strain out the elderflower. Drink three times a day as long as the fever continues.

Drink a cup of hot **ginger tea**, which also induces

sweating. To make the tea, steep a half-teaspoon minced gingerroot in 1 cup just-boiled water. Strain, then drink.

Fight Fire with Fire

🖎 Sprinkle **cayenne pepper** on your foods when you have a fever. One of its main components is capsaicin, the alarmingly hot ingredient that's found in hot peppers. Cayenne makes you sweat and also promotes rapid blood circulation.

Soak Your Socks

🖎 Try the **wet-sock treatment**, a popular folk remedy for fever. First warm your feet in hot water. Then soak a thin pair of cotton socks in cold water, wring them out, and slip them on just before going to bed. Put a pair of dry wool socks over the wet ones. This approach helps ease a fever by drawing blood to the feet, which dramatically increases blood circulation.

🖎 Another way to draw blood to the feet is with a **mustard footbath.** In a basin large enough for your feet, add two teaspoons of mustard powder to four cups of hot water, then soak.

Get Between the Sheets

🖎 An old folk remedy for treating a fever is to **soak a sheet in cold water** and wrap yourself in it. Today, doctors advise against lowering your body temperature too quickly, so if you try this remedy, use slightly cool, not cold, water. Cover the wet sheet with a large beach towel or blanket, then lie down for about 15 minutes. Unwrap yourself when the wet sheet starts to get warm.

Fill Up on Fluids

🖎 When you have a fever, it's easy to become dehydrated. Drink 8 to 12 glasses of **water** a day or enough to make your urine pale. A sports drink like Gatorade can also be helpful. It not only replaces fluids lost to dehydration but lost minerals as well.

🖎 Orange juice and other fruit juices rich in **vitamin C** are good choices, since the vitamin C assists your immune system in fighting off infection.

🖎 Cold **grapes** provide hydration—and a soothing treat.

Should I call **the doctor?**

Contact your doctor if you have a temperature of 39.4°C (103°F) or higher, if a temperature of 38.3°C (101°F) lasts longer than 72 hours, or if your pulse is above 110 beats per minute. Also, call your doctor immediately if the fever is accompanied by a stiff neck, a severe headache, extreme drowsiness, shortness of breath, burning with urination, red streaks near a wound, a severe rash, or sensitivity to light. Any fever in infants younger than six months should be brought to the attention of your pediatrician right away.

Old **wives' tale**

Forget the old saying about "starving a fever" to make it go away. (Actually, the original saying was "feed a cold, *stave* a fever," *stave* meaning to prevent.) Fasting will weaken you just as you should be preserving your strength. Even if you don't feel like eating, at least have some chicken soup and toast or other soothing foods.

Flatulence

Just bringing up the subject of flatulence starts people giggling, but when it's you who's passing gas, you probably don't regard it as a laughing matter. Instead of worrying about running to another room to avoid embarrassment, take the wind out of your sails by cutting out gas-causing foods, chewing on gas-relieving seeds after a meal, and taking steps to help your body digest food more completely.

What's wrong

The average adult passes gas between fifteen and twenty times a day. Typically, this is just the release of air we've swallowed or gases—including carbon dioxide, methane, and sulfur dioxide—produced while we're digesting food. Such gases are the odorous by-products of hungry bacteria that linger in the digestive tract, feeding off partially digested carbohydrates. If you're constipated, you might have excessive flatulence because you're not expelling gas during regular bowel movements. Also, people who can't properly digest dairy foods—a problem dubbed lactose intolerance—often have problems with flatulence.

Deflate Your Diet

➤ Certain foods are notorious for producing gas. Avoid them if they give you trouble. They include **beans, cabbage, bran, cauliflower, broccoli, onions, prunes, raisins**, and **Brussels sprouts.** Also on the list are eggs, which have some sulfur in the yolk that contributes to odorous gas.

➤ Take preventive measures before you eat. A product called **Beano**, which you can add to beans and other troublesome foods, supplies enzymes you need to digest these foods without gas. Take the Beano tablets or droplets at the start of a meal, following the label for dosage directions.

➤ Before you cook beans, **soak them overnight.** The next day, pour off the old water, then replenish with fresh water for boiling. This will remove some of the carbohydrates that cause gas.

➤ **Avoid** candies and gums that contain the sweeteners **sorbitol, xylitol**, and **mannitol.** Your body has trouble digesting them, and when they get to your colon, the resident bacteria there feed on them and produce gas.

➤ **Cut down on fructose**, a sugar found in honey, fruits, and fruit juices. Like other sweeteners that are difficult to digest, fructose stays in the colon, where bacteria feed on it and create gas-rich fermentation. Don't cut out whole fruit from your diet, but go easy on fruit juice and honey if they bother you.

➤ If you're adding more **fiber** to your diet, do it gradually. Fiber is terrific for your health, but adding a lot to your diet all at once can lead to an odoriferous end.

Look to Lactaid

If you are **lactose intolerant**, take a supplemental over-the-counter product such as Lactaid when you consume milk, cheese, ice cream, or other dairy foods. Or look for reduced-lactose milk at the supermarket. People who have trouble digesting dairy lack an adequate supply of the enzyme lactase, which breaks down lactose, the sugar in milk. Since the body's lactase supply often dwindles as we grow older, you may develop this problem in later years, even if it hasn't been an issue before.

Not sure if you're lactose intolerant? Trying **giving up dairy foods** for a few days and see if it makes a difference.

After-Your-Meal Medicine

If you've eaten a big meal that is likely to make you flatulent, drink a cup of **ginger tea.** It stimulates digestion so food won't linger in your intestines, contributing to gas. To make the tea, steep a quarter-teaspoon of powdered ginger in a cup of hot water for five minutes.

Peppermint also helps minimize gas and improve digestion. Drop dried peppermint leaves into a cup of freshly boiled water, and steep for five to 10 minutes. Strain and drink. You can use this remedy three or four times daily as needed. (*Off-limits*... if you have gastroesophageal reflux or heartburn).

Fennel seeds, which have a pleasing licorice scent, have been used for hundreds—perhaps thousands—of years to reduce gas and improve digestion. Chew half a teaspoon of the seeds after a meal, or sprinkle them on your food. You can also make fennel tea by steeping 1 to 2 teaspoons crushed dried seeds in 1 cup just-boiled water for 10 to 15 minutes. Strain, then drink. Caraway seeds have a similar effect.

Give gas the **papaya** treatment. Papaya contains an enzyme called papain that helps the body break down food. Buy papain tablets, or juice half a papaya, add an equal amount of water, and drink.

Lavender is said to be effective against gas. It can also help soothe after-meal cramps in the stomach and intestines. To make a tea, steep 1 or 2 heaping teaspoons of lavender flowers and steep for 10 minutes in a cup of boiling water, then strain and drink.

Should I call **the doctor?**

If flatulence bothers you continually, and is accompanied by diarrhea and bloating, talk to your doctor. He or she may want to examine you for other indications of the condition known as irritable bowel syndrome. Also, severe flatulence that doesn't go away can sometimes be a symptom of gallbladder problems, an inflammatory condition in the intestines, or colon cancer.

Act with Acidophilus

☙ Take an **acidophilus** supplement each day for two to four weeks. Acidophilus is one of the "friendly" bacteria that inhabit the large intestine and keep gas-causing bacteria in check. Follow the dosage directions on the label. Or eat yogurt that contains live cultures (check the label).

Curl Up for Comfort

☙ If you're feeling painful abdominal cramps, try to find a private place where you can **lie down** for a few minutes. Lying on your back, pull your knees up toward your chest. This posture allows the gas to escape more easily, relieving discomfort.

Get on the Move

☙ **Walking** is a particularly good way to encourage gas dispersal. In hospitals, it's the first thing that doctors recommend to postoperative patients to help them get bowels working again. Stroll a few blocks and see if it helps.

The Power of Prevention

☙ To reduce the swallowed air that goes into your stomach, **avoid** drinking through **straws**.

☙ **Don't chew gum.** When you do, you automatically swallow more air.

☙ **Avoid carbonated sodas** and other bubbly drinks, which carry gas into your digestive tract.

☙ **Chew food thoroughly.** When you gulp it down, you swallow more air. Also, large chunks of food take longer to digest, which means they linger in the digestive tract, where feeding bacteria launch the fermentation process.

Foot Odor

Do people turn up their noses when you slip off your shoes? Has the family dog fallen in love with your footwear? There are plenty of solutions that go way beyond baking soda to stop the sweat, eat the odor, and keep your feet from smelling like … smelly feet. In particular, many people swear by using an antiperspirant on their tootsies.

Give Feet the Underarm Treatment

⌒ It shouldn't come as a surprise that the same **antiperspirant** you use on your underarms can also keep feet less sweaty (and therefore less smelly). Simply spray or roll it on before putting on your shoes and socks.

⌒ Wash your feet daily in warm water using a **deodorant** soap or **antibacterial** soap.

Turn Up the Heat

⌒ Especially if you are prone to athlete's foot or nail fungus, blow-dry your feet with a **hair dryer** that's turned to the lowest temperature. This helps avoid infection and reduces moisture.

Soak 'Em and Scent 'Em

⌒ Try a **black tea footbath.** Boil two tea bags in two cups of water for 15 minutes. Remove the bags and dilute the tea with two quarts of water. Let the mixture cool down if necessary, then soak your feet for 30 minutes. Repeat daily. The tannic acid in strong black tea kills bacteria and closes pores to help your feet sweat less.

⌒ Make an odor-fighting foot soak by adding a cup of **vinegar** to a basin of warm water. For more odor-fighting force, add a few drops of **thyme oil.** The oil contains a strong antiseptic that kills odor-causing bacteria. Soak your feet for 15 to 20 minutes a day for a week. (*Off-limits* . . . if you have any open sores or broken skin.)

What's **wrong**

Your feet are the natural habitat of millions of bacteria, which thrive on your sweat and skin cells. By-products produced by these bacteria are what give feet that stinky smell. When you seal your feet in a pair of shoes and they pour out sweat, you give the bacteria more food to feast on. Foot odor can also be caused by poorly controlled fungal infections, such as athlete's foot. People with diabetes or heart disease, as well as elderly people in general, are often more apt to develop foot infections and foot odor due to less-than-adequate circulation.

Should I call the doctor?

If these remedies don't fix your foot odor, consult your doctor or a podiatrist. You may have an infection that requires an antibiotic or a prescription antifungal medication.

If you don't have access to thyme oil, you can easily buy a product that contains it: **Listerine.** Try adding a splash to your footbath. (The same cautions as with thyme oil apply.)

Fragrant Foot Rub

Lavender oil not only smells good, it helps kill bacteria. Rub a few drops onto your feet and massage it in before you go to bed at night. Cover your feet with socks. Before trying this remedy, check to make sure the oil won't irritate your skin by putting one drop on a small area.

Salt Your Dogs

Mix two cups of **Epsom salt** into a basin half-full with warm water. Soak your feet for 15 minutes twice a day. The Epsom salt acts as an astringent to reduce sweating, and may kill bacteria.

Try an Acne Treatment

Apply **benzoyl peroxide** 5% or 10% gel to the bottoms of your feet to fight bacteria. Why not? It works on your face.

Powder Power

Dust your feet with **talcum powder** or **foot powder** before you put on your shoes and socks. It will absorb odor-causing sweat.

To other good foot powders to try are **baking soda**, which neutralizes odor, and **cornstarch**, which absorbs moisture.

Dress Well for a Better Smell

Change your socks at least once a day, replacing them with a clean pair.

Alternate between at least **two pairs of shoes.** After you've worn one pair, set them aside and let them air out for at least twenty-four hours.

Wear shoes with **open-mesh** sides or sandals that allow your feet to "breathe." Your feet will also breathe better if you wear **cotton socks** rather than polyester.

Treat Shoes with Savvy

⮞ Check the care instructions on your athletic shoes. If they're washable, toss them into the **washing machine** at least once a month.

⮞ Store your shoes in a place that's **bright** and **ventilated**— not in a dark closet, where bacteria thrive.

⮞ Each time you put your shoes away, insert a sachet filled with cedar chips into them. You can also try products that consist of mesh pouches filled with **zeolite.** Zeolite is a natural volcanic mineral that attracts odors and traps them. Expose the reusable pouch to the sun for six hours to discharge the collected odors.

⮞ Buy odor-absorbing **insoles** and cut them to fit. Replace them every three to six months.

⮞ If your shoes have removable insoles, **take them out to dry** every time you remove your shoes. And toss them in the washer from time to time.

Did you **know?**

You have more than 250,000 sweat glands on your feet, which pump out as much as one cup of sweat each day.

Foot Pain

Sometimes foot pain has an obvious cause, like a fungal infection (athlete's foot), corn, callus, or ingrown toenail. But if the discomfort you're suffering stems simply from fatigue or ill-fitting shoes, your best friend may be water—warm or cold, with or without herbal extras—or an invigorating foot massage. No one willing to rub your feet? No problem! Read on to find out easy ways to give your tootsies a treat.

What's wrong

You spend up to 80 percent of your waking hours on your feet, and each day your feet absorb over 2,265,000 kilograms of accumulated pressure. So it's no wonder that, from time to time, your feet end up in a world of hurt. Virtually anything can cause foot pain, including shoes that don't fit, diseases like arthritis and diabetes, and poor circulation.

Toes and Teas in the Tub

⚬ For a refreshing and stimulating treat for the feet, fill one basin with **cold water** and another with water as **hot** as you can comfortably stand. Sit in a comfortable chair, and place your feet in the cold water. After 5 minutes, switch to the hot water. Repeat. This "hydromassage" alternately dilates and constricts blood vessels in your feet, boosting circulation.

⚬ To pamper your feet with essential oils—a ritual dating back to the Bible—fill a bowl with hot water and add 2 drops **peppermint oil**, along with four drops each of **eucalyptus** and **rosemary oil.** Soak for 10 minutes.

⚬ If you don't have any essential oils at home, brew up a very strong cup of **peppermint tea** and add it to the water.

⚬ Soak your feet in a warm-water footbath spiked with 15 milliliters of **arnica tincture.** The improved blood flow almost instantly results in less pain.

Massage

⚬ In health-food stores, you can buy a **roller** specially designed to massage the soles of the feet. Or you can simply roll your bare foot over a **tennis ball, golf ball,** or **rolling pin** for several minutes.

⚬ To make a **stimulating salve,** combine three drops clove oil, thought to be a mild circulation booster, and three tablespoons sesame oil. Mix the ingredients well and massage the oils into your aching feet. Another foot-rub recipe calls for

3 drops lavender oil, 1 drop chamomile oil, and 1 drop geranium oil mixed in 2 teaspoons olive oil.

Aid to the Fallen

🍃 Shoe inserts, or **orthotics**, help relieve foot pain caused by flat feet or fallen arches. They're available at medical-supply stores or from a podiatrist.

Give Feet a Workout

🍃 Scatter a few **pencils** on the floor, and pick them up with your toes. This little exercise helps relieve foot ache.

🍃 Wrap a thick **rubber band** around all the toes on one foot. Spread your toes and hold the stretch for five seconds. Repeat ten times to relieve shoe-bound feet.

Heal Your Heel

🍃 Heel pain, especially in the morning, may signal plantar fasciitis, an inflammation of the tough band of tissue that connects your heel bone to the base of your toes. To get relief, **stretch the Achilles tendon.** Stand about one meter from a wall. Place your hands on the wall, and move your right leg forward, knee bent. Keep your left leg straight, with your heel on the floor. You should feel a gentle stretch in your heel and foot arch. Hold for 10 seconds, then switch sides and repeat.

🍃 Apply an **ice pack** to the sore heel for about 20 minutes three times a day.

🍃 Pick up a **heel cup** in any drugstore. It goes inside the shoe, cushioning the heel and protecting it from pounding.

The Power of Prevention

🍃 Whenever you have to stand in one place for a long time—when you're manning a garage sale, for instance—**stand on a rubber mat.**

🍃 **Wear running shoes** whenever possible, even if you don't run. They provide the best cushioning and arch support. If you don't want to wear running shoes, at least choose shoes with thick soles.

🍃 **Shop for new shoes in the afternoon,** when your feet have expanded to their maximum size.

Should I call **the doctor?**

Occasional pain is nothing to worry about. But see a podiatrist or orthopedic surgeon specializing in feet if you find it hard to walk first thing in the morning, or if the painful area is swollen or discolored. You may have a broken bone, an inflamed tendon, or a pinched nerve. Ditto if there's a painful burning sensation in your feet, which can mean diabetes or thyroid disease. If you've already been diagnosed with diabetes, see your doctor at once if a cut, sore, blister, or bruise on your foot doesn't start to heal after one day.

Gout

The agony of gout can start very quickly. One minute, you're skipping along with a smile on your face and a song in your heart. The next, you're in excruciating pain. Your first instinct might be to reach for aspirin—a wrong move. Aspirin slows the excretion of uric acid, which only makes things worse. A better bet are the prescription drugs naproxen (Naprosyn) or indomethacin (Indocid). Then you can turn to these home remedies to further reduce pain. Pay special attention to drinking plenty of water to dissolve the uric acid crystals.

What's wrong

When too much uric acid (produced in the liver and excreted in the urine) builds up in your system, needle-sharp crystals of the compound can form in the fluid that cushions your joints. You may feel like you have shards of glass jammed into your joints. This painful inflammatory condition, known as gout, usually occurs in men over age 40 (it takes years for uric acid crystals to build up). Though it most often affects the big toe, gout can strike the wrist, knee, elbow, or another joint. Besides pain, gout can cause severe swelling.

Lift Off and Ice Down

↝ During an acute attack, try to **stay off your feet** as much as possible and keep the affected joint elevated. This probably won't be a problem. When gout is at its worst, most people can't even bear the weight of a bed sheet on the painful joint.

↝ If you can stand to, apply an **ice pack** for 20 minutes or so. The cold will dull the pain and bring down the swelling. Wrap the ice in a cloth to protect your skin. Use the ice pack 3 times a day for two or three days.

Try the Cherry Remedy

↝ **Cherries** are an old folk remedy for gout. They contain compounds that help neutralize uric acid. Cherries are also a source of anti-inflammatory compounds. So if you feel an attack of gout coming on, try eating a handful or two or cherries right away. If they aren't in season, buy canned cherries or black cherry juice (drink 1 to 2 cups; try mixing it with pineapple juice).

↝ Alternatively, you can take **cherry fruit extract pills**, which are available at health-food stores. The recommended dose is 1,000 milligrams once a day (for maintenance) or three times a day (for attacks).

↝ Don't like cherries? Some people swear by strawberries for gout.

Pill Power to the Rescue

 Daily doses of **fish oil** or **flaxseed oil** can ease the inflammation in the joints. These oils are rich sources of a potent anti-inflammatory agent known as eicosapentaenoic acid (EPA). The typical dosage of fish or flaxseed oil is 1,500 milligrams a day (about a tablespoon).

 Another way to ease inflammation is with pills containing **bromelain**, an enzyme found in pineapple. The typical dosage for acute gout attacks is 500 milligrams three times a day between meals.

 Tablets containing **celery seed extract** seem to help eliminate uric acid. The typical dosage is two to four tablets a day.

 Long advocated by herbalists to treat joint inflammation, **nettle** also helps lower uric acid levels. Experts typically recommend 300 to 600 milligrams of a freeze-dried extract a day. Don't use nettle for more than three months at a time. (*Off-limits . . .* nettle in tincture form. Tinctures contain alcohol, which aggravates gout.) Another way to use nettle is to soak a clean cloth in a tea brewed from the leaves of nettle and apply it to the tender joint. If you pick this common weed yourself, wear gloves, long pants, and long sleeves to guard against nettle's stinging leaves.

Live on Water, Not Beer

 Drink lots of **water**—at least eight 250-milliliter glasses a day. Fluids will help flush excess uric acid from your system. As a bonus, the water may help discourage kidney stones, which disproportionately affect people with gout.

 Avoid alcohol. It seems to increase uric acid production and inhibit its excretion. Beer is particularly bad—it contains more purines (see below) than other alcoholic beverages.

Should I call **the doctor?**

Anytime you develop a tender, swollen joint, call the doctor, even if you've had similar attacks in the past. Gout can mimic other conditions, such as joint infection, so the doctor should first confirm a diagnosis by drawing liquid from the affected joint and examining it under a microscope to confirm the presence of uric acid crystals. Prescription drugs for gout are available. But before you take one, make sure your doctor knows about every medication and supplement you're already taking, since some of those may be increasing your risk of gout.

The Anti-Gout Diet

High-protein foods, as well as foods that contain chemical compounds known as purines, can raise levels of uric acid in the body. If you have gout, the list of foods to avoid includes meat-based gravy, organ meats like kidneys and sweetbreads, mussels, sardines, liver, herring, fried foods, refined carbohydrates (such as white flour), oatmeal, yeast-containing foods like beer and baked goods, asparagus, peas and beans, spinach, and cauliflower.

To Tame the Pain, Mind Your Meds

∾ If you're taking a diuretic—for high blood pressure, for instance—ask your doctor about **alternatives**. Diuretics eliminate excess fluids from the body; as a side effect, they reduce the amount of uric acid that passes in the urine. Less passes, more stays, and the worse your gout.

∾ Gout can also be **triggered by niacin, or nicotinic acid**, which is often prescribed for high cholesterol. If your doctor has prescribed niacin for you, ask about alternatives.

Fast Not, Hurt Not

∾ Losing weight can help keep gout at bay, but going on a crash diet or fasting is a big mistake. Drastic dieting causes cells to release more uric acid. If you're overweight, **lose weight slowly** and sensibly—approximately one kilogram (two pounds) a week at most.

Gum Problems

If you're hurting and you want relief right now, you can walk into any drugstore and buy a tube of gel containing the topical anesthetic benzocaine. Or try a gargle or a soothing gum massage as described below. But your real war is with plaque. Control the plaque with regular visits to the dentist and dedicated brushing (use a soft-bristled brush and pay special attention to your gum line) and flossing and you should be able to give gum problems the brush-off.

Play by the Numb-ers

 To soothe gum pain and reduce swelling, swish for 30 seconds with **salt water** (one teaspoon mixed into a glass of warm water).

 Alternatively, rinse your mouth with **hydrogen peroxide** diluted 50:50 with warm water. Like salt, hydrogen peroxide dulls the pain and helps kill bacteria.

 Place a wet **tea bag** against the painful area. Tea contains tannic acid, a powerful astringent that shrinks swollen tissues and helps stanch bleeding. Think of it as a styptic pencil for your gums. If bleeding and inflammation persist, fold the bag in half and bite down on it.

 Apply an **ice pack** (wrapped in a cloth) to your cheek near the painful area. Ice helps reduce swelling, and the cold acts as a local anesthetic.

 Dab your gums with a paste made of **baking soda** and water. Baking soda kills germs and helps neutralize the acids they secrete. Don't go overboard, though; too much baking soda can damage tender gum tissue.

Rub for Relief

 What do you do for sore muscles? **Massage** them! And your gums benefit from massage too. Just grip them between your thumb and index finger, and give a series of gentle squeezes. That helps boost circulation to painful, irritated tissue, helping gums heal faster.

What's **wrong**

Are your gums puffy? Do they bleed when you brush? You probably have gingivitis, a form of gum inflammation caused by plaque, a sticky film of food particles and bacteria that accumulates on your teeth. Plaque is irritating to your gums. If it isn't removed by brushing and flossing, it can turn into hard mineral deposits that are even more irritating (and which can be removed only by a dentist). Left untreated, gingivitis eventually leads to full-blown gum disease, in which the gums pull away from the teeth. The resulting germ-filled pockets can lead to painful abscesses and chronic bad breath, and can even cause your teeth to loosen and fall out.

Should I call
the dentist?

As long as you're having
your teeth professionally
cleaned and examined
twice a year (more often
if plaque formation is a
problem), minor gum
irritation does not require
a visit to the dentist. Just
consider your irritated
gums a wake-up call that
you need to pay more
attention to brushing and
flossing. Do call your
dentist if you notice a
change in the appearance
of your gums, or if they
start bleeding. For intense
pain, schedule an
immediate appointment,
especially if you have fever
and a swelling in the neck.
You could have an abscess
that needs prompt
treatment.

✎ To enhance the soothing effect of a gum massage, try doing what practitioners of Ayurvedic medicine recommend: Massage your gums with **coconut oil.**

✎ Another way to massage your gums is with a soft wooden **dental stimulator,** which you can pick up at any drugstore. Insert it between two teeth, point the tip so it's at a 45-degree angle to the gum line, circle gently for a few seconds, then move on to the next two teeth.

✎ Buy a **Water-Pik** or another "oral irrigator," and use water pressure to clean and massage your teeth and gums where your toothbrush cannot reach.

✎ A time-tested wound healer, **calendula** may help sore gums by reducing inflammation. Simply rub the tincture directly onto the gums.

Rinse and Gargle

✎ Twice a day, gargle with a mouth rinse containing the B vitamin **folic acid.** Studies have shown that swishing twice a day with an over-the-counter folic acid solution helps with bleeding gums.

✎ Rinsing your mouth with **chamomile tea** is said to be highly effective against gingivitis. Simply pour a cup of hot water over 3 teaspoons of the herb, steep for 10 minutes, then strain and cool. Mix up a large quantity and store it in the refrigerator.

✎ Store-bought mouthwash can also help heal your gums. Choose a brand that contains **cetylpyridinium chloride** or **domiphen bromide.** These ingredients have shown significant plaque-reducing ability.

Hangover

" I will never take another drink for as long as I live!" So goes the mantra of anyone who has ever woken up with a hammering headache and a stomach rolling around like an old sneaker in a washing machine. First advice: If you feel as if you have to throw up, don't resist the urge. Vomiting is the body's way of ridding itself of toxins. And don't reach for a painkiller. Acetaminophen, and possibly aspirin and ibuprofen as well, can harm your liver if you've been drinking. To shorten the ugly shadow of a hangover, try the tips below. As for brave resolutions... well, if you do drink again, take steps to limit the alcohol's impact on your system.

First Steps for Fast Relief

➤ As soon as you wake up, drink two 250-milliliter glasses of **water** to undo the dehydration.

➤ Have a large glass of **grapefruit, orange**, or **tomato juice**. Juice contains the simple sugar fructose, which speeds the metabolism of alcohol.

➤ If you drink **coffee**, have a cup or two as soon as possible. Caffeine is a vasoconstrictor, meaning it narrows the swollen blood vessels in your head. Just be sure not to go overboard. Like alcohol, caffeine is a diuretic, and if you drink too much, you'll become even more dehydrated.

➤ **Kudzu** is a traditional Chinese remedy for alcohol poisoning, usually taken in a "morning after" tea. You can pick up kudzu extract at a health-food store. Follow the dosage directions on the package. Or you can try Intox RX, HepatoGen or another kudzu-based hangover cure available on the Internet.

Comeback Snacks

➤ Once you overcome the queasiness, fix yourself a nice bowl of hot **chicken soup** or bouillon. Either one will help replace the salt and potassium the body loses when you've been drinking.

➤ A **banana milk shake** is an especially good way to

What's **wrong**

You had too much to drink last night, and you've woken up with a wicked hangover. Your head is pounding. You're drenched in sweat. You feel like throwing up. Maybe you feel shaky or anxious too. What's going on? The alcohol in your system has left you dehydrated and depleted of minerals. It's also caused the blood vessels in your head to dilate; that accounts for the headache. Finally, alcohol makes your blood abnormally acidic (a condition called acidosis), which causes nausea and sweating.

Should I call the doctor?

Even without treatment, a hangover should last for no more than 24 hours. If you're still feeling bad after that, call a doctor. Of course, if you can't remember what happened while you were drinking, or if you get hangovers on a regular basis, you may have a drinking problem. Call your doctor to discuss treatment options.

Old wives' tale

The sixteenth-century English dramatist John Heywood suggested that the best way to recover from a hangover was to have the "hair of the dog that bit you"—meaning, another drink. The expression is a spin-off of the misguided notion that you could recover from a dog bite by plucking a hair from the cur and holding it to the wound. Unfortunately, the advice doesn't work any better for hangovers than it does for dog bites. Drink your way out of a hangover? That will only prolong your misery.

replace potassium and other nutrients lost during a night of heavy drinking. Combine a half-cup milk with a banana and 2 teaspoons honey. Whirl it all in a blender, and drink up. Banana is a good source of potassium, which was lost in your urine. And honey is rich in fructose.

🐦 If you feel well enough, eat a light meal—fresh fruit, crackers with honey. **Fruit** and **honey** are good sources of fructose. Save the bacon and sausage for another day.

Nix It with Nux

🐦 The homeopathic remedy **nux vomica** is considered an antidote to alcohol hangovers. Dissolve 3-5 pellets of the 30C potency on the tongue every four hours.

Get Moving

🐦 Although your instinct might be to stay in bed, you're better off if you can take a brisk walk or go for a run. That will boost your production of **endorphins**, the body's natural painkillers. Heavy drinking can lower endorphin levels.

The Power of Prevention

🐦 If you're headed to a social occasion where alcohol will be served, **eat something**—ideally something a bit greasy—before you go. The fatty substances help coat the intestines, slowing the absorption of alcohol. Slow absorption means less chance of inebriation, and a smaller chance of developing a hangover the following day.

🐦 If you drink hard liquor, favor **vodka** over bourbon, rum, or cognac, and white wine over red. Clear liquors like vodka don't contain congeners—naturally occurring compounds that contribute to morning-after nausea and headache. White wine contains fewer congeners than red wine.

🐦 **Drink slowly.** Your body burns alcohol at a pace of roughly 30 milliliters (one ounce) an hour. Give it more time to burn that alcohol, and less will reach your brain.

🐦 Alternate alcoholic drinks with **soda, juice**, or other **nonalcoholic** drinks.

🐦 Avoid champagne or any other alcoholic drink with **bubbles** in it (say, a rum and Coke). Effervescence puts alcohol into your bloodstream more quickly.

Head Lice

Once lice are in the hair, even a burr cut won't help. You need to get rid of the louse eggs that are attached to the hair shafts about five millimeters from the scalp. Start by using a delousing shampoo. Choose one that contains permethrin, not lindane. Lindane is a chemical cousin of the pesticide DDT and has been linked to nervous system problems (including convulsions) and brain cancer. Once you've found a killer shampoo, the remaining challenge is to use it effectively and become very nitpicky about preventing contamination. Otherwise, your whole household could get lousy.

Start with Shampoo

⁓ Use a **delousing shampoo**, and leave it in your hair for ten minutes. That's a long time to spend in the shower, so you may prefer to do your shampooing in the bathtub, where you can read or listen to music while the shampoo does its job.

⁓ After you rinse out the shampoo, rinse it again using 50% water and 50% **white kitchen vinegar**. The vinegar helps dissolve the bodies of dead nits. Rub it in vigorously, then rinse your hair a few times to dispel the odor.

⁓ Use the louse-killing shampoo again 10 days later. If you're still not getting results, mix a half-cup **vinegar** with a half-cup **olive oil**. About an hour before you take your bath or shower, apply this mixture to your hair, working it in close to the scalp. Put a shower cap over your hair. After an hour, remove the cap and take your shower, washing your hair with regular shampoo.

The Natural Approach

⁓ If you're wary of synthetic pesticides, you may be able to smother lice while you sleep. First, saturate the hair and scalp with **mayonnaise**, then put on a shower cap. The next morning, lice should be dead. Unfortunately, you can't smother the louse eggs—you'll still have to remove them by hand.

⁓ **Petroleum jelly** can have a stifling influence on roaming lice. Apply a thick layer of petroleum jelly to the scalp, then cover

What's wrong

Something is definitely moving in your hair, and the itching is driving you buggy. And that's precisely the problem: Your tresses are now a cozy domicile for the common head louse, otherwise known as *Pediculus humanus capitis*. Just 1.6 millimeters long, these wingless insects live close to the scalp, laying their eggs (nits) and feeding on your blood. When lice appear in school-age children, word usually gets around quickly, and parents are warned to be on the lookout. Lice spread via contact with contaminated hair, hairbrushes, combs, clothing, or bedding.

Should I call the doctor?

The remedies in this chapter will usually take care of a run-of-the-mill case of head lice. But you'll need a doctor's help if self-treatment fails, or if the skin on the scalp becomes cracked or inflamed.

Tried...

Before effective louse-killing shampoos came on the market, some said that the best way to kill lice was to rinse the hair with paint thinner or kerosene.

...and true

These methods were probably effective at killing lice when nothing else was available, but there are far safer options today.

with a shower cap. Leave it on overnight. In the morning, use **baby oil** or **mineral oil** to remove the petroleum jelly—and the lice along with it. Repeat several nights in a row. (One warning, though: it may take a lot of shampooing before you get all the petroleum jelly out of your hair!)

❧ Essential oils can kill lice and help soothe the itching. There are many different "recipes." One effective combination is 20 drops **tea-tree oil**, 10 drops **rosemary oil**, and 15 drops each of **lemon** (or **thyme**) and **lavender oil** mixed into 4 tablespoons **vegetable oil**. Rub the mixture into your dry hair, cover your head with a plastic shower cap, then wrap that with a towel. After an hour, unwrap your head, shampoo well, and rinse.

Be Picky

❧ No matter what you do to get rid of lice, careful inspection is also essential. If you have lice, ask your partner to go through your hair slowly with a **metal lice comb** (available at drugstores) and look for nits or lice. If your child's head is infested, you may have to use TV to get the child to sit still through this process. Nits are yellowish-white, oval-shaped, and adhere to the hair shaft at an angle. They look a bit like dandruff, but they don't drift out of your hair the way dandruff does. Mature lice grow to about the size of sesame seeds. Freshly hatched lice are clear; those approaching midlife (about a week old) are reddish-brown. If you see lice, remove them with an **emery board** or **Popsicle stick**. If you use your fingers, still-living nits might get under your nails.

Stop the Spread

❧ When someone in the family has lice, keep all **combs and brushes separate**. And make sure no one comes into contact with hats, scarves, hair ribbons, etc., that have been worn by the affected person.

❧ After treating the lice, **wash clothing, bedding** and other washables that have been used by the affected person in hot, sudsy water. Seal nonwashable items in plastic bags for a week (or three days in the refrigerator).

❧ After a coat has been worn by someone who has lice, put it in the **dryer** to make certain all lice and eggs are killed.

Headaches

Oh, my aching head! In a world of traffic jams, tight schedules, and high-speed everything, it's no wonder we find ourselves popping an occasional pain reliever. For a bad headache, choose one that contains a combination of aspirin, acetaminophen, and caffeine. (*Off-limits*...if you have a bleeding disorder, asthma, ulcers, or liver or kidney damage.) But painkillers are only part of the solution. There's much more you can do to escape the thump and wallop of a throbbing noggin.

Give It Some Good Press

⁓ With a firm, circular motion, **massage** the web of skin between the base of your thumb and your forefinger. Continue massaging for several minutes, then switch hands and repeat until the pain resolves. Acupressure experts call this fleshy area trigger point LIG4 and maintain that it is linked to areas of the brain where headaches originate.

Heat Up and Cool Down

⁓ Believe it or not, soaking your feet in **hot water** will help your head feel better. By drawing blood to your feet, the hot-water footbath will ease pressure on the blood vessels in your head. For a really bad headache, add a bit of hot mustard powder to the water.

⁓ For a tension headache, place a **hot compress** on your forehead or the back on your neck. The heat will help relax knotted-up muscles in this area.

⁓ It might sound contradictory, but you can follow up the heat treatment (or substitute it) by applying a **cold compress** to your forehead. (Put a couple of ice cubes in a washcloth or use a bag of frozen vegetables.) Cold constricts blood vessels, and when they shrink, they stop pressing on sensitive nerves. Since headache pain sometimes originates in nerves in back of your neck, try moving the compress to the muscles at the base of your skull.

What's **wrong**

Specialists have identified a few major types of headache. Tension headaches seem to be caused by muscle contractions in the head and neck, and they're characterized by dull, steady pressure. Migraines originate with constriction and expansion of blood vessels in the head. There may be throbbing pain on one or both sides of the head, often accompanied by nausea and sensitivity to light or sound. Agonizing cluster headaches are sometimes triggered by drinking or smoking, and they come episodically in groups, or "clusters," followed by periods of remission.

Should I call the doctor?

Did you know?

Here's an alternative to a cold compress: Soak your hands in **ice water** for as long as you can stand it. While your hands are submerged, repeatedly open and close your fists. This works on the same principle as an ice pack on your head—the cold narrows your dilated blood vessels.

Try the Caffeine Cure

Have a cup of **strong coffee.** Caffeine reduces blood-vessel swelling, and thus can help relieve a headache. This is why caffeine is an ingredient in some extra-strength painkillers like Excedrin. However, if you are already a heavy coffee drinker, skip this. Caffeine withdrawal can cause headaches, creating a vicious cycle.

Do Something Constrictive

Tie a **bandanna, scarf,** or **necktie** around your forehead, then tighten it just to the point where you can feel pressure all around your head. By reducing the flow of blood to your scalp, this can help relieve the pain caused by swollen blood vessels. You might try soaking the bandanna in vinegar, a traditional headache remedy.

Soothe with Scent

Certain essential oils—especially **lavender**—can help ease tension and relieve the pain of a headache. Gently massage a bit of lavender oil onto your forehead and temples, then lie back and enjoy the relaxing scent. For maximum relief, slip away to a room that's cool, dark, and quiet. The longer you can lie there quietly breathing in the aroma, the better.

In addition to lavender oil—or instead of it—use **peppermint oil.** The menthol it contains can help dissolve away a headache. Its fragrance at first stimulates, then relaxes, the nerves that cause headache pain.

If you have a vaporizer, add 7 drops **lavender oil** and 3 drops **peppermint oil,** then breathe in the relief. If you don't, try sprinkling a few drops of peppermint oil on a tissue. Inhale deeply several times.

Try wringing out two wet **peppermint tea bags** and place them on your closed eyelids or forehead for five minutes.

Swallow Some Throb Stoppers

An anti-inflammatory, **ginger** was traditionally used to treat headaches, and it seems to work. Grind up a half-teaspoon ginger, stir it into a glass of water, and drink this "ginger juice." Or pour 1 cup hot water over 1 teaspoon freshly ground ginger, let the tea cool a bit, then drink it. Ginger is especially effective against migraines, though how it works is not well understood. Doctors do know that ginger has an effect on prostaglandins, hormonelike substances that

Migraines

Migraines are characterized by throbbing, excruciating pain, usually on one side of the head. Nausea, vomiting, sensitivity to light, or visual disturbances may accompany the pain. Doctors aren't sure what causes migraines, but they suspect an association with abnormal constriction and dilation of the arteries that supply blood to the brain. The problem tends to run in families. There are many possible triggers, including sensitivities to foods or food additives, stress, hormonal fluctuations during the menstrual cycle, oral contraceptives, caffeine withdrawal, changes in the weather or season, bright lights, and odors. Migraines are more common in women than in men.

It's easier to prevent a migraine than it is to treat one. Try these techniques:

An herbal remedy from Europe called Petadolex can help relieve and prevent migraines. Take one gelcap three times daily.

Avoid foods that contain lots of the amino acid tyramine. So-called trigger foods include cured and processed meats, such as bologna, hot dogs, pepperoni and sausage, aged cheeses, nuts and peanuts. Chocolate and red wine are other sources of tyramine.

The herb feverfew has the power to reduce the intensity and frequency of migraines. Follow the dosage recommendations on the label. You'll need to take the capsules every day—possibly for several months—to maximize the herb's preventive power.

Flaxseed oil is rich in essential fatty acids, which help your body produce fewer inflammation-causing prostaglandins, hormonelike chemicals that can constrict blood vessels. Take 1 to 2 tablespoons a day. Buy the cold-pressed oil, and keep it in the refrigerator to protect it from light and heat. Good-quality flaxseed oil has a pleasant, nutty flavor; sneak it into a smoothie or add it to a salad.

Although experts aren't exactly sure how, the B vitamin riboflavin can help prevent migraines. Doctors recommend starting at a daily dose of 200 milligrams, but some people need to take up to 400 milligrams daily before they get results.

A magnesium supplement may also help. In some studies, people reported that their symptoms were much improved by taking 200 milligrams of magnesium each day. If that doesn't work, you can take up to 600 milligrams daily.

At the first sign of a migraine, take one-third teaspoon of fresh or powdered ginger. Danish researchers discovered that ginger can help prevent the onset of migraines by blocking prostaglandins.

contribute to inflammation. Ginger also helps control the nausea that so often accompanies migraines.

🍃 Try drinking a cup of **rosemary tea**; some people say it helps keep a headache from getting worse. Pour 1 cup boiling water over 1 teaspoon of the dried herb, steep for 10 minutes, strain, and drink.

🍃 At least one grandmother counted on strong **black tea** with a few bruised whole **cloves** added. Tea contains caffeine, and cloves have anti-inflammatory properties, so the brew might indeed help a headache.

🍃 Down a large glass of **water** and see if it helps. Dehydration can cause a headache.

The Power of Prevention

🍃 If you grind your teeth or clench your jaw—either when you're awake or asleep—take steps to prevent the problem. You might need to wear a **mouth guard** at night. (See Teeth Grinding, page 353, for advice.)

🍃 **Eat at regular intervals.** There's evidence that a drop in blood sugar—the result of going too long without eating—can set the stage for headaches.

🍃 At least three days a week, spend 30 minutes walking, cycling, swimming, or doing some other form of **aerobic exercise.** These exercises are great stress-relievers.

Heartburn

Heartburn is definitely punishment, but it's not always clear why you've been sentenced. Some say, "Don't eat so much" or "Don't eat so fast." Others like to blame spicy foods like fiery Szechuan or acidic foods like grapefruit and oranges. As a first line of defense, visit the pharmacy for over-the-counter antacids like Mylanta or Maalox, or acid suppressors like Zantac and Pepcid AC. But the long-term goal is to pinpoint—and avoid—your all-too-personal heartburn triggers.

Douse the Flames

∾ As soon as you feel the telltale flicker of heartburn, drink a 250-milliliter glass of **water.** It will wash the acid back down your esophagus into your stomach.

∾ To make a heartburn-easing tea, add 1 teaspoon of freshly grated **gingerroot** to 1 cup of boiling water, steep for 10 minutes, and drink. Long used to quell the nausea caused by motion sickness, ginger also helps to relax the muscles that line the walls of the esophagus, so stomach acid doesn't get pushed upward.

∾ A tea made from **anise, caraway,** or **fennel seed** can also ease the burn, according to herbalists. Add 2 teaspoons of any of them to 1 cup of boiling water, steep for 10 minutes, strain, and drink.

∾ Practitioners of Ayurvedic medicine, the traditional medicine of India, prescribe teas made of crushed **cinnamon** or **cardamom** to cool the heat of heartburn. Add 1 teaspoon of either crushed or powdered herb to 1 cup boiling water, steep, strain, and drink.

Don a Protective Coat

∾ **Marshmallow root** is one of the oldest remedies known for heartburn. It produces a gooey, starchy substance called mucilage, which coats and protects the mucous membranes of your esophagus—just what you need when you feel like it's on

What's **wrong**

When stomach acid backs up into your esophagus, you feel a burning pain. What causes acid backups? A trapdoor of muscular tissue called the lower esophageal sphincter (LES) usually keeps stomach acid where it belongs. With heartburn, it allows acid to leak upward, a problem known as reflux. Large meals as well as certain foods can lead to heartburn. You're more likely to have heartburn if you're pregnant, overweight, or a smoker, or if you have a condition called hiatal hernia. Some medications, including aspirin, certain antibiotics, and some antidepressants and sedatives, may aggravate heartburn.

Should I call the doctor?

An occasional episode of heartburn isn't serious. But frequent, bouts may be one symptom of a viral infection. Recurrent heartburn could also be a sign of gastroesophageal reflux disease (GERD), which can cause or contribute to ulcers of the esophagus, chronic cough, dental problems, and even asthma and pneumonia. See your doctor if you get heartburn three or four times a week for weeks on end, if you wheeze or become hoarse, find it difficult to swallow, or lose weight rapidly. Finally, the symptoms of severe heartburn are often similar to those of a heart attack. If they arrive after a meal and are quelled by water or antacids, it's probably heartburn. But if you have a feeling of fullness, tightness, or dull pressure or pain in the center of the chest (possibly spreading to the shoulders, neck, or arms), shortness of breath, and/or light-headedness accompanied by a cold sweat, get immediate medical help.

fire. Stir 1 teaspoon powdered marshmallow root into 1 cup water and sip it. Drink three or four cups a day.

~ You can make a similar soothing drink from **slippery elm.** Add one teaspoon of the powder to a cup of hot water, and drink a few cups throughout the day.

~ A form of **licorice** called DGL also provides soothing mucilage. Take two or three chewable wafers three times daily on an empty stomach.

Put It in Neutral

~ Saliva helps neutralize stomach acid. So chew a piece of **sugarless gum**, suck on a candy, or daydream about juicy steaks or buttery lobster—whatever it takes to get you to generate and swallow extra saliva.

~ **Baking soda** is alkaline, so it neutralizes stomach acid. Mix a half-teaspoon baking soda and a few drops of **lemon juice** in a half-cup warm water. Don't drink the baking soda by itself. You need the lemon juice to dispel some of the gas baking soda creates in the stomach when it comes in contact with stomach acid—there have been cases where baking soda produced such a rapid internal reaction that it ruptured the stomach.

~ The juices of vegetables like **carrots, cucumbers, radishes,** or **beets** help to tame the acid in the stomach due to their alkaline nature. Feel free to add a pinch of salt and pepper for flavor. If juicing vegetables is inconvenient or strange to you, just eat some raw vegetables.

The Power of Prevention

~ No matter how terrible you feel, **stay upright.** Gravity is a powerful force, and if you're standing, the earth's pull helps keep acid in your stomach. Avoid bending over after a meal, and definitely don't lie down.

~ If nighttime heartburn plagues you, eat meals at least **2 to 3 hours** before you turn in. The added time will give acid levels a chance to decrease before you lie down.

~ You might also **elevate the head of your bed** 10 to 15 centimeters with large wooden blocks. When you're tilted at an angle while sleeping, gravity helps keep acid in the stomach.

Dodge These Edibles

"Food, glorious food!" rejoiced the hero of the musical *Oliver!* But if you're prone to heartburn, it's better to avoid certain foods—and drinks as well. Limit your consumption of the following:

➤ **Beer and wine, especially red wine.** They tend to relax the LES, that important port of entry between your stomach and lower esophagus.

➤ **Milk.** The fats, proteins, and calcium it contains can stimulate the stomach to secrete acid.

➤ **Coffee, tea, and cola.** These caffeinated beverages also relax the LES, and they can irritate an already-inflamed esophagus.

➤ **Chocolate.** It's loaded with two heartburn triggers—fat and caffeine.

➤ **Soda.** The carbonation it contains can expand your stomach, which has the same effect on the LES as overeating.

➤ **Fried and fatty foods.** They tend to sit in the stomach for a long time, where they can get that acid a-churnin'.

➤ **Tomatoes and citrus fruits and juices.** They are acidic.

➤ **Peppermint and spearmint.** They relax the LES.

➤ Try **sleeping on your left side.** When you lie on your left side, the stomach hangs down and fluids pool along the greater curvature, away from the LES. Pooled fluids stay farther away from the esophagus.

➤ Eat **smaller, more frequent meals** to minimize the production of stomach acid. And avoid eating too much in one sitting; doing so can force open the lower esophageal sphincter (LES), the thick ring of muscle that separates the stomach from the esophagus and keeps stomach acid where it belongs.

➤ If you haven't done so already, **give up cigarettes.** Research shows that smoking relaxes the LES.

Healing Your Home

You've installed smoke detectors. Tested your air for radon and your tap water for lead. You've even seen to it that each bathroom has antibacterial soap and paper cups. What else can you do to protect your family against illness? Quite a lot, as it turns out—especially if you live in a tightly sealed, energy-efficient home, in which airborne toxins can quickly build up.

Use Mother Nature's Cleansers

No doubt you already know to open the windows and turn on a fan when using solvents, harsh cleansers, and other noxious chemicals. But it's an even better idea to replace these products whenever possible with homemade alternatives.

⟀ **All-purpose cleaner:** Dissolve 4 tablespoons baking soda in 1 liter warm water.

⟀ **Drain cleaner:** Pour a half-cup baking soda down the drain. Add a half-cup white vinegar. Close the drain and wait five minutes, then flush with a kettleful of boiling water.

⟀ **Toilet bowl cleaner:** Make a paste with lemon juice and borax (available in hardware stores). Apply the paste, let set for two hours, then scrub and rinse.

⟀ **Oven cleaner:** Sprinkle water on spills while the oven is still warm, then add salt. When the oven cools, scrape the spill away.

Get Bold About Mold

Many people who blame their coughing and wheezing on pet dander or pollen are actually experiencing a reaction to mold spores in their own homes. Nothing helps mold to flourish like high humidity, so do all you can to get household moisture under control. Obviously, that means keeping an eye out for roof leaks and drip-drip-dripping faucets. But you should also make sure that all space heaters, furnaces, gas logs, fireplaces, etc., are properly calibrated and well vented. In addition to producing carbon monoxide and other combustion products, these devices drench the air with water vapor.

You might want to pick up a moisture meter (hygrometer) at a hardware store. If the indoor humidity in your home regularly exceeds 50 percent, a dehumidifier should solve your problem.

Give Germs the Cold Shoulder

No matter how carefully you clean, it's impossible to get rid of *all* the germs in your home. But you can get fewer colds and other viruses simply by insisting that everyone in the household washes his/her hands before each meal and after each trip to the bathroom. Try not to touch your hands to your eyes or mouth; if germs have no way into your body, they can't make you sick. And yes, using a disinfectant spray on doorknobs and faucets does help protect the rest of the family when one of you is under the weather.

☙ **Tame your toothbrush.** One place germs love to lurk is a damp toothbrush. Many viruses, including those that cause the flu, can survive for more than 24 hours on moist bristles. Solution: Alternate between three toothbrushes, so you're using a dry toothbrush each time. If you do come down with a bad cold, replace all of them once you recover, just to be safe. Don't like the idea of so many toothbrushes? Use one and rinse it daily with hydrogen peroxide or mouthwash.

☙ **Expunge germs from your sponge.** Like toothbrushes, kitchen sponges are breeding grounds for bacteria. It's also possible to transfer food-borne bugs, such as salmonella and campylobacter, from sponges used to wipe countertops and cutting boards to dishes and cookware. To be safe, change your sponge every week and always allow it to air-dry between uses. It's also a good idea to disinfect your sponge with a mixture of one liter of water and two tablespoons of bleach.

Declare War on Dust Mites

These pesky microscopic critters feast on sloughed-off skin cells, and the droppings they leave behind can set your allergies off. How can you get rid of pests you can't see? Once a week, vacuum rugs and upholstered furniture, and wash sheets and towels in hot water. Quilts and comforters that you don't want to wash that frequently should be put through the dryer once a week.

If you place these items in storage at the end of each season, be sure to wash or dry-clean them first.

Get the Lead Out

The toxic metal isn't found only in tap water and old paint. Although leaded gasoline has been banned for decades, topsoil in many areas remains contaminated (fallout from the exhaust of automobiles that ran on leaded gas). To be safe, always assume that soil might be contaminated. Dust regularly, and make it strict policy that everyone takes off his/her shoes before coming indoors.

Newspaper ink is another surprising source of lead contamination. Always wash your hands after handling the paper. And never use newspaper to start a fire. If you do, lead dust may be left behind in the ashes. Start your fires with kindling.

Consume Less Chlorine

Most tap water is chlorinated. This is a good thing, because chlorine is such an effective germ-killer. Unfortunately, chlorinated water has been linked with some pretty nasty ailments, including cancer of the bladder and rectum.

Bottled water is getting cheaper all the time, but if you don't want to spring for it, you can dechlorinate your tap water by equipping your kitchen faucet with an activated charcoal water filter. Installing a similar filter on your showerhead will minimize the amount of chlorine-containing compounds you inhale during those long, hot showers.

Heat Rash

When your skin has been prickled by the heat, the first order of business is to cool down. For the next few days, spend as much time as you can in the cold comfort of an air-conditioned environment. Take a cool bath or shower. Have your favorite someone fan you with an ostrich feather. And while you're waiting for your skin to chill, try these other remedies.

What's wrong

The itchy red bumps dotting your neck, armpits, chest, and groin are caused by sweat with nowhere to go. Normally, perspiration evaporates, which cools your skin. But sweat trapped by fabric can't escape. The skin swells, blocks the sweat pores, and perspiration leaks into the skin, which erupts into that bumpy rash. As the bumps burst, releasing their sweat, you may feel the stinging sensation that gives heat rash its other name: prickly heat. Hot, humid weather; sweat; and constricting clothes are a recipe for heat rash. So is skin rubbing against skin, which is common in heavy folks or women with large breasts.

Pack It with Ice

Anything that cools the temperature of your skin will reduce the itching and swelling. So if you don't have time for a bath, put an **ice pack** or a **cool compress** on the rash for 10 minutes every 4 to 6 hours.

Add the Magic Powder

Sometimes it seems as if **baking soda** is good for just about anything, and it's certainly good for relieving heat rash. Soak in a tub to which you've added a few tablespoons of the powder. It will ease the itching and make you feel more comfortable while the rash heals. You can also add fine-ground **oatmeal**, which is sold under brand names such as Aveeno.

Apply baking soda or **cornstarch** directly to the rash site to absorb moisture and sweat. This is an age-old approach, recommended by many country grandmothers. Some say cornstarch is better because it is softer on the skin. Reapply every few hours, rinsing and drying the skin beforehand.

Slather to Soothe

The sticky gel of the **aloe vera** leaf has long been used to relieve itching and promote healing. Apply the gel to the affected skin two or three times a day, washing the skin before each application.

Apply **calamine lotion**. A traditional home remedy for poison ivy, the pink stuff can also ease the itching and irritation of heat rash.

Get Out in the Air

 If blisters accompany the rash, **don't cover them up.** Fresh air will speed their healing.

The Power of Prevention

 Limit your physical activity in extremely hot and humid weather. (The threat of heat rash is a great excuse to avoid a workout.) And take as many **cold showers** or **baths** as needed to cool yourself.

 Wear **loose cotton clothing.** It's more likely to keep your skin dry, making heat rash less likely to plague your tender skin. Avoid nylon and polyester fabrics and tight clothing in general, especially during the summer months.

 Avoid oily, greasy sunscreens, or formulations that contain **cocoa butter.** Choose a less greasy lotion that's hypoallergenic and blocks both UVA and UVB light.

 At the beach, perch under an **umbrella.** Your spot in the shade will be significantly cooler than a seat in the sun.

 If you could stand to **lose weight,** do. Overweight people tend to sweat more and generate more body heat, making a rash more likely to erupt.

 Increase your intake of **essential fatty acids** by eating more salmon, other cold-water fish, and flaxseed oil. These healthy fats help curtail inflammation in the body, making you less susceptible to rashes.

Should I call the doctor?

Simple heat rash is irritating but hardly serious; the itch and inflammation should clear up in a day or two. But call your doctor if the rash doesn't go away within a few days, or if the bumps become infected. You may need medication. Also seek emergency assistance if nausea, dryness, thirst, headache. and paleness accompany the rash. In severe forms, heat rash can interfere with the body's temperature-regulating mechanism and cause fever and heat exhaustion.

Hemorrhoids

Probably the only things more irritating than the burning, itching, and bleeding of hemorrhoids are the television commercials promising miraculous relief from them. Drugstore shelves are lined with products that help—creams, pads, ointments, and suppositories. As a rule of thumb, doctors say you should avoid OTC products that have ingredients ending in "caine." These have an anesthetic that provides immediate relief, but if used regularly, cause increased irritation. In addition to testing out OTCs, however, there are plenty of household remedies you'll want to try.

What's wrong

Hemorrhoids are swollen veins in or around the anus that cause pain, itching, and, occasionally, bleeding. Internal hemorrhoids, the most common type, develop inside the anus. You might have some bleeding, but no pain. External hemorrhoids are the painful ones, and they, too, can cause some bleeding. Either kind may turn into a prolapsed hemorrhoid, a soft lump that protrudes from the anus. Prolonged sitting, pregnancy, and aging all contribute to hemorrhoids. If you frequently have constipation and strain when you're having a bowel movement, you can create hemorrhoids or make them worse.

Fair Warming

⌒ Fill the bathtub with 10 to 15 centimeters of **warm water**, then ease yourself into it. You should be in a seated position, but with your knees raised, allowing maximum exposure of the anal area to the warm water. You'll find that this eases the pain. What you can't feel is how the warm water encourages increased blood flow, which will help shrink swollen veins.

⌒ When you're using this "sitz bath," you can throw in a handful of **Epsom salt** before you plunge in to help constrict the hemorrhoids. Stir the water well to dissolve the salt.

⌒ Rather than fill up a whole tub every time you want relief, you can purchase a **"sitz bath" basin** at most pharmacies and medical supply stores. Filling a small basin goes a lot faster than filling a whole tub, and since it's more convenient, you'll probably use it more often.

⌒ For external hemorrhoids, apply a warm, wet **tea bag.** You can do it while sitting on the toilet. The warmth is soothing, and you get added benefit from one of tea's main components, tannic acid. It helps reduce pain and swelling, and since it also promotes blood clotting, this treatment helps stop the bleeding.

Saddle Up on Ice

⌒ Fill a sturdy plastic bag with **ice**, wrap the bag in a thin cloth, and sit on it. The cold shrinks the swollen vessels, providing enormous relief. Sit in the chilly saddle for about 20 minutes. There's no limit on how often you can do this, but give yourself at least a ten-minute break between applications.

Do Dab, Don't Scratch

👉 Soak a cotton ball with undistilled **witch hazel** and apply to the hemorrhoids. It's rich in tannins, which cause the blood vessels to contract. Witch hazel is the main ingredient in the hemorrhoid pads Tucks.

👉 A dab of **Vaseline**, also contained in many over-the-counter hemorrhoid treatments, can help soothe the area.

👉 Liquid **vitamin E** and **wheat-germ oil** are both reputed to be effective. Put them on a cotton ball and apply it a few times a day.

👉 If you can find it in a natural foods store, try a salve containing **comfrey** or **marigold** to soothe and promote healing.

👉 Crazy as it sounds, a poultice made from **grated potato** is astringent and soothing.

Lounge Around

👉 A couple of times a day, find a comfortable couch, stretch out, and **put your legs up.** What's good for your frayed nerves is also good for your hemorrhoids. In this supine posture, you take the weight off your overstressed anal area. At the same time, you improve circulation to the roundabout that needs it. It's ideal if you can get 30-minute breaks for this assignment.

Go with the Grain

👉 Get more roughage into your diet. Research shows that **a high-fiber diet** can significantly reduce hemorrhoid symptoms, including pain and bleeding. Foods that are rich in fiber include whole-grain breads and cereals, fresh fruits and vegetables, brown rice, and nuts.

👉 When you're getting more fiber, you need to stay well hydrated to prevent constipation. Be sure to **drink enough fluids** so that your urine is pale, not dark, yellow.

Throne Room Policy

👉 Excuse yourself and **head for the bathroom whenever you have to go.** The trouble with waiting is that it leads to

Should I call **the doctor?**

Hemorrhoids don't require immediate medical attention. If you see bright red blood in the stool—a telltale sign—you first can try some self-treatment. But inflammatory bowel disease or a bowel infection can cause hemorrhoid-like symptoms. So if you see very dark blood or the stool looks black, call your doctor right away, as this is often a sign of intestinal bleeding. Also see your doctor immediately if you have significant rectal bleeding, persistent fecal incontinence, or the pain suddenly intensifies.

Did you **know?**

Hippocrates, the famous Greek physician who lived more than 2400 years ago, knew that hemorrhoids were dilated anal veins. He recommended burning them away with a red-hot iron.

Tried...

Vicks VapoRub is a little-known home remedy for hemorrhoids.

...and true

There's no harm in trying this, putting it on the outside of the anus. People say it doesn't sting—but you'll have to try it for yourself to find out.

constipation. And that, of course, means you have to strain more when you go. And that invites hemorrhoids.

✎ After a bowel movement, wipe with **plain, white, unscented toilet paper** that's been dampened under running water. Scented, colored toilet paper may have some aesthetic attractions, but any additional chemical can be an irritant.

✎ After the initial clean-up, use facial tissues coated with an **unscented moisturizing cream.**

Limit Sitting and Lifting

✎ Anyone who does a lot of sitting needs to do some standing as well. If you're tied to your desk most of the time, take a **five-minute walk** every hour or so. Every time you get up, you ease the rectal pressure that leads to hemorrhoids.

✎ Heavy lifting puts pressure on the anal area. If there's a couch or dresser that needs lifting, claim a bad back and ask for volunteers.

✎ If you usually lift weights when you work out, make sure you **skip the squat thrusts.** Every time you crouch down, then lift up again, you put direct pressure on your rectum. Also avoid any exercise that involves sitting for long periods, such as cycling on a stationary bicycle.

Hiccups

Hiccups can come at the most inconvenient times—just before you have to give an after-dinner toast or address the town planning commission, for instance. When you're in public, you might have to use some very subtle methods to control the hic-ing. Some methods involve gentle pressure; others, a glass of water. And, if you have a high threshold of embarrassment—or you can hide somewhere—there are wonderfully strange contortions that hiccup-prone people have devised to cure the contractions. Do whatever works for you.

Emergency Action in Public Places

🌿 Press the palm of your hand with the thumb of your other hand. The harder, the better. Alternatively, you can squeeze the ball of your left thumb between the thumb and forefinger of the right. The discomfort is a distraction that affects your nervous system and may put an end to the hic-cups. (And you can do it under the table, without anyone staring at you.)

🌿 **Take a deep breath** and then hold it for a while. When there's a buildup of carbon dioxide in your lungs, your diaphragm relaxes.

🌿 If you can retire from public view for a few minutes ("Sorry—have to visit the restroom!"), **stick your fingers in your ears** for twenty or thirty seconds. Or press the soft areas behind your earlobes, just below the base of the skull. That sends a "relax" signal through the vagus nerve, which connects to the diaphragm area.

🌿 As long as you're out of sight, **stick out your tongue.** This rude-looking exercise is done by singers and actors because it stimulates the opening between the vocal cords (the glottis). You breathe more smoothly, quelling the spasms that cause hiccups.

🌿 **Cup your hands** around your nose and mouth, but con-tinue breathing normally. You'll get relief from the extra dose of carbon dioxide.

What's **wrong**

Surprisingly enough—given how common hiccups are—no one really knows what causes them. But we're all hiccup-prone. Even fetuses In the womb. Something prompts your diaphragm to contract, suddenly and involuntarily, producing a spasm that gets released as a sometimes embarrassing "hic" noise. Irritating food can cause those contractions. So can swallowing air—when you get excited, for instance, or chug down carbonated soda.

Should I call the doctor?

Believe it or not, some people get hiccups that last for days. If yours continue for a long time, your doctor will want to find out what's causing them. It could be a problem with your nervous system or an intestinal disorder such as ileus (which occurs when intestinal muscles don't contract properly). You might have an ongoing stomach irritation or an infection of some kind. Doctors do have some drugs that help cure what are called "intractable hiccups"—including a number of tranquilizers and an antinausea pill, Nu-Prochlor (prochlorperazine), that relaxes the diaphragm.

Drinkable Cures

🍃 Take nine or ten **quick sips** in a row from a glass. When you're gulping a drink, rhythmic contractions of the esophagus override spasms of the diaphragm.

🍃 If you can **block your ears** when you drink, all the better. Stick your fingers in your ears and sip through a straw. You're pressing on the vagus nerve while also getting the benefits of steady swallowing.

🍃 Place a single layer of **paper towel** over the top of the glass, then drink through the towel. You'll have to "pull" harder with your diaphragm to suck up the water, and concentrated gulping counteracts spasmodic muscle movements.

Remedies to Suit Your Tastes

🍃 Put one teaspoon of **sugar** or **honey**, stirred in warm water, on the back of your tongue, and swallow it.

🍃 The sharp surprise of something sour can pucker lips and lick the hiccups. Cut a slice of **lemon** and suck on it.

🍃 Swallow a teaspoon of **cider vinegar.** This is a challenge, but if you cope with the assault on the taste buds, it's a quick cure. (Another vinegary method is to suck on a **dill pickle.**)

Take a Time-Out

🍃 Sometimes **relaxation** is the key. Lie on a bed, stomach down, with head turned and arms hanging over the side. Take a deep breath, hold it for 10 to 15 seconds, exhale slowly. After a few repeats, rest for several minutes before you get up.

🍃 If you can elicit the help of your partner, stand against the wall and ask your partner to place a fist lightly in the soft area just under your breastbone. Take a few deep breaths, and on the last one, exhale completely. Your partner should then **press gently but firmly** to help expel air from your lungs.

🍃 **A long, passionate kiss** has been known to work. (And if it doesn't? Well, no harm done.) Needless to say, it's important to choose the right partner for this remedy.

Cures in the Kids' Corner

🍃 Offer one big teaspoon of **peanut butter.** In the process of chewing and getting it off the tongue and teeth, swallowing and breathing patterns are interrupted.

With a scoop of **ice cream**, the cure becomes a treat. The chill of the ice cream, steady swallowing, and a pleasurable distraction all add up to calming the diaphragm.

The Power of Prevention

Avoid beer or **carbonated soda**, especially if they're cold. The low temperature, combined with the bubbles, creates a medley of irritations that could set off your diaphragm.

When you **eat, slow down.** Eating quickly, you swallow more air, and that can cause hiccups as well as burping.

A few medications such as **diazepam** have been known to contribute to more frequent hiccups. If you suspect a prescription drug is the problem, talk to your doctor about taking an alternative.

If a baby has hiccups, it could be because he or she swallowed too much air while feeding. So perform the same ritual you would for burping: Hold the baby against your shoulder and **pat gently on the back.** That can bring up the air and stop the hiccups. Also check the nipple of the baby bottle to see if it is allowing the right amount of fluid to flow out. Turn a full bottle upside down; you should get a regular dripping that slows and eventually stops. If too much or too little liquid comes out, that could be contributing to the hiccups.

Tried...

It's said that if you warm up a table knife, open up your mouth, and place the handle of the knife in the back of your throat, the hiccups will stop.

...and true

This stimulates the uvula, prompting the gag reflex, which really can interrupt hiccups. But it's safer to use a cotton swab rather than a table knife.

High Blood Pressure

Three out of ten people who have high blood pressure don't know they have it. Of those who do know, about seven out of every ten people don't have their blood pressure under control. So if you have no idea what your blood pressure is, ask your doctor to check it. If you've already been diagnosed with hypertension, be sure to follow the advice your doctor has given you. The cornerstones of treatment are exercise and diet changes. Even if your doctor has prescribed pressure-lowering medication, these lifestyle efforts are essential.

What's wrong

A high blood pressure reading means your heart is working harder than it should to pump blood, and your arteries are stressed. That's risky. If you don't lower your blood pressure, you'll face an increased risk for stroke, heart attack, kidney disease, and other deadly illnesses. You are considered to have high blood pressure (hypertension) when systolic pressure (the top number) is 140 or higher or the diastolic pressure (bottom number) is 90 or higher. But whenever your blood pressure readings start to creep upward, your doctor will urge you to take measures to control it.

Make a DASH for It

• DASH is short for Dietary Approaches to Stop Hypertension, and in studies, this special diet has proved remarkably effective at lowering blood pressure. The gist of the diet is this: It's **low in saturated fat, cholesterol, and total fat**, with an emphasis on **fruits, vegetables, whole grains**, and **low-fat dairy foods.** The DASH diet can produce positive results in as little as two weeks. To learn more, contact the Heart and Stroke Foundation, 222 Queen Street, Suite 1402, Ottawa, ON K1P 5V9, or visit their website at www.heartandstroke.ca, or download a copy at www.nhlbi.nih.gov/health/public/heart/hbp/dash/.

• **Ease up on the salt shaker.** Eating too much salt causes your body to retain water. The effect is the same as adding more liquid to an overfilled water balloon: pressure rises. In a follow-up to the DASH study, researchers found that the biggest drop in blood pressure came when people followed the DASH diet and also limited themselves to 1,500 milligrams of sodium a day. That's less than a teaspoon of salt a day.

• Even if you don't add salt to your food at the stove or the dinner table, you may still be getting loads of "hidden" salt in packaged and processed foods, especially snacks, meat products, and canned soups. So before buying foods, **read labels carefully** to find out the sodium content. Look for low-salt soups and crackers, and rinse canned beans before using them.

Other Dietary Do's and Don'ts

❧ Even if you don't follow the exact guidelines of the DASH diet, you'll see major benefits if you just make sure you eat lots of **fresh fruits** and **vegetables**. Vegetables can be raw or cooked. The point is to get five servings a day. You also want five daily servings of fruits—dried, fresh, frozen, or canned. Fruits and veggies are important sources of potassium, magnesium, and fiber—all of which help keep your arteries healthy.

❧ **Oatmeal** has a special ability to lower blood pressure as well as cholesterol levels, as repeated studies have shown. Its beneficial effect seems to come from a form of soluble fiber known as beta-glucan. Start every day with a bowl of oatmeal, and you'll most likely see your pressure drop.

❧ **Cut back on alcohol.** Heavy drinkers tend to have high blood pressure. If you drink, limit yourself to one drink a day if you're a woman, two a day if you're a man. One drink is 355 milliliters (12 ounces) beer (regular or light), 150 milliliters (5 ounces) wine, or 45 milliliters (1½ ounces) 80-proof liquor (like whiskey).

Liberate Some Extra Weight

❧ Carrying extra weight forces the heart to pump harder. That's why blood pressure rises as body weight increases. If you're overweight, **losing as little as five kilograms (10 pounds)** can lead to a significant reduction in blood pressure.

Stamp Out Those Cigarettes

❧ **If you smoke, quit.** Compounds in tobacco smoke contribute to hardening of the arteries by causing injury to blood vessels. And the nicotine in cigarettes causes blood vessels to constrict. That's bad for anyone, but it's especially bad for people who have high blood pressure.

Should I call
the doctor?

If you've been diagnosed with high blood pressure, call your doctor immediately if you experience chronic headache, heart palpitations, shortness of breath, fatigue, nosebleeds, blurred vision, flushed face, frequent urination, or ringing in the ears. These symptoms suggest that your blood pressure is not being adequately controlled.

Is That Blasted Honking to Blame?

We all know that driving in heavy traffic can increase our stress levels. Now a study from Germany suggests that just the sound of traffic can send blood pressure soaring. The study of 1,700 people, conducted at the Robert Koch Institute in Berlin, found that people who live in areas of heavy traffic were twice as likely to be getting treatment for high blood pressure as were people residing on quiet streets. People who kept their windows open at night, in spite of the racket, were at highest risk.

At-Home Pressure Checks

Some people get so nervous when a doctor checks their blood pressure that they experience a temporary rise in blood pressure. If you're one of them, you can get a more accurate picture of your blood pressure by buying a blood pressure monitor and taking your own readings at home. The most reliable monitors have an inflatable arm cuff and a stethoscope, but the latest generation of automatic blood pressure monitors are quite accurate as well (and easier to use). Once you get the hang of it, you can take a reading any time of the day or night. By averaging out the readings, you'll get a true picture of your pressure.

Shake a Leg

At least three times a week—and preferably five—get 30 minutes of **brisk exercise.** This advice might seem off the mark, since most kinds of exercise temporarily *raise* blood pressure. But when you work out regularly, you help keep your resting blood pressure at a safe level. Running, brisk walking, bike riding, and swimming are excellent choices.

Seek Peace

Consider **getting a pet.** Whether it's cuddling a puppy or gazing at a tankful of colorful fish, interacting with animals has been shown to bring marked decreases in blood pressure.

Watch the way you speak. Studies suggest that loud, fast talking goes hand in hand with high blood pressure. Practice **speaking in a lower tone** (and at a slower pace), even when you're upset or angry.

Learn to meditate. This isn't New Age silliness. Research shows that meditation really does affect blood pressure, apparently by lowering levels of stress hormones in your body. To begin, choose a simple word or phrase to focus on. Close your eyes and relax all your muscles. Breathing slowly and naturally, repeat your word or phrase every time you exhale. As you do this, try to assume a passive attitude. Don't try to evaluate whether you're relaxed or "doing well"—just concentrate on your words and your breathing. Do this once or twice a day for 10 to 20 minutes.

Engrossing **hobbies** such as gardening or sculpting may be just as good as meditation.

Supplement Your Efforts

➤ Take 350 milligrams a day of **magnesium.** The mineral helps relax the smooth muscle tissue that lines blood vessels, allowing them to open wide. Magnesium is especially effective at lowering high blood pressure associated with pregnancy but consult your doctor before taking any supplement when you're pregnant. Look for a magnesium supplement in the form of magnesium orotate or magnesium glycinate.

➤ Take 100 to 300 milligrams of a standardized **hawthorn** extract a day. Hawthorn has long been known to dilate arteries. It seems to work by interfering with an enzyme that constricts blood vessels. That enzyme is angiotensin-converting enzyme (ACE), the same enzyme that some blood pressure drugs target. If you currently take medication for high blood pressure, consult your doctor before taking this herb. Hawthorn may take several weeks or even months to build up in your system and have an effect.

➤ **Garlic** helps lower blood pressure, too, although it's not known why. Some experts recommend simply eating one clove of raw garlic a day. Others say to take four to six 600-milligram capsules or tablets a day, in divided doses. Choose enteric-coated capsules for best results.

➤ Take **fish-oil supplements** to boost your intake of omega-3 fatty acids. These "good" fats come from cold-water fish like mackerel and salmon, and a typical supplement contains 1,000 milligrams. Taking three or four doses a day can help to reduce high blood pressure. Omega-3 fatty acids inhibit the body's production of substances, such as prostaglandins, that narrow the arteries.

High Cholesterol

The top three places you're likely to find unwanted sludge are in your plumbing pipes, in the fuel lines of your car, and in your arteries. The first will stop your sink, the second your travel, and the third your life. To keep your arteries from getting gummed up—or to clean them out if they're already in trouble—you'll need to lower your LDL level, and also try to boost your HDL level. For every 1 percent drop in your total cholesterol, your chances of having a heart attack fall by 2 to 3 percent. And for every 1 percent increase in your HDL, your risk drops by about 3 percent.

What's wrong

Inside your arteries, a dangerous change has taken place in the balance of fatty substances that circulate in your bloodstream. There is too much of the "bad" type of cholesterol, called low-density lipoproteins (LDLs). This is the type that gums up your arteries and raises your risk for heart attack and stroke. Meanwhile, you probably don't have enough "good" cholesterol, known as high-density lipoproteins (HDLs). These are the molecules that act as "garbage trucks," carrying LDL away to the liver for disposal.

Factor Out the "Bad" Fats

 Eliminate as much **saturated fat** as possible from your diet. That means switching to leaner cuts of meats and lower-fat versions of dairy products such as milk, ice cream, cheese, and yogurt. Cut out ground beef altogether.

 Run screaming from **palm oil** and **coconut oil**, which are very high in saturated fat. These so-called tropical oils are found in some processed foods.

 Another type of fat, called trans fat, or **trans-fatty acids**, may be just as bad for your arteries as saturated fat. Store-bought cakes, doughnuts, cookies, chips, and other snack foods are often loaded with these fats, which are created when hydrogen is added to vegetable oils. To find them, look for the word "hydrogenated" on the package's nutrition label. In Canada, manufacturers will be required to list trans fats on package labels starting in December 2005.

 Eat more fresh fruits, vegetables, and **whole grains.** That's the easiest way to feel full as you cut back on meat and other fatty foods. In addition to being low in fat and cholesterol-free, plant foods contain lots of cholesterol-lowering fiber and heart-healthy vitamins and antioxidants.

 Meat lovers should consider **bison, ostrich**, and **venison.** These game meats have a fraction of the fat found in grain-fed beef (the kind in most supermarkets). In fact, they are as low-fat as most fish. Marinate them to improve their tenderness.

Get More Good Fats

❧ Numerous studies have shown that **olive oil** not only lowers LDL but also raises HDL. One study found that people who ate about 2 tablespoons of olive oil a day had lower LDL levels in just one week. Use it in garlic bread, salad dressings, in place of margarine, and in place of other oils when sautéing.

❧ Enjoy **nuts.** They are packed with heart-healthy unsaturated fats, including omega-3s. Walnuts and almonds seem to be especially good at lowering LDL. Eat a shotglass-size serving a day and watch your numbers drop. But nuts contain a lot of calories, so make sure you eat them instead of—not in addition to—other snacks.

❧ Have an **avocado** a day and you might lower your LDL by as much as 17 percent. True, avocados are very high in fat, but it's mainly the unsaturated kind.

❧ Eat **peanut butter!** That's right, peanut butter. Yes, it's high in calories, but most of the fat it contains is unsaturated. Buy a "natural" brand that contains no hydrogenated oils.

Fish for Omega-3s

❧ **Fish** is much more than a replacement for meat. It contains omega-3 fatty acids, which actually lower LDL cholesterol. Aim to eat fish three times a week—even if it's canned tuna. Your best bets are mackerel, tuna, and salmon, all very high in omega-3s. Sardines are great sources too.

❧ If you absolutely won't eat fish, take a daily **fish-oil supplement** that contains both EPA and DHA (two types of omega-3 fatty acids). Take 1,000 milligrams twice a day.

❧ Like **clams?** Indulge! Clams are high in sterols, chemicals that prevent your body from absorbing cholesterol.

❧ **Flaxseeds** are great sources of omega-3 fats. Grind them and add to your yogurt or cereal. One study found that eating 2 tablespoons of flaxseed daily cut LDL cholesterol by 18 percent. You can also use flaxseed oil in salad dressing.

Eat Your Oatmeal

❧ **Oatmeal** is a rich source of soluble fiber, which forms a kind of gel in your intestine to reduce your body's absorption of the fat you eat. Eating 1½ cups a day could lower your LDL

Should I call **the doctor?**

Your doctor should keep track of your cholesterol levels through regular screening tests. Ask your doctor for a copy of the report that breaks out LDL and HDL cholesterol so you'll know what your levels are. (The report will probably list other cardiovascular risk factors as well, such as total cholesterol and triglycerides.) If your cholesterol is high, your doctor may prescribe a cholesterol-lowering drug called a statin. But you'll still want to improve your diet, lose weight, and get more exercise.

12 to 24 percent. Choose quick-cooking or old-fashioned oats over instant oatmeal.

- Other especially good sources of soluble fiber include **prunes, barley, beans (legumes), eggplant**, and **okra.**

- Not getting enough soluble fiber in your diet? Try **psyllium**, found in dietary fiber supplements like Metamucil. Research shows that taking about 10 grams a day for eight weeks can reduce LDL by 7 percent.

Put the Squeeze on Cholesterol

- Fresh-squeezed or straight out of the carton, **orange juice** can lower cholesterol. Participants in a recent study increased their HDL levels 21 percent and lowered their LDL/HDL ratio 16 percent by drinking three glasses a day for a month.

Why Not Wine?

- **Alcohol**—no matter what kind you drink—**raises HDL levels.** "Moderate" means one drink a day for a woman, and two a day for a man. If you drink more than that, the damage could outweigh any benefits. Red wine offers additional benefits: powerful antioxidants that come from the grape skin.

Get into the Sporting Life

- Lace up your **walking shoes**, and move along briskly for 30 minutes each day. Or climb on a Stairmaster and log your 30 minutes in the temperature-controlled climate of a health club. Or join the Y and get your laps in after work. The benefits of **regular exercise** are incontrovertible. Studies show that physical activity will improve the ratio of HDLs to LDLs, decreasing your overall risk of heart disease and stroke. Plus,

Niacin: Should You or Shouldn't You?

At high doses, the B vitamin niacin can lower cholesterol. But don't take it unless your doctor recommends a particular dose and monitors your health while you're taking it. Niacin does have the effect of lowering LDLs while raising HDLs—and in this respect, it resembles prescription medications. However, the amount of niacin you need to reap these benefits is very high, and when you take excessive doses, you risk many potential side effects. Some people get uncomfortable hot flashes, and there's even a risk of liver damage. So it's unwise to take without medical advice.

Soy to the Whirl

For a delicious, cholesterol-lowering shake, blend one cup of vanilla soy milk with two tablespoons of ground flaxseed. Add some fresh or frozen berries, and mix it all in the blender. The soy protein and flaxseed help lower LDLs and raise HDLs, while the berries add cholesterol-lowering fiber.

regular exercise helps control diabetes and high blood pressure, which are independent risk factors for heart disease.

A Capsule Summary

⚭ If you aren't taking a prescription cholesterol-lowering drug, ask your doctor about **gugulipid supplements.** They seem to work by enabling the liver to take in more LDL, so that less of it circulates in the bloodstream. The usual dose is 75 milligrams of guggulsterones, the active ingredients in gugulipid, (25 milligrams three times a day). Gugulipid is often combined with other cholesterol-lowering compounds such as **garlic, niacin,** and **red yeast rice extract.**

⚭ Another alternative to prescription drugs is **red yeast rice extract.** It works by blocking an enzyme necessary to the formation of cholesterol and by speeding the removal of LDL from the blood. Follow the manufacturer's directions.

⚭ Consider taking **artichoke extract.** Artichokes contain cynarin, a compound that increases the liver's production of bile—and bile plays a key role in the excretion of cholesterol from the body. Artichoke extract is available at health-food stores. Follow label instructions.

⚭ Get your daily dose of **garlic**—either whole garlic or garlic pills. Garlic contains a compound called allicin, which is thought to be responsible for the herb's cholesterol-lowering effect. If you decide on garlic pills, look for enteric-coated tablets or capsules that provide a daily dose of at least 10 milligrams of alliin or a total allicin potential of 4,000 micrograms. (Alliin, one compound in garlic, converts into allicin inside the body.)

⚭ Four times a day, take **ginger** capsules. The typical dose is 100 to 200 milligrams. Studies suggest that the compounds in ginger help to reduce the absorption and increase the excretion of LDL.

Hives

A simple antihistamine can help reduce the allergic reaction causing your hives. Choose one of the newer drugs, such as Claritin or Alavert, that don't cause drowsiness. While you let the medicine do its work, try the handy home treatments below for added relief. You'll also want to get to the bottom of what's causing your hives so you can avoid itching in the future.

What's wrong

As small as jujubes or as large as saucers, hives are an allergic reaction that take the form of itchy red bumps or welts on the skin. They are the result of cells releasing histamine, a chemical that makes blood vessels leak fluid into the deepest layers of skin. It's not clear why some people get hives, while others don't, and the "triggers" associated with hives are so numerous, they fit the category of "everything in the world." Just for starters, hives can be caused by sunlight, heat, cold, pressure, stress, viral infections, or medications. Name anything that can cause an allergy, and it can also cause hives— including pollen, dust, dander, dust mites, shellfish, and other foods.

Drown Them with Attention

🍃 Unless you have hives that are triggered by cold (which is rare), take a **cool bath** or apply a **cold compress**. Cold shrinks the blood vessels and blocks further release of histamine. To further relieve itching, add **colloidal oatmeal** (like Aveeno) to the bathwater and soak for 10 to 15 minutes. (Be careful getting out of the tub, however—that fine-ground oatmeal turns slippery.)

A Dab Will Do

🍃 Dab the welts with **calamine lotion** or **witch hazel**. These astringents help shrink blood vessels, so they don't leak so much histamine.

🍃 Alternatives to calamine lotion are **milk of magnesia** or **Pepto-Bismol**. Because they are alkaline, they help to relieve the itching.

🍃 In a small cup, add a few drops of water to **baking soda** and stir until you get a paste. Spread the paste on the hives to help stop irritation and relieve the itching.

🍃 Do you have some **cream of tartar** in your kitchen cabinet? It might be just what you need to relieve the hives. Make a paste as above and apply.

🍃 If you just have a few small hives and want to temporarily stop the itching, apply an over-the-counter **hydrocortisone cream**. Follow the directions on the package.

🍃 Mix 1 teaspoon of any kind of **vinegar** with 1 tablespoon of lukewarm water and apply the mixture to your hives with a cotton ball or tissue to soothe the itching.

An old Chinese folk remedy for hives calls for boiling one-quarter cup **brown sugar** and one tablespoon **fresh ginger** in three-quarters cup **vinegar** for several minutes. Mix a little of this with warm water and apply several times per day.

Try a Common Weed

Herbalists recommend **nettle** as an alternative to antihistamines. Take up to six 400-milligram capsules a day. Or pick a few handfuls of the weed, steam, and eat. Wear gloves, long pants, and long sleeves to guard against nettle's stinging leaves.

Fish and the C

Take 1,000 milligrams of **fish oil** in capsule form three times a day. These capsules contain essential fatty acids that have anti-inflammatory properties. Cold-water fish like salmon, bluefish, and albacore tuna are good food sources.

Take 1,000 milligrams of **vitamin C** three times a day. At this dose, the "sunshine vitamin" has an effect that mimics the action of antihistamines. Don't take more than 1,000 milligrams a day or you might experience diarrhea.

Take Steps to Stop Stress

Stress can cause hives or make them worse. If your tension needs taming, master a nerve-calming technique such as **meditation, yoga,** or **progressive relaxation.**

Brew up a cup of **chamomile, valerian,** or **catnip tea.** All of these herbs have a sedative effect that may soothe your stress—and therefore your hives. To make the tea, stir one teaspoon of the dried herb into one cup of boiling water, steep 10 minutes, strain out the plant parts, and drink the tea.

Should I call **the doctor?**

While hives can be uncomfortable, they're usually harmless and disappear within minutes or hours. Sometimes they hang around for a few days. Seek emergency medical treatment if you develop hives around your eyes or in your mouth or experience difficulty breathing, wheezing, light-headedness, or dizziness. You may have a life-threatening condition called anaphylaxis, and the internal tissue swelling can block breathing passages. If you're prone to hives, ask your doctor if you should carry a rapid-injection form of epinephrine in case you develop anaphylaxis. And if you have chronic hives that just don't respond to milder treatments, your doctor may prescribe oral steroids.

Skin Graffiti

You probably don't think of your skin as a handy notepad, but if you have a hive condition called dermatographia, it could be. People who have dermatographia find that whenever they scratch or stroke their skin, they raise hive-like welts or swellings. That's because histamine and other chemicals are released in such a way to cause very localized redness, itchiness, and swelling. Often, people who develop dermatographia have no evidence of allergies, and the condition usually disappears without treatment—although, in some cases, antihistamines can help.

Did you **know?**

In their relentless hunt for causes of hives, doctors have discovered some very peculiar triggers. Some people get hives immediately after skin is exposed to water. Weirder still, hives can be triggered by exposure to something that's vibrating—such as the grip of a vacuum cleaner or the rapid vibration of an electric foot massager.

The Power of Prevention

To avoid hives, you need to figure out what causes them. If you don't know, start **keeping a daily diary**. The most probable suspects are things that you eat, drink, or swallow—food, drink, supplements, and medications. But even if you don't see any obvious connections, continue keeping your diary, noting other factors like weather, stress levels, clothing, or the amount of time that you spend in the sun. With careful tracking, you may link a specific lifestyle factor with the eruption of those red, itchy welts.

Foods most likely to trigger hives include **shellfish, nuts, chocolate, fish, tomatoes, eggs, fresh berries**, and **milk**. Some people react to preservatives in certain foods and wine, such as sulfites. Once you've identified a food trigger, eliminate it from your diet and see whether you have fewer outbreaks.

Common **drug triggers** include antibiotics and non-steroidal anti-inflammatory drugs (NSAIDs) such as aspirin and ibuprofen. But doctors have heard about many other triggers, including sedatives, tranquilizers, diuretics, diet supplements, antacids, arthritis medications, vitamins, eye drops, eardrops, laxatives, and douches.

Impotence

As every man knows, numerous mental and physical factors influence the hydraulics. Once you've seen the doctor and crossed out the possibility of more serious health problems, you might want to take an all-points approach to erasing erectile dysfunction. That is, take up regular exercise and, at the same time, consider some of the mental factors that might be getting in the way—including boredom or anxiety in the bedroom. There are also some renowned herbs and supplements that might prove the key to more dependable arousal.

Help Diagnose the Problem

~ Healthy men normally have several erections during a night's sleep. Doctors have devices to test this, but here's a simple way to test on your own. Before going to sleep, take a **single-ply facial tissue**, cut a strip, and wrap it relatively tightly around your penis. Tape the end. If in the morning the tissue is torn, chances are you had a nocturnal erection. That's good news—it means you probably don't have an underlying physical problem to solve, but rather, psychological matters to deal with.

Stoke Your Fire with Herbs

~ Take **ginkgo**. It can improve blood flow in vessels throughout your body, including your penis. In one study, the herb helped men have erections even after a prescription injection didn't work. The recommended dose is 60 to 240 milligrams daily.

~ Try **Asian ginseng**, sometimes called Korean or Chinese ginseng. It's long been used to bolster male virility, since it can improve blood flow to the penis, reduce fatigue, and improve energy. Take 500 milligrams daily.

~ Look for botanical formulas that contain **suma, or Brazilian ginseng** (*Pfaffia*); **maca, or Peruvian ginseng** (*Lepidium*); and **muira puama** (also called **potency wood**). One formulation, called Sumacazon, produced by the Amazon Herb

What's **wrong**

An erection is the end result of a complex chain of events. The brain sends signals to the genitals, blood vessels dilate, and the penis gets engorged. Meanwhile, the veins that normally drain away blood get blocked. When a man cannot get or keep an erection, the problem is called impotence, or erectile dysfunction (ED). Common causes include clogged arteries, diabetes, and nerve problems. Depression, anxiety, and alcoholism can also be factors—in fact, roughly 30 percent of ED cases are psychologically caused. Many medications can be blamed as well, especially those used for high blood pressure and depression.

Should I call the doctor?

If your inability to have an erection lasts for more than two months or recurs frequently, talk to your doctor. You might be a good candidate for Viagra (or similar medication), and your doctor can outline the benefits and possible side effects. Also, in reviewing the medications that you're taking, your doctor might pinpoint some that are contributing to erectile dysfunction. And a physical examination might indicate that the erection problem is a sign of a more serious circulatory condition.

Company, contains all three. These Amazon rainforest herbs have been shown to enhance virility in both animals and humans.

Supplement Your Sexual Efforts

➤ Buy **zinc** supplements and take 15 to 30 milligrams daily. This mineral increases production of testosterone, the hormone that's necessary for maintaining interest in sex.

➤ Take **vitamin C**. It helps blood vessels stay flexible, allowing them to widen when you need more blood flow. You can take up to 1,000 milligrams three times a day. Cut back if you develop diarrhea.

➤ Take a supplement containing 1,000 milligrams of **evening primrose oil** three times a day. The oil contains essential fatty acids that promote good blood vessel health. Alternatively, you can get these essential fatty acids by taking a tablespoon of flaxseed oil every morning.

➤ The amino acid **arginine** can increase blood flow to the penis by increasing the production of nitric oxide in the blood vessel walls, improving artery flexibility and helping blood vessels dilate. Ask your pharmacist for the preferred form, L-arginine. If available, take two 750-milligram capsules twice daily between meals.

Don't Weigh Up

➤ Get 30 minutes of **aerobic activity**—such as walking, jogging, swimming, or playing tennis—several days a week. Exercise helps keep excess weight off and keeps your heart and blood vessels healthier, including the ones that keep your penis operating properly.

Get Out of the Saddle

➤ **If you're a bike rider, go easy.** Too much riding, or riding on the wrong saddle, can damage delicate nerves and blood vessels in the areas you sit on. Shop for a saddle that has a respectful groove running down the center. Be sure that your knees are slightly bent when your feet are at the bottom of each pedal cycle—this puts more of your weight *on* your legs instead of *between* them. Stand up at least every 10 minutes to let blood circulate to the genital area, and also level the pedals and stand up when you go over bumps to reduce jarring to your crotch.

Lose Tobacco to Keep Your Sex Life

~ If you use tobacco in any form, **quit now.** Nicotine causes blood vessels to clamp down, impairing circulation. That means less blood can get to your penis.

Do Things Differently in the Bedroom

~ If your erectile problems are due to stress and emotions rather than something physical, there are lots of ways to get yourself back in the game. For example, have bedroom intimacy **without having intercourse.** This takes off the pressure, relieving performance anxiety. Just hop in bed and cuddle, massage each other, or think of fun things to do that don't require an erection.

~ Keep **variety in your activities.** Boredom with the same-old, same-old can hinder your ability to have an erection. Try new positions or do it elsewhere than in the bedroom. Check your bookstore or adult novelty store for books or games that offer suggestions.

~ **Have sex in the morning.** You may have more spark since your testosterone level is higher at this time of day. Plus you shouldn't be as fatigued and frazzled as at the end of a long day.

Keep Up the Discussion

~ If you keep the problem to yourself, you might be making it worse. Instead, **talk about it** with your partner. You can both brainstorm potential reasons why this may be happening—perhaps a bothersome disagreement or old aggravation is keeping you from performing properly. Not only will you find out your partner's point of view, you also benefit from having two people thinking of possible solutions.

~ Let it go. Worrying about it too much will only make it worse. **Focus on other parts of your life** for a while, such as work, your hobbies, or your kids.

Should You Revise Your Rx's?

~ Blood-pressure medications can contribute to erectile dysfunction, especially **beta-blockers** such as **metoprolol (Lopresor)** and **calcium channel blockers** such as **nifedipine (Adalat).** If you're taking these drugs, ask your

Skip it!

Alcohol helps relax you and stoke the fires of your desire, but it makes you less likely to be able to perform. Limit your consumption to two drinks a day or fewer.

Is It All in Your Mind—or Farther South?

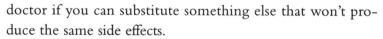

Knowing if your erectile dysfunction is rooted in your mind or body will help you know how to solve it:

It's probably psychological if ... you still have erections sometimes—for example,

when you wake up in the morning.

It's probably physical if... the problem came on gradually, and you have other problems in your genitals, such as difficulty urinating or numbness in your penis.

doctor if you can substitute something else that won't produce the same side effects.

🔊 Digitalis drugs for heart ailments, such as **digoxin (Lanoxin)**, can also present problems. But don't change the dosage until you have a chance to talk to your doctor.

🔊 Men taking certain antidepressant medications such as **Elavil, Prozac, Paxil,** and **Zoloft** frequently report erection problems. Since side effects are not predictable, your doctor may be able to "try you out" on a different antidepressant.

🔊 If you're taking the ulcer drug **cimetidine** and also experiencing erectile dysfunction, be sure to let your doctor know. This, too, is one of the common culprits.

Get Plenty of Rest and Relaxation

🔊 Try to get at least **six to eight hours** of sleep each night. Being fatigued definitely puts a damper on your ability to have an erection.

🔊 **Reduce your stress levels.** Anxiety and anger aren't conducive to the frame of mind needed for sex—plus, anxiety causes your body to make a form of adrenaline that interferes with the physical process behind an erection.

🔊 If you have trouble winding down, regularly engage in **meditation** or other forms of stress relief. For instance, you might spend a few minutes each day doing deep-breathing exercises—that is, just focusing on breathing in and out.

Incontinence

Whenever you hear about ways to curtail incontinence, the word Kegel pops up. Named for Arnold Kegel, M.D., the doctor who first advocated the technique, Kegel exercises are an easy way to strengthen the muscles that retain your urine. They're not a cure-all, but they can help both women and men overcome mild incontinence. Of course, you've also got to pay attention to what you drink and when, what medicines you take, and even how much patience you have in the bathroom.

Make Like a Cricket

➤ If you suddenly get the urge to go, sit down at once and rub your right ankle down the shin of your left leg (or vice versa). Keep steady pressure all the way. Rubbing your legs together like this **inhibits bladder contractions** by putting pressure on a sensory nerve (called the dermatome L5) that affects the need to urinate.

Learn the Number One Exercise

➤ Do **Kegel exercises** regularly to strengthen the "pelvic floor" muscles that run from your tailbone to your spine, holding up the bladder. To pinpoint these muscles, stop your flow while urinating; the muscles you use to do this are the ones you want to strengthen. (Do this just once. Repeatedly stopping the urine flow is bad for the bladder.) Squeeze the muscles for a second or two, and then relax them. Repeat 10 times three to five times a day. Since all of the action is internal—imperceptible to anyone else—you can do Kegels while shopping, driving, taking a shower, watching television and so on. As your pelvic floor muscles get stronger, start holding the contraction for five seconds. Gradually work your way up to 15 seconds.

➤ If you feel that you're about to laugh, cough, sneeze, or do anything else that could create pressure in your abdomen, quickly do a Kegel exercise to help keep you from having an accident.

What's wrong

There are two types of urinary incontinence. In stress incontinence, urine leaks out as you bear down while laughing, sneezing, coughing, or lifting something heavy. In urge incontinence, you feel the need to urinate but can't get to the restroom in time. Incontinence is more common among women, since childbirth can damage the structures that help retain urine, and can also damage the nerves that tell the bladder neck to contract. In men, incontinence is often caused by an enlarged prostate. Other causes of incontinence include muscle relaxants, urinary tract infections, Parkinson's disease, and multiple sclerosis.

Should I call the doctor?

If there's blood in your urine, or if urination causes pain or a burning sensation, check with your doctor. These might be signs of a bacterial infection, kidney stones, or bladder cancer. You should also check with your doctor if incontinence makes it hard for you to undertake everyday activities, or if you suspect that a medication you take might be causing your problem.

Drinking Lessons

If you've been bothered by urge incontinence, **cut back on caffeinated beverages** or avoid them altogether. Caffeine, a diuretic, makes your body produce more urine. It can also make bladder muscles contract, causing accidents. Have no more than 200 milligrams of caffeine a day. That's a bit less than the amount in two cups of coffee.

Avoid alcohol. Like caffeine, it increases your body's production of urine. Have no more than one beer, glass of wine, or mixed drink a day.

Don't go without drinking fluids in an effort to produce less urine. You can become dehydrated, particularly if you're a senior. And you'll increase your risk for kidney stones.

Eat Only Bladder-Friendly Foods

Cut out **strawberries, rhubarb**, and **spinach** from your diet and see if it makes a difference. These foods are rich in bladder-irritating compounds called oxalates.

Avoid **artificial sweeteners** and **coloring agents.** They, too, can irritate the bladder.

Set a Schedule

If you've been bothered by urge incontinence, **urinate every three hours**, whether you need to or not. Wear a digital watch and set the alarm if you need a reminder. Some people go too long without urinating, failing to realize that their bladder has filled up. Urinating on schedule helps you avoid this problem.

Can't go for three hours without urinating? Go at the **beginning of each hour**. Every few days, try holding off a few more minutes before going to the restroom. Eventually you should be able to make it the full three hours between bathroom breaks.

Spend a Bit More Time Here

Once you've reached the smallest room of the house, **don't rush to empty your bladder.** If you're a woman, stay seated until you feel that your urine is fully drained. Then sit a while longer. If you do, the cystocele—the place where the bladder presses against the vaginal wall—will spontaneously contract, emptying out the additional urine. For men, you'll get all the urine out if you just stand for a while, relax, and see what else happens. Some men find it helpful to sit on the toilet to urinate. By spending a bit more time in the bathroom to make sure your bladder is completely empty, you'll avoid accidents later on.

For Women Only

🔹 If you have mild stress incontinence, place an **extra-absorbent tampon** in your vagina. The tampon presses against the urethra, helping it stay closed. To ease insertion, dampen the tampon with a little water. Be sure to remove it before going to bed. Wear a tampon only for exercising if that's when your stress incontinence typically occurs.

🔹 Another option: Consider trying vaginal muscle "weight training" with the help of a **cone-shaped weight** that you insert and hold in the vagina. They're available in drugstores and come in various sizes.

Get Some Exercise

🔹 Carrying extra weight puts more pressure on the bladder. Exercise will help you **shed unwanted weight.** (Of course, so will watching what you eat.)

Did you **know?**

Some doctors are now using Botox injections to treat urinary incontinence. The strategy is to paralyze certain muscle groups along the urinary tract to equalize pressure.

Indigestion

Great-Grandma and Great-Grandpa tamed their tummies with some of these comforting cures, and you may have luck with them too. No matter which teas or chewables you choose, though, you'll certainly want to cast a critical eye over the foods you eat—as well as how often and how much you munch. There's no free parking for the traffic in your GI tract. Once it's in, you pay the price.

What's wrong

The term "indigestion" covers a lot of ground, but mostly it means food isn't headed through your digestive tract smoothly and comfortably. Instead, you're experiencing nausea or possibly acid reflux as stomach acid backs up into your esophagus. Or maybe the problem is abdominal pain or bloating. There are many possible causes of indigestion, including eating too much or too quickly, eating foods that don't agree with you, and having too much or too little acid in your stomach.

Well-Rooted Traditions

🌿 **Ginger** is justifiably famous for settling stomach upset and improving digestion. You have three options: Take one or two 250-milligram capsules of ginger with meals, eat a few pieces of candied ginger as needed, or brew up a cup of ginger tea. To make the tea, stir 1 teaspoon grated gingerroot in 1 cup hot water, steep for 10 minutes, and strain.

🌿 **Chamomile**, an age-old treatment for indigestion. It calms the stomach and soothes spasms in the intestinal tract. Take a half-teaspoon chamomile tincture up to three times daily, or drink a few cups of chamomile tea throughout the day. Make it by stirring half to 1 teaspoon of dried herb into 1½ cups boiling water. Let it steep for 10 minutes, then strain and drink.

Pamper Yourself with Peppermint

🌿 **Peppermint oil** soothes intestinal muscle spasms and also helps relieve nausea. Take one or two capsules containing 0.2 milliliter of oil per capsule three times a day, between meals. Note that if you have heartburn, peppermint is *not* the cure for you.

🌿 If you'd prefer a steaming cup of **peppermint tea**, make it by steeping 1½ teaspoons of the dried herb in 1 cup hot water.

Chewable Resources

🌿 Chew and swallow a spoonful of **fennel** or **caraway seeds** when you're having indigestion (or you've eaten a big or especially spicy meal that might cause indigestion). These seeds contain oils that soothe spasms in the gut, relieve nausea, and help control flatulence. That's why some Indian restaurants set out dishes of fennel seeds for customers.

- ∾ Make a cup of **fennel tea.** Steep 2 to 3 teaspoons of crushed seeds in hot water for 10 minutes. Strain, then drink. You can also make the tea with anise seeds if you have them on hand.

- ∾ Take **deglycyrrhizinated licorice, or DGL,** sold in health-food stores. This product soothes stomach upset and indigestion by coating the lining of the stomach. Chew the tablets as needed, following label directions.

Sour Solution

- ∾ Try drinking 1 teaspoon of **apple cider vinegar** mixed with a half-cup of water, especially if you'd overindulged in a large meal. It will help you digest the food if you don't have enough acid in your stomach. Add a little honey to sweeten the taste.

The Soda Solution

- ∾ Stir a teaspoon of **baking soda** into a glass of water and drink it. If your stomach is too acidic, this solution neutralizes stomach acid and also helps relieve painful gas. Because in very rare cases baking soda can explode in the stomach and cause tears, some experts recommend adding a few drops of **lemon juice** to dispel some of the gas before it hits your stomach. (*Off-limits* … if you're on a low-sodium diet, since baking soda is high in sodium.)

Sip This

- ∾ Some people claim that drinking a plain old cup of **hot water** eases indigestion.

- ∾ Warm **ginger ale** or **lemon-lime soda,** or **flat Coca-Cola,** are also said to soothe an upset stomach.

Beware of Juice and Dairy

- ∾ Though it's touted as a health drink, fruit juice can actually cause abdominal pain and gas. It contains fructose, a sugar that passes undigested into the colon. When bacteria in the

Should I call **the doctor?**

If indigestion lasts for more than two weeks despite self-care approaches, talk to your doctor. Seek immediate medical attention if you have nausea accompanied by sweating or an ache in the chest; you may be having a heart attack. Other danger signs include abdominal pain that's accompanied by black or bloody stools or vomiting. (Black stools sometimes come from iron supplements or Pepto-Bismol, or from eating certain foods, but they may also be a sign of gastrointestinal bleeding.) Finally, call your doctor if you have any trouble eating, or if food won't go down.

colon finally break down the sugar, you're likely to get gas and bloating. If you drink juice, have **no more than 180 milliliters** at a time, and drink it **with a meal** so you can digest it better.

～ If dairy foods make you feel gassy and bloated, the problem could be lactose intolerance—an inability to digest lactose, a sugar found in milk. To find out for sure, take this test: Drink 2 glasses of milk and see whether you get the symptoms that have been bothering you. If so, eliminate dairy foods from your diet or look for **lactose-free products** (or take an supplement containing **lactase**, the enzyme that digests lactose).

Eat Slowly, End Early

～ **Eat slowly** and deliberately. Wolfing down your food puts big chunks of material into your digestive system, and you also swallow air, which can contribute to bloating and flatulence. Plus, when you eat too fast, food doesn't get fully coated with saliva. That interferes with the digestive process.

～ Eat your last big meal of the day at least **three hours before bedtime.** You digest best when you're up and moving about, not while you're sleeping.

Infertility

When nature takes its course, eventually a baby results. Except that sometimes it doesn't. Doctors now know that men and women are equally likely to be infertile. The home-remedy "assignments" below are separated by sex. But no matter who is "to blame" for an inability to conceive, couples must work together to find a solution. Making a baby is, after all, a collaborative undertaking. Here are ways to help make it successful.

FOR WOMEN

Know When Your Egg Is Ready

⁓ Check your **cervical mucus.** You are most fertile five days before and one day after ovulation. When your cervical mucus turns thin and clear, ovulation is about to begin. (Thin mucus makes it easier for sperm to reach the egg.) Periodically wipe your vaginal area with a tissue: If the secretion is stretchy and looks like egg white, the getting is good for getting pregnant.

⁓ You should make sure that you're actually ovulating. To do that, buy an **ovulation test kit** at the drugstore. Like a pregnancy test kit, it requires only a urine sample. If the test kit fails to indicate ovulation during three months of use, see your doctor.

Trim Down—or Bulk Up

⁓ If you have some **weight to shed**, your desire to conceive should be a real motivator. Body fat can produce estrogen, and if your estrogen level is too high, it can throw off your ability to conceive.

⁓ **Being too thin** is another cause of infertility in women. Without enough body fat, you may not ovulate normally, or your uterus may be unable to accept implantation of a fertilized egg. If you worry that you're too thin to conceive, add more healthy calories to your diet—lean protein, whole-grain foods, and beneficial oils such as olive oil.

What's wrong

Infertility is defined as an inability to become pregnant after having unprotected sex for a full year. In women, infertility has many possible causes, including sexually transmitted diseases, endometriosis, uterine fibroids, irregular menstruation, a deficit of healthy eggs, and hormone trouble. Some women are infertile because of a hidden birth defect affecting the uterus or fallopian tubes. Others experience irregular ovulation. In men, a low sperm count is just one possible cause of infertility. The sperm might be misshapen or unable to swim properly to the egg.

Should I call **the doctor?**

If you're female and over age 35, you'll want to let your doctor know you're trying to conceive. If after six months you're still not pregnant, it's time to begin doing what you can to improve your chances. If you're under 35 and trying to get pregnant, you might prefer to wait up to a year before seeking medical help. Of course, any woman who has had a problem that could be interfering with fertility should talk to her doctor as soon as it becomes clear that it's taking a while to conceive. Men should consult a urologist at the same time their partners consult a fertility specialist.

Take Things Easy

If you're already making lots of physical demands on your body, it may be less capable of "accepting" the demands of pregnancy. In particular, **exercising for more than an hour a day** can interfere with ovulation. If you usually exercise strenuously, take it down a notch.

Go easy on your work schedule. Research shows that women who work at a hectic pace in stressful jobs have trouble getting pregnant. Set reasonable work goals, and try to leave office stress behind when you head home. Consider **meditation** or **yoga** as a way of keeping stress in check.

Check Your Medicine Cabinet

Try to **avoid antihistamines and decongestants.** The drugs are designed to reduce the amount of mucus in your sinuses, but they affect your cervical mucus as well. And you need that mucus to help sperm reach the egg.

Also **skip ibuprofen** (Advil, Motrin) when you're trying to get pregnant. These painkillers can interfere with ovulation and prevent a fertilized egg from attaching to the wall of your uterus. For pain relief, try aspirin or acetaminophen.

Herbal Insurance

Take **chasteberry** each morning at a dose of 175 milligrams in capsule form or 40 drops of tincture. This herb, which is said to mimic the effects of the female hormone progesterone, helps regulate the menstrual cycle. That can make ovulation a bit more predictable. Chasteberry also contains substances that strengthen the uterine lining. As soon as you think you might be pregnant, stop taking it.

Each day, take 5 to 15 drops of tincture of **false unicorn root.** Regular use of this estrogen-like herb can make your menstrual cycle more regular—especially if your estrogen levels have begun to ebb.

FOR MEN

Stock Up on Sperm

Say no to sex for a few days before your partner begins to ovulate. You want to inseminate her with the maximum possible number of sperm; the longer it's been since your last ejaculation, the greater that number will be.

⮑ Wear **boxers** instead of briefs. Snug-fitting underwear traps heat, and too much heat reduces the number of healthy sperm produced by the testicles. Ditto for tight denim. So if you've got fatherhood in mind, keep things loose. And skip hot baths and steam rooms.

Take Baby-Making Supplements

⮑ Each day, take 30 milligrams of **zinc.** The mineral boosts your testosterone level, increases your sperm count, and helps give sperm a little extra oomph. Because zinc interferes with your body's absorption of copper, also take 2 milligrams of copper per day if you're taking zinc.

⮑ Protect your sperm with antioxidants in the form of 1,000 milligrams of **vitamin C** a day and 400 IU of **vitamin E** twice a day. Vitamins C and E help protect sperm by blocking the action of free radicals, rogue oxygen molecules that cause cell damage throughout the body. If you're taking an anticoagulant or another drug that interferes with blood clotting, talk to your doctor before taking vitamin E.

⮑ Take **selenium.** Studies suggest that men who take 100 micrograms a day for three months experience a marked increase in sperm motility (swimming ability), although there seems to be no effect on sperm count.

⮑ Try **pycnogenol**, an extract from the bark of a pine tree that grows along the coast of southwestern France. A potent antioxidant, it may improve the health of sperm in men with fertility problems. One recent study found that men with fertility problems who took 200 milligrams of pycnogenol daily for three months significantly improved the quality and function of their sperm. Pycnogenol is sold as an over-the-counter supplement in drugstores.

⮑ Consider taking a daily dose of **flaxseed oil**. There's some preliminary evidence that this oil, an excellent source of essential fatty acids, can help keep sperm healthy. Even if it doesn't boost your fertility, it will work to lower your cholesterol and help protect against heart disease. Take one tablespoon a day with food. You can mix it into juice, yogurt, or anything else.

Old **wives' tale**

Some women have been told that douching helps clean the vagina, creating better conditions for egg fertilization. In fact, douching changes the vagina's acid-alkali balance, and that makes the environment less hospitable for sperm.

FOR WOMEN AND MEN

Steer Clear of Smoke

🍃 Smoking not only **decreases fertility** in both sexes but also increases the **risk for miscarriage.** The number of healthy eggs in the ovaries dwindles more quickly in smokers than among nonsmokers. In men, sperm counts decrease, and there are more damaged sperm.

Lose the Booze

🍃 **Avoid alcohol.** Alcohol in a woman's bloodstream compromises the egg's ability to move. In men, alcohol can impair ejaculation.

Timing Is Everything

🍃 When ovulation is imminent, **have sex** at least once a day for three days.

🍃 If you've chosen not to track ovulation—either by examining cervical mucus or using an ovulation test kit—have sex at least every other day from days 8 through 20 (counting from the first day of menstruation). Sperm have a three-day life span. By having sex that often, you improve the chances that sperm will be ready and waiting when ovulation occurs.

Inflammatory Bowel Disease

Doctors tend to treat IBD with powerful steroids and other prescription medications, and these drugs can be very helpful, especially during flare-ups. But there are steps you can take on your own to reduce the severity of your symptoms, such as favoring foods that are kind to your bowels and taking measures to manage stress.

Boost Beneficial Bacteria

⁓ Boost the population of beneficial bacteria in your gut. You can do this by taking an OTC bacteria supplement known as a **probiotic**. In healthy people, the colon is home to "good" bacteria (such as *Lactobacillus acidophilus* and *Bifidobacteria bifidum*) that prevent overgrowth of harmful bacteria. But when these bacteria are killed off—often, by antibiotics—the resulting overgrowth of "bad" bacteria and yeast can cause inflammation. Probiotics help maintain an optimal balance. If you don't want to take a supplement, try eating yogurt with active cultures.

Fuel Your Body with Care

⁓ Favor bland food—**cooked carrots, white rice, apple-sauce**, etc. If you're already suffering from diarrhea and abdominal pain, eating lots of spicy foods will only make matters worse.

⁓ **Cut back on dietary fat.** Fried foods, fatty meats, and other sources of fat can trigger contractions in your intestine, which can exacerbate diarrhea.

⁓ **Eat less dietary fiber** during flare-ups. Ordinarily, high-fiber foods like bran, whole grains, and broccoli are good for the system. But during flare-ups they increase your risk for painful gas. Once you feel better, resume a normal fiber intake.

⁓ Many people with Crohn's disease are unable to digest lactose, a form of sugar found in dairy foods. If you feel gassy and bloated, try **avoiding milk** and all other dairy foods for a few days. If your symptoms go away, you may have lactose

What's **wrong**

The term "inflammatory bowel disease," or IBD, encompasses several conditions. The two most common ones are ulcerative colitis and Crohn's disease. Ulcerative colitis causes sores on the lining of the colon and rectum. Crohn's disease is more extensive—sometimes affecting the intestines, stomach, esophagus, and mouth—and tissues can become much more deeply inflamed. Symptoms are similar for both colitis and Crohn's: diarrhea, abdominal pain, and blood or mucus in the stool. These problems can flare up, then go away, with remissions sometimes lasting years.

Should I call the doctor?

If you have IBD, you should be under the care of a gastroenterologist. Alert the doctor if you experience a flare-up of symptoms, especially if you have diarrhea that contains blood or mucus. That could be an indication of cancer or another potentially life-threatening condition.

intolerance. Switch to lactose-free dairy products, take pills containing lactase (the enzyme needed to digest milk), or avoid milk products altogether.

Track What You Eat

🔹 Keep a **food journal.** Record what foods you eat, what reactions you have, and the severity of your discomfort. At the end of a month, review your journal to get a sense of how well you tolerate dietary fiber and potentially troublesome foods like dairy products. You'll also find out whether you need to avoid any particular foods entirely.

Stress Less to Digest Best

🔹 Stress can trigger IBD symptoms. So every day, practice **yoga, meditation, deep breathing, visualization,** or another stress-reduction technique. For example, you might sit in a quiet spot for 20 minutes or so and visualize a healing blue light slowly pouring down the length of your digestive tract, soothing the inflammation. Imagine that as this blue light travels through you, it leaves healthy tissue behind.

Do Some Interior Work

🔹 Take a daily **multivitamin/mineral.** This helps restore the nutrients that can be depleted by persistent diarrhea.

🔹 A daily dose of a naturally occurring vitamin-like compound called **PABA (para-aminobenzoic acid)** may help ease inflammation within your intestines. During flare-ups, take 1,000 milligrams of PABA three times a day. Once your condition goes into remission, cut back to 1,000 milligrams twice a day. PABA is sold over the counter at drugstores.

🔹 Certain antioxidant nutrients help ease symptoms of IBD, although exactly why is unclear. Good choices include **grape-seed extract** (100 milligrams once or twice daily), the amino acid **NAC** (ask your pharmacist for N-acetylcysteine and take 500 milligrams twice daily), and **vitamin C** (1,000 milligrams twice a day).

🔹 Give the amino acid **L-glutamine** a try. An old folk remedy for intestinal inflammation calls for drinking lots of cabbage juice, which is rich in L-glutamine. But if that doesn't sound particularly appetizing, you can ask your doctor for a prescription of L-glutamine pills (500 milligrams a day). L-glutamine helps heal ulcers in the gut.

Because it combats inflammation, a type of **licorice** called **DGL** may help ease symptoms of inflammatory bowel disease. Chew two wafers (380 milligrams) three times a day between meals when you have a flare-up. Don't try to substitute licorice candy; most licorice candy contains no "real" licorice. And unlike DGL, "real" licorice can raise your blood pressure.

Oil Your Inflammation Away

Omega-3 fatty acids are essential for good digestion. Good sources include **flaxseed oil** (one tablespoon a day taken straight or mixed into salad dressing or cereal) and **fish oil** (1,500 milligrams to 3,000 milligrams of fish-oil capsules daily). One Italian study found that fish oil reduced the frequency of intestinal attacks in people with Crohn's disease.

Teatime Again

Peppermint and **chamomile** contain antispasmodic compounds that help curb cramps and ease pain caused by abdominal gas. To make a tea, drop a teaspoon of either dried herb into a cup of boiling water, and let it steep for 10 minutes. Strain and drink. If you're susceptible to heartburn, choose chamomile over peppermint.

Marshmallow tea soothes by coating the mucous membranes in the digestive tract. Use 1 to 2 teaspoons of dried herb per cup of hot water. Steep for 10 to 15 minutes, then strain.

Tried...

People with IBD used to be advised to eat onion skins.

...and true

Onion skins contain quercetin, a naturally occurring antihistamine that helps block the allergy-like reactions that IBD sufferers have to certain foods. When cooking soup, you can add a whole onion to the pot; the quercetin will seep out of the skin. (Just be sure to remove the skin before eating the onion.) Don't like onions? Quercetin supplements are sold over the counter at drugstores. Follow instructions on the label.

Ingrown Hairs

If we didn't shave, we'd have far fewer problems with ingrown hairs. But for men who don't wish to resemble Rip Van Winkle and for women who favor glamorous gams, shaving is inevitable. Fortunately, a little prep work before you apply razor to skin can help. So can changing the kind of shaver you use. But even with those precautions, from time to time you'll need some tricks to wrest a hair from its nest.

What's wrong

You have another ingrown hair, but why? Maybe a too-close shave has damaged the tiny rootlike structure (follicle) from which the hair sprouts, causing it to grow into your skin through the side of the follicle. But a hair can also become ingrown simply if it curls sharply and grows back into the follicle. In either case, you're left with a sore red bump. People with curly body hair are especially prone to ingrown hairs; the problem is common among African Canadians.

A Hairy Operation

➤ If a hair has curled back and grown into your skin, you'll probably want to remove it. First, place a **washcloth soaked with hot water** over the area. Leave it on for about five minutes to soften the hair. Using **tweezers**, gently pull the tip of the hair away from the skin. Then use **nail scissors** to trim off the curl.

Skin Shavers

➤ If ingrown hairs keep recurring, a simple **shaver-swap** might do the trick. If you normally shave with a blade, switch to an electric shaver. If you already use an electric shaver, switch to a blade.

➤ Many razors now feature double or even triple blades for an ultra-close shave. But when it comes to preventing ingrown hairs, an old-fashioned **single-bladed razor** is often better. Two-bladed razors tend to tug the stubble away from the skin before cutting it. Hairs "snap back" a bit, and can wind up jammed below the surface.

➤ If an ingrown hair becomes infected and you shave with a razor, **changing blades** should speed the healing process by helping you avoid re-exposing your skin to the germs that caused the infection in the first place. If you don't want to spring for a new blade each day, sterilize the blade by dipping it in **rubbing alcohol**. Be sure to rinse off the alcohol or you might burn your skin.

Prep Your Skin

↝ Before your next shave, briskly rub the area with a dry **loofah** or washcloth. You'll brush away dead skin cells that might block hair follicles—a process called exfoliation—and lift hairs away from their follicles.

Watch How You Mow

↝ **Shave with the "grain"** of your hair growth. When men shave the neck, for instance, they should go down rather than up. When shaving their legs or bikini area, women should follow the same policy. This might not give the closest shave, but you won't cut the hair so short that it gets under your skin.

↝ If you shave your underarms, **don't make the mistake of pulling the skin taut** before applying the razor. That makes the hairs protrude slightly, and after you slice off the ends, they pull back under the skin surface. For the same reason, men should not pull on facial skin when shaving.

Bump Off Bumps

↝ To reduce inflammation, apply an OTC cream containing **hydrocortisone.** Follow the directions on the label.

↝ **Benzoyl peroxide**, an ingredient in many acne creams and face washes, can help minimize hair bumps.

↝ Lotions that contain **alpha-hydroxy acids (AHAs)** exfoliate your skin and help cut down on the number of hairs that get trapped under your skin. Apply an AHA lotion morning and night to the skin that you shave regularly. One of these applications should be right after you shave. Watch out, though: AHAs can be irritating, especially if the skin is wet. When you start using an AHA lotion, put it on every other night until you see how well you tolerate it.

Ways Around Shaving

↝ Give up the quest for a close shave. The closer the shave, the greater the risk of ingrown hairs.

↝ As an alternative to shaving, some women use a **depilatory lotion.** Similar products are now available for men. Be sure to follow the instructions carefully. Use the product no more than twice a week to minimize skin irritation.

Should I call **the doctor?**

If the pain and redness seem to be getting worse, call the doctor. The ingrown hair may be getting infected.

Skip it!

Waxing may be the best way to get an elegant bikini line or magnificently smooth legs, but it's not a good idea if you're prone to ingrown hairs. After a wax job, hairs tend to grow back at an angle instead of straight out, which means they're even more likely to become ingrown.

Ingrown Toenails

Toenail care is probably not high on your list of skills to master, but when an ingrown nail is bothering you, it's amazing how quickly you can develop an interest in the subject. Of all the minor ills in our lives, this is among the most preventable. But once an ingrown nail is on the cutting edge of your concerns, follow these steps to put it in its place.

What's **wrong**

Ingrown toenails are usually a big-toe problem. A thick, sharp nail starts growing into the tender skin at the corner of the nail, cutting the skin as it grows. The incised area becomes red, painful, and vulnerable to infection. Some people have toenails that just naturally grow in ways that set the stage for this problem. But there are other contributing factors—wearing tight shoes or socks, for instance, or trimming toenails improperly. And you're more likely to have ingrown toenails if you have the structural irregularities known as bunions or hammertoes.

Soak Your Feet

Fill a large basin with about eight liters of **hot water.** Add several spoonfuls of **salt** and stir until the salt dissolves. Soak your problem foot for 15 to 20 minutes each day. Hot water softens the skin around the ingrown nail while the salt helps combat infection and reduces swelling.

Try This Cotton-Pickin' Technique

After you've soaked your feet, wash off the salt with **warm, soapy water**, rinse, and let your feet dry.

Pull a small piece of **cotton** from a cotton ball and smear it with some **antibiotic ointment** such as Neosporin. Roll the cotton into a thin tube between your fingertips. This little tube needs to get between the sharp edge of the nail and the tender skin it's cutting into.

Dip a clean **toothpick** into **alcohol** to sterilize it. Use the toothpick to carefully poke the cotton underneath the edge of your toenail. With the edge of your nail cushioned by cotton instead of cutting into your skin, you should feel less pain.

If you find that pressure from the cotton creates extra pain, use less. Undo your first attempt, and try again with a smaller roll.

Keep Your Feet Clean

Put on a **clean pair of socks** every day. While you can't keep feet completely germ-free, you reduce risk of infection if you keep them as clean as possible.

⤙ Whenever you take a bath or shower, be sure to scrub your feet well with a **soapy washcloth.** Afterward, smear an **antibiotic ointment** onto your toe.

Display Your Toe Tips

⤙ Wear shoes that are **open at the end**, like sandals. Tight shoes just exacerbate the problem because you're jamming the nail ever deeper into skin that already hurts.

The Power of Prevention

⤙ Before cutting your nails, soak your feet in warm water for a few minutes to **soften the nail.** When you trim toenails, always **cut them straight across**, leaving a little extra nail on each side. Then **file the corners** very slightly—just so they're not sharp. While you should cut all your toenails this way, pay special attention to the big one, since it's the most vulnerable.

⤙ **Don't pick** at your toenails. You're more likely to tear off the corners, and the remaining edge of the nail can grow into your toe.

⤙ To make sure you buy shoes that fit properly, have your **feet measured** each time you buy new shoes. Your feet get longer and wider as you age, and shoes that would have fit at one time might be real toe-squeezers.

⤙ **Buy your shoes** at the end of the day. Your feet often swell from the day's pounding, and they are at their largest come evening.

⤙ Pay more attention to how you **lace your shoes.** The point is to keep your foot from sliding inside the shoe, so that your toes don't keep running into the end of the toe box. To best achieve that, make sure the laces are tightest (but not uncomfortably so) near the top of your midfoot.

⤙ Believe it or not, tight socks or stockings can affect toenails too, even if the shoe is loose and comfortable. Pick **socks that don't squeeze** your toes together.

Should I call **the doctor?**

See your doctor or a podiatrist if your toe is oozing pus, a sign of infection. You'll also need medical attention if an injury to the nail bed is making the nail grow out crooked. Redness, particularly streaks running up the foot, can be a sign of serious infection, whether or not it's accompanied by fever. If you have diabetes, see a doctor or podiatrist any time you have an ingrown toenail: Like any foot problem, it could lead to serious complications.

Skip it!

Don't wrap a bandage or gauze tightly around the wounded toe. That's just going to press the sharp nail harder into the skin.

Insect and Spider Bites

If you live near a polar ice cap, you'll never have to worry about mosquitoes, bees, wasps, or spiders. For the rest of us, confrontations with these pesky predators are as inevitable as the summer solstice. For some bugs, insect repellent is an effective deterrent. Others, however, seem eternally bold, and their bites are as bad as their buzz. Here's how to recover from sneak attacks and protect your skin from further affronts.

What's wrong

Some bugs bite you because they're hungry and they see you as food. Mosquitoes, ticks, fleas, and chiggers are on this team. Others sting you because they regard you as a threat. This club includes spiders, wasps, fire ants, yellow jackets, and bees. Mosquitoes inject you with a little saliva that leaves a maddeningly itchy bump, while bees and wasps penetrate skin with a poison that makes you yelp and run. Worst, of course, are venomous spiders—but fortunately, they're the rarest of foes.

WASP AND BEE STINGS

Get Out the Credit Card

🐝 If you've been stung by anything larger than a mosquito (a honeybee, for instance), **scrape away the stinger** as soon as possible using the edge of a credit card, a knife blade, or your fingernail. As long as it remains in your skin, this little sac of poison keeps pumping its contents into your body. Don't use tweezers or pinch the stinger with your fingertips, since you'll squeeze more venom into your skin.

Pamper the Sting Site

🐝 As soon as you have the stinger out, soak the area in **apple cider vinegar** for a few minutes. Dip a cotton ball in vinegar and tape it to the sting site. It will help relieve redness and swelling.

🐝 Treat the area with **meat tenderizer** right after you're stung. It contains enzymes that break down the venom, reducing swelling and inflammation. Take a few spoonfuls of meat tenderizer powder, add enough water to form a paste, smear the paste on, and leave it on for an hour.

🐝 Apply an **aspirin paste** to stop the itching. Using the back of a spoon, crush one or two aspirin on a small plate or cutting board. Add just enough water to make a paste, then dab the paste on the sting site. Ingredients in aspirin help to neutralize the venom.

🐝 Apply an **ice pack** to numb the area and help slow the

Spot the Spider

If you know you've been bitten by a spider, try to memorize its appearance. Some spiders can cause serious symptoms affecting your whole body, while others just create a localized reaction. Whether or not you have a severe reaction, get medical attention right away.

swelling. If you have a towel or washcloth between the ice pack and your skin, you can leave the ice pack in place for up to 20 minutes.

✎ **Papaya** contains enzymes that neutralize insect venom. If you happen to have this fruit in your lunch basket, simply lay a slice on the sting for an hour.

✎ **Baking soda** can bring relief. One method of application is to mix baking soda with a skin lotion, then apply it to the sensitive area. The baking soda helps relieve inflammation, and the skin lotion keeps it in place. Alternatively, you can mix one teaspoon of baking soda in a glass of water, let it dissolve, then apply the mixture with a cotton pad or washcloth. Leave the compress in place for 20 minutes.

✎ Cut an **onion**, then rub it over the sting site. Doctors aren't quite sure how this works, but the onion contains enzymes that seem to break down inflammatory compounds. Other people swear by smearing a crushed clove of garlic over the skin.

✎ **Sugar** works too. Just dip your forefinger in water, dab it in sugar, then touch the sting site.

✎ To help reduce swelling, try **bromelain**, a protein-digesting enzyme derived from pineapple. On an empty stomach take 500 milligrams containing at least 2,000 GDU or 3,000 MCU. You can take several doses in a single day. Stop taking it when the swelling goes down.

✎ **Tea-tree oil** will also help reduce the swelling. Apply one drop several times a day.

✎ To stop the itching, dab on a drop or two of **lavender oil**. Wait about fifteen minutes to allow the oil to take effect. If the area starts to itch again, apply more—but just one or two drops at a time.

Should I call **the doctor?**

If you've been bitten by a spider, call the doctor immediately. If you've been stung by a bee or wasp and then have trouble breathing, feel faint, or have swelling in your mouth or throat, a rapid pulse, or hives, get to an emergency room. You could be having a potentially fatal allergic reaction called anaphylaxis. And see a doctor if you develop a bull's-eye rash, muscle aches, fever, and headache within three weeks after getting a tick bite; these could be signs of Lyme disease, which can lead to mental confusion and arthritis if not treated.

If you're been in tick territory, be sure to follow this advice.

🍃 After you've been in the woods or weeds, strip off your clothes and check yourself from head to toe. (Have your spouse or partner check parts of your body you can't see.)

🍃 If you find a tick that hasn't attached to your skin, grasp it with a napkin or piece of toilet paper, and flush it down the toilet.

🍃 If a tick has already latched onto your skin, use tweezers to grab it by the head, as close to your skin as possible. Slowly pull upward until it lets go. If you yank it off, the head can break off in your skin and remain there until infection sets in.

🍃 Preserve any tick that has been embedded in your skin in a zipped-up plastic sandwich bag. If you develop a rash, your doctor can analyze the tick to see whether it carries Lyme disease. A rash can show up from three days to a month later, so keep that bagged tick for a while before flushing it away.

INSECT BITES

Instead of Scratching...

🍃 Rub an **ice cube** on the bug bite right away. This helps decrease the inflammation that causes itching.

🍃 **Sea Breeze astringent** for oily skin will stop the itching from mosquito bites. In addition to alcohol, its contents include camphor, eucalyptus, clove oil, eugenol, and peppermint oil. Dab a small amount on a cotton pad or tissue, and apply it to the site.

🍃 **Underarm deodorants** have ingredients that reduce skin irritation. If you get a bug bite, try any deodorant and see if it works.

🍃 Apply a drop or two of **peppermint oil**. It has a cooling effect, and also increases circulation to the bite, speeding the healing process. Alternatively, if you have toothpaste that contains peppermint oil, apply a dab.

🍃 Look for an anti-itch spray or gel that contains **menthol**, a classic skin-soother. Keep the product in the refrigerator until you're ready to use it. The coolness will provide extra itch relief.

🍃 Buy anti-itch cream that contains a topical anesthetic to numb the area. Some also contain **hydrocortisone** to stop the swelling and **antihistamine** to counter the allergic reaction.

🍃 Use a **bug-bite relief patch**, which looks like a small bandage and goes directly on the skin. Each patch contains concentrated numbing medicine.

The Power of Prevention

☙ Use a bug spray that contains **DEET**, the most effective insect repellent for use on the skin. Adults can safely use any DEET product (following directions on the label). Children should not be exposed to a cream that exceeds 6% DEET.

☙ Before heading into the deep woods, treat your clothing with one of the many insect repellents that contain **permethrin**. Permethrin is a synthetic version of a bug-repelling compound found in chrysanthemum plants. Apply it liberally to outdoor-wear clothing, and it should remain effective even after a washing. Permethrin only goes on clothing, but not for safety reasons: The compound loses its effectiveness when it's applied to skin.

☙ You can also use products made with **p–Menthane 3, 8-diol**, a chemical derived from the eucalyptus plant. **Off! Botanicals** is one product that contains this ingredient.

☙ **Citronella**, an oil that comes from a type of grass, is found in bug-repelling candles, as well as bug sprays. Follow label directions.

☙ Several days before you take a camping or hiking trip into bug-filled territory, start eating **garlic**. Have a clove or two every day. As you sweat out the garlic odor, it repels many insects.

☙ To **keep bees away**, avoid wearing perfumes or scented products, keep food and soda covered, and don't wear bright clothing, especially floral patterns.

Skip it!

Tick bite? Smearing the tick with petroleum jelly or oil won't cause it to come loose, as some would have you believe. Removing the head with tweezers is the effective way to get the job done.

Insomnia

Insomnia can become a real nightmare as the clock ticks on into the night and you're awake to notice. What to do? Try counting sheep. Seriously. If that doesn't work, you could follow Mark Twain's advice: "Lie near the edge of the bed and you'll drop off." Better yet, try the other approaches listed below. A relaxing cup of tea, a whiff of lavender oil, smarter scheduling of sleep, and other tactics can summon the sandman and help you awaken less tired and cranky come morning.

What's wrong

Insomnia can take three forms: (1) You toss and turn instead of falling asleep; (2) You fall asleep okay, but then wake up repeatedly during the night; or (3) You wake up too early and can't fall asleep again. Whatever the form of sleep thievery, you've been set up for grogginess and irritability the next day. The most common causes of insomnia are emotional stress and depression. Other reasons for poor sleep include pain or illness, medications (such as decongestants), eating a heavy meal late at night, drinking caffeine or alcohol too near bedtime, or simply trying to sleep in an unfamiliar bed.

Before-Bed Bites

🌑 Have a slice of **turkey** or **chicken**, or a **banana** before heading to bed. These foods contain tryptophan, an amino acid that's used to make serotonin. And serotonin is a brain chemical that helps you sleep. Keep the portion small, though, or your full belly may keep you awake.

🌑 Carbohydrates help trytophan enter the brain. Try a glass of **warm milk** (milk contains tryptophan) and a **cookie**, or warm milk with a spoonful of **honey**. A sprinkling of **cinnamon** couldn't hurt, and might add mild sedative properties of its own.

🌑 **Avoid big meals** late in the evening. You need three to four hours to digest a big meal, so if you eat a lot within four hours of your bedtime, don't be surprised if intestinal grumblings and groanings keep you awake.

🌑 Spicy or sugary food, even at suppertime, is usually a bad idea. **Spices can irritate your stomach**, and when it tosses and turns, so will you. Having a lot of sugary food—especially chocolate, which contains caffeine—can make you feel jumpy.

Call on Herbs for Help

🌑 **Valerian** helps people fall asleep faster without the "hangover" affect of some sleeping pills. It binds to the same receptors in the brain that tranquilizers such as diazepam bind to. The herb itself stinks (think sweaty old socks), so we don't recommend trying to make a tea. Instead, take one-half to one teaspoon of valerian tincture or two capsules of valerian root an hour before bed.

 Take 4,000 to 8,000 milligrams of dried **passionflower** capsules. Passionflower is widely used as a mild herbal sedative.

 Or you can combine forces, taking a supplement that includes both **passionflower** and **valerian**. "Natural" sleep remedies often include other herbal ingredients as well, such as **hops** and **skullcap**. Whatever the formulation, follow the package directions.

Smell Your Way to Sleep

 Lavender has a reputation as a mild tranquilizer. Simply dab a bit of the oil onto your temples and forehead before you hit the pillow. The aroma should help send you off to sleep. You can also add lavender oil to a diffuser or vaporizer to scent your bedroom. Or place a lavender sachet near your pillow.

 Put a drop of **jasmine** essential oil on each wrist just before you go to bed. In studies conducted at Wheeling Jesuit University in West Virginia, researchers discovered that people who spent the night in jasmine-scented rooms slept more peacefully than people who stayed in unscented—or even lavender-scented—rooms.

 Try a soothing aromatic **bath** before bedtime. Add 5 drops **lavender oil** and 3 drops **ylang-ylang oil** to warm bathwater and enjoy a nice soak.

Be a Slave to Schedule

 Wake up at the same time each day, no matter how little sleep you got the night before. On weekends, follow the same schedule, so your body adheres to the same pattern all week long. You'll fall asleep faster.

 Every morning, **go for a walk**. It doesn't have to be a long walk, but it should definitely be outdoors. The presence of natural light (even if the day is overcast) tells your groggy body it's time to wake up for the day. With your body clock set by the great outdoors, you'll sleep better at night.

 Try not to nap during the day, no matter how tired you feel. People who don't have insomnia often benefit from

Should I call **the doctor?**

If you've tried the following self-care strategies and still can't get a good night's sleep, talk to your doctor. And waste no time getting to your doctor if sleep deprivation is harming your work performance or endangering your life—as in, causing you to fall asleep at the wheel. You may need to be evaluated overnight at a sleep clinic.

Tried...

A hops pillow can help relieve insomnia.

...and true

Hops—flowers of a plant used in beer-making—release a mild sedative into the air. To make your own pillow, sew two 20-centimeter (8-inch) squares of fabric together along three sides to form a pocket. Stuff it full of dried hops and sew the fourth side shut. Put the pillow near your head so you can smell it at night. You may need to periodically dampen it with grain alcohol to reactivate the herb.

a short afternoon nap. However, if you're napping in daytime only to turn into a wide-eyed zombie at night, there's a good chance that that afternoon snooze is disrupting your body clock. If you absolutely must nap, catch a half-hour of zzz's at the most.

Pillow Tricks

🙳 Once you get into bed, imagine your feet becoming heavy and numb. Feel them sinking into the mattress. Then do the same with your calves, and slowly work your way up your body, letting it all grow heavy and relaxed. The idea is to **let yourself go**, in gradual phases, all the way from head to toe.

🙳 If you're still awake after this progressive relaxation exercise, **count sheep**. Sound like an old saw? The whole point is to occupy your mind with boring repetition, and, not to cast aspersions on sheep, there's nothing more boring or repetitive than counting a herd of them. Any repetitive counting activity will lull you.

🙳 If you prefer lullabies, listen to **calming, relaxing tapes** as you drift off.

🙳 If you just can't sleep, **don't lie in bed worrying about it**. That will only make sleep harder to attain. Get up, leave the bedroom, and grab a book or watch TV. Recommended reading, at this time of night, is some mind-numbing tome about the history of Swiss watch-making or macroeconomic theory. And if you decide to watch TV, look for a channel showing coverage of a recent zoning-board hearing or something equally soporific. The goal is to bore yourself into oblivion—so sleep becomes a sweet release.

Prep Your Bedroom

🙳 If you find yourself tossing and turning as you try to get comfortable, consider purchasing a special **neck-supporting pillow**. They are specially designed for people who have neck pain or tension that prevents sleep.

🙳 **Turn your alarm clock** so that you **can't see it** from bed. If you're glancing at the clock when you wake up—and it's almost impossible not to—you'll soon start wondering how you can function tomorrow on so little sleep tonight. For truly accomplished insomniacs, just one glance at a glowing digital dial is enough to set a whole anxiety-train in motion.

🖎 **Turn your thermostat down** a few degrees before heading to bed. Most people sleep better when their surroundings are cool.

🖎 If you share your bed, consider buying a **queen- or king-size mattress** so you don't keep one another up. Some new models are designed so that when your partner moves—or if a bowling bowl drops on his or her side of the bed—you feel nothing. Or consider sleeping in separate beds. (If you value the relationship, of course, be sure to emphasize that your wish for separate beds is based on pragmatism rather than preference.)

Check the Label

🖎 Be cautious about taking an over-the-counter painkiller before bed. Some of them, like Excedrin, contain **caffeine**. Read the label first.

🖎 Check labels of decongestants and cold remedies too. In addition to caffeine, they may contain ingredients, such as pseudoephedrine, that rev up your nervous system and leave you unable to fall asleep. Look for a **nighttime formula**.

Don'ts and More Don'ts for Better Dozing

🖎 **Avoid exercising** within four hours of bedtime—it's too stimulating. Instead, exercise in the morning or after work. An exception is **yoga**. A number of yoga postures are designed to calm your body and prepare you for sleep.

🖎 **Avoid caffeinated beverages**, particularly within four hours of bedtime. Though people have varying ranges of sensitivity to caffeine, the stimulating effects can be long-lasting.

🖎 Also **avoid alcohol** in the evenings. While a glass of sherry might help you fall asleep a bit faster than usual, the effects soon wear off, and you're more likely to wake up during the night.

🖎 If you **smoke** within four hours of your bedtime, look no further for the **cause of your insomnia**. Nicotine stimulates the central nervous system, interfering with your ability to fall asleep and stay that way.

Skip it!

Avoid sleep inducers containing kava. Though derivatives of this plant root reduce anxiety and relax your muscles, kava supplements have been linked to liver toxicity in recent years. They have been pulled off the market in Canada as well as in many other countries.

Irritable Bowel Syndrome

Since there's no sure cure for IBS (also called "spastic colon"), people develop their own ways of living with the enemy. The key: Don't become discouraged. Dietary changes and stress-relief tactics should provide a significant dose of relief. For more insurance, combine them with one of the alternative therapies noted below. Once you have a system for controlling your symptoms, IBS will surely put less of a cramp in your style.

What's wrong

Normally, food travels through your digestive system propelled by wavelike contractions of the intestinal muscles. But if you have irritable bowel syndrome, or IBS, the contractions are irregular—fast and spastic, causing diarrhea, or slow and weak, causing constipation. Other symptoms include abdominal pain and gas. Causes are unknown, but doctors have discovered that elevated stress, along with certain foods, aggravate IBS. Women are twice as likely as men to get the syndrome.

Cut the Stress Connection

⮞ Since stress is one of the factors known to trigger an IBS flare-up, learn to short-circuit it with **meditation**, **yoga**, or a **simple breathing exercise** like this one. Sit comfortably, or lie down. Turn your attention to the air going in and out of your body. When upsetting or anxiety-producing thoughts intrude, focus completely on your breathing. Practice this daily. Then, whenever you feel yourself becoming tense and anxious, use it to calm yourself.

⮞ **Keep a diary** of your IBS symptoms, noting what types of problems you have and how severe they are. In this journal, also jot down any stressful events you face in your day. Occasionally look back at your diary. If you see more IBS symptoms just before airplane flights or meetings with your boss, for instance, there may be a connection. Once you've detected situations that seem to trigger IBS symptoms, look for ways—like using the breathing technique above—to cope with them better.

Go Easy on Your Intestines

⮞ **Minimize fried foods**, meats, oils, margarine, dairy foods, and other fatty foods. They cause your colon to contract violently, which can lead to diarrhea and abdominal pain.

⮞ **Stay away from spicy foods**. The capsaicin in hot peppers, for example, makes your large intestine go into spasms, which can cause diarrhea.

- **Cut down on caffeine.** It can worsen IBS by irritating your intestines.

- Avoid foods known to cause flatulence, including **cabbage, Brussels sprouts,** and **broccoli.**

- Don't chew gum or candy that contains artificial sweeteners. Among the common sweeteners in these products are **sorbitol** and **mannitol,** which can have a laxative effect. They're very difficult to digest. When bacteria in your colon eventually break down these "nonabsorbed sugars," you get gas and diarrhea.

- **Stop smoking.** Nicotine contributes to IBS flare-ups. Also, when you smoke, you swallow air, and people with IBS are very sensitive to having air in their gut.

Fit In More Fiber

- Soluble fiber soaks up liquid in your intestines, helping to prevent diarrhea. Good sources are **beans, oatmeal,** and some **fruits,** such as **apples, strawberries,** and **grapefruit.**

- If you can't seem to get enough soluble fiber in your diet, take a daily supplement of **psyllium,** the main ingredient in dietary fiber supplements like Metamucil. Unlike chemical laxatives, psyllium is safe to take long-term. Follow the label for dosage directions.

- If constipation is your main complaint, fill up on **insoluble fiber,** found in **whole wheat, bran,** other **whole grains, salad greens,** and other foods. Insoluble fiber bulks up stool, which speeds its passage through the intestines.

- If you haven't had much fiber in your diet, **increase the amount you eat gradually.** Adding too much fiber all at once can actually give you gas and bloating. Start with 8 grams of fiber daily—about what you'd find in two pears—and increase by 3 or 4 grams each day until you're up to 30 grams daily.

Should I call **the doctor?**

Call your doctor if you notice blood in your stool, you start losing weight when you're not trying to, or your IBS symptoms are so severe that you can't even leave your home. If you're over 50 and start to have IBS symptoms, you should get a doctor involved. And if you've had IBS for many years but note a change in a previous pattern, make the call. Among other things, the doctor should ask you about prescription or OTC medications to find out whether a change in bowel habits is related to drug side effects.

Cowed by Dairy?

Many people who think they have IBS actually have lactose intolerance, a problem in which the body can't properly digest the lactose sugar that's found in dairy foods. An easy way to self-diagnose this is to drink two cups of milk. If you are lactose intolerant, you will get cramps, gas, and diarrhea. If you get these symptoms, you know it's time to drop all dairy foods from your diet. Instead of pouring milk on your cereal in the morning, use Lactaid, which is almost entirely lactose-free.

Skip it!

Avoid using medications to affect your bowel habits—either laxatives for constipation or drugs to fight diarrhea—if you have IBS. These can make you swing wildly back and forth between constipation and diarrhea.

➤ Drink at least six to eight glasses of **water** each day to keep fiber moving smoothly through your system.

Graze, Don't Gorge

➤ Eat **smaller meals** more frequently rather than a couple of large meals each day. Taking in too much food at once can overstimulate your digestive system.

➤ If you usually bolt down your meals, **go more slowly** and pay more attention to chewing your food. Fast eaters often swallow too much air, which turns into bothersome intestinal gas.

Eat Yogurt

➤ Having diarrhea can drain away good bacteria that help prevent harmful bacteria from growing out of control. When you're having IBS-related diarrhea, eat plenty of **yogurt** containing active bacteria, such as acidophilus. Or take supplements of **acidophilus**. The usual daily dosage is one pill containing 1 to 2 billion live organisms. Take it on an empty stomach.

Steep Well

➤ Every day, drink a cup or two of **peppermint tea**, which relaxes your intestines, reduces spasms, and relieves gas pain. Make sure to buy the kind that contains real peppermint, rather than black tea with peppermint flavoring. (*Off-limits . . .* if you have heartburn.) Alternatively, you can take enteric-coated **peppermint-oil** capsules. The coating ensures that the oil reaches the intestine instead of breaking down in the stomach. Take one or two capsules three times a day, between meals.

➤ Drink **ginger tea**. Ginger soothes all manner of digestive problems, including IBS. For the freshest tea, grate a half-teaspoon of ginger into a cup, then pour in hot water, let it steep for 10 minutes, strain out the ginger, and drink the tea. Ginger tea bags are also available. Drink four to six cups a day.

Exorcise with Exercise

➤ Whenever possible, get at least 30 minutes of noncompetitive **exercise** such as walking. Exercise helps relieve stress, releases natural painkilling endorphins, and keeps your body—including your digestive system—working smoothly.

Jock Itch

If you don't believe jock itch is common, walk into any drugstore and survey all the over-the-counter antifungal remedies. Active ingredients in these products run the gamut from miconazole and tolnaftate to terbinafine. OTC remedies generally work well, and if the first one you try doesn't work, you can always try another that has different ingredients. Of course, you're not confined to drugstore products. Many traditional remedies work as well—or better. Read on for some suggestions.

A Few Dabs a Day

What's wrong

This annoying itch can visit the sedentary scholar as well as the serious athlete—and despite its name, women as well as men can get it. Most of the time, the red, itchy, chafed area in the groin is caused by the fungal infection tinea cruris. But jock itch can also be caused by the fungus of athlete's foot (tinea pedis) that has spread to the groin. Other causes include yeast or bacteria, or it might be simply skin irritation: The groin is a hot, sweaty place where a lot of friction occurs, so skin problems there are almost inevitable.

~ Soak a cotton ball in **thyme tea**, and apply it to your groin. Thyme contains thymol, a potent fungus fighter. To make the tea, stir 2 teaspoons fresh or dried thyme in 1 cup boiled water, and let it steep for 20 minutes. Once the tea cools, it's ready to apply.

~ Another good herb for chasing away fungus is **ginger**. It contains a total of 23 antifungal compounds, including caprylic acid, which is especially effective. Stir 2 tablespoons grated gingerroot into 1 cup boiled water, and steep for 20 minutes. When the tea is cool, apply it using a cotton ball.

~ Licorice also contains antifungal components and has long been used in traditional Chinese medicine as a remedy for jock itch. Stir 6 teaspoons powdered **licorice root** in 1 cup boiled water, and let it steep for 20 minutes. As soon as it's cool, dab it on the groin.

~ **Tea-tree oil** is a germ-fighting and fungus-fighting antiseptic. Rub a thin layer of the oil onto your skin three times a day, and continue using it for two weeks after the jock itch clears up. If the pure oil irritates your skin, dilute it first; mix 10 drops into 2 tablespoons **calendula cream**. Apply it to the affected site twice a day. Never ingest tea-tree oil.

What to Wear

~ Wear **loose, breathable clothing**. Body-hugging clothes heat up your groin, making jock itch more likely.

Should I call the doctor?

If the itchy area has blisters, or if the itch doesn't clear up after a few weeks of self-treatment, talk to your doctor. You might have something other than jock itch, such as an allergic reaction to some irritant in your clothing or the laundry detergent you use. In rare cases, jock itch is associated with serious illnesses such as diabetes or cancer.

Tried...

Apple cider vinegar is a useful remedy for jock itch.

...and true

Vinegar is acidic, and fungi cannot thrive in an acidic environment. Using a fresh cotton ball, apply vinegar to the jock itch once a day.

🍃 For men who wear a jock strap while working out, it's a good idea to wear **cotton underwear** under the jock strap. The cotton absorbs sweat and protects tender skin.

🍃 The **socks** you wear should be made of **acrylic** or other fabric that wicks away perspiration.

Clean and Dry Does the Trick

🍃 After a workout (or any other activity that leaves you hot and sweaty), **don't linger in sweat-soaked clothes**. Shower promptly, then put on fresh underwear and clean clothes. The idea is to get the fungus-fueling sweat away from your skin as soon as possible. Likewise, don't stay in a wet bathing suit any longer than necessary.

🍃 Always **wash exercise clothes** before wearing them again.

🍃 If you have athlete's foot, **put your socks on before your underwear**. Otherwise, when you pull on your underwear and it touches your bare feet, you might be spreading fungus to your groin.

🍃 Don't dig a towel out of the laundry basket and use it again. Fungus thrives in moist, dark conditions, and you're likely to get another infection.

🍃 After bathing, dry your groin using a **hair dryer** set on its coolest setting.

Take a Powder

🍃 When you get dressed or change your underwear, dust your groin with **talc or baby powder**. It will absorb moisture and help keep the skin dry.

🍃 **Goldenseal powder** is a kind of "grown-up" version of baby powder; in addition to absorbing moisture, it contains substances with anti-inflammatory and antibacterial properties. Look for it in health-food stores.

Look to Lose Weight

🍃 If you're overweight and have extra skin folds, **shed some pounds**. Folds of skin tend to be warm and damp, providing more areas for fungus to set in.

Kidney Stones

It's been said that the pain of passing a kidney stone is comparable to that of giving birth. Whether that's true or not, you'll probably want to stay home and take over-the-counter pain relievers to take the edge off this experience. You can also place a hot-water bottle over the painful area to provide some measure of relief. After that, it's a waiting game. The stones might pass in a few hours, but sometimes it takes days. Fortunately, you can take measures to speed up the process a little.

Flush It Out

🌱 To flush the stone into the bladder, drink at least **three liters of water** a day. If you're gulping enough water to do the job, your urine should run clear, with not a trace of yellow.

🌱 During an attack, drink as much **dandelion tea** as you can. A strong diuretic, dandelion stimulates blood circulation through the kidneys, increasing urine output and helping to flush out the stone. To make the tea, add 2 teaspoons dried herb to 1 cup boiling water. Steep for 15 minutes, then drink.

🌱 Consider drinking two or three cups daily of **corn silk, buchu, or couch grass tea.** Like dandelion, these herbals have diuretic properties to help flush out and prevent kidney stones.

Stepping Stone

🌱 When you have a kidney stone, the slightest move is likely to be painful. But if you can bear to **take a walk**, try to do it. Walking may jar the stone loose. Despite the discomfort, you might pass the stone more quickly if you just keep moving.

An Old Saw

🌱 As soon as you have symptoms of a kidney stone, take two 160-milligram capsules of **saw palmetto.** If the stone does not pass right away, continue taking the same daily dose until it does. The blue-black fruit of the saw palmetto, which has been called "plant catheter" and "old man's friend," has long been used as a home remedy for urinary and prostate prob-

What's wrong

The pain in your back and side is so excruciating that you feel as if you might vomit. The cause: A nasty nugget formed from crystals that separate from the urine and build up on the inner surfaces of the kidney. Now that tiny stone wants to exit via the ureter, the spaghetti-thin tube that empties the bladder. Up to 80 percent of stones are made of calcium in combination with oxalate or phosphate. Less common are stones composed of uric acid or cystine. Heredity, chronic dehydration, repeated urinary tract infections, and a sedentary lifestyle are all thought to contribute to kidney stone formation.

Should I call **the doctor?**

Most stones pass without a doctor's help, but the first time you get one, it's inevitable that you'll call the doctor. With pain like this, you definitely want to report your symptoms. They include nausea and vomiting, bloody or cloudy urine, needing to urinate but not being able to, a burning sensation upon urination, or fever and chills (which may indicate infection). Even if you've had kidney stones before, call your doctor if the pain becomes excruciating. Severe cases may require hospitalization and narcotic painkillers.

lems. Saw palmetto relaxes the ureter, which makes it easier to pass a stone.

The Power of Prevention

◦ Many experts believe that the single most important thing you can do to prevent kidney stones is the same thing you do to make them pass more quickly—that is, drink enough fluids. Anyone who is prone to kidney stones should drink at least **8 to 10 cups of water a day**, every day. The more you drink, the more you dilute the substances that form stones.

◦ Stick to a **low-sodium diet** to reduce the calcium in your urine, which may reduce your risk of forming new stones. A good start: Limit your consumption of fast foods, canned soups, and other processed foods. The target is less than 2,400 milligrams of sodium a day.

◦ Drink two 250-milliliter glasses of **cranberry juice** each day. Research suggests that it may help reduce the amount of calcium in the urine. In a study of people with calcium stones, cranberry juice reduced the amount of calcium in the urine by 50 percent.

◦ If you don't like cranberry juice, drink **orange juice** or **lemonade**—200 milliliters at each meal. The citric acid these juices contain will raise the citrate level in your urine, helping to keep new calcium stones from forming.

◦ **Magnesium** has been shown to prevent all types of kidney stones. Eat more foods rich in this mineral, such as dark-green leafy vegetables, wheat germ, and seafood. You can also take 800 milligrams a day in supplement form.

◦ Ramp up your intake of fruits and vegetables, which are rich in **potassium**. In studies, people who ate a lot of produce

Strain and Tell

As distasteful as it may sound, most experts recommend that during an acute attack, folks with kidney stones urinate through a piece of gauze, cheesecloth, or a fine-mesh strainer. Why? So you can catch a stone, should you pass one, and take it to your doctor. The doctor will have it analyzed to find out whether it's composed of calcium oxalate, calcium phosphate, uric acid, or other substances. Based on that analysis, you can make specific dietary changes to prevent a recurrence.

slashed their risk of kidney stones by half. If you suffer from stones regularly, ask your doctor whether potassium supplements might help you ward off future attacks.

꙳ **Cut back on coffee**. Caffeine increases calcium in the urine, which increases the risk of stone formation.

꙳ If you know your stones are made of calcium oxalate (a urine test can tell you), **cut back on foods rich in oxalates**. These foods include spinach, chocolate, wheat bran, nuts (especially peanuts), strawberries, and raspberries. Also avoid black tea, which is high in oxalates.

꙳ If you have had uric-acid stones in the past, you need to keep your urine as alkaline as possible to prevent a recurrence. **Avoid foods that raise acid levels**, including anchovies, sardines, organ meats, and brewer's yeast. Also, don't eat more than 100 grams of meat or more than one serving of oatmeal, tuna, ham, lima beans, or spinach a day.

꙳ **Calcium** in the diet may help prevent calcium oxalate stones, probably because calcium combines with oxalate in the intestine and so prevents the body's absorption of pure oxalate. Foods rich in calcium include milk, cheese, yogurt, dark green leafy vegetables, nuts, and seeds. Taking calcium supplements during or just after meals may have a similar effect, but taking them between meals can increase the risk of stones.

Laryngitis

If you have laryngitis, the best way to recover your voice is to spend a week at the library. In other words: Shhhhh! As in … don't even whisper. (It seems strange, but a whisper strains vocal cords as much as a shout.) Resting your vocal cords will help keep them from developing more serious problems, such as bleeding or the formation of nodules, polyps, or cysts. And as you give your voice a time-out, try one or more of these soothing remedies.

What's wrong

Your throat is sore and you can't make a sound. You've got laryngitis, an inflammation of the larynx (voice box), the part of the windpipe that houses your vocal cords. Normally, the vocal cords open and shut when you speak. When the vocal cords swell, they vibrate differently, which causes hoarseness. Along with overusing your voice, laryngitis can be caused by colds and other viral infections, smoking, allergies or a sinus infection, exposure to irritants like dust or fumes, and some medical conditions such as bronchitis and heartburn.

Don't Clear the Air

🌿 Whatever you do, **resist the urge to cough** or clear your throat. Either can damage your vocal cords. Try to squelch the feeling by sipping a glass of water or simply swallowing.

Float Your Throat

🌿 Drink at least six to eight glasses of warm or lukewarm (not hot) **water** a day. Fluid keeps your larynx moist, which is critical to curing laryngitis.

🌿 Other warm liquids, such as **chicken broth**, can also help ease the discomfort.

🌿 Herbalists recommend soothing laryngitis with teas made from **horehound** and **mullein**. Horehound, a hairy-leaved plant in the mint family, is a source of the famous horehound candy that has long been a cough remedy. Mullein contains gelatinous mucilage, which soothes irritated tissues. To make the teas, put 1 or 2 teaspoons dried herb (available in health-food stores) in 1 cup boiling water, steep for 10 minutes, strain, and drink. Drink one to three cups a day.

🌿 An old folk remedy for laryngitis is to drink a mixture of 2 teaspoons **onion juice** followed by a "chaser" of 1 teaspoon **honey**. Take those 3 teaspoonfuls every 3 hours. To get onion juice, press an onion half between two plates and collect the juice that runs out.

🍃 Try mixing up a tablespoon of **honey**, some **lemon juice**, and a pinch of **cayenne pepper** and sip the mixture. Repeat as often as necessary.

Steam Your Vocal Cords

🍃 **Inhale the steam** from a bowl of hot water for 5 minutes, two to four times a day. To help trap the steam, drape a towel over your head, forming a tent around the bowl, and breathe in deeply. The steam will help restore the lost moisture in your throat and accelerate healing.

🍃 For more powerful healing, add four to six drops of antiseptic and anti-inflammatory essential oils, such as **lavender, sandalwood,** or **chamomile,** to your bowl of hot water.

🍃 Make a **hot compress** using mullein, sage, thyme, or hyssop tea. Apply the compress to your throat, then wrap a dry towel around your neck to keep the heat in.

The Power of Prevention

🍃 **Breathe through your nose.** Your nasal passages are natural humidifiers. Mouth-breathing, on the other hand, exposes the voice to dry, cold air.

🍃 Use a **cold-air humidifier** in your bedroom. Your vocal cords are lined with mucosa that needs to be kept moist in order to repel irritants.

🍃 When you travel by plane, chew **gum** or suck on **lozenges.** The cabin air is excessively dry, and your vocal cords suffer. If you keep your mouth closed and increase saliva production, you help prevent dehydration.

🍃 Check with your doctor to see if a drug you're taking might be the cause of your hoarseness. Certain **drugs**, including **blood-pressure** and **thyroid medications** and **antihistamines**, can be very **drying to your throat**.

🍃 **If you smoke, quit**. It's a major cause of throat dryness. And avoid smoky bars, clubs, and restaurants too.

Should I call **the doctor?**

Usually laryngitis isn't serious, and you'll have your voice back in a few days. But if you're still hoarse after four or five days, let your doctor know. Persistent, unexplained hoarseness needs evaluation, especially if you're a smoker or tobacco chewer. It can be a sign of cancer. Also make the call if you're coughing up blood or wheezing. And see a doctor immediately if your laryngitis is accompanied by pain so severe that you have trouble swallowing. The upper part of your larynx may be swelling so much that it could block your breathing passages and become life threatening.

Memory Problems

Do you remember the title of the last book you read? Do you scratch your head and wonder whether you've taken your pills this morning? Are names sometimes just beyond your brain's reach? While forgetfulness isn't necessarily a sign that something's wrong, it can be frustrating. Memory boosters and simple do-it-yourself remedies can help sharpen your memory now and keep it honed for years to come.

What's wrong

Whether you have "senior moments" when you can't remember where you put your keys or glasses, or you forget names, memory lapses can be disconcerting. Aging is the main culprit. As we get older, there are changes in the way the brain stores information, making it harder to recall facts. Physical problems, including thyroid disorders, can affect memory, as can medications, including those for high blood pressure and anxiety. Alzheimer's disease also causes memory problems, but the symptoms are much more severe than the more common, normal memory lapses.

Catch a Whiff

At a health-food store, purchase a small bottle of either **rosemary** or **basil** essential oil. Tests of brain waves show that inhaling either of these scents increases the brain's production of beta waves, which indicate heightened awareness. All you need to do is put a trace of the oil in your hair, wrists, or clothing—anywhere you can get a whiff. Or put some of the oil in a diffuser, and let it fill the air.

Count on Coffee

If you drink **caffeinated beverages**, you'll get a short-term boost in your ability to concentrate. And there may be long-term benefits as well. At the Faculty of Medicine in Libson, Portugal, researchers concluded that elderly people who drink three or four cups of coffee a day were less likely to experience memory loss than people who drank a cup a day or less.

Give It Oxygen!

Take 120 milligrams of **ginkgo biloba** a day. The herb appears to improve blood flow to the brain, which helps brain cells get the oxygen they need to perform at their peak. In Germany, where the government's Commission E reports regularly on the effectiveness of herbal medicines, a standardized extract of ginkgo is frequently prescribed to prevent memory loss as well as stroke. If you're perfectly healthy, you probably won't see any effect from ginkgo. But if you have diminished blood flow to the brain, it may help.

Another way to increase the flow of blood to the brain is to **get moving**. There's even some evidence that exercise may increase the number of nerve cells in the brain. Any type of regular exercise, but especially aerobic exercise like walking and biking, will do. Exercise also helps prevent illnesses like diabetes, stroke, and high blood pressure, all of which can contribute to memory lapses.

Keep Your Blood Sugar Steady

New research has uncovered a link between mild glucose intolerance and age-related memory loss. Food converted by the digestive system to glucose (blood sugar) is the main fuel that powers the organs, including the brain. But many people, especially those past their youth, have poor glucose tolerance, meaning they have trouble processing glucose out of the bloodstream and into cells. According to the new research, even mild, nondiabetic glucose intolerance appears to reduce short-term memory in middle age and beyond. What to do? Eat **reasonably sized meals** at **regular hours**, emphasizing fiber-rich **whole grains** and **vegetables** over "white" carbohydrates such as white pasta, white bread, potatoes, and white rice.

Focus on good fats—those found in **vegetable oils, nuts, seeds, avocados**, and **fish**. They help keep your blood sugar steady without clogging your arteries.

Lace up your walking shoes! **Regular exercise** is another way to prevent blood sugar problems.

Smarten Up Your Diet

The brain is 85 percent **water**. So if you're not drinking at least eight 250-milliliter glasses a day, it's time to get into the habit. Dehydration leads to fatigue, which can take its toll on memory.

Make sure that you get enough of the **B vitamins** in your diet. These include vitamins B_6, B_{12}, niacin, and thiamin. These nutrients help make and repair brain tissue, and some of them help your body turn food into mental energy. Bananas, chickpeas, and turkey are rich in vitamin B_6; whole grains and meat are good sources of all the Bs. Nuts and seeds, wheat germ, and fortified breakfast cereals are other good sources of B vitamins.

While you're eating more of the good stuff, **cut back on foods high in saturated fat**. You probably already know that

Should I call **the doctor?**

There's really no way that you, on your own, can determine the seriousness of memory problems. So schedule an appointment with your doctor if you feel that your memory has gotten significantly worse in the past six months. Make an immediate appointment (or have a loved one or a friend make one for you) if you have trouble remembering how to do things you've done many times before or can't remember how to get to a familiar place. Also call if you have trouble accomplishing activities that involve step-by-step instructions, such as following a recipe.

it clogs the arteries that feed the heart. But high-fat foods also clog arteries that feed the brain, which reduces the supply of oxygen that reaches your noggin. Just as bad as saturated fats are the **trans fats** found in soft margarine and many packaged baked goods and snack foods.

🖚 Eat **fish** two or three times a week. Cold-water fish such as salmon, mackerel, herring, and tuna contain omega-3 fatty acids. You probably know these fats are good for your heart because they help "thin" the blood and prevent clogged arteries; they're good for your brain for the same reasons.

Buy Extra Insurance

🖚 Take a **multivitamin** every day. Make certain it has 100 percent of the DV (daily value) of folic acid and B$_{12}$, as it's difficult to get enough of these vitamins in your diet. Even moderate shortfalls may contribute to mental decline.

Sound Out the Problem

🖚 **Listen to music** often, and sample various types. Researchers have found that listening to music can improve your ability to concentrate and help you remember what you've learned. Some types of music actually cause brain neurons to fire more quickly. The faster the beat, the more the brain responds.

Challenge Your Thinker

🖚 If you're really motivated to sharpen your memory, take up a **musical instrument.** Whether you want to play the drums or the piano, learning to play will develop your motor skills while it fine-tunes your brain's ability to analyze and focus.

🖚 Go out of your way to stay mentally active. A study conducted on nuns, known as the Nun Study, found that those with the most education and language abilities were less likely to develop Alzheimer's. But what really counts is not the amount of schoolbook learning you did—it's how much you actively use your mind. **Doing crossword puzzles, learning a second language**, or **playing Scrabble** can tickle your brain.

Put Stress in Its Place

🖚 Find ways to **reduce stress.** Tense people have high levels of stress hormones in their bodies. Over time, these hormones

Mental Gymnastics

Try these fun exercises to challenge your brain and help you perfect the art of recall:

MEMORY BOOSTER #1

Want to grow some new brain circuitry? Several times a day, use the "wrong" hand to do an everyday task. For example, if you normally brush your teeth with your right hand, use your left instead. If you always zip up your jeans with your left hand, use your right. The brain "knows" when you're using the wrong hand, because of the sensory and motor information it receives from that hand. It's that "confusion" that stimulates new brain circuits, as the brain struggles to master a new task. (Stick to the simple tasks, though. You don't want to try this when you're using a power drill.)

MEMORY BOOSTER #2

If you're trying to remember how to spell a word, think of the word as an acronym and expand it into a sentence. Many kids learned to spell "arithmetic" by remembering the line "A Rat In The House Might Eat The Ice Cream." You can use the same trick to memorize lists. Need to stop at the Library, Post Office, and Drugstore? Make up a phrase like "Larry Plays On the Drums." Or you may have a shopping list that includes Jam, Apples, Paper towels, Eggs, Milk, and Cheese. How about "Jane And Polly Eat Moldy Cheese"?

MEMORY BOOSTER #3

Need to remember which errands you have to run? Make up a short story—the more fantastic, the better—about them. Suppose your list includes bank, library, drugstore, and a stop at your friend Fred's to return a book you borrowed. The story might go like this: "Frantic Fred, a renowned drug addict, robbed the bank at gunpoint and then hid in the library."

can affect the hippocampus, the part of the brain that controls memory. You don't have to chant or meditate—just do something that's simple and fun, from swinging in a hammock to finger painting with your children or grandchildren.

⤳ Consider taking **Siberian ginseng**, which helps protect the body from the effects of stress and is said to heighten mental alertness. Buy a liquid extract and follow the dosage directions on the label.

Favorite Food of Elephants

⤳ **Gotu kola**, an herb elephants love, has been used to increase mental acuity for thousands of years. There is some research to support the use of the herb to boost memory. Buy a standardized extract and take 200 milligrams three times a day.

Menopause Problems

You may feel as if your body is out of control and you never know what unpleasant surprise it may hold in store for you. Maybe you awaken in the middle of the night drenched in sweat, or you suffer from irritability, annoying mental "fuzziness," and memory lapses. First, remember that menopause doesn't last forever. Then try these approaches for relief in the meantime.

What's wrong

A woman is officially done with menopause when she hasn't menstruated for one year. But in the years preceding menopause, called perimenopause, her ovaries are producing less of the female sex hormones estrogen and progesterone, while ovulation (the monthly release of an egg) also becomes less frequent. This hormonal ebb can result in a variety of uncomfortable symptoms, including hot flashes and night sweats, vaginal dryness, mood swings, sleep problems, and unusually light or heavy periods.

Say Yes to Soy

🌭 Eat 200 to 250 grams of **tofu** every day. Tofu is high in phytoestrogens—compounds with mild estrogen-like qualities that have been found to ease menopausal symptoms. Certain kinds of phytoestrogens, called isoflavones, found in soy products can help ease hot flashes and vaginal dryness. The recommended amount is 60 milligrams a day of isoflavones, which is what you'll get by eating 200 to 250 grams of tofu.

🌭 One 50-milligram supplement of **isoflavones**, taken daily, can meet most of your needs when you can't eat a lot of tofu. Look for brands that contain genistein and daidzein. One widely available brand, Promensil, has both of these components and is often recommended by doctors.

🌭 **Flaxseeds** are another source of phytoestrogens. Grind some in a spice grinder and add 1 to 2 tablespoons to cereal or yogurt.

Don't Sweat It

🌭 To help control hot flashes and night sweats, take ½ to 1 milliliter of **black cohosh** in tincture form two to four times a day. To make it more palatable, add the tincture to half a glass of juice or water. Research has shown that the herb helps control hot flashes by lowering blood levels of luteinizing hormone (LH), which dilates blood vessels and sends heat to the skin. You might get other benefits as well, since some women have found that black cohosh can relieve vaginal dryness, nervousness, and depression. For maximum effectiveness, take black cohosh for 6 weeks, then take four weeks off before resuming it again. Then repeat the cycle—6 weeks on, 4 weeks off.

➤ To tame night sweats, take 3 to 15 drops **sage tincture** three times a day in a half-cup water or tea. The genus name of this herb, *Salvia,* comes from the Latin *salvere* (to heal), and the extract of salvia leaves has been used to treat more than 60 different health complaints. The herb has astringent qualities that can help quell profuse sweating.

➤ Some women find that taking **vitamin E** can help to relieve hot flashes and night sweats as well as mood swings and vaginal dryness. The recommended dose is 800 milligrams a day (400 milligrams twice a day). Consult your doctor before you start taking it regularly. This is especially important if you have diabetes, bruise easily, or have high blood pressure.

➤ To help stay cool, wear lightweight clothing made of **natural fibers**. And carry a small, battery-powered **fan** with you to cool off the hot flashes.

➤ Some women find that taking a **tepid bath** in the morning for 20 minutes prevents hot flashes all day long.

Exert Yourself

➤ Increase the amount of **aerobic exercise** you get until you're getting at least twenty minutes a day. Besides helping you lose weight, exercise has other positive effects for women going through menopause. Studies show that daily vigorous physical activity decreases hot flashes and night sweats, helps improve mood and sleep, and improves the balance of hormone levels. Weight-bearing activities like walking, running, and resistance training also help keep your bones sturdy.

Should I call the doctor?

Menopause isn't a disease, of course. It's a milestone. And some women don't even have symptoms. But many women do, and the discomfort can run the gamut from mildly annoying to extremely bothersome. If you're experiencing changes in your cycle—like irregular periods or unusual flow— see your doctor to make sure the changes are related to menopause and not a medical problem. If you have urinary discomfort, see a doctor to check for bladder infections, which occur more frequently among women who have vaginal dryness. Also, schedule an appointment if you miss a period or you develop vaginal bleeding between periods, or if you just don't feel like yourself because of your symptoms.

A Liver Saver

If you take synthetic hormones, you might have symptoms related to excess hormone levels—such as breast tenderness, bloating, or headaches. But some of these symptoms can be alleviated with milk thistle, an herb that helps the liver clear away some byproducts from the synthetic hormones. Milk thistle also helps repair and regenerate liver cells. The recommended dose is 420 milligrams a day in divided doses. Take that amount for 6 to 8 weeks, then taper down to 280 milligrams a day in divided doses.

Skip it!

Some women turn to progesterone creams or suppositories to ease menopause symptoms. But doctors and researchers are concerned that overuse of progesterone might raise the risk of breast cancer. Talk to your doctor before using the cream.

Stay Chaste

☙ The berries of the **chaste tree** have been used by women for some 2,000 years. They help restore progesterone levels, which decrease significantly during menopause. Chaste tree may be particularly useful for combating very heavy bleeding, which some women experience during perimenopause. It may also help with other symptoms, including hot flashes and depression. Take 1 to 2 teaspoons of a standardized extract once a day.

Meal Plans

☙ If you've been getting hot flashes, **stay away from alcohol, coffee, spicy foods**, and **hot drinks**. Many of these foods are triggers.

☙ To help prevent accelerating bone loss—osteoporosis—make sure you get enough **protein**. It doesn't take much chicken, fish, or meat to supply your daily requirement for protein. As long as you have a serving that's about equal to the size of a deck of cards, you're getting enough. Also make sure you get 1,500 to 2,000 milligrams of **calcium** per day plus **vitamin D**. Low-fat dairy products are good sources. A cup of skim milk, for instance, provides 300 milligrams of calcium, as well as supplemental vitamin D. But to be on the safe side, take 1,500 milligrams in supplement form a day.

Look to Lubricants

☙ Vaginal dryness, the result of waning estrogen levels, may dampen your interest in sex. Try a **water-soluble lubricant**, such as K-Y Silk-E or K-Y Jelly. Avoid oil-based lubricants such as petroleum jelly. Studies suggest that the oil-based kind don't work as well and can actually increase irritation if used long-term.

Menstrual Problems

Long ago, people used to believe that the presence of a menstruating woman could turn milk sour and make meat go bad. Beliefs have changed—now the assumption is that menstruation turns moods sour and makes tempers go bad. Preconceptions aside, there are ways to make the cycles easier. When you need quick relief from cramps or lower-back pain, ibuprofen (the active ingredient in Advil and Motrin) can help. In addition, there are many other ways to find relief and—with patience and foresight—prevent next month's discomfort.

Take Anti-Cramp Action

What's **wrong**

⤸ When you feel cramps coming on, go for a walk or run. Or jump in the pool for a swim. Or get on an exercise bike. Any kind of **exercise** (including sex!) helps inhibit prostaglandin production and boosts the release of painkilling endorphins. As a bonus, exercise can also help relieve bloating.

⤸ Soak in a tub of **hot water**. The warmth helps relax knotted-up muscles in the uterus. Or lie down with a hot water bottle or heating pad on your abdomen.

⤸ Try a homeopathic remedy. For severe cramps experts recommend **mag phos** (phosphate of magnesia). Take five pellets of 6C or 12C every hour for five doses. If the cramps don't improve, take the same dosage of **nux vomica** or **pulsitilla**. Nux vomica is usually recommended for cramps that are accompanied by constipation and extreme irritability, and pulsitilla is advised when you find yourself not only cramping, but weeping as well.

Tame Cramps with Tea

⤸ During the day, have three cups of warm **red raspberry-leaf tea**. (Look for raspberry-leaf tea bags at the grocery store or a health-food store.) Raspberry leaves contain fragrine, a substance that tones the uterus and helps ease cramping. It can also lighten excessive bleeding.

⤸ As its name implies, **cramp bark** (*Viburnum opulus*) can

Cramps, bloating, backache, nausea, headache, and fatigue—any or all of these menstrual problems can result from hormonal fluctuations in a woman's monthly cycle. Some of them are related to prostaglandins, hormone-like substances that cause the muscles in the uterus to tighten, leading to cramping. During the 7 to 10 days before your period, there's also a drop in production of the hormone progesterone, which causes your body to retain salt and water. And an imbalance between progesterone and the hormone estrogen contributes to emotional symptoms such as depression, anxiety, and irritability.

Should I call the doctor?

Give your doctor a call if your cycles are shorter than 21 days, or if you go more than 35 days between menstrual periods. You'll also want to contact the doctor if you bleed heavily for more than a week, quickly soaking through your tampons or pads, or if you pass large clots of blood. (Small clots, no larger than the size of a quarter, are normal.) And the doctor might help if you experience severe cramps that over-the-counter medication can't relieve.

take the edge off cramps. Buy the dried bark and make a tea using 1 teaspoon bark in 1 cup water, or buy the tincture and follow the dosage directions on the label.

～ Good old **chamomile tea** has antispasmodic properties to unclench your uterus. Use 2 to 4 teaspoons of herb per cup of hot water, or buy chamomile tea bags. Peppermint is another antispasmodic herb.

～ **Ginger** is another tried-and-true cramp remedy. It's thought to work by inhibiting the production of prostaglandins. To make the tea, grate 1 teaspoon fresh gingerroot, add 1 cup hot water, steep for 10 minutes, then strain.

Beat the Bloat

～ To deal with bloating, **reduce the salt** in your diet and take **vitamin B$_6$** during your period. During the week before your period, use the saltshaker as little as possible and also cut back on other high-sodium foods, such as packaged meats, canned soups, and salty snacks. Meanwhile, take 25 to 50 milligrams of vitamin B$_6$ every day. This vitamin appears to have a mild diuretic effect.

Manage the Flow

～ Every day take 1,000 milligrams of **vitamin C** and 1,000 milligrams of **bioflavonoids** in divided doses—500 milligrams of each in the morning, then another 500 milligrams in the evening. Both supplements help strengthen the walls of the blood vessels to reduce excessive bleeding. Bioflavonoids are found in grape skins, blackberries, blueberries, and citrus fruits, especially in the pulp and white rind.

～ **Chaste tree**, typically used as a PMS remedy, also helps regulate the menstrual cycle by balancing levels of sex hormones. (In men it can lower libido, so in days of old it was fed to priests, hence the name chasteberry.) Try it to lighten a heavy flow. The dosage is 40 drops (in tincture form) or 225 milligrams (in capsule form) a day.

The Power of Prevention

～ Every day take 1,000 milligrams of **calcium citrate**. Calcium is a natural tonic and muscle relaxer. It helps to reduce

the ferocity of menstrual cramping. (Avoid coral-derived calcium, as it is subject to contamination with heavy metals.)

 Take 200 milligrams of **elemental magnesium** two or
three times a day. The supplements come in the form of magnesium glycinate, magnesium citrate, and magnesium oxide. All
help prevent menstrual cramps, but the citrate and oxide forms
also have a laxative effect. Use glycinate if you don't need to
worry about regularity.

 Essential fatty acids slow the production of prostaglandins, which contribute to cramps. Get your fill by taking
1,000 milligrams of **evening primrose oil** three times a day or
1 tablespoon of **flaxseed oil** a day (use it in salad dressings in
place of other oils).

 During the last 2 weeks of your cycle, take 15 drops of
black cohosh in tincture form three times a day. This herb is
an antispasmodic, which means it relaxes the uterus and reduces
cramping.

Did you know?

Women who enjoy
camping may be deterred
by rumors that the smell
of menstrual blood can
attract wild bears. A look
at the statistics suggests
otherwise. Judging from
records of campers who
have been attacked by
black bears or grizzlies,
menstruation is not a
factor in bear behavior.

Morning Sickness

You may be joyfully embracing the notion that a new life is growing inside you, but your body seems to be doing anything but. Considering how queasy you're feeling, you have a perfect right to mutter a few unprintable words and snap at your significant other now and then. But you also have a right to some relief. When your stomach feels like it's riding the seven seas, try these strategies to calm, soothe, and settle. But first, check with your doctor before ingesting any home remedy while you're pregnant.

What's wrong

When a pregnant woman has daily bouts of nausea, it's no surprise. But that doesn't mean it can be explained. Doctors think morning sickness—which doesn't necessarily occur in the morning—may be the result of rising levels of estrogen, mild dehydration (not enough water intake to keep your body wet enough on the inside), or the lower blood sugar characteristic of early pregnancy. Stress, traveling, some kinds of food, prenatal vitamins, and certain smells can aggravate the problem.

Give Your Tummy a Tasty Treat

⤺ Nothing beats morning sickness like a cup of **ginger tea**. The same spicy herb is used to counter motion sickness. To make ginger tea, boil 30 grams dried root (available in health-food stores) in 1 cup water for 15 to 20 minutes, strain, and sip.

⤺ Herbal teas made with **chamomile, lemon balm**, and **peppermint** are also known to reduce nausea. Use 1 to 2 teaspoons of dried herb per cup of hot water. Avoid peppermint tea if you have heartburn, however.

⤺ Brew yourself a cup of **red raspberry-leaf tea**. The herb is popular for a number of pregnancy problems, including morning sickness, and has been shown to relax the smooth muscles of the uterus. Use 1 to 2 teaspoons of dried herb per cup of hot water. But with this remedy in particular, check with your doctor before taking it. There is some evidence that raspberry leaf can cause uterine contractions, so your doctor might advise against taking it later in the pregnancy or if you're at increased risk for miscarriage.

⤺ Drink flat, room-temperature **ginger ale** to settle your stomach. Although no one knows why (there's not enough ginger in commercial ginger ale to have an effect), it works for many nauseated moms-to-be. Don't drink ginger ale with fizz, though. The bubbles promote the production of more stomach acid—just what you don't need.

⤺ Chew on **anise** or **fennel seeds**, which are known to soothe upset stomachs.

Feel Better with Bs

🍃 In studies, women who took 25 milligrams of **vitamin B$_6$** three times a day (a total of 75 milligrams per day) for three days reduced nausea and vomiting associated with pregnancy. As with other vitamins, if you're pregnant, don't take B$_6$ without your doctor's consent.

Wristy Business

🍃 Try wearing the **acupressure wristbands** designed for people who get seasick. Available in drugstores, they apply constant pressure to acupressure points for nausea.

🍃 If you can't find a wristband, **use your fingers to apply pressure**. Turn your arm over, forearm up. Locate the point about 4 centimeters (1½ inches) away from the base of your hand, dead center between the ligaments. Press this point with your thumb while you count slowly to 10. Repeat three to five times, or until the nausea subsides.

Drown the Queasies

🍃 **Water** is the best medicine! Amazing as it seems, women who drink a glass of water every hour have a lot less morning sickness. Also, drink a glass of water every time you get up in the night to go to the bathroom. This helps ensure you start your day feeling as good as you can. Peek at the toilet water before you flush. If you are drinking enough water, urine should be almost clear. If it's dark, sinks to the bottom, or has an extra-strong smell, you need to drink more.

🍃 If nothing wants to stay down, treat yourself to a **frozen-fruit bar**. It helps replace sugars lost through vomiting. And since a fruit bar is made with frozen water, it also helps keep you hydrated.

Should I call **the doctor?**

Despite how miserable you feel, morning sickness becomes cause for concern only If you can't keep down any foods or fluids and begin to lose a lot of weight. Give your doctor a call if nausea or vomiting continues after four months and home remedies aren't working. Call immediately if you are vomiting blood or a substance that looks like coffee grounds; if you lose more than one kilogram (two pounds); or if you have prolonged, severe vomiting, which can cause dehydration and malnutrition.

Is Morning Sickness Really a Good Sign?

People have long believed that if you suffer from morning sickness during pregnancy, you're less likely to miscarry. But is it true? Researchers at Penn State University say it is, but not because there's any direct connection between nausea and healthy nativity. As it turns out, older pregnant women are less likely to have morning sickness than are their younger counterparts, and they are also more likely to miscarry. So age is the real factor.

When Life Hands You Morning Sickness . . .

❧ Sniff a slice of **lemon**. Some pregnant women report that, for unknown reasons, it helps with morning sickness.

❧ You might also try drinking water with lemon or another **lemon-based drink**.

❧ Grate a bit of **grapefruit, orange**, or **tangerine rind** and add it to your tea.

Don't Run on Empty

❧ In the morning, you might be able to prevent nausea by putting something in your stomach before you even get out of bed. Keep some **crackers** by your bed and have a few as soon as you wake up.

❧ Eat a number of **small meals** throughout the day. Small amounts of food are much easier to tolerate than a large meal. In fact, you might want to have a snack every hour or two, keeping the servings small. Peanut butter on apple slices, a few nuts, or a slice or two of cheese are all good choices.

❧ **Take your prenatal vitamins with food** to help them stay down. Even a saltine cracker or wheat thin can help.

❧ **Avoid fried, fatty foods**, which tend to cause and intensify the nausea. It's not known why—perhaps because fatty foods are digested more slowly.

Smell No Evil

❧ If you're extremely sensitive to odors during this time, try to stay in **well-ventilated rooms** that don't accumulate cooking odors or cigarette smoke. And it's okay to ask your partner to brush his teeth more often to help you avoid nausea due to bad breath! This sensitivity usually passes by the twelfth to fourteenth week . . . so you're not going to be finicky forever.

Muscle Cramps

Something as simple as heat or massage can strong-hand cramps into submission. Once the agony is over, it's important to mount an anti-cramp campaign. Your body is probably yearning for potassium, magnesium, and calcium—the trio of minerals that helps regulate activity in your nerves and muscles. (You have potassium aplenty if you eat fruits and veggies, but you may be potassium poor if you're on a high-protein diet.) You'll also need to drink plenty of water and stretch your limits regularly.

Put the Heat On

⤆ Place an electric **heating pad** or a **hot washcloth** on the misbehaving muscle to relax the cramp and increase blood flow to the affected tissue. Set the pad on low, apply for 20 minutes, then remove it for at least 20 minutes before reapplying.

⤆ Take a long, warm shower, or soak in the bath. For added relief, pour in a half-cup **Epsom salt**. The magnesium in Epsom salt promotes muscle relaxation.

Press Out Pain

⤆ Find the epicenter of the cramp. Press into this spot with your thumb, the heel of your hand, or a loosely clenched fist. Hold the pressure for 10 seconds, ease up for 10 seconds, then press again. You're doing it right if you feel some discomfort, but not excruciating pain. After a number of repetitions, the pain from the cramp should start to diminish.

Rub It In

⤆ Mix 1 part **wintergreen oil** with 4 parts **vegetable oil**, and massage it into the cramp. Wintergreen contains methyl salicylate (related to aspirin), which relieves pain and stimulates blood flow. You can use this mixture several times a day, but not with a heating pad—you could burn your skin.

Banish Nighttime Leg Cramps

⤆ Before bed, drink a glass of **tonic water**, which contains quinine, a popular remedy for leg cramps. Research has sup-

What's wrong?

Sometimes you get a cramp during a workout. But it can also happen after some part of your body has remained frozen in one position for hours—say, gripping a pen or a paintbrush. In either case, the cramps are caused by overuse of a muscle, dehydration, stress, or fatigue. But if calves cramp painfully when you're trying to sleep, or a muscle often locks up for no apparent reason, the root cause is a faulty chemical signal from the nervous system that "tells" the muscle to contract. Often the problem is linked to an imbalance of potassium and sodium.

Should I call the doctor?

Muscle cramps are usually temporary and don't cause permanent damage. But give your doctor a call if the cramp or spasm lasts for more than a day, or if it continues to bother you despite trying home remedies. And call immediately if the spasm occurs in the lower back or neck and is accompanied by pain that radiates down your leg or into your arm, or if abdominal cramps occur in the lower-right-hand part of your belly, which could signal appendicitis.

ported the use of quinine for nocturnal leg cramps, but **don't take quinine tablets**; they can have serious side effects, such as ringing in the ears and disturbed vision. Quinine is not readily available in Canada because it can be dangerous to heart function.

➤ To prevent nighttime calf cramps, **try not to sleep with your toes pointed**. And don't tuck in your sheets too tightly—this tends to bend your toes downward, activating cramps.

➤ Take 400 to 800 IU of **vitamin E** to prevent nocturnal leg cramps. Studies suggest that taking vitamin E improves blood flow through the arteries.

Mind Your Minerals

➤ Low levels of minerals known as electrolytes—which include potassium, sodium, calcium, and magnesium—can contribute to cramps. You probably don't need any more sodium in your diet, but you may need more of the others. Good food sources of **magnesium** are whole-grain breads and cereals, nuts, and beans. You can get **potassium** from most fruits and vegetables, especially bananas, oranges, and cantaloupes. And dairy foods supply **calcium**.

➤ If you change your diet and you still get cramps, take 500 milligrams of **calcium** and 500 milligrams of **magnesium** twice a day, for a total of 1,000 milligrams of each supplement. Some people who get leg cramps due to a magnesium deficiency find fast relief from taking supplements. Don't take magnesium without calcium; the two minerals work as a pair.

➤ Taking a diuretic for high blood pressure? Your increased need to urinate may be robbing you of potassium. The result: a condition called **hypokalemia**, which can cause fatigue, muscle weakness, and muscle cramps. Ask your doctor if you can switch to a blood-pressure medication that isn't a diuretic.

Drink Your Fill

➤ Cramps are often caused by dehydration, so if you're getting frequent cramps, drink more **water**.

➤ If you tend to get cramps during exercise, drink at least 2 cups of water two hours before each workout. Then stop and drink 125 to 250 milliliters every 15 minutes during your exercise sessions. If you're sweating a lot, consider a **sports drink**, such as Gatorade, that replaces lost sodium and other electrolytes.

Do-It-Yourself Healing: Cramp-Quelling Stretches

Next time you get a cramp, stretch it out with one of these moves. Hold each stretch for 10 to 20 seconds and repeat three times.

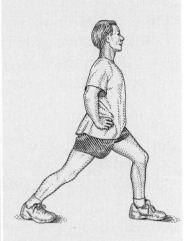

Nocturnal Cramps

If calf or foot cramps awaken you at night, do this stretch three times a day, especially before bedtime. Stand about 75 centimeters (30 inches) from a wall. Place your palms on the wall near eye level. Keeping your heels on the floor, gradually move your hands up the wall until you're reaching as high as you can. Hold, then return to the first position.

Calf Cramp

Stand with your legs apart, feet facing forward. Shift your weight to the front leg, keeping the back leg straight.

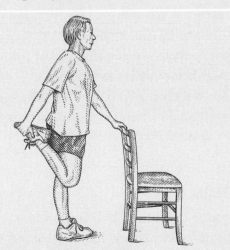

Front-Thigh Cramp

Holding on to a chair, bend the cramped leg and grab the foot, bringing the heel as close to your buttock as you comfortably can. Keep the knee pointing down.

Hamstring Cramp

Place the heel of the leg with the cramp on a low stool or step. Slowy lean forward from the waist until you feel a stretch at the back of your leg.

Nail Problems

There are people who really care for their nails, while others couldn't care less. Whether or not you're the manicure type, though, you'll want to seek some help when fingernails or toenails turn into eyesores. Here are some ways to get them back in shape fast with better nutrition, selected supplements, and fungus-fighters.

What's wrong

Apart from ingrown toenails (see page 248), nail fungus is probably the most disagreeable nail problem. When you get this affliction—usually on a toenail—the nail turns thick, discolored, and crumbly. Other nail problems include brittle nails, which can be the result of age or too much or too little moisture, or nutritional deficiencies. And certain skin diseases can affect the nails, including psoriasis (it can cause a thickening and pitting of the nails) and the patchy hair loss known as alopecia areata (it can cause ridged, pitted, rough nails).

Foil Fungus

To fight stubborn nail fungus, try **tea-tree oil**. A powerful antiseptic, it can help make nail fungus disappear. In fact, in one study it proved to be as effective as a prescription antifungal medicine. Once or twice a day, apply a drop or two to the discolored nail. A good time to do it is after you bathe or shower, when your skin is softest.

Alternatively, you can use an **antifungal powder** that absorbs moisture and prevents fungus. Some good ones are Tinacten powder or Dr. Scholl's powder. You can sprinkle a medicated antifungal powder into your socks too.

If your feet are sweaty when you get home, change into a **fresh pair of socks** right away. And if you have an office job, take along a pair of clean socks—especially on hot summer days—so you can change before you start work.

Don't clip your cuticles. When you do this, you're removing your nail's protective barrier. Fungi and bacteria find it easier to get a grip around the base of the nail after the cuticle is removed.

Say No to Weak Nails

Take 300 micrograms of **biotin**, a B vitamin, 4 to 6 times a day with food. Long ago, veterinarians learned that this vitamin could strengthen horses' hooves—and the hooves are made primarily from keratin, the same material that makes up human nails. If your nails are weak or brittle, biotin might be all you need to strengthen and thicken them. But it doesn't work right away. You'll need to take this treatment for six months or more before you see a noticeable difference.

➤ Drink a cup of **horsetail** or **nettle tea** once a day. These herbs are high in silica and other minerals that nails need to grow.

Eat for Beautiful Nails

➤ If your nails are brittle or flaking, try getting more essential fatty acids. These are found in foods such as **fatty fish** and **flaxseed** or **flaxseed oil**. If you don't eat much fish, take 1 tablespoon flaxseed oil a day (use it in place of other oil in salad dressing), or sprinkle ground flaxseeds on your cereal or other food.

➤ **Evening primrose oil** is another source of essential fatty acid. Take 1,000 milligrams three times a day with meals.

➤ If your nails have white spots, you may be deficient in **zinc**. Nuts, root vegetables, whole grains, meat, and shellfish are good sources of this mineral.

Moisturize and Protect

➤ For dry, brittle nails, rub **petroleum jelly** or a thick cream into your nails to hold moisture around and under your nails. If you do this at bedtime, slip a pair of thin cotton gloves on your hands before you to sleep.

➤ Wear **vinyl gloves** every time you wash dishes or do other household tasks that require you to immerse your hands in water. (Vinyl is best, because people with nail problems tend to have skin that is sensitive to rubber.)

➤ Avoid polish removers that contain acetone or formaldehyde. They're terribly drying to nails. Use **acetate-based** removers instead.

Should I call **the doctor?**

Unless you suspect you have an underlying nutritional deficiency, brittle nails are cosmetic issues rather than health issues. As for nail fungus, it's tenacious, and it can take months—or years— to clear up on its own, so ask a doctor if you might benefit from prescription medication.

Fake Nails Breed Fungus

For women who have problems with weak, soft, brittle nails, artificial nails can seem like a godsend. But if you want to avoid nail fungus, forgo the fakes, no matter how much you long for elegant nails. Artificial nails are glued on top of your real ones, and the gap in-between creates a breeding ground for fungus. Even worse, this is an area where you can develop a painful bacterial infection. Artificial nails are the most common cause of nail fungus in women.

Nauseau

When nausea tells you that something inside your stomach wants to get out, doctors agree that you shouldn't try to induce vomiting. But if it's going to happen naturally, then go ahead and let it. If you have a milder case of queasiness, try these tummy tamers to get your stomach feeling like it's back on dry land instead of tossing on stormy seas.

What's wrong

Nausea happens when the nausea and vomiting center in the brain stem is activated. It can be caused by motion sickness, morning sickness that accompanies pregnancy (see page 278), and the stomach flu. Sometimes it's a natural reaction to something you've eaten—something bad the body wants to get rid of. A concussion, heart attack, some types of cancer, and chemotherapy can also trigger nausea. So can prescription drugs and OTC medications.

Teas for the Queasy

🍃 One of the oldest and perhaps the best remedies is ginger, proven to allay both nausea and motion sickness. Try a warm cup of **ginger tea**. Peel away the root bark, then chop or grate the whitish part of the root until you have one full teaspoon. Put the gratings in a mug, add a cup of boiling water, cover with a saucer, and let it steep for 10 minutes. You can drink the tea when it's still warm or after it has cooled down a bit. If you don't have any fresh gingerroot, try eating a few gingersnaps or a piece of crystallized ginger.

🍃 Second to ginger is **peppermint**, which has a calming effect on the lining of the stomach. There are many brands of peppermint tea, sold in bags or loose-tea form, and you can drink a cup anytime you feel nauseous.

Sip Sweet Stuff

🍃 Drinks containing sugar are likely to calm a shaky stomach. One recommendation is **cola syrup**, which can be found in some pharmacies. If your drugstore doesn't have it, just open a bottle of cola and let it go flat, shaking it every once in a while to dispel the fizz. Drink it at room temperature.

🍃 Some people get great results with flat **7-Up** or **ginger ale**.

🍃 Create a homemade **anti-nausea syrup**. Put a half-cup white sugar and a quarter-cup water into a saucepan, turn the heat to medium, and stir steadily until you have a clear syrup. After the syrup cools to room temperature, take 1 to 2 tablespoons as needed.

Refill Your Fluids

If nausea leads to vomiting, you may lose a lot of salts and fluids. To recover—and avoid dehydration—you need to replace what you've lost. One way is to make a rehydration drink by dissolving 8 level teaspoons sugar and 1 teaspoon salt in 1 liter water. Drink small sips to start, then more as your stomach settles down. Alternatively, a sports drink such as Gatorade will do the trick.

Be Still

✎ When you're nauseated, **lie still**. Moving around disturbs the balance mechanism in your middle ear, which can worsen nausea and lead to vomiting. While you're lying down, place a cool washcloth on your forehead and focus on your breathing so you don't think as much about your stomach.

Press the Anti-Nausea Point

✎ Try this **acupressure** trick: Place your right thumb on the inside of your left forearm, about two thumb-widths from the crease of your wrist. Press firmly for about a minute, then move your thumb a little closer to your wrist and press for another minute. Repeat on the other forearm.

Calm with Carbs

✎ If you're hungry (despite the nausea) and you think you can handle it, eat some **toast** or a few **crackers**, foods that are high in carbohydrates. As your stomach starts to calm down, add a bit of light protein—cooked chicken breast, for instance. But don't eat foods that contain fat until you're feeling a lot better.

Should I call **the doctor?**

If you've been queasy for several days, tell your doctor. And be sure to call the doctor if you start to vomit profusely, if the vomit is bloody, if you've been unable to keep food or liquids down for 24 hours, or if you've taken a bad fall or had a severe blow to the head. Heart attacks are sometimes accompanied by nausea, so call immediately if your nausea is accompanied by severe, sudden chest pain.

Putting the Pressure On

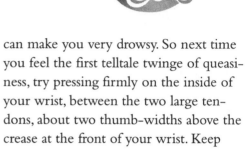

Who knew you could stop a toothache simply by pinching the web of skin between your thumb and index finger? Or fall asleep faster simply by pressing your index fingers against the center of your forehead, between your eyebrows?

Plenty of practitioners of acupressure, that's who. Think of this 5,000-year-old therapy as a do-it-yourself, no-needle version of acupuncture.

Acupressure requires nothing more than applying some pressure with your fingertips. When you press on specific points on your body, you rebalance or unblock qi (pronounced "chee"), a subtle form of energy that flows along pathways that crisscross the body like so many highways. At least that's the explanation given by practitioners of traditional Chinese medicine.

Western-trained doctors still aren't sure exactly how acupressure works, though recent studies suggest that these energy pathways do indeed exist and that finger pressure can cause the body to release natural painkillers known as endorphins. These morphine-like compounds ease muscle tension and promote better blood circulation while triggering a wonderful sense of well-being.

Acupressure is no substitute for proper medical care, nor does it guarantee push-button relief. But here's a sampling of what it can do for you:

Fight Nausea

When your stomach is topsy-turvy, you want relief—fast. Unfortunately, anti-nausea drugs don't always work, and they can make you very drowsy. So next time you feel the first telltale twinge of queasiness, try pressing firmly on the inside of your wrist, between the two large tendons, about two thumb-widths above the crease at the front of your wrist. Keep pressing until you feel better.

If you're planning a long trip by car or boat, you might want to pick up a set of the acupressure wristbands that are sold in many drugstores and marinas. These elastic bands have a small bead that automatically presses against the anti-nausea point in the wrists.

Acupressure is so effective at relieving nausea that some surgeons now use it to relieve nausea caused by anesthesia. In a recent study of 80 women who had undergone surgery, 40 received acupressure, while the other 40 received a sham treatment (finger pressure on a non–acupressure point). Only 16 of the women in the acupressure group continued to feel nausea, compared with 28 in the placebo group.

Tame Back Pain

What did you do the last time you threw out your back? If you're like most people, you swallowed a few painkillers and

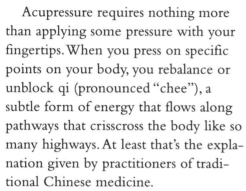

Pressure Pointers

How hard should you push when doing acupressure? Hard enough to cause mild pain, but no more. Skilled practitioners say the sensation is somewhere between strong pressure and outright pain.

If you bruise easily, have a history of orthopedic injuries, are taking a blood-thinning drug, have osteoporosis, or are pregnant, check with your doctor before trying acupressure.

crawled into bed. But painkillers can have side effects, and doctors now know that bed rest is just about the worst thing you can do for a bad back.

Many people have found that they can ease the pain with acupressure. All you need to do is press against the creases in the skin behind each knee while lying on your back with your knees bent and your feet flat on the floor. Next, lift your feet, gently rocking your legs back and forth for a minute or two.

Soothe Repetitive Strain Injuries

If you spend a lot of time writing, working a cash register, or surfing the Internet, there's a good chance you'll develop pain and tingling in the wrists, hands, or elbows. Acupressure is no panacea for this condition (known as repetitive strain injury, or RSI). But it can ease the pain a bit once it starts, and it is even more effective at preventing RSI in the first place.

- **Elbow pain:** Bend your arm so that your palm is facing your chest, then press against the elbow for a minute or two.

- **Hand pain:** Press against the web of skin on the back of the hand between the thumb and forefinger.
- **Wrist pain:** Press against the center of the crease on the back of the wrist.

Conquer Cold Symptoms

Acupressure helps fight colds in two ways. It stimulates the immune system, improving its ability to fight off cold viruses, and it helps ease nasal congestion.

Start by reaching over each shoulder (one at a time) to press the tender spots in the upper back. You're aiming for a spot between the spine and the tip of the shoulder blade. These points help stimulate the body's natural resistance to infection.

To ease congestion, press the inner corner of each eye (just next to the bridge of the nose) and then against the points at which the nostrils meet the upper lip. This four-point acupressure technique also helps relieve itching, burning eyes.

Ease Headaches

When headache pain strikes, it's only natural to rub your eyes. And no wonder. The area around the eyes is one of the main acupressure points for easing pain from tension headaches and migraines.

For maximum relief, press a spot about one centimeter above each eyebrow, directly above the pupils. Don't press too hard, or your headache might get worse. Next, apply pressure under the cheekbone, directly below the pupils. Press upward into the notch on the bottom of the cheekbone.

Neck and Shoulder Pain

Most of us have slept in a funny position or sat for too long in front of a computer or a project such as knitting or woodworking, only to endure painful neck or shoulder stiffness as a result. Or maybe you gabbed on the phone with the handset cradled between your ear and shoulder. Anti-inflammatory drugs such as aspirin or ibuprofen can help. But there are other ways to tame the tension.

What's wrong

Neck pain usually results from nothing more aggressive than staying in the same position too long. Shoulder pain is often caused by tendinitis—the inflammation of the cord that connects muscle to bone. But it could also be bursitis, resulting from inflammation of the sac, or bursa, that encases the shoulder joint. (See Bursitis and Tendinitis, page 96.) And sometimes shoulder pain is "referred pain"—it starts in the neck, but you feel it in the shoulder. Injury, arthritis, and Lyme disease are other causes of neck and shoulder pain.

Heal with Heat

🍃 Heat helps relieve pain, relaxes the muscles, reduces joint stiffness, and speeds healing. You can use a **heating pad** set on low, a **hot-water bottle**, or a **heat pack**. Or simply take a hot shower.

🍃 Moist heat eases a stiff, sore neck caused by muscular tension. Make a **neck compress** by soaking a towel in hot (not boiling) water. Fold the towel and wring it out well. Unfold and place it over the back of your neck and shoulders. Cover the wet towel with a dry one, and leave both in place for 10 minutes.

🍃 For easy, fast relief, simply set a **hair dryer** on warm and blow the air on your neck.

Go to Press

🍃 Try this simple trick: With your thumb or fingertips, apply **steady pressure** on the painful spot on your neck for three minutes. By the end of those 180 seconds, your pain should have lessened significantly.

🍃 A gentle **massage** can work wonders on neck and shoulder pain. Place the fingers of your left hand on the right side of your neck just below your ear, and stroke the muscles in a downward motion toward your collarbone. Do this three times and repeat on the other side. Use a massage oil or lotion and add a few drops of **lavender** or **geranium oil** to enhance the soothing effects.

Pick the Pepper Cure

- Apply an over-the-counter cream made with **capsaicin**, the compound in hot peppers. (Zostrix or Menthacin are available in drugstores.) Researchers with the U.S. Army in Texas found that people with chronic neck pain showed significant improvement when they used the cream four times a day for five weeks.

The Power of Prevention

- If you usually sleep on your stomach, you can do your neck a favor by **changing your nighttime posture**. Sleep on your back instead. And try using a special **neck-supporting pillow**, available at department stores and medical supply stores. You may also want to buy a new mattress if yours is old and lumpy.
- Make sure you sit in chairs that give you **good back and head support** (buy a lumbar support roll if you need one, or use a rolled-up towel or small pillow behind your lower back), and be sure not to hunch forward.
- Whether you're standing or sitting, keep your ear, shoulder, and hips in a **straight line**.
- Do you wedge your phone in the crook of your neck? To avoid neck strain, use a **headset** or **speakerphone** instead.
- If you're a woman with large breasts, an **athletic bra** can help relieve neck and shoulder pain. The bra offers more support, and because it has wider straps than a regular bra, it distributes the weight more evenly across your shoulders.
- Don't overload your shoulder bag. The bag not only puts weight on the shoulder, it also throws your posture out of alignment. The best alternative is a **fanny pack**. Then, for dressy occasions, carry a strapless purse.
- If you spend hours at a computer, make sure the **screen is set up** so that you don't have to bend your neck or tilt your head to see it.
- **Avoid wearing high-heeled shoes**. They contribute indirectly to neck pain by tilting your spine out of alignment, making your neck jut forward.
- **Wear a scarf** whenever the weather is cold and damp. Raw conditions can aggravate neck stiffness and pain.

Should I call **the doctor?**

If home remedies don't work and the pain lasts for more than three days, call your doctor. And let the doctor know right away if shoulder or neck pain starts immediately after a fall or accident. You'll probably need a doctor's help if you have the kind of pain that prevents you from lifting your arm above your head, or if you can't move your shoulder. And seek immediate attention if neck pain is accompanied by new—and sudden—head pain. It's rare, but you may have meningitis.

Do-It-Yourself Healing: Neck and Shoulder Pain

Shoulder Stretches

The best way to shrug off shoulder pain is to keep your shoulder muscles strong and flexible. The following exercises can be done in one session.

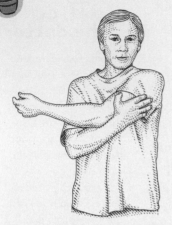  

Cross your left arm in front of your body. Use your right hand to press on the outside of the biceps and push the arm toward your collarbone. Press for 15 seconds, then release for 15 seconds and press again. Repeat five times, then switch sides.

Raise your left arm and bend it behind your head so your left hand touches the right shoulder blade. Then place your right hand on your left elbow and pull that elbow toward the right. Hold for 15 seconds, release for 15 seconds, and repeat 5 times. Switch sides.

To help resolve shoulder pain, hold a small soup can in one hand. Bend over, letting the weight-bearing arm hang straight. Keeping your shoulder relaxed, slowly trace a figure-eight with the soup hand. Repeat 10 to 20 times. Stop if you feel numbness, pain, or tingling.

Easy-Does-It Neck Relief

To relieve a sore neck, try these two stretches. Stretch slowly and smoothly, without any jerky motions that could tear a muscle or ligament.

Relax your neck muscles and let your head tilt to the left as far as it will go without straining your neck or lifting the shoulder. Hold for ten seconds. Return your head to an upright position. Then tilt your head to the right, hold it, and return to the upright position. Repeat four times.

Keeping your shoulders relaxed, slowly drop your head forward. Hold for 10 seconds. Repeat four times.

 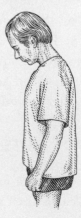

Nosebleed

They tend to occur at the most inopportune moments, and the sudden gushing of blood from your face can be both embarrassing and frightening, especially since a small amount can seem like liters when it's soaking tissue after tissue with crimson. Don't panic. Usually you can halt a nosebleed—and save face—in a matter of minutes. Here are some effective ways to do it.

Pinch, Press, and Spray

⮑ The simplest remedy for a bloody nose is the time-honored **pinch cure**. Sit up straight with your head tilted slightly forward (to keep the blood from running down your throat). Gently blow out any clots that could prevent a vessel from sealing. Then pinch the soft part of your nose and press firmly toward your face. Hold that position for at least 10 minutes.

⮑ Tired of pinching? Use a **clothespin**.

⮑ Still dripping? Wad up a small piece of **tissue or gauze**, then stick it between your gums and upper lip in the area right under your nose. Leave it there for 5 to 10 minutes. The tissue puts pressure on the blood vessels that are sending blood to your nose. There are countless versions of this remedy—pouring vinegar, witch hazel, or lemon juice on the tissue; using a small square of brown paper from a bag sprinkled with salt; even placing a dime or a small, flat button under your upper lip instead of a tissue.

⮑ Apply an **ice pack** alongside the bleeding nostril. The cold narrows the blood vessels in the nose to slow the spurting.

⮑ If your nose still doesn't stop dripping, sniff some **nasal spray**, such as Otrivin or Dristan Nasal Mist. Like ice, it will constrict the vessels in your nose, stanching the flow of blood.

The Power of Prevention

⮑ If you want to avoid nosebleeds, keep your mucous membranes moist by drinking eight 250-milliliter glasses of water a day. You are well hydrated if your urine is pale, not dark.

What's **wrong**

Maybe you ran into a door or blew your nose too hard. Now your nose is leaking—or pouring—blood. Regardless of the precipitating factor, a nosebleed occurs when blood vessels rupture inside a nostril. Often, that happens when the sensitive inner lining of the nose becomes irritated by dry indoor heat or air conditioning. People with high blood pressure or hardening of the arteries (atherosclerosis) are particularly vulnerable to bloody noses, along with those who take certain medications, including anti-inflammatory drugs such as aspirin or ibuprofen or blood thinners such as warfarin (Coumadin).

Should I call the doctor?

Call your doctor if your nosebleed is the result of a blow to the head, especially if the blood appears thin and watery (it suggests the presence of cerebral fluid). Also call if the nosebleed doesn't stop within 30 minutes, if you feel weak or faint, or if your nose bleeds frequently for no apparent reason. Anyone who has been diagnosed with high blood pressure should call his doctor if a nosebleed continues for more than 10 minutes.

➳ **Don't overdo the AC.** Air-conditioning dries out the air, leaving you more prone to nosebleeds.

➳ In winter, add moisture indoors by running a **humidifier**.

➳ Dab the insides of your nose with **petroleum jelly**, or spritz your nostrils liberally with a **saline nasal spray**. Either method will help keep nostrils moist. This approach is helpful if you're about to take a plane flight, if you've just recovered from a cold or sinus infection, or if you live in a very dry climate.

➳ **Watch your aspirin intake.** Aspirin can interfere with blood clotting, and of course that's not a good thing if you get frequent nosebleeds.

➳ If you have **nasal allergies**, treat them promptly. Between the constant irritation caused by allergens and the damage done by blowing your nose, nasal membranes take a real beating when you're having an allergic reaction.

➳ If you often have trouble with nosebleeds, take 1,000 to 1,200 milligrams of **vitamin C** every day to help prevent them. Vitamin C helps strengthen capillary walls and is also a vital component of collagen, a substance that gives your nostrils a moist, protective lining. Along with vitamin C, take 500 milligrams daily of a **bioflavonoid supplement** such as grape-seed extract, pine-bark extract, pycnogenol, or proanthocyanins. Flavonoids are known to heal capillaries.

Oily Hair

Does it look like someone put Vaseline in your hair? Are you weighed down by the weight of it? First, don't blame your hygiene habits, because your problem is probably hereditary. Fight back with the right shampoo—wash, rinse and be sure to *repeat*—and special oil-stopping rinses you make yourself.

Read Your Shampoo Bottle

ও Select a shampoo that's high in sodium lauryl sulfate and low in any kind of conditioners such as lanolin. What you want are **clarifying shampoos** that tend to strip oil from the scalp and the hair shaft.

ও Even if you don't have dandruff, you might get good results with a dandruff shampoo that contains **coal tar**. The formulas used for dandruff shampoos tend to dry out even the oiliest hair.

Do the Daily Double

ও It may seem obvious that you need to shampoo every day. But beyond that, you should **shampoo twice** every time you take a shower. Lather up, leave the shampoo on your hair for several minutes (that gives it time to remove the oil), rinse thoroughly, then repeat. Even on the second round, leave the shampoo in your hair for a few minutes before you rinse.

Change the Rinse Cycle

ও Rinsing your hair with water is fine, but you'll get even better results if you use a strong **rosemary tea**. Wonderfully aromatic, this herb contains essential oils that help control overproduction of oil on the scalp. To make the rinse, pour 1 cup boiling water over 2 tablespoons dried rosemary. Steep for 20 minutes, strain, cool, and pour into an empty plastic bottle. Keep the bottle in the shower and splash your hair with the tea after each shampoo. As long as the fragrance agrees with you, there's no need to rinse away the tea.

What's **wrong**

Your hair is lank, limp, matted to your head. It may even look dirty, although you washed it yesterday (or just hours ago). But don't blame your hair. Blame the oil-producing sebaceous glands that lie just beneath the surface of your skin. They secrete sebum, a mixture of fatty acids that protects your scalp. Some people's sebaceous glands pump out so much sebum that each hair becomes coated with the stuff. Genetics, stress, hormones, or a poor diet can contribute to the problem, as can birth-control pills that contain mostly androgen, a male sex hormone.

Can't Lather Up? Powder Up!

You're running late—there's no time to shower. But your hair looks like an oil slick. For an emergency "dry" shampoo, turn to your bottle of talcum powder. Sprinkle a small amount onto your hair, one section at a time. Lightly massage the powder first onto the scalp, then through your hair. The powder will absorb some of the oil. Voilà—an instant "shampoo." Remember: a *small* amount. Use too much, and you'll end up with dull tresses that appear just a shade whiter.

Should I call the doctor?

As physical challenges go, oily hair isn't a serious problem. Still, greasy hair can be embarrassing. If you're troubled by your hair's appearance, and the advice in this chapter doesn't solve the problem, you may want to schedule an appointment with a dermatologist.

🌿 Make a **lemon juice** rinse. Blend juice from 2 lemons into 2 cups of distilled water and pour into an empty shampoo bottle. After you shower, blot your hair dry and apply the mixture to your scalp. Leave it on 5 minutes, allowing the acidic lemon juice to work on the oil. Then rinse with cool water.

🌿 **Vinegar**, which is also acidic, can de-slick your hair too. Mix 1 cup vinegar with 1 cup water, then pour over your hair as a final rinse. Concerned about smelling like a salad? Don't worry, the smell will quickly fade.

Extreme Measures: Mouthwash

🌿 If your hair is extremely oily, you can mix a solution that will help slow your scalp's production of sebum. In a small cup, mix equal parts **witch hazel** with any commercial **mouthwash**. Both ingredients are astringents, which means they help tighten skin pores as they dry. Dip a cotton swab in the solution, then dab the swab on your scalp (not your hair) after you finish shampooing and rinsing.

Oily Skin

Look on the bright side: Oily skin tends to age better and develop fewer wrinkles than dry or normal skin. But it does require more attention, since you need to keep cleansing those overproductive pores. The key is a firm but gentle hand. You want to wash away dead skin cells, dirt, and excess oil without scrubbing so hard that you cause irritation. (Ironically, if you overdo the scrubbing, your skin produces even more oil.)

Washing Well

~ Wash your face with **hot water**. It dissolves oil more effectively than cool or lukewarm water.

~ Choose the **right cleanser**. Whether you prefer bar soap or liquid cleansers, avoid products, like Dove, that have added moisturizers. Bar soaps like Ivory, Dial, or Lever 2000 are perfectly effective, though you can also use cleansers formulated specifically for oily skin (they're likely to be more expensive).

~ If you're having acne outbreaks, choose an antibacterial soap formulated with **benzoyl peroxide** or **triclosan**. These discourage growth of acne-causing bacteria.

~ Use a liquid face wash that contains **alpha-hydroxy acids (AHAs)**, such as citric acid, lactic acid, or glycolic acid. The AHAs work in several ways, helping to slough off dead skin cells, reduce the oil in your pores, and combat infection.

Make Your Own Toner

~ After you've washed your face, soak a cotton pad in distilled **witch hazel** and dab it all around. Use it twice a day for two to three weeks. After the third week, apply it once a day. Witch hazel contains tannins, which have an astringent effect, making the pores tighten up as they dry.

~ The herbs **yarrow, sage**, and **peppermint** also have astringent properties. To make a homemade skin toner that will improve the look and feel of oily skin, put a tablespoon of one of these herbs in a cup, then fill to the top with boiling water. Let steep for 30 minutes. Strain the liquid and let it cool before

What's **wrong**

If you have oily skin, your sebaceous glands are pumping out an overabundance of sebum, the waxy substance that protects your skin. When there's too much, skin looks oily, and that overabundance of sebum may contribute to acne. Heredity plays a part: For instance, people with dark hair make more oil than fair-haired folks. But there are other contributing factors, including stress and changes in hormone activity. Pregnant women and those taking oral contraceptives are more likely to have problems with oily skin.

you dab it on your face. Whatever's left over can be stored in a squeeze bottle. It will stay fresh for three days at room temperature, or five days if you keep it in the refrigerator.

~ **Hyssop**, a member of the mint family, also makes an excellent herbal toner. In folk medicine it's considered good for the complexion. Add 1 tablespoon hyssop to 1 cup water. Boil for ten minutes, then strain. Let the mixture cool. After cleansing your skin, apply the toner with a cotton ball.

~ A combination of **lavender** and **neroli** essential oil (derived from orange blossoms) acts as a skin cleanser and toner. Pour some lavender floral water in a hand sprayer, and add a drop of neroli oil. Spray the mixture on your skin several times a day.

Give Your Face a Massage

~ A fine-grain powder can help absorb oil and get rid of dead skin cells that clog pores. Grind and sift 2 teaspoons of **dry oats**, then moisten with some **witch hazel** to form a paste. Using your fingertips, massage this paste gently into your skin, then rinse it away with warm water.

~ Several times a week, massage your face with **buttermilk** after washing it. The active cultures in buttermilk contain acids that help to clean away dirt and tighten pores. Leave it on for a few minutes, then rinse.

Use a Grease-Cutting Facial Mask

~ **Clay masks** or **mud masks** reduce greasiness and help tone your skin and draw out impurities. The masks are available at most drugstores. Or you can make your own using facial clay (like **bentonite**, available at natural foods stores and on the Internet) and **witch hazel**. Don't use pottery clay; it won't have the same effect. Add 1 tablespoon witch hazel to 1 teaspoon facial clay, and stir until they're blended. If you like, add 2 drops cypress oil and 2 drops lemon oil for fragrance and to help control overactive oil glands. Sit back, relax, leave the mask on for 10 minutes or until the clay is dry, then rinse it off.

~ Egg-white masks are said to firm the skin and soak up oil. Mix one teaspoon of **honey** with an **egg white** and stir well. Then add just enough flour to make a paste. Apply the mask to your face, avoiding the eye area. (Be careful not to ingest any of the egg mixture.) Let it dry for about ten minutes, then wash it off with warm water.

~ Some Indonesian women use **mango** to make a face mask to dry and tone the skin. To make the mask, mash a mango until it turns into soft pulp, massage it into your skin, leave it on to dry for a few minutes, then rinse off. It is said to help unclog the pores.

~ **Lemon juice** is used in another grease-cutting mask, along with astringent herbs and a chopped **apple** as the base. Place the apple in a pot, add water to cover, then simmer until it's soft. Mash the apple, add 1 teaspoon lemon juice, then 1 teaspoon of either dried **sage, lavender,** or **peppermint.** Apply this mixture to your face, leave it on for 5 minutes, then rinse with warm water.

Take the Shine Off

~ Throughout the day, powder your face with **loose face powder,** which will blot up excess oil. Don't use pressed powder—it contains oil and it may foster blemishes or make existing acne worse.

~ **Clinac OC** is a cream that can be used several times a day to absorb oil. You can buy it as an over-the-counter medicine at the pharmacy, as well as on the Internet.

~ Look for foil-wrapped packets of **alcohol-saturated wipes** for oily skin. You'll find them in the skin-care section of the drugstore. Keep some in your handbag or briefcase, so they're handy when you need them. The alcohol cuts through the oil to temporarily de-shine your face.

The Power of Prevention

~ Take 1 tablespoon of **flaxseed oil** a day. While it may sound kooky to add oil to your diet, there's good rationale. Flaxseed is high in essential fatty acids, which have been shown to help improve many skin conditions, including oily skin. You'll find flaxseed oil in health-food stores. To protect it from light and heat, buy the cold-pressed oil in an opaque container and store it in your refrigerator.

Palpitations

About 36 million times a year, your heart beats exactly when it's supposed to. So why sweat it if your ticker occasionally marches to a different drummer? Because palpitations can be unnerving. Fortunately, there are ways to stop them almost as soon as they start. Better yet, prevent them from happening in the first place by practicing stress-reducing techniques, screening your medications, and adding some heart-healthy foods and supplements to your menu.

What's wrong

Spurred on by a steady series of electrical impulses, your heart normally beats with such regularity that you don't even notice it. But if this electrical system develops a glitch, you may experience palpitations— a fluttering or pounding sensation in your chest as your heart beats too fast or "skips a beat." Palpitations do sometimes indicate a serious problem with your heart. But most cases are caused simply by fatigue, anxiety, illness, or stress. While worrisome, they generally don't require medical treatment.

To Calm a Flutter...

As soon as you notice an irregular heartbeat, sit down and prop up your feet. Breathe slowly and deeply, letting your belly expand with each inhalation. If you focus on **slow, steady breathing**, your heartbeat will probably return to its normal rhythm right away.

If the fluttering continues, do the **Valsalva maneuver**: Pinch your nose, close your mouth, then try to exhale. Since you can't—because your nose and mouth are closed—you'll bear down as if you were forcing a bowel movement (or pushing out a baby during childbirth). The brief rise in blood pressure that results should help reset your heart. The Valsalva technique is named after seventeenth-century Italian anatomist Antonio Maria Valsalva.

Cough forcefully. Like the Valsalva maneuver, coughing increases pressure inside your chest. Sometimes that's all you need to restore your heart to its regular rhythm.

Spring to the Tap

Take a few **gulps of cold water**. No one knows exactly why this helps, but some people get instant results. One theory is that the swallowed water causes your esophagus to press against your heart, and that nudge restores the rhythm.

Alternatively, **splash ice-cold water** on your face. The shock might be enough to do the trick.

Eat, Drink, and Be Moderate

 Eat plenty of fish. **Salmon** and **mackerel** in particular contain high levels of heart-healthy omega-3 fatty acids.

 Avoid eating too much at one time. Forcing your body to digest a huge load of food diverts blood from your heart to your digestive tract. That can lead to palpitations.

 Cut back on caffeine. In some people, drinking caffeinated coffee, tea, or soft drinks triggers palpitations.

Soothe Stress and Get Sleep

 If you are experiencing palpitations, there is a good chance that stress is to blame. In fact, palpitations can be the body's way of alerting you that your stress level has exceeded the safe range. **Meditating** helps get your stress level back down. So set aside 30 minutes each day just to let your body relax and your mind unwind.

 Soothe yourself with aromatherapy. Sprinkle a few drops of relaxing **lavender oil** onto a handkerchief, and inhale the pleasant aroma. Or try rubbing two drops of **bitter orange oil** on your chest.

 Get at least **seven hours of sleep** each night. Being tired can set the stage for out-of-rhythm heartbeats.

Warm Up and Get Moving

 Get at least 30 minutes of **aerobic exercise** three or four times a week. Walking, running, and tennis are all excellent choices. Just be sure you don't become too focused on beating your previous time or outscoring an opponent—that will increase your stress. Exercise at a pace that allows you to comfortably carry on a conversation.

 Warm up for 10 minutes before each workout and for 10 minutes afterward.

Help Out the Rhythm Section

 Many people with irregular heart rhythms are low on **magnesium**. So you might try taking 400 milligrams of magnesium twice a day. (*Off-limits* . . . if you have kidney disease.)

 Take **coenzyme Q$_{10}$.** This naturally occurring substance, sold over the counter in pill form, helps keep your heart

Should I call **the doctor?**

Unless you have a history of heart disease, there's generally no reason to alert your doctor that you're having palpitations, unless they occur more than once a week, become more frequent, or are accompanied by a feeling of light-headedness or dizziness. Of course, if you pass out or experience tightness in your chest accompanied by nausea and sweating, call an ambulance at once. You might be having a heart attack.

Tried...

Many people claim that cutting back on sweets will help prevent palpitations.

...and true

Any food that causes sharp changes in blood sugar can contribute to palpitations. If you're a "sweet food junkie" and you have palpitations, try cutting back. You may find that palpitations diminish or cease.

rhythm regular, especially if you have heart disease. Take 150 milligrams once a day with food.

 If you're not eating much fish, take 2 to 3 grams daily of cold-pressed marine **fish oil**, which is high in beneficial omega-3 fatty acids.

 The amino acid **taurine** helps quell irregular electrical impulses in the heart. Take 1½ to 3 grams daily. Taurine is available by prescription.

Check Your Meds

 Many prescription and over-the-counter drugs can cause palpitations, so **check the package insert**. It might say something like: "Do not use this product if you have heart disease or high blood pressure." Or it might give a specific warning about the drug's effect on heartbeat. Pay close attention to over-the-counter cold and allergy medications that contain decongestants. One ingredient that is frequently implicated is pseudoephedrine.

 Some **bronchodilators** for asthma, such as terbutaline (Bricanyl), can increase the risk of palpitations. So can **antihistamines** like loratadine (Claritin). If you've been taking these, ask your doctor about switching to different medications.

 Avoid any diet remedy or supplement containing the ingredient **ma huang**, or **ephedra**. This can sharply increase your risk of irregular heartbeat or palpitations—sometimes with dangerous consequences.

Poison Ivy

No one would knowingly touch a toxic plant, yet generations of even sharp-eyed outdoors people, not to mention kids wandering in the woods, have picked up the itch. If you know you've been exposed, you may be able to wash off the allergy-inducing urushiol before it's too late. And there are many ways to ease the itching and dry the blisters if you do get poison ivy. But avoidance is by far the best approach—especially if you're one of those people driven nuts by itching.

Rush to Wash

☙ Run for the shower—or the nearest creek, if you're hiking—and **wash away the resin** before the allergic reaction takes hold. Once you come into contact with poison ivy, the clock starts ticking: You have about 15 minutes to get rid of the urushiol. Use soap and warm water, if they're available. If you have a choice of soaps, use one that does not contain moisturizers. Skip the washcloth, since it can spread the oil around your body.

☙ If it's impossible to wash right away, clean your skin with **rubbing alcohol** to dissolve the urushiol. If none is handy, you can use any product (or beverage) that contains alcohol.

☙ Alternatively, you can clean off the urushiol with **Tecnu**, an over-the-counter solvent (available on the Internet) that's designed especially to remove urushiol from the skin. Tecnu is very effective at removing the resin, but be sure to rinse it off immediately or you risk skin irritation.

A Gem of a Cure

☙ If you know what the **jewelweed** plant looks like (it has tall, translucent stems and hanging, trumpet-shaped yellow or orange flowers) and there's one growing nearby, crush a handful of the leaves and stems and smear the juice on the affected area. Also known as impatiens and touch-me-not, this plant sometimes grows near poison ivy. There is some research to support the old folk notion that it works against poison ivy rash.

What's wrong

Seven out of ten people are allergic to poison ivy, making this the world's most common allergy. People who have the allergy are sensitive to urushiol, an irritating resin that's found in poison ivy, poison oak, and poison sumac. If you so much as brush one of these plants, urushiol can get on your skin. Within as little as two hours, you'll develop an itchy rash that will have you scratching for three weeks or more. You can also get the rash by touching clothes or other items that have been contaminated with urushiol. And if there's urushiol on your fingers, you'll be spreading the rash around your body every time you scratch.

Should I call the doctor?

If you're in extreme discomfort, or if you have severe blistering, swelling, or redness, call your doctor. You should also alert the doctor if you might have inhaled the smoke of burning poison ivy plants, particularly if you become short of breath. Seek medical attention at once if the rash is on your eyes, nose, mouth, throat, or genitals.

Other Plant Remedies

- Slice a leaf of a fresh **aloe vera** plant, scoop out the gel, and apply to the affected areas. Aloe is not only for sunburn; its anti-inflammatory and antibacterial properties make it great for poison ivy as well. Commercial aloe vera gel products are fine if they are made mostly from pure gel from the plant.

- Pick a few leaves from the common lawn weed **plantain,** wash them, mash them, and apply as a poultice to the affected skin. Plantain contains a chemical (called allantoin) that is anti-inflammatory and antimicrobial.

Stop the Spread

- **Wash the clothes** you were wearing when you touched poison ivy in the washing machine with warm water. This should get out all the urushiol so the rash won't spread.

- **Rinse off your shoes.** If you were wearing washable sneakers when you came into contact with the plant, put them through a separate cycle after washing your clothes.

- **Dogs and cats** don't get poison ivy, but their **fur** can become coated with urushiol. So if Fido followed you into the woods, you can either avoid him for the next few days or give him a bath in soapy water. The bath is a real chore, however, since you'll have to wear rubber gloves and a raincoat to avoid getting urushiol on your skin.

Attack the Itch

- Use a **vinegar** compress to dry the rash and relieve itching. Mix a half-cup white vinegar with 1½ cups water. Chill in the refrigerator. When you need cool relief, moisten a cloth in the solution and press it onto the rash.

- Dab **calamine lotion** onto the rash. This classic poison ivy remedy relieves itch and will help dry up blisters. If you find the lotion too runny, just mix in a little **cornstarch**.

- Soak a cloth in **cold milk** and hold it against your skin. Cold milk is more soothing to itchy skin than cold water. Exactly why milk relieves itching is unknown, but perhaps it's the milk fat.

- Using a cotton ball, treat your rash with **witch hazel**, which has a great reputation as a skin soother. The kind that comes in an alcohol solution cools your skin as it evaporates.

Moisten a plain old **tea bag** (black or green, it doesn't matter) and apply it to the itchy skin. The tannic acid in tea, which is astringent, helps contract inflamed tissue and relieve the itching.

Take a warm bath to which you've added a few table-spoons of **colloidal oatmeal** (like Aveeno) or plain oatmeal ground in a blender. The oatmeal will help dry a rash that has started to blister, and also relieves the itch. Be careful when getting out—oatmeal makes the tub very slippery.

To dry out the rash, relax in a bath containing **Epsom salt**. Follow the label directions.

The Power of Prevention

Whenever venturing out into the wilds where you may come into contact with poisonous plants, wear **long pants** and a **long-sleeved shirt**.

Get a plant-identification book, and **learn to recognize poison ivy, oak, and sumac**. Many people recognize poison ivy for its "leaves of three." But they may fail to recognize that poison ivy can grow as a shrub or tree-clinging vine as well as a ground cover. In the spring, its leaves are reddish. Late in the season, it bears pale white berries.

Before going out, rub some **Stokogard** outdoor cream on exposed skin. This claylike lotion, available on the Internet, forms a protective barrier that guards skin against urushiol.

Don't go near any burning brush pile. If there's poison ivy in the pile, the oil takes to the air and can get into your lungs. You can develop a serious lung infection, as well as a rash over your entire body.

Tried...

Before there was calamine lotion, people used white shoe polish on poison ivy rash.

...and true

Shoe polish in the old-fashioned shake-up bottle contains pipe clay, which is similar to one of the main ingredients in calamine.

Old **wives' tale**

Poison ivy blisters sometimes become filled with fluid, and some people think that the fluid spreads the rash. Not true. It's harmless. Only oil from the plant can cause the rash.

Pregnancy Complaints

As the months march along, pregnancy can start to feel more like a burden than a wondrous event in the making. Morning sickness is just the beginning. (For ways to overcome nausea, see Morning Sickness, page 278.) When the new you is someone with heartburn, stretch marks, back pain, swollen feet, and varicose veins, you may even begin to wonder whether this was such a good idea. Every pregnant woman can use some sound ideas, like the ones here, for coping with the challenges.

What's wrong

As a fetus grows inside the womb, Mom can start to feel pretty uncomfortable. Carrying around the extra weight can cause back pain and fatigue. And as the bulging uterus encroaches on the stomach and intestines, heartburn and constipation can crop up, along with hemorrhoids. Then there is fluid retention—causing swollen feet and even carpal tunnel syndrome, among other things—and unsightly varicose veins. As breasts and abdomen swell, stretch marks are all but inevitable.

Ease Fatigue

↝ Take a **half-hour nap** each day. As you slumber, make sure your feet are raised higher than your heart; that helps take pressure off your legs. Don't feel guilty about needing to rest. Building a baby is hard work.

↝ Get some **exercise** every day, as long as your doctor says it's okay. Aerobic activity, such as walking or swimming, gives you more energy. And labor and delivery will be easier if you've been exercising regularly.

Deflate Swollen Feet

↝ Improve circulation to aching feet with alternating **hot and cold footbaths**. The hot water summons blood to your feet, and the cold moves it back out. Fill two basins with water—one comfortably hot, the other cold. Plunge your feet into the hot water for 3 minutes, then in the cold water for about 30 seconds. Switch back and forth six times, ending in the cold water.

↝ After your footbaths, rest for at least ten minutes with your feet propped up.

Get Heartburn Under Control

↝ When you're pregnant, the growing pressure on your abdomen can force stomach acid up into the esophagus. **Antacids** help neutralize this acid. Ask your doctor to recommend a brand.

Eat **almonds**. Chemical compounds in the tasty nuts help keep stomach acid in the stomach by strengthening the valve between the stomach and esophagus. Watch out, though: At about 10 calories per nut, almonds are very high in calories. To avoid gaining too much weight, you'll need to give up some high-calorie food in exchange.

Avoid foods that relax this valve. They include **coffee, citrus juices, fried foods, peppermint, tomato products**, and **alcohol**.

Beat Back Back Pain

Avoid standing for long periods, particularly in the latter months of pregnancy. As the baby grows and the joints in your pelvic area soften, backaches become common; standing increases the pain.

When you must stand for any length of time, keep your weight **evenly balanced** between your feet. If you cock one of your hips, you'll put sideways pressure on your lower spine.

When you're in a chair, **sit up straight**. Press your lower back against the chair back and repeat this several times every day to help strengthen muscles that support your back.

If you're working at a desk, keep your feet slightly elevated on a **footrest** or a **small stool**.

Control Carpal Tunnel Syndrome

Many women are bothered by numbness or tingling in the fingers during pregnancy, typically because water retention causes pressure on nerves in the wrist. To ease the discomfort, **exercise** your arms and wrists for five minutes or so every hour. (See the exercises on page 113.)

Don't bend your limp wrist in an effort to control the discomfort. That will only make matters worse.

Pick up a **wrist splint** at a drugstore or medical supply store and wear it to bed. That will keep you from bending your wrists as you sleep.

Say So Long to Stretch Marks

Nearly every pregnant woman gets stretch marks—streaks on the skin that turn from reddish to white. They're inevitable, because the skin has to stretch to allow for the

Should I call **the doctor?**

Fortunately, most pregnancy complaints end with the end of pregnancy. Contact your doctor if you're losing weight, if you can't keep down food or fluids and worry that you're getting dehydrated, if you have lingering headaches or double vision, or if the fetus moves less often or stops moving.

expanding belly and breasts. The stretching occurs in the collagen layer of skin, which is beneath the surface, so skin-care products do not help. But if you can avoid **putting on excess weight**, you'll keep the marks to a minimum.

Say "Vamoose" to Varicose Veins

🐛 Varicose veins form because you're building up an extra volume of blood to feed the fetus. To keep them at bay, wear **supportive knee-high socks**, sold at medical supply stores.

🐛 Minimize the appearance of varicose veins by using a **cold compress** on your legs. Mix 6 drops each of essential oil of **cypress, lemon**, and **bergamot** in a cup of distilled **witch hazel**. Chill in your refrigerator for at least an hour. Prop up your feet, soak a washcloth in the liquid, and apply it for 15 minutes. This combination of oils helps shrink swollen blood vessels and reduce swelling.

Combat Constipation

🐛 Pregnant women are more susceptible to constipation, so you'll want to **increase your fiber** intake. High-fiber foods include beans, bran and other whole-grain breads and cereals, ground flaxseeds, leafy vegetables, and broccoli.

Premenstrual Syndrome

It's not just the mood swings and headaches. Not just the pain and bloating. What's most annoying is the inevitability of it all—this month's symptoms repeated the next, and the next after that. When you're looking ahead to cyclical misery, anything that can break the pattern is worth trying. One approach is to start taking two 200-milligram doses every 8 hours of a pain-reliever such as ibuprofen (Advil, Motrin), starting 3 to 5 days before your period begins. But there are many other ways to prepare for PMS and to get some relief when it hits.

Keep Moving Along

⌐ Get at least 20 to 30 minutes of **aerobic exercise** daily throughout the month. Walking and swimming are shoo-ins. But if those forms of exercise seem tame for you, there's always in-line skating, karate, kickboxing, water aerobics, swing dancing, and much more. Try to exercise to the point of perspiration. If you keep up the good work, you'll lower the level of free-circulating estrogen that's in your system. Exercise is both a stress reliever and mood enhancer, because it boosts your body's natural painkilling endorphins while also relaxing your muscles. Women who exercise regularly find that fluid retention is less of a problem.

Get Your Diet In-Line

⌐ **Eat less salt** throughout the month, but especially in the week before your period. With more salt comes increased fluid retention, hence more bloating. Processed foods such as canned soups and packaged snacks are especially high in sodium, so avoid them whenever possible.

⌐ Also **cut back on alcohol** and **caffeine**, both of which can contribute to PMS.

⌐ **Eat lots of fiber**. High-fiber foods help to escort surplus estrogen out of your body. Load up on whole grains like barley, oats, and whole-grain breads; vegetables; and beans.

⌐ **Drink more water**. When you do, more "extra" salt

What's **wrong**

PMS may start a week or two before the beginning of menstruation. Common symptoms are breast tenderness, mood swings, headache, backache, and bloating. Experts still don't know why some women feel the effects of PMS worse than others, but the problem is thought to be linked to out-of-balance hormones. Estrogen and progesterone are the chief suspects. Levels can soar just before menstruation, then come crashing down. It may be that these fluctuations throw levels of the mood-regulating chemical serotonin out of kilter.

Should I call the doctor?

If your PMS is interfering with your ability to enjoy a normal life, talk to your doctor about it. He or she might be able to recommend prescription PMS-control medications.

Old wives' tale

Some have claimed that the reason women crave chocolate when they have PMS is that they're deficient in magnesium, which chocolate provides. Scientific research has shot this theory down. After all, wheat germ and green leafy vegetables are high in the mineral, and few people crave those. Nonetheless, chocolate cravings are common. If you must indulge, satisfy your urge with dark chocolate, which has less sugar and fat than milk chocolate.

leaves in your urine, and that helps stop swelling and bloating. Go for eight 250-milliliter glasses a day.

  ❰ **Cut out sugary snacks**. Cravings for sweets trend upward when you have PMS, but candy and cookies send your blood sugar levels spiking. When you have a blood sugar crash later on, you'll feel tired and irritable. If you limit your sugar supply, you'll set the stage for a steadier mood.

Calcium and Beyond

  ❰ Take 1,200 milligrams of **calcium** at bedtime, or take two Tums (which contains calcium) after every meal. The mineral reduces headaches, mood swings, and muscle cramps. It also helps make you sleepy, which is one reason to take the large dose just before you go to bed.

  ❰ Also take 800 milligrams of **magnesium**. Many women with bad PMS symptoms are low in the mineral. Magnesium works with calcium to help control muscular activity, and taking a combination of both can help contain symptoms.

  ❰ Take 50 to 100 milligrams each day of **vitamin B_6** when you have PMS to reduce irritability and depression. Among its other powers, B_6 can help calm jittery nerves by increasing your supply of serotonin, the mood-regulating brain chemical.

  ❰ Take 500 to 1000 milligrams of **evening primrose oil** every day throughout the month. It contains essential fatty acids that reduce breast tenderness, bloating, and irritability. The supplement comes in gel-filled capsules, available at health-food stores.

Balance Your Hormones

  ❰ Chase down some **chasteberry** supplements. This herb is prized for its ability to improve PMS symptoms by bringing hormones back into balance. Take one or two 225-milligram capsules each day throughout the month. It can take up to six months before you get the full effect. Once your symptoms have subsided, stop taking the herb.

  ❰ Use **black cohosh** the two weeks before your period. Take two 20-milligram capsules of extract daily, or two to four droppers of tincture in water three times a day. This herb works by bringing your estrogen to a proper level—if it's high, the herb blocks its effects, and if it's low, the herb helps do the work of the missing estrogen.

Prostate Enlargement

Here's another example why "aging gracefully" is an oxymoron. After years of doing bathroom business with due dispatch, many a male turns grim-faced when the usual stance turns unproductive. First? Check your medicine cabinet for OTCs such as antihistamines and decongestants that might be making the problem worse. Then, after you've cleared out those troublemakers, try some supplements and check your diet. For the male in a bind, many of these remedies, used alone or in combination, can make the trouble far more tolerable.

Gladden Your Gland with Herbs

➤ Take 160 milligrams of **saw palmetto** in capsule form twice daily. Look for an extract containing 85% to 95% fatty acids and sterols. This supplement, which contains extracts of the berries of the saw palmetto plant, seems to block the action of a hormone called dihydrotestosterone, which stimulates growth in the prostate gland. There is evidence that it also decreases inflammation.

➤ Twice a day, take 50 to 200 milligrams of **pygeum africanum**, a supplement that comes from the bark of an African tree. Like saw palmetto, it has a long history of relieving benign prostatic hyperplasia (BPH), apparently by interfering with dihydrotestosterone.

➤ You may find that taking a supplement containing **both saw palmetto and pygeum** works better than taking either of the herbs alone. If you go this route, look for a brand containing about 320 milligrams of saw palmetto and about 100 milligrams of pygeum.

➤ Look for supplements containing extract of dried **nettle root** extract and take 200 to 400 milligrams in capsule form three times a day. Nettle root helps shrink the prostate, and when taken with pygeum, it seems to help that supplement work better.

➤ The antioxidant **lycopene** decreases inflammation and swelling of the prostate gland. The effective dose is 10 to 20

What's **wrong**

After age 40, many men start to notice that their personal plumbing isn't working properly. Urine comes out with difficulty, the flow is weak, and urination ends with dribbles. Most irritating of all, nature calls during the night, and sleep suffers. The cause is often benign prostatic hyperplasia (BPH). This is a noncancerous swelling of the prostate, the gland that produces seminal fluid. Since the prostate surrounds the urethra— the tube running from the bladder out through the penis—when that gland swells, it blocks the flow of urine. After age 60, at last half of all men have some degree of prostate swelling.

Should I call
the doctor?

When you have trouble starting to urinate, a weak urine stream, a feeling that your bladder can't totally empty, and a frequent need to go during the night, you should have a checkup. The doctor can tell whether you have BPH and rule out other conditions, particularly prostate cancer. More severe symptoms call for an emergency room visit. If you can't urinate, even with straining, for more than 8 hours, this is urinary obstruction. You need immediate treatment to prevent kidney failure.

milligrams daily, taken in combination with other supplements that help control BPH. Try a brand-name supplement such as Jamieson Lycopene-Rich Tomato Concentrate, or you can purchase a formula with a combination of other BPH relievers such as serenoa, pygeum, urtica, and zinc chelate.

Give Your Prostate the Food It Needs

Eat a handful of unroasted **pumpkin seeds** each day. The seeds, which are an old folk remedy for prostate enlargement still often recommended today, are a rich source of zinc.

Eat lots of **tomatoes** or tomato-based products—as many as 10 servings per week. Tomatoes are rich in lycopene, the prostate-friendly antioxidant described above. **Watermelon** and **apricots** also are rich in lycopene.

Twice a day, mix a tablespoon of **flaxseed oil** in your food. It is a rich source of omega-3 fatty acids. These and other essential fatty acids decrease inflammation in the prostate gland (and thus reduce swelling) by limiting the concentration of the hormone prostaglandin.

Be a Picky Drinker

Cut back on fluids in the evening, as you'll more likely have to get up in the night. You need plenty of fluids, but **drink before dinnertime**, not after.

If you're already having trouble urinating, **limit** the number of caffeinated drinks you consume, such as **coffee, tea**, and **sodas**. Caffeine tends to make the outlet from your bladder tighten, creating a roadblock that interferes with urine flow. It's also a diuretic, which is exactly what you don't want if you're already getting up to urinate during the night.

Also **cut back on alcohol**—or, better yet, forgo it completely. Like caffeine, it causes constriction at the neck of the bladder, and acts as a diuretic.

Keep Your Prostate Running on Empty

Ejaculate regularly, either through intercourse or alone. The prostate gland produces the nutrient-rich fluid in which the sperm are bathed, and ejaculation helps to relieve the internal fluid pressure. It also helps keep the gland from becoming inflamed.

Lounge in the Tub

⮑ Sit in **warm water**. The heat will increase blood flow in the prostate gland, which helps reduce swelling and inflammation. If you can, spend 20 to 45 minutes in the tub every day.

Let It Flow

⮑ Urinate **whenever you get the urge.** Some men seem to think it's best to exercise bladder control and avoid trips to the bathroom. But when the bladder is too full, urine gets into the prostate, irritating it.

⮑ When in the bathroom, **urinate as much as possible,** relax for a few minutes, and then urinate again. Doctors call this "double voiding." It's a good way to guarantee that you have emptied your bladder completely.

⮑ **Try sitting on the toilet** to urinate rather than standing. The combination of the new position and the more relaxed situation can make for a more effective bathroom visit.

⮑ **Relax in the bathroom.** This is not a contest, no one is judging, no one is timing you. Read something, ponder something, take ten slow, deep breaths in a row. Why? Tension and anxiety trigger stress hormones that can cause the bladder muscles to tense up. If you are putting too much psychological pressure on yourself to "perform," that alone can stop the performance. No reason to turn a physical problem into a psychological one as well.

Tried...

Some men say you should get up and walk around as much as possible to help deal with a problem prostrate.

...and true

When you remain sitting, you put pressure on your prostate. In fact, men who sit for long periods while they work—such as truck drivers—report more BPH than those who are frequently moving around. If you have a desk job, get up and pace every once in a while.

Psoriasis

There are good days and there are bad days, and if you're troubled with psoriasis, you know the difference all too well. On the good days, you hardly need to pay attention to what your skin's doing. On the bad ones, red itchy patches are crying for attention. Here are ways to make good days better and the bad more bearable.

What's wrong

Your skin is growing too fast. Normally, new skin cells need about 28 days to migrate from deep within your skin to the surface, where they replace dead cells that fall away. But if you have psoriasis, the cycle is compressed into about four days. Skin cells pile up, causing distinctive red, bumpy patches covered with white scales. These frequently develop on the knees, elbows, and scalp. The cause is unknown, but psoriasis seems to be more prevalent in some families than in others. People with psoriasis tend to have flare-ups, when the rashes get worse, followed by intervals when the condition is far less severe.

See the Light

🔹 **Sunlight** is an excellent remedy for psoriasis. Every day, spend 15 to 30 minutes in the sun, and you should see results in less than six weeks. While doctors don't have the full explanation, research shows that sunlight decreases the activity of the skin's T cells. These specialized cells produce substances called cytokines, which initiate a cycle of inflammation. When you expose T cells to sunlight, it quells their action, breaking the cycle.

🔹 Protect yourself from burning by wearing **sunscreen** with an SPF of at least 15 on healthy areas of skin.

Go Skin Dipping

🔹 Take a good, long soak in warm water...then add some **vegetable oil**. Here's why: A long bath can soften scaly patches and soothe itching, but bathing can also dry your skin and make itching worse. So sit in the tub for about 10 minutes, letting your skin get thoroughly soaked, but about 5 minutes before you get out, add a few spoonfuls of vegetable oil. That's all it takes to seal the water into your skin. (Be careful getting out of the tub, because oil makes the tub slippery.)

🔹 To relieve itching, try a cool-water bath, adding **vinegar** to the bathwater. Many people find that vinegar helps psoriasis, even though doctors aren't sure why. What's known is that acetic acid in vinegar kills bacteria—and one theory holds that psoriasis is made worse by bacteria.

🔹 Fine-ground **oatmeal** is another good ingredient for itch relief. You can sprinkle in an oatmeal product specially made for bathing, such as Aveeno. Or put unflavored oatmeal in a blender, grind it until it turns into a fine powder, then sprinkle it in the water.

Don Another Layer

～ After bathing, spread on a moisturizing cream to lock in your skin's natural moisture. Make sure to add a thick layer to the psoriasis patches. This helps prevent cracking. Avoid liquid lotions, which dry up too quickly, and instead choose a heavy cream or ointment. Among the best are **Lacticare** or **Amlactin**, which contain lactic acid to prevent skin from drying out, or **Dermal Therapy**, which contains urea to help loosen scales.

～ Try **Bag Balm**, a product originally designed for use on cows' udders. It's gained a reputation for soothing dry, cracked skin. Look for it in farm-supply stores or pharmacies.

～ Try a cream that contains **chamomile**, if you can find one. This plant has a long-held reputation for reducing inflammation and soothing flaky skin.

～ Rub a few drops of **tea-tree oil** into your psoriasis patches several times a day. This Australian remedy is useful for relieving itch and softening psoriasis patches, especially if you have a mild case. However, some people have an allergic reaction to tea-tree oil, so be sure to test on a small patch of skin. Also, the skin covered with tea-tree oil may have increased sensitivity to sunlight.

～ To soften the skin and remove scaly patches, you can also use **petroleum jelly**. Apply it as often as necessary.

Get Oiled

～ Mix a tablespoon of **flaxseed oil** into your cereal, yogurt, or other food each day. This isn't for flavoring—it's for your psoriasis. Flaxseed oil is high in omega-3 fatty acids, and these compounds help to block a chemical in your body called arachidonic acid, which causes inflammation.

～ Oily fish are also high in omega-3s. If you like **salmon**, it's a good idea to have it at least once a week. Other fish that are high in omega-3s are **sardines** and **mackerel**.

～ You can also get these fatty acids by taking 1,000 milligrams of **fish oil** three times a day. Large amounts of fish oil can "thin" the blood, so check with your doctor first if you're taking a blood thinner such as aspirin, coumadin.

Should I call **the doctor?**

If an outbreak covers a wide area of skin, or affects the palms of your hands and soles of your feet, you'll want to see the doctor. You also need a doctor's attention whenever you see signs of infection, such as pus or a yellow crust on your skin. If your psoriasis is accompanied by joint pain, a condition called psoriatic arthritis, you need to be under a doctor's care. And if you develop widespread bumps containing pus and have a fever, it's an emergency: Call a doctor to deal with the infection immediately.

If you have an **aloe vera** plant on your shelf, break a stem and apply the gel several times a day to itchy patches of skin. Aloe has anti-inflammatory compounds, and the gel contains magnesium lactate, which helps control itching.

Avoid Getting into Scrapes

Keep your hands off the red spots. Even minor damage to your skin can worsen your psoriasis symptoms. If you pick and scratch the itchy patches, you'll damage your skin, which can lead to more extensive outbreaks.

Always use an **electric shaver** instead of a razor if you have psoriasis on your legs, face, or other areas where you shave. A sharp razor nicks your skin, no matter how careful you are, which raises your risk of new outbreaks. Shavers are gentler.

The Ticket to Scalp Care

If you get psoriasis on your scalp, it's time to shop for special shampoos. You want a product that contains **salicylic acid** or **tar**. Effective shampoos (with 2% tar) include Neutrogena T/Gel Extra Strength or DHS Tar. Use daily at first, then twice a week—alternating with regular shampoo—as symptoms subside. When you apply the shampoo, leave it in contact with your scalp for 10 minutes before rinsing.

Keep a list of several shampoos that you like. Whenever you finish one kind, rotate and choose another. Your scalp may become tolerant to one kind of shampoo that becomes less effective if you use it long-term. People report better results if they **switch shampoos**.

Adopt a **short hairstyle**. With a simple do, it will be a lot easier to treat your scalp.

Simmer Down

Get regular **exercise**. It's a great stress reducer—and stress is known to contribute to outbreaks. If you can take a 30-minute walk every day, you may be surprised at how effectively that token amount of exercise distracts you from things that are getting you keyed up.

Practice a relaxing mental exercise, such as **meditating** or **deep breathing**, a few minutes each day.

Razor Burn

You've done a bad job shaving, and now your skin is chafed, red, and irritated. Here are several ways to relieve the burn that don't involve expensive face creams or aftershave lotions. Just as important, we've provided some hints on how to drag a sharp gadget across your skin without pain in the future.

Soothe the Burn

～ **Aloe vera** is among the best natural ingredients for irritated or burned skin. If you have an aloe plant, snap off the tip of a branch, squeeze out some of the clear liquid, and apply directly to the skin just like a store-bought lotion. Or use a commercial skin product that contains the herb. Best is 100% pure aloe vera gel.

～ **Avocado** is rich with vitamins and oils great for the skin. You can apply this tropical fruit directly to the skin for razor-burn relief.

～ **Cucumbers** have a long folk history as a cure for skin problems. Apply a slice directly to the burn. Or, peel a cucumber, throw it into a blender, and apply the puree to the area. Even better: Throw some avocado into the blender at the same time.

～ Rub **calendula** cream on the affected area. Creams containing extracts of this flower have a long history of treating damaged skin, including razor burn.

Analyze Your Razor

～ **Change your razor blade** after three or four uses. If a razor's edge is slightly dulled, you have to press harder, causing more irritation. Disposable razors should be tossed after the third use.

～ Better yet, **alternate** between using a regular razor and an electric shaver. Use one for about a month, then switch to the other. Dermatologists don't know the reason, but by switching between the two, you reduce razor burn.

What's wrong

Shaving gets more than hair. You also scrape away cells from the skin's surface. Blood flow increases to the chafed skin, making it red. And without the outermost skin layer, which retains moisture and acts as a protective barrier, the skin beneath grows dry and irritated. Shaving quickly and incorrectly increases the risk of razor burn, and certain people, such as African Canadians and men with curly beards, are especially prone to bumpy reactions on their faces from shaving. For women, shaving underarms and legs can create similar problems—dry, chafed, irritated skin that can turn bumpy in places.

You'd be amazed at the items that can stand in for shaving cream when you discover you're out. Here are substitutes actually tested and suggested by frugality experts as well as everyday folk. All make some sense: Many are oil-based, which provides the moisture and protection you seek in a shave. Still, only use in a pinch:

- Cheddar cheese spread, such as Cheez Whiz
- Cream rinse or hair conditioner
- Toothpaste
- Whipped-cream substitutes, such as Cool Whip
- Peanut butter (creamy, not chunky)
- Butter
- Moisturizing cream
- Mayonnaise
- Cooking spray.

Should I call the doctor?

If the razor burn is really bothering you or interfering with your ability to stay groomed, talk to your doctor about it or get a referral to a dermatologist. If you get severe razor burn that refuses to clear up, you might be having an allergic reaction to something contained in shaving creams. Occasionally a bacterial or fungal infection causes the problem. It is sometimes difficult to distinguish allergic reactions from infections, but a dermatologist can make a diagnosis and recommend treatment.

Use Sheer Skill

- If you shave with a blade, do it when your skin and hairs are **wet**. Soak in the bathtub or hold a warm washcloth on your face for about 10 minutes prior to shaving. When skin is wet, the hairs stand up straighter, which makes them easier to shear off. (If you use an electric shaver, just the opposite is true: Your hair should be completely dry.)

- Select the **right shaving cream**. Pick one made for sensitive skin—ideally, with aloe vera as one of the ingredients. Avoid perfumed products and products with benzoyl peroxide or menthol. These can irritate your skin. And don't shave with soap. Shaving creams are thicker and more moisturizing, providing more skin protection.

- Shave *with* your hair growth, not *against* it. Though you won't shave as closely this way, you'll remove less skin and cause less irritation to the skin and hair follicles. Generally, shaving *down* your legs or face is the right way to go.

- **Avoid aftershaves**. These contain lots of alcohol, which will dry your skin and make the chafing worse. A nice alternative is witch hazel, which contains just a bit of alcohol and leaves your skin feeling softer and soothed. You can also use it if your nick yourself to clean the cut.

- An **exfoliating mitt, sponge**, or a **loofah** pad, used daily, can help prevent ingrown hairs. (See also Ingrown Hairs, page 246.) Sometimes these hairs cause bumps to form, and when the razor or shaver passes over the bumps, you end up with razor burn.

Restless Legs Syndrome

Of all our body's mysteries, this is surely among the quirkiest. When you're otherwise ready for rest, why should your legs keep running? When every fiber of your being says, "Settle down!" why are you gamely kicking your bedmate? Since RLS seems to be related to mineral imbalances, perhaps the best place to end the night race is with supplements. But if they don't stop your in-place pacing, you'll want to develop some pre-bed rituals to help those legs settle down.

Run Out for Supplements

~ Each day, take 500 milligrams of **magnesium**, 800 to 1,000 milligrams of **calcium**, and 800 to 1,000 milligrams of **potassium**. A shortage of any of these minerals can make your legs more twitchy.

~ Drink mineral water that's high in **magnesium**. The optimum magnesium level is in the range of 100 milligrams per liter of water.

~ Bump up your intake of **folic acid**, a B vitamin (also called folate). Folic acid helps build red blood cells, which in turn helps oxygenate the body. That's an important benefit, since RLS is associated with a decrease in oxygen. Food sources of folic acid include leafy green vegetables, orange juice, and beans. You'll also find folate in most multivitamins.

~ Eat **iron-rich** foods such as dark green vegetables, liver, wheat germ, kidney beans, and lean beef. Iron is part of the myoglobin molecule, which is a protein that stores oxygen in the muscles until it's needed. Without iron, myoglobin can't hold enough oxygen, and muscle problems may develop.

The Home Stretch

~ When you get the urge to move your legs, start **rubbing** them, or **stretch** them to their full length and **point your toes**. These intentional movements send signals to your brain that can override the strange tingling sensations of RLS. But be sure to stop if the stretching produces a charley horse or leg

What's wrong

The name restless legs syndrome (RLS) pretty much describes what this condition is. But it fails to capture how distressing RLS can be. When you lie down to sleep or rest, you start feeling a maddening "creepy-crawly" sensation in your legs. Generally, the only way to stop it is to move the legs or walk around. Older people, pregnant women, and people with diabetes or lumbar disk disease are more susceptible. While causes are unknown, the high-risk groups all have low levels of magnesium. RLS symptoms are also associated with sugar, caffeine, and alcohol consumption, as well as some prescription drugs.

Should I call the doctor?

If RLS is causing severe sleep loss or interfering with your work or daily activities, talk to your doctor. Because the condition is associated with mineral and vitamin deficiencies, you may also want to consult with a practitioner who specializes in nutrition, such as a naturopathic doctor.

Tried...

Drinking tonic water can quench those restless feelings in the legs.

...and true

This drink contains quinine, which does relieve symptoms in some people.

cramps: Those are strong indications of magnesium deficiency and can't be alleviated by stretching.

❧ Sit on the edge of the bed and firmly **massage** your calves to give the muscles deeper stimulation.

❧ If those treatments don't calm your legs, get up and go for a brief **walk** around your home. Take long steps and bend your legs to stretch the muscles.

Before You Go to Bed

❧ Sit in a tub filled with comfortably **hot water** for 10 to 15 minutes before you go to bed.

❧ Chilling your legs may also help. Rub a **cold pack** on your legs before you go to bed.

❧ Or combine the **heat and cold** treatments. Dip your legs in a comfortably hot bath for two minutes, then apply the cold pack to your legs for a minute. Repeat several times before bed.

Make Steady Progress

❧ After you get into bed, practice the calming ritual known as **progressive muscle relaxation**. Breathe deeply for a few minutes, then tense the muscles in your feet. Hold the tension for a few seconds, then relax. Next, tense your calf muscles, hold, and relax. Then do the same with your thigh muscles. Repeat the tensing-and-relaxing pattern, working all the way up your body to your neck and face muscles. When you're finished, your whole body should feel relaxed.

Dip Into Homeopathy

❧ Homeopathic doctors recommend **Causticum** at the 12C dilution for legs that are restless during the night.

❧ Another option is a 12C dilution of **Tarentula hispanica**, three times a day until you see improvements in symptoms.

The Power of Prevention

❧ In the evening, **avoid alcoholic or caffeinated drinks**, which stimulate the muscles and nerves in your legs.

❧ Studies have found that **smokers** are more likely to have RLS than people who don't smoke.

❧ **Avoid cold and sinus medications**, which can make RLS symptoms much worse.

Ringworm

Any fungal infection spreads easily, and ringworm—once thought to be an actual worm lurking beneath the skin—is no exception. It all begins with prevention—keeping your feet and groin dry—and taking quick action with an over-the-counter antifungal medication when you see the first suggestion of an outbreak. Also try the home remedies below.

Use an Antifungal First

🍂 Look for over-the-counter **antifungal remedies** that contain ingredients such as miconazole, ketoconazole, clotrimazole, or terbinafine (Lamisil). Most need to be applied twice a day. If you follow the label directions, ringworm should start to clear within a week. Used twice a day for at least 8 weeks, OTCs like Zeasorb-AF powder—specifically for the feet and groin—are sure to get rid of the infection.

A Real Nut Case

🍂 If ringworm strikes in the fall, you might be able to resolve the problem with a green-hulled harvest from a nearby **black walnut** tree. Black walnuts have a distinctive-smelling thick green rind. Crush the rind into a pulp and apply it to ringworm up to four times a day until the condition clears up. (But that pulp is toxic if you eat it, so make sure it just goes on your skin.)

The Curry Cure

🍂 Turn ringworm away with **turmeric**. The main ingredient in curry powder, turmeric contains curcumin, which has helped many people who have inflammatory conditions like arthritis. It's not clear why turmeric should work so well on a fungal skin problem, but Asians have long used this spice to fight ringworm. Stir enough water into a teaspoon or two of powdered turmeric to make a paste. Smear it on the affected area and cover it with a bandage or piece of gauze. After 20 minutes to

What's **wrong**

Ringworm is actually a fungal infection of the skin that tends to creep insidiously along the groin, scalp, feet, and face. It often starts out as a round, itchy red patch that grows outward. As it expands, the middle area heals, but all around is a red ring where infection continues to spread. If it's on your scalp, count on some flaky skin and patches of hair loss. The condition is contagious, thrives in warm, moist environments, and is often spread when people touch an infected surface such as a shower floor.

Should I call
the doctor?

If your symptoms don't improve after a few weeks of self-care treatments, or the ringworm continues to spread, talk to your doctor. If you have ringworm in the groin area, the doctor might prescribe an antifungal powder such as Nystatin. For ringworm of the scalp, you'll need to get a prescription drug that's taken orally. And if you have diabetes, it's essential to get ringworm treated by a doctor as soon as possible. It can cause skin cracking, and if bacteria enter the skin, you could end up with a serious infection.

an hour, remove it. You can repeat this three or four times a day, but stop the treatment if turmeric irritates your skin.

Treat the Ring Right

◦ Be sure you keep the affected patch **clean and dry**.

◦ If the infection starts to ooze or blister over, apply cool or warm **moist compresses**. Or soak in water with dissolved **Epsom salt** or a proviodine solution to help dry the oozing rash. Take care not to break the blisters, and make an appointment with a doctor as soon as possible.

The Power of Prevention

◦ **Don't share shoes or used towels** with other people—they can spread an infection.

◦ If family members have ringworm, make sure that **no one shares clothing** or grooming items, such as **hairbrushes**.

◦ Wash in hot water any clothes, towels, washcloths, and bedclothes that may have come in touch with the infected area.

◦ Be sure to dry your feet completely soon after swimming or bathing, using a **hair dryer** whenever possible. The area between the toes is the most common place for fungus to start growing.

◦ Instead of going barefoot at a public swimming pool, wear **flip-flops** or **sandals** to avoid picking up fungus.

◦ Use a powder such as **Zeasorb-AF** in your shoes or your groin area to absorb excess moisture. The powder contains an antifungal ingredient for extra protection.

◦ Pets can carry ringworm that can be transferred to humans. If you see a **hairless spot on your dog or cat**, take your pet to the vet as soon as possible for a ringworm treatment.

Tick Off This Possibility

The ring created by the ringworm fungus resembles the "target" around a tick bite that's symptomatic of Lyme disease. So how can you tell the difference? If you're concerned, examine the "ring" area for some telltale signs. When ringworm has not yet been treated, it tends to be scaly, and the ring in the center is clear. Lyme disease, in its earliest stage, looks like a bull's-eye or target, and it has no scale. Also, if you have Lyme disease, the center of the ring is likely to be red or purplish at the site of the original tick bite.

Rosacea

You look like you're blushing, even when you're not. Or worse, you look like a teenager with a bad case of acne. Take heart. If Princess Diana could cope with her rosacea—you probably didn't even know she had it—so can you. Try these approaches to prevent mild flare-ups and flushing. Should your condition get worse, combine forces with a dermatologist to keep your ruddiness under control.

A Wetting List

❧ When your face gets warm and red, your first instinct is the right one: Cool it down. The easiest way is to soak a washcloth in **ice-cold water** and lay it on the red areas for about ten minutes. The cold tightens blood vessels.

❧ Chamomile, applied to the skin, has anti-inflammatory effects. Rather than using chamomile oil, which is highly concentrated and might cause a skin reaction, use dilute tea. Steep several **chamomile tea** bags in three cups of boiling water for 10 minutes. Strain the liquid and chill it in the refrigerator. When your face is flushed, dip a cloth into the tea and apply it to the red area.

Wash on the Mild Side

❧ Use a cleanser designed to be particularly gentle, such as **Cetaphil** or **Aquanil**, or **Dove soap for** sensitive skin, whenever you wash your face. You want to avoid soap that might be rough or irritating. What all these cleansers have in common is that they are moisturizing and contain no perfumes and few preservatives, which are the ingredients most likely to irritate skin.

❧ **Avoid** any **exfoliating skin washes** or **acne cleansers**. These contain harsh ingredients, and acne treatments can actually make rosacea worse.

❧ If you pick up a cleanser that lists **salicylic acid, benzoyl peroxide, or alcohol** as an ingredient, return it to the shelf—it will just **make rosacea worse**. Also steer clear of any abrasive cleaning products.

What's **wrong**

Sometimes rosacea looks no worse than a bothersome blush. But the condition can gradually worsen until it resembles severe acne. If you have rosacea, tiny blood vessels in the face widen and fill with blood until portions of the face seem suffused with red. The redness fades after a few hours, but if rosacea isn't treated, the face can take on a bumpy, sunburned look; blood vessels can become visible through the skin; and the nose may become red and enlarged.

Should I call the doctor?

Avoid Face Flushers

~ **Give up** the spiciest of spicy foods, including such south-of-the-border treats as **hot sauce, chili, and jalapeño peppers**. After you eat such foods, your face not only feels like it's flushing, it is. The fine arteries expand in reaction to the spicy food.

~ **Alcohol also makes your blood vessels widen.** Take note of any flushing after you drink. If your face tends to turn redder when you've had a cocktail or a glass of beer or wine, opt for soda or water at the next social occasion.

~ **Stay out of hot tubs and saunas.** Their heat can trigger flushing of the skin on your face.

A Whiter Shade of Pale

~ Stay out of the direct sunlight as much as possible, particularly in the middle of the day when the sun is at its hottest. **Sunlight can lead to flare-ups of rosacea**, since it warms your skin, dilating the blood vessels in your face.

~ If you do have to be outside on a sunny day, wear a **wide-brimmed hat** that provides shade for your ears and cheeks as well as your nose. A baseball cap isn't enough.

~ Use **sunscreen**, and plenty of it. For anyone with rosacea, the best sunscreens contain **titanium dioxide** or **zinc oxide,** which physically block the sun's rays rather than absorbing them chemically.

Don't See Red

~ When tempers flare, so do blood vessels, and that can lead to an outbreak of rosacea. One of the best ways to keep a fiery response in check is simply to **count to ten**. Take it a step further by inhaling deeply as you count. Exhale fully while you count to ten again. After you've done this a few times, you'll find that you can handle the situation much more calmly.

Shaving Face

~ Men with rosacea need to take special care not to irritate their faces while attacking their whiskers. Use an **electric shaver** instead of razor blades. The shaver is less irritating.

~ If you use an aftershave, **stay away from** products that contain **alcohol, witch hazel,** or **menthol**.

Seasonal Affective Disorder (SAD)

When some people hear about the symptoms of SAD, their first reaction is, "Oh, *that's* what my problem is!" Indeed, if the depths of winter have always seemed especially gloomy, it may be reassuring to know that you're not the only one suffering the seasonal blues. If your mood turns so black that you feel like you can't function normally, don't hesitate to tell your doctor or a therapist. But if your symptoms are mild, the remedies below can help light up your life.

Brighten Up!

⌒ Do everything you can to **increase the amount of natural light** that comes into your home. Keep curtains and blinds open. If tree branches block your windows, trim them back. For a room that's dim, consider having a skylight installed, especially if it's the kitchen or a living area where you spend a lot of time.

⌒ On sunny winter days, **take walks outdoors**. Even if winter light doesn't have midsummer intensity, a dose of real sun is far more effective than indoor bulbs. In fact, one study showed that an hour's walk in winter sunlight was as effective at reducing SAD symptoms as two and a half hours walking under bright artificial light.

⌒ Plan your longest vacation during the winter months, and get away to a **warm, sunny climate** if at all possible. Just one or two weeks of escape from winter gloom can provide welcome relief from SAD symptoms.

Join a Gym or Strap On Skis

⌒ While research shows that **exercise** helps relieve depression, it's hard to get motivated in the winter. If you join a health club and set up a regular time to go, you're more likely to get the exercise you need to boost your mood.

⌒ Better yet, adopt a **winter sport**. Obviously, you're a lot more likely to get outdoors if there are things you enjoy doing, even when the weather is chilly. If you haven't explored winter

What's **wrong**

Seasonal affective disorder (SAD) comes on in the late fall or winter, when sunlight is in short supply. Symptoms include blue mood, low energy, prolonged sleep, cravings for sugar and starch, and weight gain. SAD has been linked to the hormone melatonin, produced by the pineal gland in the brain. Low levels of light result in increased melatonin production. Another theory holds that sunlight affects levels of mood-regulating brain chemicals such as serotonin.

Should I call the doctor?

If you experience severe depression and changes in your eating and sleeping habits, schedule an appointment with your doctor or a therapist. Many treatments for severe depression are available, including antidepressants. If the doctor determines that your depression is seasonal, you may benefit from light therapy in addition to other forms of treatment.

sports before, consider ice-skating, snowshoeing, or cross-country skiing. Even on gray days, you'll manage to soak up some sunshine if you're outdoors exercising.

An Anti-Worry Wort

To help lift your mood, take 40 to 60 drops of tincture of **St. John's wort** in a glass of cold water three times a day. Once called "God's grace" or "the blessed herb," this home remedy now has a venerable reputation as a mild antidepressant. Within the last twenty years, studies have shown that one of its components indirectly helps to increase the mood-boosting brain chemical serotonin. One drawback of St. John's wort, however, is that it increases skin sensitivity. When you're taking it, be sure to slather on sunscreen before you head outdoors.

Other Mood Boosters

Take a daily multivitamin and mineral supplement that contains **vitamin B$_6$, thiamin**, and **folic acid**. Studies have shown that all of these B vitamins can benefit mood.

Don't overdo cookies, candy, and other sugary foods. That refined sugar may give you an initial lift, but afterward your energy plummets and so will your mood. Opt for **protein-dense meals** that can help increase alertness—an egg-white omelet for breakfast, for instance, with a chicken-breast sandwich for lunch.

Tell your family and friends about your SAD, and enlist their **support**. If they're aware that you're more susceptible to blue moods on dark days, they can help plan activities.

To prevent mood swings, **stay away from alcohol**. A drink or two might help dispel anxiety or relieve stress for a short while. But because alcohol is a depressant, your mood plummets when the buzz wears off.

Let There Be Light

If self-treatment for SAD symptoms doesn't work, ask your doctor about light therapy, which uses extremely bright artificial light to compensate for the lack of natural sunlight. You'll sit a few meters from a special lamp that's 10 to 20 times brighter than ordinary indoor lights. Sessions may last from 30 minutes up to several hours a day. Light therapy is thought to alter levels of both melatonin and serotonin, so it has a positive influence on sleep patterns and feelings of well-being.

Shin Splints

You exercised because it's good for you, and in return you got an excruciating pain in your shin. For immediate relief, your best bets are ice and an over-the-counter pain reliever such as ibuprofen or aspirin to ease the tenderness and swelling. You'll also want to change your exercise habits. Runners usually develop shin splints when they've been running on hard surfaces or when they've been faithful to worn-out running shoes for too long. Stretching is essential, and so is moderation, if you want to prevent recurrent pain.

Numb the Pain

⤙ Ice the injured shin to bring down swelling and dull the pain. Use a flexible **ice pack** or a bag of **frozen vegetables** and keep it on for up to 20 minutes. To make sure you don't get frostbite, put a towel between the ice pack and your skin.

⤙ Instead of an ice pack, you can apply a lump of ice. **Freeze water in a foam cup**, then peel away the cup and press the solid ice to the shin. As the ice melts, just peel away more of the cup. If you use this method, however, limit applications to under 8 minutes at a time. And give the chilled skin a chance to warm up before you apply that ice a second or third time.

Stretch the Point

⤙ Sit or lie down with your knees slightly bent. **Flex the foot** of the painful leg up and down, in and out, and in circles. Your leg should remain still. Repeat each motion ten times.

⤙ For a **leg stretch** that relieves pain, start out in a seated position on the floor. Keep the painful leg outstretched, and the knee slightly bent. Loop a towel around the ball of your foot and, with the knee still bent, gently pull the towel toward your body. Hold for 15 to 30 seconds, then relax. Repeat 3 times.

⤙ As a follow-up, stand and place your hands against the wall at eye level. Keep your painful shin back, with the heel on the floor, and the uninjured shin forward. Turn your back foot slightly inward, as if you were pigeon-toed. Slowly lean into

What's **wrong**

If you run regularly or do any kind of exercise that hammers the lower leg, there's a chance you'll develop shin splints. During exercise, muscles in the lower leg swell and press against the gap formed by the tibia and fibula, the bones that extend from the knee to the ankle. This pressure irritates nearby muscles, tendons, or ligaments, causing pain along the outer calf (anterior shin splints) or inner calf (posterior shin splints). Posterior shin splints are common among people with flat feet, because leg muscles have to work hard to support the foot's arch.

Should I call the doctor?

You can usually treat shin splints on your own. But if the pain lingers for more than three weeks, give your doctor a call. You may need further evaluation or treatment by a podiatrist or orthopedist, especially if he or she suspects you have a stress fracture. Though it's just a tiny crack in the bone, a stress fracture usually causes pain in a small area inside the shinbone, accompanied by swelling and tenderness. It can get much worse without treatment. To positively identify a stress fracture, the doctor will probably have to do an X ray or other imaging test.

the wall until you feel a stretch in the back of your calf. Hold for 15 to 30 seconds.

- Repeat the same standing stretch, but this time cross the back leg behind the front one so most of your weight is on the outside edges of your feet. Hold for 15 to 30 seconds.

- In a standing position, with one hand against a wall or chair for balance, bend the knee of your injured leg and grab the top of your foot. Pull the toes of that foot toward the heel to create a stretch in the front part of your shin. Hold for 15 to 30 seconds. Repeat 3 times.

- Holding a chair or counter for balance, rise up onto your toes, hold for 5 seconds, then come down slowly. Repeat 10 times. Then do two more sets of 10.

- Alternate walking on your heels for 30 seconds with 30 seconds of regular walking. Repeat four times.

The Power of Prevention

- It's vitally important to **stretch your calf muscles** before you exercise. Whether you're running, doing aerobics, or playing a fast-action team sport, consult with a trainer or doctor to find out what type of leg stretches are most appropriate. Then do them religiously before and after each workout.

- Choose the **softest available surface** for exercise. If you run, use a dirt or cinder track rather than concrete sidewalks. If you do aerobics, use a soft mat instead of a hard floor.

- Buy well-cushioned shoes with excellent arch support. Ask a podiatrist about **arch supports** or **heel inserts**.

- When you're **buying sports shoes, get advice about what kinds are best for your feet**. For instance, if you roll your ankles inward (this is called pronation) when you run, it forces your tendons to compensate, increasing your risk of shin splints. You need shoes that help correct for that tendency.

- If you are a regular runner, buy a **new pair** of running shoes before the old ones have a chance to wear out. If you run more than 40 kilometers per week, you'll probably need new shoes every 2 or 3 months. Even if you run less than that, it's a good idea to check the wear on your shoes after 4 months.

- Anyone with flat feet should visit a **runner's specialty store** for proper footwear. You want to make sure you have adequate cushioning and shock-absorbing inner supports.

Shingles

First step: Call your doctor, who will likely put you on a prescription antiviral drug. Meanwhile, you'll want all the relief you can get from the burning and pain. You can try acetaminophen or ibuprofen, plus the remedies in this chapter. But if the pain is more than you can stand, don't hesitate to call your doctor, who can prescribe stronger medication.

Beat the Blisters and Ditch the Itch

To help dry the blisters, apply **calamine lotion**. As the wet solution evaporates from your skin, it also draws moisture from the blisters.

If you have an **aloe vera** plant in your home or garden, cut a leaf and smooth the liquid over your skin. The milky liquid inside the leaves may help soothe the blisters. Or use an over-the-counter aloe vera gel (make sure it's 100% aloe).

A paste of **baking powder** and water will dry up blisters and soothe the itching. Add enough water to dry baking powder to create a paste, then apply it liberally to the affected area.

Another remedy for drying blisters and soothing inflammation is a paste made from **Epsom salt** and water. Apply directly to the affected area. Repeat as often as you wish.

Brew a tea of **lemon balm**, an herb from the mint family that European studies suggest fights herpes viruses. To make it, boil 2 teaspoons dried herb in 1 cup boiling water. Use a cotton ball to dab it directly onto the affected areas. Some herbalists recommend bolstering the brew with **rose oil** or mints such as **peppermint, spearmint**, and **sage**.

Reach into your pantry, where you probably have the ingredients for another shingles solution: **vinegar** and **honey**. Mix them together to form a paste and dab it onto your sores.

Send the Pain Packing

Dip a washcloth or towel into **cold water**, squeeze it out, and lay it over the affected area. Alternatively, you can use

What's wrong

Shingles occurs when the dormant herpes zoster virus, which causes chicken pox, re-awakens in nerve cells and makes its way to the skin. About 20 percent of people who had chicken pox will later develop shingles, usually when they're over age 50. The infection causes a burning, blistering rash—often on the torso, face, and neck—which appears as a band or patch of raised dots. Itching, tingling, or pain can be mild or severe. Within a week or so, small, fluid-filled blisters form, dry up, and crust over. Anything that lowers resistance to infection, such as illness or stress, can awaken the virus. On average, the rash and pain last 2 to 4 weeks, but sometimes the pain lingers for months.

Yes, and quickly. You should contact the doctor within 72 hours if you develop the typical symptoms. Starting antiviral drugs immediately can help reduce the severity and duration of an attack and may also stave off postherpetic neuralgia, the painful aftereffects of shingles. Call, too, if you're unable to endure the pain of a current outbreak of shingles, or if your shingles have disappeared but the pain hasn't. If you get shingles on your nose, forehead, or anywhere else near your eyes, call your doctor immediately for treatment, as there is a risk of going blind.

cold milk instead of water. Some people say that the milk is especially soothing.

Made from the extract of hot pepper, **capsaicin cream** can quell pain that lingers after the rash is gone. Zostrix is one brand to try. When you first put it on, you'll feel a burning sensation, but as long as you're not using it on an open rash, the burning will diminish as you continue using it over the next few weeks. (Just don't use the cream if the skin is broken or you have an open rash—it will burn intensely.)

If you still have pain after the blisters have healed, fill a bag with **ice** and use it to gently stroke your skin. Experts don't know why the cold treatment is helpful, but it does work.

Put Brakes on Breakouts

As long as you have your doctor's approval, and a prescription, take 500 to 1,000 milligrams of supplemental **lysine** three times a day during an outbreak. This amino acid prevents viruses from replicating and may speed healing.

Take two 250-milligram capsules of **echinacea** three times a day to help your body fight the infection.

Try taking **cat's claw**, an herb long used for a variety of purposes among indigenous people of Peru and now considered a promising treatment for viral disorders, including shingles. Follow the dosage directions on the package.

The Power of Prevention

To protect others from the virus, **wash your hands often**, especially if you have an oozing rash. The blisters contain the varicella virus, so you could infect someone with chicken pox. Or cover the blisters with an antibiotic ointment and wrap them with gauze.

Pain After the Pain

Many people who develop shingles experience lingering pain in the affected area months or even years after an attack. This is called postherpetic neuralgia (PHN). If you have PHN, be sure to see your doctor, who can prescribe a medication such as Neurontin (gabapentin), an effective oral drug approved for shingles. Other treatments include the Lidoderm patch (not yet available in Canada), which feeds medication into damaged nerves under the skin, and an injection with local anesthetic.

Sinusitis

You're stuffed up, your face hurts, and the pressure is getting to you. If a bacterial infection is the cause of your sinusitis, your doctor can give you antibiotics that will help. Otherwise, oral or nasal decongestants can give you temporary relief. (Don't use them for more than three days or the swelling in your sinuses could get worse.) Of course, you don't have to dash off to the drugstore every time your sinuses swell. There are plenty of other ways to reopen blocked passages and help yourself feel better.

Do Some Steam Cleaning

⮞ **Steam** can relieve the painful sinus pressure. Take a long, hot shower, inhale the steam, and let the water spray on your face. Then snort and swallow the hot water until your sinuses are clear.

⮞ Give your congested sinuses a mentholated steam treatment. Boil a pot of water to which you've added a few drops of **eucalyptus oil**, then remove the pot from the stove. Drape a towel over your head and shoulders, then lean forward so it forms a tent over the pan. Keep your face about 45 centimeters above the water as you breathe in deeply. As the vapor rises, it carries droplets of oil into your sinuses and loosens secretions.

⮞ Don't have any eucalyptus oil on hand? No problem. Just add a teaspoon of **Vicks VapoRub** to the water instead.

Sniff a Salt Solution

⮞ Another method of loosening mucus and reducing swelling is irrigating the sinuses with a **saline solution**. Make the salt solution by mixing one-third teaspoon of table salt and a pinch of baking soda in a cup of warm water. Then fill an ear-bulb syringe with the solution. Closing one nostril with your thumb, tilt your head back and squirt the solution into one nostril while you sniff. Blow your nose gently, then repeat with the other nostril.

⮞ You can also use a device called a **neti pot**, available at health-food stores. (It looks like a small watering can with a

What's **wrong**

The sinuses—air-filled cavities on either side of the nose—are lined with a superthin mucous membrane. When the membrane becomes inflamed and infected, it swells, blocking channels that allow mucus to drain into the nose. The resulting pressure can cause headache, nasal congestion, yellow-green nasal discharge, and cheekbone pain. Sinusitis that lasts three weeks or less (acute sinusitis) may result from a bacterial infection, a cold or the flu, or swimming in contaminated water. Chronic sinusitis is often caused by a deviated septum, irritation from dust or cigarette smoke, or fungal infections.

narrow spout.). To use the neti pot, place half the liquid in the device. Standing over a sink, place the spout into one nostril, then tilt your head to the side and down, away from the spout. Pour the saline solution into the nostril. The liquid will come out of the other nostril. Once it has drained out, blow your nose gently into a tissue. Repeat with the other nostril using the other half of the saline solution.

Heat Those Cavities

🍃 Inhale freshly grated **horseradish**. The pungent root contains a fiery substance that helps to thin mucus.

🍃 Alternatively, mix equal amounts of grated **horseradish** and **lemon juice** and eat 1 teaspoonful an hour before breakfast. Take another teaspoonful an hour before dinner.

🍃 If you're a fan of spicy-hot foods, add some chili peppers to your meals. The peppers contain **capsaicin**, a compound that breaks up congestion and promotes the drainage of mucus. And when you're all out of chilis, you can sprinkle on cayenne pepper instead; it, too, has all-powerful capsaicin.

🍃 Many studies show that a substance in **garlic** called allicin is a potent antibacterial and natural antibiotic. Crush 1 clove of garlic, drop it into a quarter-cup of water, and swish it around. Then use an eyedropper to extract some of this garlic water and put 10 drops in each nostril. At the end of 3 days, your infection should be well on its way to healing.

Enter the Land of Ahhhs

🍃 A cup of hot **tea** can help thin nasal mucus. **Chamomile tea** was once considered a folk remedy for sinusitis. If you like it, try it. Another herbal tea to try is Red Zinger from Celestial Seasonings. We heard that one opera singer swears by it for sinus problems. It contains rosehips and lemongrass. Drink several cups a day as soon as you feel an infection coming on.

🍃 **Get plenty of rest.** When you're lying down, however, be sure to keep a pillow under your head to help your sinuses drain. Lying flat on your back without a pillow can make your congestion worse.

🍃 Apply a **warm washcloth** over your eyes and cheekbones. Leave it in place until the cloth cools. Then warm it up again and repeat as often as needed until you get some relief.

Become a Nose Masseur

🌿 Giving your sinuses a **mini-massage** will increase blood circulation to the area and help to chase away the pain. Using your index fingers, press hard on the outer edge of your nostrils at the base of the nose.

🌿 Another pressure-relieving move: Apply your thumbs to both sides of your nose, about halfway up, and press firmly on the cartilage. Hold for 30 seconds, then release. You can repeat this as often as you like.

🌿 For sinus relief using **acupressure**, use your left thumb and index finger to press the areas next to the inner eyes on both sides of the bridge of your nose. At the same time, use your fingers and the heel of your other hand to grab muscles on both sides of the spine at the back of your neck. Put pressure on all four points for about one minute.

Bring In the Herbal Bouncers

🌿 **Echinacea** and **astragalus** are two herbs that can boost immunity and sometimes banish bacteria and viruses. For echinacea the recommended dosage is 200 milligrams standardized to 3.5% echinacosides, taken four times a day. Astragalus capsules should also be 200 milligrams, standardized to 0.5% glucosides and 70% polysaccharides. Take astragalus twice a day between meals. If you have the kind of sinusitis that comes on suddenly after a cold or flu, take the full dosage of both these herbs for a few weeks or until the sinusitis gets better. For chronic sinusitis—the kind that drags on and on—alternate taking echinacea one week and astragalus the next.

🌿 Try taking 250 to 500 milligrams of **goldenseal** three times a day. This herb is thought to fight infections and is

Did you **know?**

If you blow both nostrils at a time when you blow your nose, the pressure could force bacteria farther up into the sinus passages. Blow one nostril, then the other.

New Flight Plan

Some frequent fliers have problems on the way up; others, on the way down. When a plane takes off, air pressure is reduced and the pressure builds in your head, blocking your sinuses (or the Eustachian tubes in your ears). In mid-flight you might be all right, but on the way down, the pressure changes again, and your sinuses take the punishment. To avoid the pain, use a decongestant nasal spray or ask your doctor about a prescription inhaler you can use before you endure the ups and downs of another flight.

sometimes combined with echinacea. Goldenseal tea can be either drunk or used as a nasal wash. To make it, boil one half to one gram of goldenseal in a cup of water. Don't use goldenseal for more than one or two weeks at a time, though.

The Power of Prevention

Run a **cold-mist humidifier** in your bedroom at night to keep your nasal and sinus passages from drying out. Just make sure you clean the humidifier once a week so mildew or fungi can't set up shop.

Cut down on your consumption of **alcoholic beverages.** Alcohol causes swelling of nasal and sinus membranes.

Avoid swimming in a chlorinated pool—and never dive. Chlorine irritates the lining of the nose and sinuses. Diving forces water from nasal passages up into the sinuses.

Stay away from smoke-filled rooms. Cigarette smoke dries out nasal passages, and bacteria get trapped in the sinuses.

Snoring

If you're the snorer in your household, lucky you. After all, you're the only one who can sleep right through the thunderous racket. For the sake of household harmony, show your partner the tips in the "Self-Defense" sidebar (page 337). Then try the following preventive measures. Changing your sleeping position may be all it takes, but a larger project—namely, losing weight—is often the real ticket to tranquil nights.

Put Yourself in a Good Position

↝ Buy yourself a few extra pillows and **prop yourself up** in bed, rather than lying flat on your back. You'll prevent the tissues in your throat from falling into your air passages.

↝ **Elevate** the head of your bed. An easy way to do it is to place several flat boards under the legs at the top end of the bed. A couple of short lengths of two-by-eights or two-by-tens under each leg should raise the bed enough to do the trick.

↝ **Sleep on your side**. Of course, there's no guarantee you'll stay in that position, but at least start on your side with your arms wrapped around a pillow. There's a good reason you don't want to sleep on your back: In that position, your tongue and soft palate rest against the back of your throat, blocking the airway.

↝ If hugging a pillow doesn't help, you can ace the problem with service from a sewn-in **tennis ball**. Here's how: Sew a little pouch on the back of your pajama top and tuck a tennis ball inside. At night, if you start to roll on your back while you're sleeping, you'll get a nudge from that tennis ball, prompting you to get back on your side.

Don't Be So Nosy

↝ If nasal congestion is causing your snoring, take a **decongestant** or **antihistamine** before you turn in.

↝ Tape your nose open with **nasal strips**, available at most drugstores. They may look odd, but who's watching? Following the directions on the package, tape one of the strips to the out-

What's wrong

When you snore, structures in the mouth and throat—the tongue, upper throat, soft palate, and uvula—vibrate against the tonsils and adenoids. There are many possible causes. Overweight people are more likely to snore, and experts think it's because the extra fatty tissue compresses the air passages. Drinking alcohol before bedtime is another factor: It causes throat muscles to relax and tissues to sag. And whenever you have nasal congestion from a cold or allergies, you're more likely to snore, because inflamed tissues and extra mucus interfere with airflow.

Should I call **the doctor?**

side of your nose before you fall asleep. They'll lift and open your nostrils to increase airflow.

Gargle with a **peppermint mouthwash** to shrink the lining of your nose and throat. This is especially effective if your snoring is a temporary condition caused by a head cold or an allergy. To mix up the herbal gargle, add one drop of peppermint oil to a glass of cold water. (But *only* gargle—do not swallow.)

Chin Up

It sounds extreme, but some people have used a **neck brace**—the kind people with whiplash wear—to stop their snoring. It works by keeping your chin extended so your throat doesn't bend and your airway stays open. You don't have to use a stiff plastic brace, however. A soft foam one, available at drugstores or medical supply stores, is less restraining and will work just as well.

Axe Allergies

Reduce bedroom allergens (dust, pet dander, mold) to alleviate nasal stuffiness by **vacuuming floors and drapes**. Change sheets and pillowcases often.

If your snoring is a seasonal problem—and you know you're allergic to pollen—try drinking up to three cups of tea made from the herb **stinging nettle**. Herbalists recommend it for soothing inflammation caused by pollen allergies. To make the tea, pour 1 cup boiling water over 1 tablespoon of the dried leaf (available in health-food stores). Cover the tea and let it steep for 5 minutes. Strain and drink. Drink one cup of tea just before bedtime.

Watch Your Mouth

Don't eat a heavy meal or drink alcoholic beverages within three hours of turning in. Both can cause your throat muscles to relax more than normal.

Snoring improves as you **shed some weight**. Losing 10 percent of your body weight can help by easing constriction of the upper airway.

A Short Course in Snoring Self-Defense

If you're living with someone who snores, there's a better than even chance the nightly sonorities are fraying your relationship. But remember, other spouses and partners have dealt with this too—and survived. So before you head for the hills, consider some practical methods to deal with the rumblings of your otherwise lovable bedmate.

- Buy yourself a pair of earplugs. They are inexpensive and quite comfortable, once you get accustomed to them.

- A white-noise machine can make nights with a snorer more bearable. These electronic devices produce a consistent sound that muffles other noises.

- Turn in well before your snoring spouse. That way, at least, you have a head start on a good night's sleep. Some well-practiced partners can sleep right through the full-scale thunder of Rip Van Winkle.

- **Quit smoking.** Tobacco smoke irritates mucous membranes, so your throat swells, narrowing the airway. Smokers also have more problems with nasal congestion.

- If you're regularly taking any kind of **medication**, talk to your doctor about alternatives. Some drugs can make snoring worse, including sleeping pills and sedatives.

- Dry air can contribute to snoring. There are lots of ways to do battle with dry air. A **humidifier** or **steam vaporizer** in the bedroom can keep your air passages moist; just be sure to clean it regularly, following the manufacturer's instructions. Another approach: Just before bedtime, fill a bowl with hot water, drape a towel over your head, bend over the bowl so your nose is roughly 15 centimeters from the water, and breathe deeply through your nose for a few minutes.

Teatime

Do you drink tea? If not, now may be a good time to dust off your teakettle. A growing body of evidence suggests that it's possible to prevent and control many common ailments simply by savoring a daily cup or two.

You may already be familiar with the remarkable story of green tea. This minimally processed variant of black tea (both come from the same shrub, *Camellia sinensis*) has been shown to boost immunity, lower cholesterol levels, fight tooth decay, and even help ward off cancer. It contains EGCG, one of the most potent antioxidants ever discovered. Ordinary black tea confers health benefits too. (See page 421 for more on tea.)

Herbal teas have powerful medicinal properties all their own. They are perfect for people who want the healing benefits of herbs without taking capsules. Most are remarkably free of side effects (though it's always a good idea to check with your doctor first, especially if you're pregnant or if troublesome symptoms persist for more than a few days). Did you know, for example, that tea made with the leaves and flowers of the hawthorn plant is considered a tonic for the heart? That raspberry tea helps curb traveler's diarrhea? Certain teas, such as chamomile, are even useful in compresses to speed the healing of wounds and relieve inflammation.

Many herbal teas are surprisingly tasty, though some do call for a dollop of honey. And, of course, tea is easy to make. You simply add to boiling water some fresh or dried herb you pick up from your local grocer or health-food store. The following recipes call for dried herbs. If you use fresh herbs instead, you'll need to use three times as much.

Antioxidant tea. During World War II, pilots in the RAF were known to eat lots of bilberry jam. Seems word had gotten out that the berries contained compounds that would improve their eyesight. Bilberry is a rich source of anthocyanosides, compounds that may protect the retina against macular degeneration, a leading cause of blindness. Because bilberries are astringent, the tea is also useful against diarrhea. (Bring some along with you on your next international voyage.) It also appears to strengthen veins (useful if you have varicose veins), and may lower blood sugar in people with diabetes.

Rx: *Steep one teaspoon of ground bilberry in hot water for 15 minutes. Drink up to four cups daily.*

Tummy-taming brew. An aromatic blend of cardamom and three other spices makes a tasty way to stop cramps and gas pains, especially when you overindulge at mealtime. Drink it at the first sign of pain or—even better—about 15 minutes before mealtime. This tea is also great for children's stomachaches.

Rx: *In a mug, mix a quarter-teaspoon cardamom spice, a half-teaspoon ground fennel seed, a half-teaspoon ground caraway seed, and half a slice of fresh gingerroot. Pour in one cup boiling water. Steep for 10 minutes. Add a cinnamon stick if you have one on hand.*

Hot-flash help. If you're eager to curb menopausal symptoms without subjecting yourself to the risks of hormone replacement therapy, consider black cohosh. Drinking tea made from this bitter herb helps ease hot flashes and other menopause symptoms by lowering levels of luteinizing hormone. Talk to your doctor before taking black cohosh in the long term.

Rx: *Boil a half-teaspoon of powdered root per cup of water for 30 minutes, then strain. Take two tablespoonfuls every few hours throughout the day. Honey and lemon help tame the bitter taste.*

Before-bed beverage. For occasional insomnia, there's nothing wrong with taking a sleeping pill. But why risk becoming dependent on pills when this yummy chamomile-lavender tea makes a natural substitute? You can drink the tea several times a day, or once at bedtime.

Rx: *Combine two parts chamomile flowers, two parts lemon balm herb, one part catnip herb, one part lavender flowers, one part peppermint leaf, one part rose petals and a pinch of nutmeg to taste. For one cup of tea, mix two teaspoons in one cup of boiling water. Steep for five minutes.*

Cold and cough busters. Hot tea is a natural choice when it comes to fighting colds and congestion. Especially good are hyssop tea for coughs, horehound tea for coughs and congestion, and marshmallow tea for a sore throat.

Rx: *Use two teaspoons of powdered hyssop or dried horehound per cup of hot water. Add honey to offset the bitter taste. To make marshmallow tea, use two teaspoons of chopped root per cup of hot water, gently boil for 15 minutes, then strain.*

Queasies calmer. Ginger works so well at combating nausea that some cancer specialists now recommend it as a way to counteract the severe nausea associated with chemotherapy.

Rx: *Steep two teaspoons powdered dry ginger or grated fresh gingerroot in a cup of hot water for 10 minutes. The tea works better at preventing nausea than at stopping nausea once it starts.*

Beneficial nettle. A daily cup of pleasant-tasting nettle tea offers several benefits. For men plagued by a weak urine stream and the need to wake up repeatedly during the night to urinate—signs of an enlarged prostate—the tea can help by slowing the growth of prostate tissue. A powerful diuretic, nettle can also help control high blood pressure and bloating caused by premenstrual syndrome. Drinking nettle tea regularly may also help against hay fever.

Rx: *Steep two teaspoons of dried leaves in a cup of hot water for 10 minutes. Drink a cup or two daily.*

Sore Throat

An over-the-counter pain reliever like ibuprofen or acetaminophen will give you temporary relief. But the quickest way to simmer down a searing gullet is with gargles, teas, or a coating of honey. Here are the best combinations:

Get Gargling

➤ For fast and effective relief, nothing beats an old-fashioned **saltwater gargle**. Salt acts as a mild antiseptic, and also draws water out of mucous membranes in the throat, which helps to clear phlegm. Dissolve a half-teaspoon salt in a glass of warm water, gargle, and spit out. Repeat up to four times a day.

➤ For a spicier gargle, substitute a few drops of **Tabasco sauce** for salt.

➤ Alternatively, gargle with a **baking-soda** solution. Dissolve one-half teaspoon of baking soda in a glass of warm water.

Tonight, Honey

➤ **Honey** has long been used as a sore-throat remedy. It has antibacterial properties, which can help speed healing. It also acts as a hypertonic osmotic, which means that it draws water out of inflamed tissue. This reduces the swelling and discomfort. Add several teaspoons to 1 cup of hot water or herbal tea.

➤ **Hot lemonade with honey** can also relieve pain. Combine the juice of half a lemon with hot water.

Capital Teas

➤ **Horehound** reduces the swelling of inflamed throat tissue. It also thins mucus, which makes it easier for you to clear it from your throat. To make the tea, steep 2 teaspoons chopped herb in 1 cup boiling water for 10 minutes; strain and drink.

➤ **Slippery elm** contains mucilage that coats the throat and eases the soreness. Steep 1 teaspoon of the inner bark in 2 cups boiling water, strain, and drink.

Like slippery elm bark, **marshmallow root** (*Althea officinalis*) contains throat-coating mucilage. To make the tea, steep 2 teaspoons dried herb in 1 cup boiling water for 10 minutes; strain and drink. Drink three to five cups a day.

Throw Down the Gullet

Take 1,000 milligrams of **vitamin C** three times a day. Whether your sore throat is caused by a cold, the flu, or strep, this vitamin will help boost your immune system and fight off infection. Reduce the dose if you develop diarrhea.

Take 200 milligrams of **echinacea** in capsule form four times a day. This herb's antibacterial and antiviral properties will speed healing. Make sure the echinacea you buy is standardized to 3.5% echinacosides.

As another aid to fight off infection, take 400 to 600 milligrams of **garlic** in capsule form, four times a day. Dried garlic has potent antibacterial and antiseptic properties. Take the capsules with food.

Take one **zinc** lozenge very two hours until your sore throat is gone—but never for longer than a week. In one study, people who sucked on a lozenge containing about 13 milligrams of zinc every two hours got rid of viral sore throats three to four days quicker than those who didn't. But too much zinc can actually compromise immunity, which is why you shouldn't take the lozenges for a long time.

The Power of Prevention

During cold and flu season, **wash your hands often** and make an effort to keep them away from your eyes, nose, and mouth. You'll be less likely to catch a cold or the flu.

Should I call **the doctor?**

You can usually take care of a common sore throat, and it should clear up on its own within a day or so. But see a doctor if the pain lasts more than two days, if the soreness is accompanied by a fever of 38.8°C (102°F) or higher, or if you also have an earache. These are signs that you might have a strep infection. Call, too, if you find it difficult to swallow or have swollen glands in your neck. If not treated, strep can lead to potentially serious conditions, including inflammation of the kidneys and rheumatic fever, which can affect the heart, brain, and joints.

Could It Be Reflux?

One of the more unusual causes of a sore throat is acid reflux. If strong stomach acids back up into your throat while you're sleeping, you'll wake up with what feels just like a sore throat. To prevent acid backup, put a few short pieces of two-by-six boards under the legs at the head of your bed. With the bed tilted 15 to 20 centimeters above the horizontal, reflux will flow downhill during the night—away from your throat and toward your stomach.

A Lozenge Hazard

When you feel the scratchiness of a sore throat, your first impulse might be to buy throat lozenges that numb the tissue. But be sure to read the labels first. You want to avoid phenol, a chemical that can be toxic, according to government health reports. Some of the side effects of phenol—if taken internally—are liver and kidney damage and heart problems.

Tried...

According to frontier folk tradition, you could cure a sore throat if you took three tablespoons each of honey, lemon, and red or white vinegar, three times a day, for three days.

...and true

While there's nothing special about the "threes" in this recipe, the ingredients can soothe your throat and help fight off infection.

🙠 Run a **cool-mist vaporizer** or humidifier in your bedroom. Adding moisture to the air will help keep the air from drying out and prevent the lining of your throat from becoming too dry.

🙠 If you don't have a humidifier, place a **bowl of water** on your radiator or heating vent each night. It will work as well as a store-bought device.

🙠 **If you smoke, quit**. Cigarette smoke is extremely irritating to the lining of the throat.

🙠 **Breathe through your nose**, rather than your mouth. It's a natural way to humidify the air you breathe.

🙠 If you're plagued with a sore throat that seems to come back time and time again, **buy a new toothbrush**. Bacteria collect on the bristles, and if you injure your gums as you brush, they can enter your system and re-infect you.

🙠 **Bolster your immune system** during cold and flu season with vitamins, herbs, and good nutrition. The obvious supplement candidates are **vitamins C and E,** the minerals **zinc and magnesium,** and immune-boosting herbs such as **goldenseal** and **astragalus**. Also cook or supplement with **garlic, ginger, shiitake mushrooms,** and **reishi mushrooms,** all of which have immune-boosting properties.

Splinters

You may remember as a child having a needle-wielding parent dig a splinter out of your skin while you wiggled and winced. The sharp prick of the needle was probably worse than the splinter itself. Alas, a sterilized needle and a set of tweezers are still standard tools for splinter removal today. But try these tricks to help coax slivers out of skin with less pain and suffering.

Try a Tape Trick

 If part of the splinter—however small—is protruding from the skin, try using some tape before you go to work with tweezers and needle. Put **adhesive tape** over the splinter and press down gently so the adhesive catches it. As you lift the tape again, the splinter might come away with it. This is particularly effective if you have a number of tiny splinters that aren't very deeply embedded.

Summon Splinters to the Surface

 For a splinter on the tip of your finger, carefully fill a wide-mouthed bottle with **boiling water** to within one centimeter of the top. Place the part of the finger with the splinter over the top of the bottle and press down lightly. As you press directly down, the heat from the water will "draw out" the splinter.

 Some doctors suggest putting a **wart removal disk** containing **salicylic acid** (found in drugstores) over the splinter site. Change the disk every 12 hours or so. After a few days under the wart plaster, the splinter may come out or work itself close enough to the surface for you to grab it with tweezers.

A Swell Idea

 If the splinter is a sliver of wood, it might pop out on its own if you can get it to swell up. For 10 or 15 minutes, soak the area of skin where the splinter is buried in a cup of warm water to which you've added 1 tablespoon of **baking soda**. Do

What's wrong

Almost anything can embed itself in your skin—a needle-sharp piece of wood, a sliver of glass, or a piece of metal. But tiny slivers can cause a big hurt, especially if they lodge in a sensitive spot, such as under a fingernail. And there's the possibility of infection if they're not removed carefully and completely.

Back in the good old days when people split cords of wood to keep home fires burning, everyone got splinters. But woodcutters had a special way of removing them. They would spread warmed pine sap on the skin, then peel it away after it dried, lifting out the splinter at the same time. No reason why it won't work—if you want to try it. But if you have other implements, like tweezers, there's really no reason to go scouting for sap.

Should I call **the doctor?**

You can usually treat a splinter at home. But if it's deeply embedded, or if it's underneath your nail or in the facial area, you should probably let a doctor handle it. Also call your doctor if you notice an infection brewing, usually a sign that some of the splinter is still lodged in your skin. Typical infection warnings include pain, swelling, redness, or red streaks. Finally, make the call if the splinter is metal and you haven't had a tetanus shot within the past 5 years.

this twice a day. A tiny splinter might swell up so much that it comes right out. If it's larger, perhaps more of it is protruding, and you can use tweezers to extract it.

Tweezer Tips

◦ If it looks as if the splinter isn't going to come out on its own, use **tweezers**. Sterilize them first by holding the end of the tweezers over a match or cigarette lighter. Gently pull out the part of the splinter that's poking through the skin. Use a magnifying glass if you need to.

◦ If the splinter is buried under the skin, use a **needle** too. Sterilize the needle over flame, then use the tip to gently lift the bit of skin that covers the end of splinter. Holding up the skin with the needle tip, use tweezers to pull out the splinter.

◦ Check to see whether you got the entire splinter. If you did, wash the area with soap and water, blot dry, and cover it with a bandage. If some of the splinter remains embedded in your skin, you'll need to repeat the process.

Recipe for Relief

◦ Way back when, cooks who got a splinter used a ready remedy, **bacon fat**, to draw it out. This still works. Softening the skin around the splinter—with bacon fat or any other fat or oil—helps the splinter glide out.

Sties

Perhaps the biggest challenge when you have a sty in your eye is resisting the temptation to rub it. It's a natural reaction, but no amount of rubbing will get rid of that something-in-my-eye feeling, and the bacteria that infected the follicle can spread to others. Instead, use moist heat to bring the sty to a head. And follow our tips to keep your eyelids clean and clear of future irritations.

Have a Heated Exchange

Apply a **warm compress** to the affected eye for 10 to 15 minutes four times a day for two or three days. For a compress, you can use a soft washcloth, a piece of clean cotton cloth, a gauze pad, or even a tea bag. Run warm water over the item, close your eye, and hold the moistened compress against the eyelid. Once you get used to the heat against your eye, you can moisten the compress a few more times with ever-warmer water. The heat will cause a sty to come to a head and rupture sooner. Once you've used a compress, it should either be thrown away or (if it's a washcloth) washed in very hot water before you use it again. Otherwise, you might re-infect your eye with the bacteria.

To give a hot compress extra infection-fighting power, soak it in tea made from **calendula** flowers. Put 2 teaspoons dried flowers in a bowl, add 2 cups boiling water, and steep for 20 minutes. Then strain out the flowers.

There's another way to bring heat to a painful peeper. Boil an **egg** until it's hardboiled, then take it out of the hot water and wrap it in a clean cloth. Hold the hot egg against the outside of your eyelid. It stays hot longer than the compress. (And when you're done, you can make an egg salad sandwich out of your sty remedy.)

Hot **potatoes** work too (but not as leftovers). Microwave a potato, cut it in half, and put it on a cloth over your eye. It stays hot for a long time, so you can relax, recline, and enjoy the break.

What's wrong

Sties are red, inflamed, painful bumps on the upper or lower edge of the eyelid that look much like pimples. They occur when an eyelash follicle gets clogged with dirt or oil, then infected by bacteria. (If a gland on the eyelid is clogged, you have a chalazion instead of a sty.) Your eye may water, or you may feel like there's something in it. Normally, a sty enlarges with pus over the course of several days, then ruptures and heals. The sty may disappear completely once the infection is over, or it may leave a small fluid-filled cyst that requires medical treatment.

When Is a Sty Not a Sty?

A chalazion—an enlarged, blocked oil gland in the eyelid—looks like a sty for the first few days, but it becomes larger and lasts longer. You can tell it's not a sty because it's farther from the edge of the eyelid, and it's likely to turn into a hard, painless, round bump. Most chalazions go away with lots of hot compresses that melt the thickened oil and allow it to drain from the pores of the eyelid. But if it lingers for weeks or months, you might want to visit your doctor for a steroid cream or antibiotics that will help it heal. In some cases, doctors recommend minor surgery to remove chalazions.

Should I call the doctor?

Although sties are painful and annoying, they're usually harmless. Call a doctor if the sty starts to bleed, grows very large very quickly, or doesn't begin to heal after two days. You may have a more serious eyelid infection called cellulitis.

Beat Back Bacteria

To boost your immune system and help fight infection-causing bacteria, take 200 milligrams of **echinacea** three or four times a day and continue until the sty goes away.

Eat one clove of fresh **garlic** a day. It may not be your favorite appetizer, but it has antibacterial properties. If you can stand to, eat it raw for best effect.

The Power of Prevention

If you are prone to sties, you may want to bathe your eyelids once a day to keep the follicles clear. An easy way to do this is to gently rinse your closed eyelids with a mixture of **no-tears baby shampoo** and warm water.

Every couple of days, apply a **warm compress** to your eyelids to prevent oil glands from becoming blocked.

Take a tablespoon of **flaxseed oil** every day, or take two flaxseed-oil capsules. It can help prevent follicles from clogging. If you want to get the most benefit from pure flaxseed oil, add it to salads or put it on bread, but don't cook it. Heat breaks down its nutrients.

To prevent spreading infection to other members of your family—or re-infecting yourself—when you have a sty, **wash your hands frequently** and keep them away from your eyes. For the same reason, **don't share your washcloths** or towels with other family members. Change your towel and pillowcase often.

Make sure you get enough **vitamin A** by taking a multivitamin or eating foods such as broccoli, cantaloupe, spinach, and swordfish. If sties are a problem for you, it may be a sign of vitamin A deficiency.

Stress

Your body is designed to handle brief periods of stress from time to time. But too much isn't good for body or soul. Fortunately, even when you can't change a stressful situation, you have some control over the way you deal with it. So if you're pulling out your hair, biting your nails to the quick, or worrying yourself into a tizzy, try these techniques to loosen stress's grip and restore a sense of sanity.

Dose with De-Stressors

~ Ever since ancient Greeks began enjoying **chamomile tea**, it has been praised for its healing properties. Today, when an estimated one million cups are drunk each day throughout the world, herbalists and naturopathic doctors praise chamomile as a wonderful remedy for stress. Drink one cup three times a day.

~ You can also add chamomile, along with other calming herbs such as **lavender** and **valerian**, to bathwater for a nerve-soothing soak. Wrap the dried herbs in a piece of cheesecloth and hold it under the faucet while you fill the tub.

~ Get more **vitamin C**. In one study, under-pressure people who took 1,000 milligrams of C had milder increases in blood pressure and brought their stress hormone levels back to normal more quickly than people who didn't take it.

~ Look to **Panax ginseng**, an herb valued for its ability to protect the body from stress. It has been shown to balance the release of stress hormones and support the organs that produce them (the pituitary gland, the hypothalamus, and the adrenal glands). Take 100 to 250 milligrams twice a day during times of stress. Experts recommend that you stop taking it for a week every two or three weeks.

Bring Something to Mind

~ Closely studied by Herbert Benson, M.D., of Harvard University, the **relaxation response** has been clinically proven to short-circuit stress. Sit in a comfortable position in a quiet

What's wrong

Your body is on the alert, telling you something's wrong and you need to fix it. Stress can cause your endocrine system to pump out high levels of certain hormones that weaken immunity, damage the heart and blood vessels, and increase susceptibility to colds and other illnesses. Your mind can be assaulted as well. Stressed-out people become irritable or easily angered, experience extreme anxiety, and lose their ability to concentrate. They may also experience insomnia, have a chronically upset stomach, and suffer from headaches and fatigue.

Should I call **the doctor?**

Seek the help of your doctor or a therapist if stress-related symptoms are affecting the quality of your life. Symptoms to look for include overwhelming anxiety, inability to fall or stay asleep, chronic or severe headaches, back pain, neck pain, or thoughts of suicide. The consequences of long-term stress may include increased vulnerability to high blood pressure, heart attack, stroke, and other diseases.

Skip it!

Kava kava, an herb that contains kavalactones (which help relax tense muscles), is sometimes recommended as a natural sleep aid, particularly in times of stress. Following many reports of liver toxicity and some fatalities, sales of kava kava have been banned in Canada and other countries until further research can be done.

place. Close your eyes. Now choose a word or phrase to focus on ("It's okay," for example). As you concentrate on breathing in and out, repeat the phrase each time you exhale. If you get distracted by other thoughts, gently put them out of your mind and return to your word or phrase. Continue for 10 to 20 minutes. Practice at least once a day.

⌒ Research has found that **music** can reduce heart rate, blood pressure, and even levels of stress hormones in the blood. Take a break and listen to music you find soothing, whether it's classical, jazz, or something else.

⌒ Do a **time-travel exercise**. When you're feeling knotted up with some immediate concern, remember something that had you feeling equally tense a year ago. How important does it seem today? Now try to project a year into the future, and look back on your present dilemma. Chances are, that "leap forward" in time will give you a better perspective on what you're going through now.

Take a Progressive Approach

⌒ When you feel especially tense, try a technique called **progressive relaxation**. Sit or lie down in a quiet, comfortable place. Close your eyes. Now curl your toes as hard as you can for 10 seconds. Then relax them. After your toes, tense and relax your feet, legs, belly, fingers, arms, neck, and face. In other words, progressively "work" the tension all the way from the tips of your toes to the top of your head, and then "let it go."

The Power of Prevention

⌒ Get out for a walk or do some other form of **exercise** for at least 20 minutes, three times a week. Exercise boosts feel-good brain chemicals called endorphins, which lift your mood and make you feel less anxious.

⌒ **Limit** your consumption of **alcohol, caffeine**, and **sugar**; and **if you smoke, quit**. All of these substances can fire up your body's fight-or-flight response, contributing to physical symptoms of stress like a racing heart, trembling, clammy hands, anxiety, and irritability.

⌒ Take up a **calming hobby**. Knitting, working on puzzles, reading, or some other favorite pastime can help you take a breather from the stresses of life.

Sunburn

If you have the complexion of boiled lobster and you're in significant pain, take aspirin, ibuprofen, or some other over-the-counter anti-inflammatory drug to reduce the swelling and relieve the pain. And of course, do what you'd do for any other type of burn: Cool it with cold water to stop the sizzle. You may also want to use one of the sunburn sprays, sold in the drugstore, that contain numbing ingredients. Finally, make sure to learn your lesson and remember to wear sunscreen next time you venture out into the sun.

Dip In

~ For immediate relief, soak the sunburned areas in **cold water** (but not ice water) or with cold compresses for 15 minutes. The cold reduces swelling and wicks away heat from your skin.

~ If you're burned all over, take a soak in a cool bath to which you've added **oatmeal**. You can either buy a colloidal oatmeal product such as Aveeno or simply grind up a cup of oatmeal in a food processor and add it to your bath.

~ Brew up a pot of **green tea** and let it cool. Soak a clean cloth in the tea, and use it as a compress. The tea contains ingredients that help protect the skin from ultraviolet radiation damage and reduce inflammation.

~ Use the cooling, aromatic qualities of **peppermint** to quell the scorch of a sunburn. Either make peppermint tea or mix two drops of peppermint oil with a cup of lukewarm water. Chill the concoction and gently bathe the burned area.

Pantry Painkillers

~ For extra-painful spots of sunburn, rub the area gently with sliced **cucumber** or **potato**. They contain compounds that cool the burn and help reduce swelling.

~ **Vinegar** contains acetic acid—one of the components of aspirin. It can help ease sunburn pain, itching, and inflammation. Soak a few sheets of paper towels in white vinegar, and

What's **wrong**

The outer layers of your skin have become inflamed by overexposure to the sun's ultraviolet (UV) rays. With a first-degree burn, the skin may be hot and tender as well. Small, fluid-filled blisters indicate second-degree sunburn. Worst of all are third-degree burns, which cause blistering, red or purple skin discoloration, chills, fever, nausea, and headache. With repeated severe sunburns, your skin ages more rapidly, and risk of skin cancer increases. Fair-haired people with light skin are more at risk for sunburn, as are those who take certain medications such as sulfa drugs, some antibiotics, and oral diabetes medications.

Should I call **the doctor?**

Most sunburns are first-degree burns. The pain will ease in one to four days. But call the doctor if your sunburned skin starts to blister, you run a fever or develop chills or nausea, or if the pain becomes unbearable.

Tried...

Many people report that putting milk on a sunburn is extremely soothing.

...and true

Milk has a high fat content, and it doesn't seal the skin the way lard does. If your burn feels cooler that way, go ahead and milk the remedy for all it's worth.

apply them to the burned areas. Leave them on until the towels are dry. Repeat as needed.

 If the sunburn itches, take a cool bath, but add 2 cups of **vinegar** to the bathwater before you get in.

Put On a Coating

 Mix **baking soda** and **vinegar** to make a thick paste, and slather it over the sunburned areas. Apply the salve before bedtime, and leave it on overnight.

 Sprinkle your sheets with **cornstarch** to minimize painful chafing. (Use this technique only for bad sunburns, since you'll have to wash the sheets afterward.)

 Apply a light coating of pure **aloe vera** to the painful skin, using either a fresh piece from the plant or in the gel form you can buy at the drugstore. If you buy the gel, make sure it's 100% pure aloe vera.

 Try applying an oil or ointment of **St. John's wort** as a burn balm: The herb has antiseptic and painkilling properties, and is thought to help heal skin wounds. If you're taking the herb internally, however, stay out of the sun: It makes skin more sensitive to damaging rays.

The Power of Prevention

 Always slather your skin with a **sunscreen** that contains a sun protection factor (SPF) of 15 or higher, at least 30 minutes before going outdoors. Insist that your loved ones do the same.

 Between 10 A.M. and 3 P.M., **limit your exposure to the sun.** This is when the sun's rays are at their strongest.

 If you burn easily or have been diagnosed with skin cancer in the past, take no chances: **Cover up in the sun.** That means long pants, long sleeves, a wide-brimmed hat, and sunglasses.

Swimmer's Ear

"But I'm not a swimmer!" you say. You don't have to be. The infection can get started when you're just taking a shower. But you can be quite sure it's swimmer's ear if you feel a piercing pain when you push on the triangular flap that covers the opening to the ear canal. To deal with the pain, your easiest option is an over-the-counter painkiller such as aspirin or acetaminophen. Also try heat to ease the ache and take steps (described below) to dry out the ear canal and make it unfriendly to the bacteria or fungi that caused the infection.

Warming the Cockles

For soothing relief, treat your ear to heat. Use a **hot-water bottle** or a **heating pad** set on low. If you're using the bottle, wrap it in a towel so it feels comfortably warm, not super hot. If you're using a heating pad, for safety's sake, be careful not to fall asleep with that electric pad nestled against your ear.

Drop In Center

Take advantage of garlic's potent antibacterial properties and use this herb in eardrops. You can buy **garlic oil** in health-food stores, or make your own. Grate three medium cloves of garlic and place them in a shallow dish. Cover them with olive oil and let the mixture stand overnight. Strain out the garlic and apply 3 drops in the affected ear.

If your infection itches but doesn't hurt, mix equal parts of **rubbing alcohol** with **distilled white vinegar**, and use a clean eyedropper to put a few drops in your ear. Tilt your head so the mixture flows into the ear canal, then tug your earlobe to make sure it flows all the way in. Keep your head tilted (or lie down) for a few minutes, then sit erect and tilt your ear toward your shoulder to let the excess drain out. (You'll need a tissue or handkerchief to catch the runoff.) Because vinegar creates an acid environment—inhospitable to bacteria and fungi—it helps to clear infection. And the drops also help dry

What's **wrong**

Swimmer's ear is an infection of the outer ear canal. It happens when water gets trapped in your ears and allows bacteria or fungi to flourish. At first, the affected ear feels blocked and may itch. If you leave it untreated, the infection can cause swelling, accompanied by some drainage of fluid. The condition can be quite painful. Often, the area that hurts the most is the triangular piece of cartilage called the tragus that covers the front of the ear canal.

Usually swimmer's ear is easy to treat and goes away, never to be heard from again. But not always. In about one percent of all cases, it comes back again no matter what you do to prevent a recurrence. Some particularly hard-to-treat bacteria has set up home in your ear, and all you can do is try to keep it under control. If you have this problem, be sure to keep your doctor informed. In rare cases, the infection can spread into nearby tissue around the ear (a severe condition called malignant otitis externa). People with diabetes and those with compromised immune systems are most susceptible.

Should I call the doctor?

If you've ever had a ruptured eardrum or had tubes put in your ears, see your doctor for any kind of earache. Otherwise, you can usually treat a mild case of swimmer's ear at home. But if you develop sudden, severe ear pain, or hearing loss, get to the doctor. You'll also need a doctor's help if you have signs or symptoms of a punctured eardrum (blood, discharge from the ear, very intense pain followed by sudden relief). For swimmer's ear that doesn't respond to home remedies, a doctor can prescribe antibiotics.

out the ear canal, because they contain alcohol, which evaporates rapidly.

✎ If your ear is painful, skip the alcohol. Just use **vinegar** blended with a few drops of water.

✎ If your ear itches, mix a few drops of **lavender oil** with a teaspoon of **olive oil** and rub the mixture in your outer ear. You don't need to use much.

The Power of Prevention

✎ Wear wax or silicone **earplugs**, available at most drugstores, to keep your ears dry when you're swimming or showering. The earplugs can be softened and shaped to fit snugly into your outer ear canal.

✎ After you swim or shower, shake your head to remove any water that remains in your ears. Better yet, gently **blow-dry** your ears. Pull the flap of your ear to create an open airway to your ear canal. Set the hair dryer on the lowest setting and direct the airstream into your ear for 30 seconds. The nozzle of the hair dryer should be about 45 centimeters away.

✎ Dilute a small amount of **apple cider vinegar** with an equal amount of **distilled water** and use 1 drop in each ear after you swim or shower. The vinegar is good for preventing bacterial and fungal infections as well as clearing them up.

✎ Don't try to get all the wax out of your ears. In normal amounts, earwax coats the ear canal, which protects your inner ear from moisture.

Teeth Grinding

You had a stressful day and you unleashed your tension by grinding your teeth at night—maybe grinding so forcefully that you woke up the household. And perhaps you paid the price the next day with a headache. For head and facial pain caused by teeth grinding (also called bruxism), you can get temporary relief from over-the-counter pain relievers like aspirin or acetaminophen. But that doesn't get to the root of the problem. For that you'll want to consult with your dentist. In the meantime, here are some ways to minimize the daily (or nightly) grind.

Enjoy Your Retiring

 Avoid stressful thoughts, activities, and movies in the hours before bedtime. You probably don't realize it, but just before bed is the worst time to pay the bills, watch *Die Hard* reruns, or talk about your in-laws. Get to your finances, violent movies, and sensitive subjects early in the evening. If you are bothered by worries, jot down things that you need to address the next day. Then take a **long, warm bath** before you go to bed.

 While you're in the bath—or even when you're lying in bed—cover your jaw with a washcloth that's been soaked in hot water. The extra warmth will relax your jaw muscles.

 Practice **progressive muscle relaxation** before you go to sleep, so tension doesn't lead you to grind at night. When you're lying in bed, tense, then relax the muscles in your feet. Repeat with your calf muscles, then thigh muscles, and so on, progressively tensing and relaxing each set of muscles all the way up your body. By the time you tense and relax your neck and jaw muscles, you should feel as limp as a rag doll.

 Avoid eating within an hour of bedtime. Digesting food while you sleep makes you more likely to grind your teeth.

Be Guarded

 A protective **mouth guard** made for boxers and defensive linebackers will work for teeth grinders too. Many types of protective mouth guards are available at sporting-goods

What's **wrong**

You may respond to stressful situations during the day by clenching or grinding your teeth at night, without even realizing you're doing it. This presents a problem, since your teeth are designed to touch briefly when you're chewing and swallowing. They aren't built for the punishment of constant grinding. Common triggers are tension and anger. Nighttime grinding can lead to cracked teeth and headaches, as well as the neck and jaw pain called temporomandibular disorder (TMD).

Should I call the doctor?

If you wake up with pain in your jaw, neck, or shoulder, or have morning headaches, talk to your dentist or doctor. This is particularly important if your bedmate reports that you grind your teeth at night. And you need to see the doctor immediately if you have a broken tooth from the grinding. For severe teeth grinding, you can be fitted with a very effective appliance called the NTI-tss (nociceptive trigeminal inhibition–tension suppression system). It protects you from the damaging and often migraine-producing clenching on back molars.

Did you know?

When you grind, you may be putting as much as 545 kilograms (1,200 pounds) of pressure on the crowns and roots. That recurring pressure is what can break or loosen your teeth.

stores. Follow directions on how to mold it to your bite, then wear it to bed at night. The rubbery material will absorb pressure and save your teeth from damage. (If you find that the mouth guard keeps falling out, or you wear it right through, talk to your dentist about a customized mouth guard.)

Give Your Jaw a Break

➤ During the day, make a conscious point of **keeping your jaw relaxed and your teeth apart**. As a reminder to yourself, rest your tongue between your top and lower teeth—so if you start to bite down, you'll chomp on some nerve endings. Doctors have observed that people who can break the daytime teeth-grinding habit are less likely to do it unconsciously at night.

➤ **Avoid excessively hard or chewy foods**—not only gum and hard candy, but also steak or dried foods that require a lot of jaw action. And if you're in the habit of chewing on the end of your pencil, try to stop. When you work your jaws during the day, the pattern is likely to continue in your sleep.

Watch What You Imbibe

➤ **Keep alcohol consumption to a minimum**—or, better yet, stop drinking altogether. This is especially important in the evening. Though sleep experts aren't sure why, people who drink heavily at night are more likely to grind their teeth when they sleep.

➤ **Avoid caffeinated drinks**. Since caffeine is a stimulant, if you drink coffee, black tea, or caffeinated soft drinks, you're far more likely to grind your teeth.

Get Mineral Power

➤ Take powdered **magnesium** and **calcium**—in a two-to-one ratio—every day. These minerals help your jaw muscles relax, particularly at night. Dosages range from 600 milligrams of calcium along with 300 milligrams of magnesium to 1,000 milligrams of calcium with 500 milligrams of magnesium daily. Start at the lower dose, and if you don't get relief after a couple of weeks, increase the dosages. Calcium/magnesium tablets are also available, but they don't dissolve as readily. When you use the powdered form, dissolve the mineral supplements in an acidic liquid like orange or grapefruit juice.

Teething

When a baby cuts a new tooth, both baby and parents suffer. The baby-care section in your local drugstore offers over-the-counter products like Infants' Tylenol that can ease the pain, but be sure to consult with your pediatrician and follow label directions. Of course, that's just one option for relieving your child's teething troubles. For plenty more, see the remedies below. But whatever you try, the main ingredient will be parental patience during those fussy weeks when the first teeth emerge.

Help Your Baby Chill Out

🐭 Pick up a water-filled **teething ring** at the department store or baby store, chill it in the refrigerator, and let your baby chew on it. The cold temperature numbs the gums and brings pain relief. Just don't put it in the freezer. Objects that have been frozen can cause frostbitten gums.

🐭 Babies older than six months can chew on a **clean washcloth** soaked with cold water.

🐭 Wrap an **ice cube** in a clean cloth, and rub it gently on the baby's gums. Be sure the ice itself doesn't touch the gums, and keep it moving so it doesn't get any spot too cold.

🐭 If your baby is just cutting her first tooth, you can use a **chilled spoon** to help ease the pain. Chill a spoon in the refrigerator (not the freezer) and apply the rounded part of the spoon to your baby's gums when she's fussy. As with a cold teething ring, the chilled spoon helps numb the areas that hurt most. But once a tooth comes in, don't use the cold-spoon approach, as your child could chip a tooth.

🐭 **Cold food** can help relieve gum pain. Cut up a bagel, put the pieces in a sandwich bag, and store it in the freezer. When your baby is uncomfortable, give her a piece to gnaw on. The coldness helps numb the gums, and the edges of the bagel will massage your baby's gums as she chew on it. Just be sure to stay nearby and take away the bagel when it turns mushy.

🐭 Offer your baby a **frozen banana** (peeled, of course). The banana thaws quickly as your baby chews on it, and the cool

What's **wrong**

Between the ages of four and eight months, as the first teeth begin to emerge, a baby's gums grow red, tender, and swollen. Some babies grow fussy and irritable and have difficulty sleeping. Most put their fingers in their mouths, and you can expect to deal with a lot of drooling. Teething problems are usually most noticeable with the first two to four teeth. But some children continue to have pain when the other teeth come in, which can continue up to the age of three.

Should I call **the doctor?**

Contrary to common belief, teething should not cause fever, diarrhea, vomiting, or loss of appetite. If your child develops any of these symptoms, they're probably signs of some other health problem, so call your pediatrician. It's especially important to call the doctor if your child has a temperature— even low-grade—that lasts more than two or three days.

Skip it!

One old folk remedy for teething is to rub liquor on the baby's gums. However, giving alcohol to babies and children isn't a smart idea. Use another, safer remedy instead.

fruit soothes the gums. As with the bagel, however, you want to take away the banana when it becomes mushy.

Have a Bonding Experience

⤚ Sometimes giving your baby some **extra affection** can ease teething pain. Give the little one some cuddling time, or carry him around the home to distract him from his discomfort.

⤚ **Massage** her gums with a clean finger for a few minutes. The pressure feels good, and the attention from a parent will be comforting.

Spice Up the Gums

⤚ Make a clove-oil gum soother by mixing four drops of **clove essential oil** with at least 1 tablespoon of **vegetable oil**. Before you give it to your baby, try the mixture on your own gums to make sure it's not too strong. If you feel any irritation, add more vegetable oil. Never use straight clove oil on your baby's gums; it's much too strong.

⤚ Place one or two drops of **chamomile oil** on a wet cotton swab and apply to the gums twice a day. The blue oil has a soothing effect on irritated skin and gums.

Frequent the Pharmacy

⤚ A cherry-flavored gel called **Baby Orajel** can help ease teething pain. Another option: **Orajel cotton swabs**. They have the same nonalcoholic painkilling medicine and flavor as the gel. Any of these products should be used in very small amounts. They not only numb the gums, they also numb the "gag reflex," which means that swallowed food can be aspirated into the airways without producing the normal gagging or vomiting response.

Start a Teeth-Cleaning Routine

⤚ As soon as the teeth emerge, start **regular cleaning**. Twice a day, rub the gums very gently with a soft toothbrush or clean washcloth. This helps control bacteria in the mouth, which reduces teething irritation as well. Also, it's important to get your child accustomed to the feeling of having his teeth cleaned.

Temporomandibular Disorder

If you have pain when you chew or yawn—or even when you say "temporomandibular disorder"—you know the discomfort of TMD. Your first lines of defense are heat, cold, and an over-the-counter anti-inflammatory drug such as ibuprofen. And try the other approaches below. No matter which avenue you take, you'll also need to give your mouth a rest (that means no more biting pencils, gnawing on beef jerky, or chewing gum). Use it as an excuse not to answer the phone!

Global Cooling and Warming

⁓ When you feel occasional sharp pain in your jaw joints, apply a pair of **cold packs**. The cold numbs your nerves, dulling pain messages that go to your brain. Wrap a couple of soft packs in thin towels and hold them on both sides of your face for about 10 minutes or so (not longer than 20 minutes, though, or you could cause mild frostbite). Repeat every two hours as needed.

⁓ If you're experiencing a dull, steady ache rather than sharp pain, **heat** is better than cold. It increases blood circulation to the area and relaxes jaw muscles. Soak a couple of washcloths in warm water and hold them to your face for 20 minutes or so. (You'll want to run them under hot water a few times to keep them hot.)

Go Ahead—Rub It In

⁓ **Massage** the areas around your jaws to relieve muscle tightness and enhance blood flow to the area. Several times a day, open your mouth, then rub the muscles by the ears near your temporomandibular joints. Place your forefingers on the sore areas, and swirl them around, pressing gently, until the muscle relaxes. Close your mouth and repeat the massage.

⁓ With a clean **forefinger**, reach in your mouth until you can feel the sore muscles that are inside. Pressing firmly with your forefinger, massage one side, then the other, getting as close to the joints as you can.

What's **wrong**

A pair of hinges—temporomandibular joints—attach your jawbone to your skull. These structures are surrounded by muscles and ligaments. In temporomandibular disorder, or TMD, the muscles around the joints become tight and inflamed. TMD is marked by pain in the joints, a clicking or popping noise when using your mouth, headaches, and aching in your neck and shoulders. Common triggers include emotional stress, chewing tough foods, and jaw clenching or teeth grinding. Less often, people get TMD as a result of arthritis or a blow to the jaw.

Should I call
the doctor?

If you have symptoms
after two weeks of self-
help remedies, call your
doctor. And you'll want
prompt medical attention
if it's too painful to open
your mouth or brush
your teeth. For severe
TMD doctors may
prescribe muscle-relaxing
drugs or, if you have
inflammation, inject
corticosteroids into the
joints. A dentist can
prescribe a customized
mouth guard to wear at
night to reduce clenching
or grinding if that's
contributing to TMD pain.

◢ Finally, **massage** the muscles on the sides of your neck. Those muscles don't directly control your jaw, but by massaging them you help to reduce tension that contributes to jaw pain.

Don't Be Inclined

◢ When you're sitting in a chair most of the day, it's especially important to **sit up straight** rather than lean forward. Your back should be well supported. Make sure your chin doesn't jut out in front of your body. If you are angled forward, you're putting strain on your neck and back, and that creates jaw pain.

◢ Use a **document holder** when you type so you don't have to crane your neck or lean forward to read the text.

◢ If you spend a lot of time on the telephone while you're using your hands for other tasks, get a **headset**. Cradling the telephone receiver between your shoulder and cheek puts a lot of strain on your neck and jaw.

Put Your Guard Up

◢ If nightly teeth grinding or clenching is contributing to your TMD, try wearing the type of inexpensive **mouth guard** that can be found in any sports store. This isn't as good as a custom-designed mouth guard that dentists can provide. But even a sports-store product can be molded for a good fit. Follow package directions to make it fit your mouth.

Table Matters and Manners

◢ Try to **steer clear of extremely crunchy and chewy foods**, such as apples, carrots, beef jerky, and hard dinner rolls. You want to spare your jaws from overwork, particularly when the aching and clicking are severe. What you want are soups, pastas, and other easy-to-eat foods.

◢ Don't take big bites. Cut your food into **smaller portions**, so you don't have to overwork your jaw.

◢ **Skip tea and coffee**. Caffeine and TMD don't go well together, since caffeine can increase muscle tension. Switch to decaffeinated drinks.

Put Some Teeth in Your OJ

◢ Add 500 milligrams of powdered **calcium** and 250 milligrams of powdered **magnesium** to your morning orange juice. These minerals work together to promote muscle relax-ation, which can help reduce tension in your jaw muscles. You can take capsules if you can't find the powders, but the pow-dered form—which dissolves quickly—is more easily absorbed by your body.

A Yawning Trap

🔹 If you see someone yawning, resist the temptation to join in. Under those circumstances, it's extremely difficult to stifle a yawn, but that's exactly what you want to do if you have TMD. A **big, wide yawn is sure to cause pain**. If you can't stop a yawn, try to suppress it by opening your mouth as little as possible.

Give Your Jaw a Rest

🔹 **Avoid chewing gum**. Every time you chew, you tense your jaw muscles and give your temporomandibular joints an exhausting workout.

🔹 **Avoid biting your fingernails or chewing on a pencil**. Instead, find a non-jaw-related way to get rid of your nervous energy—such as fiddling with "worry beads" or twisting a paperclip.

🔹 **Sleep on your back or side**. If you're on your stomach, with your head turned to one side, the misalignment produces neck strain that's transferred to your jaw.

🔹 If you put in a lot of desk time, take a few minutes to hide out and **meditate**. Focus on the muscles in your face and neck, allowing them to relax and grow slack.

🔹 Get 20 to 30 minutes of **aerobic exercise** at least three or four times a week. Not only does exercise reduce stress, it helps your body produce endorphins, which are its natural painkilling chemicals.

🔹 When you're under stress, make a point to not respond by grinding your teeth or clenching your jaw. If it helps, **hold your tongue between your teeth** to ensure that you don't grind your teeth together.

🔹 If you often carry a monstrous purse or briefcase on one shoulder, **lighten your load**. The weight throws your spine and neck out of alignment—indirectly contributing to jaw pain. If you absolutely need the heavy tote, move it from shoulder to shoulder as you're walking along.

Did you **know?**

The temporomandibular joint is so named because it connects the mandible (or lower jaw) to the temporal bone at the side of the head.

Toothache

Toothaches range from throbbing to excruciating, but with a good dentist as your ally, the pain should be short-lived. If you can't get an appointment right away, you can stop at the pharmacy for a pain-relieving gel like Anbesol or Orajel. (The active ingredient they have in common is benzocaine—the same topical pain reliever is found in products that relieve sunburn.) For general pain relief, you can also take aspirin or acetaminophen (Tylenol). And try the following approaches.

What's wrong?

Cavities often cause tooth pain, and you get cavities from bacteria in the mouth that are thriving on sugary and starchy foods that cling to teeth and gums. The bacteria produce acids that damage your teeth, and when the damage reaches a nerve, misery sets in. But there can be other causes as well—a filling that's come loose, a cracked tooth, an abscess (a pocket of infection at the gum line), or a sinus condition. Any infection that reaches the root is sure to cause pain.

Get Cloves to the Pain

⬥ Dab some **clove oil** directly on your bad tooth. Clove oil has remarkable bacteria-slaying properties—and it also has a numbing effect, which is why it's a longtime folk remedy for toothache. In the 1800s, when toothpaste was scant and dentists employed tools of torture, every doctor carried a good supply of clove oil. Today we know that this extract from the clove bud contains eugenol, which acts as a local anesthetic. The oil may sting at first, but then blissful relief sets in.

⬥ You can get the same numbing effect from **whole cloves**. Put a few in your mouth, let them moisten until they soften, bruise them a bit between your non-hurting molars to release their oil, then hold the softened cloves against your painful tooth for up to half an hour.

⬥ If you don't have any cloves, make a paste of **powdered ginger** and **red (cayenne) pepper**. Pour the powdered ingredients in the bottom of a cup, then add a drop or two of water to make the paste. Roll a small ball of cotton into enough paste to saturate it, and place it on your painful tooth. (This can irritate the gums, so keep the cotton on the tooth.) In addition to using the spices together, you can try them separately. Either one can help relieve tooth pain.

Swish Channels

⬥ Rinse your mouth with a **tincture of myrrh**. The astringent effects help with inflammation, and myrrh offers the added benefit of killing bacteria. Simmer 1 teaspoon of powdered myrrh in 2 cups water for 30 minutes. Strain and let cool. Rinse with 1 teaspoon of the solution in a half-cup water five to six times a day.

🍃 **Peppermint** tea has a nice flavor and some numbing power. Put 1 teaspoon dried peppermint leaves in 1 cup boiling water and steep for 20 minutes. After the tea cools, swish it around in your mouth, then spit it out or swallow. Repeat as often as needed.

🍃 To help kill bacteria and relieve some discomfort, swish with a mouthful of **3% hydrogen peroxide solution.** This can provide temporary relief if the toothache is accompanied by fever and a foul taste in the mouth (both are signs of infection), but like other toothache remedies, it's only a stopgap measure until you see your dentist and get the source of infection cleared up. A hydrogen peroxide solution is only for rinsing. Spit it out, then rinse several times with plain water.

🍃 Stir a teaspoon of **salt** into a glass of warm water and rinse for up to 30 seconds before you spit it out. Salt water cleanses the area around the tooth and draws out some of the fluid that causes swelling. Repeat this treatment as often as needed.

Compresses for Comfort

🍃 Place a small **ice cube** in a plastic bag, wrap a thin cloth around the bag, and apply it to the aching tooth for about 15 minutes to numb the nerves. Alternatively, that ice pack can go on your cheek, over the painful tooth.

🍃 A warm, wet **tea bag** is a standard folk remedy for toothache that's worth a try. Black tea contains astringent tannins, which may reduce swelling and give you temporary relief.

🍃 Another country cure calls for soaking a small piece of **brown paper** (from a grocery or lunch bag) in **vinegar,** sprinkling one side with **black pepper,** and holding this to the cheek. The warm sensation on your cheek may distract you from your tooth pain.

A Gentle Brush-Off

🍃 Use a **toothpaste that's designated "for sensitive teeth."** If you have a problem with shrinking gums, this could relieve a lot of the pain you probably experience from hot or

Should I call **the doctor?**

Whatever else you do, make an appointment to see your dentist. The home remedies in this chapter can provide temporary relief, but your dentist needs to do some exploration and find out what's causing this toothache. Odds are, you have a problem that requires treatment. If you don't find out what's causing the ache, it will only get worse.

Tried...

According to folklore, if you massage your hand with an ice cube, you can help relieve a toothache.

...and true

When nerves in your fingers send "cold" signals to your brain, they may override the pain signals coming from your tooth. Just wrap up an ice cube in a thin cloth and massage it in the fleshy area between your thumb and forefinger.

cold foods. When gums shrink, the dentin beneath your teeth's enamel surface is exposed, and this material is particularly sensitive.

➤ Switch to the **softest-bristled brush** you can find to help preserve gum tissue and prevent further shrinking.

Caulk It

➤ If you've broken a tooth or have lost a filling, you can relieve some pain by covering the exposed area with softened **chewing gum**. This might work with a loose filling, too, to hold it in place until you can get to the dentist. To avoid further discomfort, avoid chewing anything with that tooth until you can have it repaired.

Press Here for Relief

➤ Try an **acupressure** technique to stop tooth pain fast. With your thumb, press the point on the back of your other hand where the base of your thumb and your index finger meet. Apply pressure for about two minutes. This helps trigger the release of endorphins, the brain's feel-good hormones. (*Off-limits*. . . if you're pregnant.)

Ulcers

This is one of those ailments that make us all too happy to take advantage of today's antibiotics, which can wipe out *Helicobacter pylori*, the bacterium that causes most ulcers. (Gone are the days when stress, all by itself, was thought to wear holes in the stomach.) If *H. pylori* is the culprit in your case, you'll probably get a 10- to 14-day course of treatment. Complete recovery takes about eight weeks. In the meantime, there are many steps you can take to relieve discomfort and prevent a recurrence. Don't use any of the herbal medicines until you've finished all the antibiotics.

Put Acid in Neutral

~ The quickest and easiest pain relievers are over-the-counter **antacids**, such as Maalox or Mylanta, which will help neutralize stomach acid, and **H$_2$ blockers**, such as Pepcid, Ranitidine, and Zantac, which reduce stomach acid secretion. In fact, these drugs may even heal your ulcer over time. For antacids, take two tablespoons after every meal, at bedtime, and any other time you feel your ulcer starting to act up. With H$_2$ blockers, follow label directions. If you begin to get constipated or show signs of diarrhea, you're overmedicating. Try cutting the dose in half.

~ **Eating** may also help temporarily relieve your discomfort. That's because your stomach acid becomes neutralized as food is digested. But if you have a duodenal ulcer, eating will actually make your pain worse . . . *unless* you eat a high-fiber diet. Fiber slows down the digestive process. Duodenal pain is alleviated when food travels more slowly through the stomach, allowing more time for stomach acid to be neutralized.

~ Some animal studies suggest that **ginger** may help reduce the release of digestive fluids in the GI tract. It also works against inflammation. You can swallow capsules or break them open and dissolve them in water or juice. Take no more than 1 teaspoon per day, as too much can have a reverse effect and cause irritation. You can try eating some candied ginger (avail-

What's **wrong**

Peptic ulcers are pitlike sores in the lining of your stomach or the uppermost section of your small intestine, the duodenum. They occur when pepsin, a digestive enzyme, begins to digest your own tissue. Your gastrointestinal (GI) tract usually protects itself from digestive juices with a thick layer of mucus and natural antacids. But bacteria that might be living in the wall of your GI tract, called *Helicobacter pylori*, can break down this defense system. So can long-term use of nonsteroidal anti-inflammatory drugs such as aspirin and ibuprofen.

Should I call the doctor?

See a doctor if you have any ulcer symptoms—a burning sensation in your belly, belching, bloating, pain, red blood in your stool, black blood in your stool (indicating digested blood), or unexplained nausea. If you vomit blood (which looks like dark or black coffee grounds, or is bright red or maroon), have tarry black stool (which indicates internal bleeding), or feel extreme pain, your ulcer may have perforated—that is, opened a hole all the way through the stomach or duodenum. This development could be life threatening. See a doctor or get to the emergency room immediately.

able in health-food stores). Commercial ginger ales probably don't contain enough ginger to do much good.

Don a Protective Coat

⮞ Licorice, which forms a protective coating between your stomach lining and your stomach acid, has been proven to help ulcers heal. Make sure you use a form of licorice known as **deglycyrrhizinated licorice (DGL)**, since regular licorice can send your blood pressure through the roof. Chew one or two DGL wafers about 30 minutes before each meal. You shouldn't take it if you're still on antibiotics. (*Off-limits*... if you use any kind of snuff or chewing tobacco containing licorice filler. You might put too much licorice in your system.)

⮞ Also used to coat sore throats, the inner bark of the **slippery elm** produces a lot of mucilage, a transparent, sticky, gelatinous substance, which can help protect the lining of your stomach. As long as you're not taking medication, you can take 700 milligrams of slippery elm in capsule form after every meal. Or, if you prefer to take it in tea form, steep 1 to 2 teaspoons of the dried bark in a cup of hot water for 20 to 30 minutes, then strain. Drink three cups a day.

⮞ Chew and swallow a teaspoon of **flaxseed**. Like slippery elm, the seeds create a soothing mucilage in the stomach. And they're a top-notch source of heart-healthy omega-3 fatty acids, which will help lower your cholesterol.

⮞ Try **aloe vera juice**. A popular European folk remedy for ulcers, the juice seems to quell gastrointestinal inflammation and may reduce stomach acid secretions. Drink one-third cup three times a day.

Favor Ulcer-Fighting Foods

⮞ Indulge in some **raw-cabbage juice.** It's probably not your beverage of choice, but if you have a peptic ulcer, it might hit the spot. Folk healers used it for years before a 1950s research team at Stanford University, led by Dr. Garnett Cheney, M.D., showed it to be an effective treatment. In one of the follow-up studies that confirmed Cheney's findings, people's ulcers disappeared in only seven days. The active substance in cabbage is probably glutamine, an amino acid that nourishes cells of the GI tract. If you don't have a home juicer, you can pick up raw-cabbage juice in health-food stores. Drink a quart every day for three weeks for best results.

🍃 Do you hate cabbage? **Pineapple** is another good source of glutamine.

🍃 Eat plenty of **onions**. They contain sulfur compounds that may help to neutralize *H. pylori*.

🍃 Help yourself to **honey**. Some studies show that honey can discourage the growth of ulcer-causing *H. pylori* bacteria. Spread some honey on your morning toast, use it instead of sugar on cereal, or add it as sweetener to herbal teas.

Honor Other Herbals

🍃 **Astragalus** is an immune enhancer, natural antibiotic, and anti-inflammatory that you can use when you're not taking antibiotics. Take 2 grams in capsule form every day.

🍃 Another member of the ginger family, **turmeric**, also seems to protect the gastrointestinal lining, and it also reduces gas. Take one-third teaspoon of powdered root between meals, or use it to season your food. (Turmeric doesn't make a good tea because it won't dissolve in water.) Don't overdo it, as too much turmeric can upset your digestive system rather than help it. (*Off-limits* . . . if you have gallstones. Excessive turmeric can make them worse.)

Put the Kettle On

🍃 **Chamomile tea** is an old-time favorite for soothing the stomach because it calms inflammation. Pour a half-cup boiling water over 2 teaspoons chopped flowers. Steep for 5 minutes, then strain.

🍃 **Peppermint** is another anti-inflammatory that can relieve pain and help you heal. To make tea, pour one cup of boiling water over a tablespoon of chopped leaves, steep for a couple of minutes, then strain out the leaves out. (*Off-limits* . . . if you have a problem with gastroesophageal reflux disease, which can be aggravated by peppermint.)

Cease Stressing

🍃 Practice **deep breathing**, **meditate**, listen to soothing **music**, practice **yoga**, inhale **calming scents**—whatever you

Skip it!

People say it works. Seems like it should work. Even kind of feels like it works. What is it? Plain old milk. Once thought to soothe ulcer pain, milk actually increases production of stomach acid, so in the long run, it will make you feel worse rather than better.

can do to take the edge off the stress in your life. In the days before we knew about *H. pylori*, ulcers were thought to result from excessive emotional stress. Now we know better, but doctors have found that stress can trigger pain by increasing production of stomach acid. And if you already have *H. pylori* in your system, the opportunistic bacteria take advantage of your reduced defenses—and get started on ulcer formation.

If you're going through a particularly tough period, spring for a weekly **massage**. There's no more enjoyable way to relax and melt away stress.

The Power of Prevention

Vitamin C may slow down the growth of *H. pylori* if you have colonies of these bacteria in your stomach. Take a 1,000-milligram supplement twice a day. Citrus fruits and vegetables, especially tomatoes, are good dietary sources.

Vitamin A is a must. People who get plenty of it are the least likely to develop duodenal ulcers. Try to get at least 10,000 IU a day, in a combination of supplements and diet. The best way to consume enough vitamin A is to add a broad range of fruits and vegetables to your diet and take a daily multivitamin.

Eat plenty of **yogurt** containing active cultures, especially *Lactobacillus acidophilus,* beneficial bacteria that inhibit *H. pylori.* It's an especially good idea to eat plenty of yogurt while you're taking antibiotics, since these drugs diminish the levels of the "good" bacteria in your gut that keep "bad" bacteria in check.

Go easy on alcohol, which can irritate the stomach lining. Two 90-milliliter glasses of wine a day for a man, and one for a woman, is the limit.

Be moderate in your use of **aspirin, ibuprofen**, and other nonsteroidal anti-inflammatory drugs. They can contribute to ulcer formation.

Avoid caffeine and tobacco. Both increase production of stomach acid, and tobacco makes antibiotics less effective.

Urinary Tract Infections

You know that burning sensation when you urinate means another urinary tract infection. One in five women suffer from at least one such infection at least once a year. If your doctor has prescribed antibiotics, it's important to finish all the pills. But in the meantime, drink your cranberry juice—it really does work—and follow these other steps to cut short an infection and ease its sting.

Drink Up

~ At the first sign of infection, mix a cold and frothy drink with **baking soda**. Dissolve one-quarter teaspoon of baking soda in 120 milliliters of water. Drink two glasses of water, then the mixed drink. The baking soda helps create a more alkaline (less acidic) environment in your bladder, making it more difficult for bacteria to thrive.

~ Throughout the day, have a **glass of water every hour** or so. When you flood your urinary tract with water, you flush out bacteria. Also, the more water you drink, the more you dilute your urine, so it's less irritating.

~ It's not an old wives' tale: Research has shown that **cranberry juice** does help women get rid of urinary tract infections faster. (It also helps prevent them.) There's nothing in the juice to stop bacteria from multiplying, but it does contain an acid that prevents bacteria from sticking to the lining of the urinary tract. If they don't stick, they are easily flushed away by your urine. Drink a 250-milliliter glass daily, both as a way to prevent UTIs and to treat them.

~ **Avoid citrus drinks, tomato juice, coffee, and alcohol.** All of these drinks may make urination more painful.

Steep Well

~ Help yourself to **garlic tea**. Garlic contains powerful bacteria-killing compounds that make it ideal for battling the bugs that cause UTIs. Peel a couple of fresh garlic cloves, mash them well, then drop them in warm water. Let them steep for five

What's **wrong**

Women get urinary tract infections (UTIs)—a term that includes bladder infections—much more often than men. Often the problem is a combination of cystitis, an infection of the bladder, and urethritis, an infection of the urethra. UTIs typically occur after bacteria in the anal area get pushed into the urethra, often during intercourse. UTIs are more likely to occur after menopause, since tissues in the vagina and urethra grow thinner and drier and are more prone to infection. Symptoms include fever, burning during urination, a feeling of bladder fullness, and frequent need to urinate. Men usually get UTIs as a consequence of a swollen prostate gland, which obstructs their urine flow.

Did you **know?**

Even though few men suffer from urinary tract infections, any male with an enlarged prostate has a higher-than-average risk. Fortunately, there are a number of remedies that can help manage this problem. (See Prostate Enlargement, page 311.)

minutes. Alternatively, you can make a tea by stirring a teaspoon of garlic powder in hot water.

To help your immune system fight the infection—and boost your fluid intake at the same time—make **echinacea tea** using tea bags or by steeping 2 teaspoons of the raw root in hot water. Drink three cups of tea a day.

Make a tea of **lovage** (a member of the carrot family) by pouring a cup of boiling water over 2 teaspoons of minced, dried root. Steep for 10 minutes, then strain and drink. This garden herb contains components with anti-inflammatory and bacteria-killing powers.

Try drinking **nettle tea**. Nettle is a diuretic. It will make you urinate more, which will help flush bacteria out of your system. Use 1 teaspoon of the dried herb and step in a cup of hot water. Drink one cup a day.

Herbal Antiseptics

Uva ursi (also called bearberry because bears like its red berries) is a short shrub whose leaves have been used for hundreds of years to treat urinary tract infections because of their antiseptic properties. If you take capsules containing powdered leaves, you'll need 500 to 1,000 milligrams three times a day. If you use a standardized extract, take 125 to 250 milligrams three times a day. Stop taking this herb when you feel well again, since it may not be safe for long-term use. If you're taking uva ursi, don't also take vitamin C; it will make your urine more acidic, which will compromise the effects of the herb.

Goldenseal is a natural weapon against the *E. coli* bacteria, the culprit behind so many cases of UTIs. It not only fights the bacteria, but also stimulates your immune system and helps heal inflammation in the urinary tract. Take 500 to 1,000 milligrams of goldenseal-root extract once a day for up to a week.

The Power of Prevention

Vitamin C, vitamin A, and **bioflavonoids** all render your bladder more impervious to clinging bacteria. Take 1,000 to 1,400 milligrams of vitamin C and 300 to 600 milligrams of bioflavonoids daily. A helpful dose of vitamin A is 50,000 IU daily, but this much can be toxic over long periods and requires a doctor's supervision.

~ If you use spermicides or a diaphragm, consider **another type of birth control**. These can contribute to UTIs by altering the bacteria in the vagina, which can then get into the urethra.

~ Many doctors advise women to **wash their genitals** before sex and **urinate afterward**. Urine will flush away bacteria that can be pushed up into the urethra during intercourse.

~ When underwear is warm and damp, it's an ideal breeding place for bacteria. Instead of synthetics, wear loose-fitting **cotton underwear** that "breathes."

~ For the same reason, don't loiter in a wet, tight-fitting bathing suit. Change into **dry clothes** as soon as possible after you take a swim.

~ A recent Finnish study found that women who frequently eat **cheese and yogurt** have fewer UTIs, possibly because these foods contain beneficial bacteria that help keep troublesome bacteria in check.

Varicose Veins

Bluish, bulging blood vessels can mar the appearance of otherwise great gams—and they can itch and hurt. If you really want them to go away, doctors have several methods that are generally considered safe and effective. They can inject chemicals that shrink the veins, or perform surgery to "strip" the veins. But many less-drastic measures can reduce the prominence of varicose veins and help prevent them from getting worse. Just for starters, how about stretching out with your feet up?

What's wrong

"Varicose" refers to blood vessels that are dilated, knotted, and tortuous, and when your veins are varicose, that's exactly how they look. Veins are the one-way channels that transport blood toward your heart. Along these are valves that shut down and resist if blood backs up and tries to reverse direction. When the valves weaken, it's usually in the legs, where gravity causes the blood to pool. The veins expand and take on a thick, lumpy appearance. Varicose veins are twice as common in women, especially pregnant women. But people who spend a lot of time on their feet—especially standing in place—are always at risk.

Put Your Feet Up

 Lie back on a couch or easy chair, with your **legs higher than your heart**. Varicosity is the result of blood pooling in your veins, and if you prop up your feet, it lets those "pools" drain downhill toward your heart. If you're at home, take a break periodically for this couch-potato assignment. Even at work, you may be able to tip back your chair and put your feet up for a while.

 For a more active approach, try this simple **yoga** move: Lie on your back near a wall, propping your feet against the wall with your knees straight so that your legs are at a 45-degree angle. Hold the position for three minutes, breathing deeply and evenly.

Give Your Veins Aid

 For three months, take 250 milligrams of **horse chestnut** twice a day. A traditional herbal remedy for varicose veins—one that is recommended by experts today—horse chestnut improves blood-vessel elasticity and also seems to strengthen the valves inside veins. After your third month on horse chestnut, take it once daily.

 Take 200 milligrams of **gotu kola** three times a day. This herb enhances the strength of blood vessel walls and the connective tissue that surrounds veins. In an Italian study, people who were taking gotu kola showed measurable improvements in the functioning of their veins.

Add some **lemon peel** to citrus drinks or to your tea. The peel contains a substance called rutin, a type of flavonoid that helps prevent leakage from small blood vessels.

Take **vitamin C** daily. This vitamin helps your body maintain strong connective tissues that support your veins, keeping them flexible and strong. Take at least 500 milligrams daily—and as much as 3,000 milligrams—but cut back to lower doses if you find you start to get diarrhea.

Seek out a family of compounds known as **oligomeric proanthocyanidin complexes (OPCs)**. They appear to strengthen blood vessels and make them less prone to leakage. In one study, varicose veins improved in 75 percent of people who took OPCs versus 41 percent of people who didn't. A typical dose is 150 to 300 milligrams daily, but you can also get OPCs in **cranberry, blueberry**, and **bilberry**.

Be a Water Runner

Run **hot and cold water** over your legs. With alternating temperatures, blood vessels expand and contract, improving blood circulation. Next time you're standing in the shower, direct the water stream onto your legs and run hot water for one to three minutes. Then switch to cold for the same length of time. Repeat three times, ending with cold.

Stock Up on Stockings

If you have small varicose veins, slip on a pair of **support hose** at the start of the day. These put pressure on your legs, which helps prevent veins from swelling. Support hose can be found in drugstores and department stores.

If your varicose veins are large, you'll need **graduated compression stockings**. These are tight at the ankle and somewhat looser further up the leg. That graduated pressure helps to push blood upward toward the heart. To find these more specialized stockings, look in a medical-supply store, check catalogs, or order online. You don't need a prescription for graduated compression stockings that provide mild or moderate support: Select the highest amount of pressure you can tolerate. For women, the pantyhose styles are the most effective. Many companies have special pantyhose-style compression stockings that widen out at the waistline and belly for pregnant women.

Should I call **the doctor?**

Varicose veins are more of a cosmetic annoyance than a health problem. However, call your doctor if you develop sores or if the skin over a varicose vein begins to peel off. Notify your doctor immediately if a vein ruptures and bleeds, or if walking becomes painful. Blood clots may be developing if there's swelling, pain, and redness in one leg, or if you detect swelling in both legs, so contact your doctor at once if you notice these symptoms.

Skip it!

If your legs are aching at the end of a long day because of varicose veins, you might be tempted to soak in a hot tub. Resist the temptation. While alternating hot and cold water is a useful treatment, when you sit in hot water for a long time, your veins swell larger.

Keep Your Blood Moving

~ **Avoid standing or sitting still** for long periods. If you are dormant in either position, blood will pool in the legs.

~ When you get any kind of break, spend time **walking around**. As long as your legs are moving, you're helping blood to move upward.

~ Whether standing or sitting, take a break about once an hour and **flex your feet**. For about ten minutes, lift and lower the balls of your feet to work your calf muscles. Since those muscles are adjacent to your veins, their flexing helps squeeze the vessels and move blood upward toward your heart.

~ Whenever you're sitting, make sure you **don't cross your legs**. When you put one leg on top of the other, you're putting undue pressure on your veins and blocking the return route to your heart.

~ Be sure to get at least 20 minutes of **aerobic exercise** three days a week to help you stay in shape as well as lose weight. (If you're overweight, you're putting more pressure on the veins in your legs.) Walking is particularly good for varicose veins, since you help pump blood to the heart each time you contract your leg muscles.

~ Give your legs a gentle **massage** to stimulate blood circulation by pressing both thumbs into the muscle (but not the veins directly) and stroking upward toward the heart.

~ Treat your legs (or other affected areas) with cloth compresses soaked in a strong tea made from **white oak bark**, which is thought to stimulate blood flow.

Clear Up Constipation

~ Eat a diet rich in **high-fiber foods** such as apples, carrots, kidney beans, and sweet potatoes to avoid straining due to constipation, which obstructs blood flow from the legs and puts pressure on veins.

Warts

You don't have to touch a toad to get a wart—and you don't have to see a doctor to get rid of one, although there are several medical approaches to doing so. Warts can be frozen with a squirt of liquid nitrogen or burned off using lasers or an electric needle. At the pharmacy, you'll find several wart cures, including liquids and plasters containing salicylic acid, which has a peeling effect. (They can be harsh, so be sure to follow the directions on the label.) In the panoply of wart-removal techniques, however, these are only the tip of the iceberg. In fact, folk remedies for warts could fill an entire book. Here are some of the best.

Irritate Warts to Death

Cover the wart with a small piece of **duct tape**. According to a recent study, duct tape works even better against warts than cryotherapy (using liquid nitrogen to freeze them off). Cut a piece that will just cover the wart. Stick it on and leave it there for six days. When you take the tape off, soak the area in water for a few minutes, then use a disposable emery board or pumice stone to file down the dead, thick skin. Leave the wart uncovered overnight and apply a new patch in the morning. Repeat the procedure until you're wart-free. How does duct tape help? It's likely that the mild skin irritation it causes spurs your immune system to fight off the virus once and for all.

Apply freshly crushed **garlic** directly to the wart and cover with a bandage. The caustic effect of the garlic will cause the wart to blister and fall off in as little as one week. Apply new garlic every day, avoiding contact with healthy surrounding skin. (Smearing the area around the wart with **petroleum jelly** can help.) For an added effect, some herbalists suggest eating raw garlic or taking three garlic capsules a day to help the immune system fight the virus.

Apply a compress or cotton ball soaked in **vinegar** and tape it down on the wart with an elastic bandage for at least one or two hours daily.

Pull a **dandelion** from your yard, break the stem, and

What's wrong

If you have a wart, it means the human papillomavirus (HPV) has invaded a tiny cut in the skin. HPV is really an umbrella term for many strains of a virus that can show up all over the body. Some types of warts are found singly; others, in clusters. Generally, the wart appears as a pale skin growth with a rough surface. Plantar warts, which grow on the bottom of the feet, can be so painful that walking is difficult. Genital warts, found around the genital and anal area, are very contagious and can increase the risk of cervical, penile, and other cancers.

Should I call **the doctor?**

Genital warts require immediate medical attention, and if your partner has them, you both need treatment. They are potentially serious and should never be treated exclusively with home remedies or OTCs. But the warts that appear on other parts of your body are not dangerous, and you can try any number of remedies before turning to a doctor or dermatologist. If you're over 45 and develop a new wart, however, it's a good idea to get the growth looked at by a doctor to rule out skin cancer.

squeeze some of its liquid onto your wart. Do this daily as needed. The sap is mildly irritating, so it stimulates your immune system to take care of the wart. Don't use dandelions that have been treated with herbicides during the previous few years.

Acidic Approaches

 Grind up a few **vitamin C** tablets, mix with enough water to make a paste, and dab it onto your wart. Cover the paste with a bandage or tape. Because the tablets are highly acidic, they can help wear the wart away and also fight the virus itself.

 If a piece of **birch bark** is available, dampen it with water, and tape it over your wart with the inner side of the bark facing your skin. The bark contains salicylates, which are also found in many over-the-counter wart treatments.

 You can also make a tea from **powdered birch bark**, available from health-food stores. Steep a teaspoon of bark in a cup of boiling water for 10 minutes, let it cool, soak a cloth in it, and press it on the wart.

Kitchen Cures

 Tape a piece of **banana peel**, inner side down, over the wart before you go to bed. A chemical in the peel can slowly dissolve the wart.

 Do the same with a piece of **lemon peel**. An oil in the peel seems to discourage warts.

 Papaya contains an enzyme that digests dead tissue. Make shallow cuts on the surface of an unripe papaya, collect the sap that runs out, and let it coagulate. Mix the thickened sap with water, then apply morning and night.

 A popular folk remedy is to rub a juicy, freshly cut slice of **raw potato** over a wart. (Pennsylvania Dutch tradition says this remedy won't work unless you bury the used potato, but others report no need to give the spud a send-off.) We can't vouch for the efficacy of this cure, but it can't hurt.

 Crush a fresh **basil** leaf and tape it over your wart with waterproof first-aid tape (or even regular tape in a pinch). The leaves contain virus-killing compounds. Replace with fresh basil daily for up to a week.

Imagining Warts Away

The power of suggestion has proved to be amazingly useful in making warts disappear. Odd folk remedies over the years have included rubbing the wart with dung, saliva, a penny, or raw meat—and many actually seem to work!

One doctor pretended to bombard a patient's warts with powerful X rays. Although the man was in fact given no radiation at all, his warts fell off the next day. Spend a few minutes each day just imagining that the warts are shrinking. If your child has a wart, make up an elaborate wart-curing ritual, such as rubbing the wart with a rock, placing the rock in a box, then burying it. If your child believes it will get rid of the wart, it just might.

Rub-On Remedies

 Several times a day, apply a tincture of **goldenseal**, an herb that contains compounds that fight off bacteria and viruses.

 Rub **castor oil** into your wart daily. The oil can make warts disappear, perhaps by keeping them moist so the skin cells in the wart just come apart.

 Vitamin E oil is also said to work against warts. Once a day, pierce a vitamin E capsule and rub the contents into the wart.

 If you have an **aloe vera** plant on the windowsill, break off a leaf and squeeze a few drops of gel onto the wart. Repeat daily. Some people report success with this remedy, perhaps because of the malic acid in aloe vera gel.

Give Feet the Water Cure

 Plantar warts are sensitive to heat and may disappear in a few weeks if you soak your feet in **hot water** (43° to 45°C) for about 15 minutes a day, a remedy published by a medical journal in the 1960s, but long since forgotten. For an added kick, pour one part **vinegar** into four parts hot water.

The Power of Prevention

 Wear sandals around swimming pools and in the locker room. Wart viruses thrive in warm, moist environments.

 Be sure to **dry off your wart** after you wash your hands, to reduce the chance of the virus spreading to someone else. When warts are wet, they seem to be more contagious.

 Don't scratch or pick at warts. You can transfer the virus when you scratch other areas of skin.

Water Retention

Doctors typically treat water retention with diuretic drugs that push excess fluid out of the body. But these medications can also cause you to lose important minerals that, among their other functions, keep your heart beating properly. While diuretics might be necessary for serious medical conditions such as congestive heart failure, simple self-help remedies—altering your diet, drinking herbal teas, and getting outside for a long walk several times a week, for starters—may provide all the help you need.

What's wrong?

Fluid that should travel through blood vessels and lymph channels ebbs into cells and the tiny spaces between them. Sometimes the cause of fluid retention is easy to identify: Knee-high stockings, or too much salt in your diet, which causes fluid to move from the bloodstream into intracellular spaces in your body. But the causes of fluid retention before menstruation are more complex: fluctuating hormone levels that change the function of blood vessels and lymph glands. More rarely, fluid retention is related to kidney disease, liver disease, or congestive heart failure.

Fight Water with Water

↪ It may sound strange, but you may need to **drink more water** to solve the problem of fluid retention. If you're dehydrated, your body may be storing up water to cope with what it sees as a dry spell. Also, when you drink more water, you'll urinate more and pass more salt from your body. Put 2 quarts of water in the refrigerator every morning, and try to finish the pitcher by the end of the day.

Adjust Your Salt-Potassium Balance

↪ Keep **sodium** intake under 2,400 milligrams a day. Most of the sodium in your diet doesn't come from the saltshaker, but from processed foods like soups, sauces, and packaged snacks. Favor unprocessed fresh foods such as fruits, vegetables, and whole grains—foods that don't come in a box, bag, or can. When you do eat processed foods, try to get versions that are labeled low-sodium.

↪ Get more **potassium**. This mineral does not work directly as a diuretic, but the right balance of potassium and sodium is crucial for regulating your body's fluid levels. (Most people get too little potassium and too much sodium.) Aim for 5,000 milligrams a day of potassium if you're retaining water. Nonprescription potassium supplements come in a maximum dosage of 99 milligrams per capsule, so you won't get to 5,000 milligrams by taking them. Instead, eat plenty of fruits and vegetables that are high in potassium, such as bananas, avocados, and citrus fruits. One large banana has more than 500 milligrams, and an avocado has more than 1,000 milligrams. Potassium is also present in high levels in most kinds of meat.

Flush Out Fluid the Natural Way

🍂 Drink two to four cups of **dandelion tea** daily. Dandelion leaf is a natural diuretic, allowing your kidneys to drain away more water. The herb is also a rich source of potassium. To make the tea, add 1½ tablespoons dried dandelion (available in health-food stores) to 1 liter water and boil. Simmer for 15 minutes, strain, and let cool before drinking.

🍂 Try drinking tea made from **nettle**, also called **stinging nettle**. Nettle is a natural diuretic. To make the tea, place 1 heaping teaspoon powdered root in 1 cup cold water. Bring to a boil, boil for one minute, then remove from the heat and let steep for 10 minutes. Drink a cup four times a day.

🍂 **Corn silk tea** has a mild diuretic effect, possibly because of its high potassium content. Put 1 teaspoon of corn silk in cold water. Boil for two to three minutes, then strain. Drink 1 cup several times a day.

🍂 While you're loading up your plate with fruits and vegetables for their potassium content, save extra room for **celery**, **watermelon, asparagus**, and **cucumbers**. All contain chemicals that work as natural diuretics.

🍂 The spice **turmeric**, an ingredient in curry powder known to have anti-inflammatory qualities, may have the power to inhibit water retention, according to research in China. Use it liberally in your cooking.

Beat Menstrual Bloating

🍂 If you have problems with fluid retention before menstruation, take a daily dose of 200 milligrams of **vitamin B₆** during the five days before your period. The vitamin is a diuretic, which means it helps you get rid of more urine (therefore lowering your body's water supply). It also helps balance a woman's estrogen and progesterone levels. Doctors advise not to take over 50 milligrams a day long-term, since excessive B₆ can cause nerve problems. To increase your intake throughout the month, eat more spinach, poultry, and bananas.

Should I call **the doctor?**

If fluid retention causes swelling in your abdomen or limbs that persists more than a week, call your doctor. Also seek medical attention if water retention causes bloating so severe that poking your skin with your finger leaves a dent in it. If your fluid retention is the result of congestive heart failure or another serious disease, you should be under the care of a doctor.

Restrain the Swell

✎ Get regular **exercise** to relieve swelling in the legs, which is a common result of fluid retention. Because gravity pulls water downward, you may find that your lower legs and ankles get swollen, especially at the end of the day. If you do the kind of exercise that works the muscles in your calves, more fluid gets pumped up from your legs through your veins. Get at least 20 to 30 minutes of walking, jogging, biking or other leg-pumping exercise most days of the week.

✎ Another way to help reduce swelling in your legs is to pull on a pair of **support hose** first thing in the morning. The hose fit snugly on your legs and minimize swelling.

✎ To help squeeze fluid from your lower legs, do a gentle **self-massage**. Start by sitting on the floor with your knees bent. Grasp your shin just below the knee with fingers on your calf and thumbs placed along your shinbone. Move your hands slowly toward your ankle while applying gentle pressure with your thumbs. Next, place both thumbs on the inside of your ankle and stroke back up toward your knee. Finally, wrap your hands around your calf and perform a squeeze-and-release massage down your leg. Repeat on the other leg.

✎ If you have swollen lower legs and feet, when you get home from work, **lie down** on a couch and lift your legs so they're higher than the level of your heart. Excess fluid stored in your legs will work its way back into your bloodstream, travel to the kidneys, and pass from your body in urine. Keep your feet up an hour or two daily if possible.

Wrinkles

Dermatologists have many tools for tackling those little lines that mark the passage of time. One is Retin-A, a prescription cream that increases your body's production of collagen near the surface of your skin. Chemical peels use acid to burn away the top layers of wrinkled skin. And injections of the toxin Botox paralyze facial muscles temporarily so you can't wrinkle your skin with certain facial expressions. But perhaps the best option is to protect your skin just as it is, and help keep it healthy.

De-Etch with Acids

◆ Use a lotion or cream that contains **alpha-hydroxy acids**, or AHAs. AHAs come from milk, fruit, and sugarcane, and clear away dead cells on the surface of your skin. These products encourage collagen growth, which fills in wrinkles. They also counteract free radicals, which are rogue oxygen molecules in your body that can damage your skin. Since AHAs can sometimes cause irritation, try a touch of the product on a small patch of skin first. If the patch doesn't turn red by the next day, the moisturizer is safe for you to use.

◆ Soak a washcloth in **milk** and apply it to your skin. Milk contains alpha-hydroxy acids.

◆ Apply fresh **aloe vera gel**, which contains malic acid. Cut off a leaf at the base and slit it open with a knife. Scrape out the gel with a spoon, taking care not to rupture the green rind, and apply.

◆ **Papayas** are chock-full of enzymes that can etch away the top layer of your skin, reducing the appearance of wrinkles. Wash and peel a papaya, then thoroughly mix two tablespoons of it with a tablespoon of dry oatmeal to help exfoliate your skin. Apply it to your skin and leave it on for 10 minutes. Scrub off the mixture with a washcloth.

Plump Up Skin

◆ Apply a **moisturizer** every morning. When you add moisturizer, dry skin expands a bit, which helps hide the wrinkles. Also, moisturizers make your skin softer and more elastic.

What's **wrong**

After the age of thirty or so, some of the connective tissue in your skin starts to break down, oil production slows down, and wrinkles develop. Those are facts of life. But wrinkles are also caused by factors that you can control. Smoking is a major culprit; it slows circulation, so your skin doesn't get as much oxygen. Sun exposure is another. The sun's ultraviolet rays do direct damage to connective fibers in the skin. And they release rogue oxygen molecules called free radicals, which wreak havoc on cell membranes.

Should I call the doctor?

If you'd like to see more improvements than you're getting from self-help treatments, talk to your doctor or a dermatologist about medical options for treating your wrinkles.

Skip it!

Will goofy facial exercises treat wrinkles? Some beauty books and magazines claim so. But smiles, grimaces, and other facial contortions just contribute to further wrinkling.

Try an **avocado** facial for moisture as well as **vitamin E**, an antioxidant. Puree the pulp, smooth it on your face, and leave it on for 20 minutes.

Eat , Sleep, and Move for Smoother Skin

Eat fish like **salmon, sardines, tuna**, and **mackerel** several times a week. These are rich in omega-3 fatty acids, which are very nourishing to your skin.

Another good way to get omega-3s into your diet is to eat a teaspoon of **flaxseed oil** each day. You can mix the oil with juice or cereal, or drizzle it over a salad.

Pile your plate with plenty of **fruits, vegetables, nuts**, and **seeds**. These offer vitamins A, C, and E—antioxidants that block harmful free radicals before they can cause skin damage.

Even if you're getting more **vitamin C** in your diet, go a step further by putting it directly on skin. Research presented at a recent international dermatology conference shows that using 5% vitamin C cream can boost the skin's production of collagen and help erase signs of aging after six months.

Get in the habit of **sleeping on your back**. When you sleep on your side or stomach, you bury your face into the pillow, "pressing in" wrinkles and crevices.

Exercise 20 to 30 minutes most days of the week. Maybe you've noticed that exercise can cause flushing—a sure sign that oxygen and nourishment in your blood are reaching the capillaries in your skin.

The Power of Prevention

Don't smoke.

Drink enough **water** so that your urine is very pale. Drinking a lot of water really does help keep your skin moist.

Every day, apply **sunscreen** to your face, neck, and other areas of exposed skin before you head outdoors.

Never use a tanning salon. A half-hour there does more damage than lying on the beach all day without sunscreen.

Wear **sunglasses** to avoid wrinkles around your eyes, a.k.a crow's-feet. The wrinkles come from squinting. Even if you've already started to have crow's-feet, the lines can disappear after several months of consistently wearing sunglasses.

Yeast Infections

Most women suffer the itching and discomfort of a vaginal yeast infection at least once in their lives. Some of them get them often enough that they know the symptoms at once and head to the drugstore for an over-the-counter antifungal cream such as Gyne-Lotrimin or Monistat. (If you need a stronger treatment, your doctor can prescribe an oral antifungal drug.) Whatever medication you're taking, other measures are also helpful, not only for treating vaginal infections but also for preventing a recurrence. Most of the remedies in this chapter are specifically for *vaginal* infections.

Rinse or Soak

⤷ Douche twice a day, for two days in a row, with a mixture of 2 tablespoons white **vinegar** in 1 liter water. This slightly acidic solution creates an environment that's unwelcome to yeast. But you should only do this for two days, and only when you have a yeast infection. If you use a vinegar douche when you don't need to, you actually rinse out the beneficial bacteria that keep infections at bay.

⤷ Sprinkle a cup of **sea salt** in a tub of warm water, stir the water around until the salt dissolves, then take a nice soak. You can do this every day, as long as it helps relieve itching and pain. The saltwater soak also speeds up healing.

Pick the Stinking Rose

⤷ Eat a few cloves of **garlic** each day. "The stinking rose," as it's sometimes called, has been used for several millennia to combat everything from colds to intestinal infections. Its antifungal action makes it useful against yeast infections. It's most effective if crushed and eaten raw. If you don't relish the idea of eating a whole clove, chop it up and sprinkle it on salads, or stir it into pasta sauce.

⤷ Some people recommend inserting a gauze-wrapped garlic clove into the vagina. But most women will prefer using an **antifungal cream**—especially since the garlic can sting.

What's wrong?

We all carry small amounts of yeast. Called *Candida albicans*, it inhabits various moist parts of our bodies, usually without causing problems. But occasionally something triggers yeast cells to multiply. One trigger is antibiotics, which can kill off beneficial bacteria that keep yeast populations in check. Most women will have a vaginal yeast infection at some point in their lives. Symptoms include itching, redness, and a white, lumpy discharge (sometimes with an unpleasant smell). Another type of yeast infection, thrush, occurs in the throat, and can afflict both men and women.

Should I call the doctor?

If you're a woman who has been previously treated for vaginal yeast infections, you're probably familiar with the symptoms, and can treat them on your own. Otherwise, always see a doctor to rule out other problems, such as a sexually transmitted disease. You should also get medical care if you have a discharge that's bloody or very foul-smelling, feel pain during urination or intercourse, or have symptoms that don't go away after you've been treating them for five days. And if you've been taking antibiotics for another infection, talk to your doctor about an alternative treatment, since use of antibiotics is often associated with yeast infections.

Battle Yeast with Bacteria

☙ Every day, eat a cup of plain, unsweetened **yogurt** that contains live *Lactobacillus acidophilus* bacteria. *L. acidophilus* has been shown to cut down on yeast overgrowth in the vagina and the intestines. Note that if what you have is a bacterial infection and not a yeast infection, yogurt will actually make matters worse.

☙ Buy capsules or tablets of *Lactobacillus acidophilus*. Look for a supplement that contains one to two billion live organisms per pill. You can either take two pills daily, or you can use the supplement as a vaginal suppository. (To help prevent infection, many women use a single dose of acidophilus every month on the last day of their menstrual period.)

Other Fungus Fighters

☙ Prepare a solution of **cinnamon**, which research suggests has strong antifungal properties. (In fact, German researchers concluded that impregnating toilet paper with cinnamon would completely suppress the fungus responsible for yeast infections.) Add 8 to 10 broken sticks of cinnamon to 4 cups of boiling water and let them simmer for about 5 minutes. Take the pot off the burner and let the cinnamon steep for about 45 minutes. Some herbalists suggest using the lukewarm solution as a douche, but others say drinking cinnamon tea can also help control yeast infections.

☙ Try supplements of **lapacho tree bark** (also known as **pau d'arco** and **taheebo**), which is thought to be a potent infection fighter. (It's even been researched as an anti-cancer agent.) You can make a tea by boiling 2 tablespoons of the herb in 1 liter of water and storing it in the refrigerator before straining and drinking. But some natural medicine practitioners say certain ingredients in the bark don't dissolve in water, making capsules more effective. A standard dose is 300 milligrams taken three times daily.

☙ To help your immune system fight the infection, take three 200-milligram doses of **echinacea** three times a day, or a dropper of tincture in a half-cup of water four times a day. Take echinacea daily for up to two weeks, then stop taking it for two weeks.

To Eat and Not to Eat

🍃 When you have an infection, cut way back on sugary foods and starches. **Avoid white bread, pasta, honey, molasses, and fruit juices.** These foods raise the level of blood sugar (glucose) in your body, and yeast feed on glucose.

🍃 **Avoid alcohol.** Yeast digests alcohol, too—and you don't want well-fed yeast if you're trying to end an infection.

The Power of Prevention

🍃 **Go without underwear at night.** Since yeast flourishes in warm, moist environments, the ventilation will help you avoid infections. When you do wear underwear, go with cotton or with cotton-lined panties. They allow for better air circulation than synthetic fibers.

🍃 For the same reason, **leave tight pants in the closet.**

🍃 **Don't linger in a wet bathing suit** after swimming. Shower promptly and change into dry clothes.

🍃 Use a **hair dryer** on cool setting (never hot!) to dry the external vaginal area completely after you've been bathing or swimming.

🍃 **Don't use soap** or very hot water to cleanse the vaginal tissues. If you do, you'll remove healthy natural skin barriers that help to control yeast.

🍃 **Refrain from using scented tampons**, feminine deodorants, and douches. The chemical used to create pleasant fragrances can upset the delicate environment in the vagina and allow yeast to take over.

🍃 Also **avoid perfumed dusting powders.** Some women develop an irritation when using these powders—and the additional irritation makes them more prone to yeast infection.

🍃 Make a point of **urinating after intercourse.** Mucous membranes of the vagina normally are slightly acidic, but semen is alkaline, making it friendlier to yeast. Urinating will help make the area less inviting to infectious growth.

Did you know?

Couples can pass a yeast infection back and forth during sex. If you have a vaginal yeast infection, be sure your partner isn't also infected, which most often happens in uncircumcised men. The most likely sign of a yeast infection in males is inflammation on the head of the penis.

Skip it!

Refrain from dusting your vaginal area with any product that contains cornstarch. Though cornstarch acts as a drying agent, yeast feed on it.

Part

Honey

Two

20 Top Household Healers

What do you do when life hands you lemons? How about using them to prevent kidney stones, strengthen veins, and stave off skin cancer? You probably know that aloe vera soothes a sunburn, but did you know you can also use it for acne and psoriasis? Or that garlic juice can kill the fungi that cause ear infections? Here you'll discover the amazing healing virtues of 20 common herbs, foods, and kitchen staples. Find out how to use chamomile tea to soothe inflamed gums, Epsom salt to treat sprains and bruises and soothe tired feet, ginger to short-circuit migraines and ease arthritis pain, lavender to take the itching out of insect bites, and mustard to kick athlete's foot. Plus learn the big benefits of good old baking soda, handy honey, versatile vinegar, and nine more healers.

Aloe Vera

Every kitchen should have a potted aloe vera plant on the windowsill. Aloe vera has been used medicinally since prehistoric times. Today the clear gel inside aloe vera leaves is among the most popular herbal remedies for sunburns, minor wounds, and other skin problems. It's even been used for hemorrhoids and insect bites because it's rich in anti-inflammatory substances and the gel forms a cool, soothing coating on itchy, irritated tissues.

What's it **good for?**

- Acne
- Age Spots
- Athlete's Foot
- Blisters
- Canker Sores
- Dry Hair
- Dry Skin
- Heat Rash
- Psoriasis
- Razor Burn
- Sunburn
- Shingles
- Warts
- Wrinkles

Aloe vera enthusiasts swear that the gel—or a juice that contains a high concentration of aloe vera—can be taken internally as a treatment for arthritis, diabetes, ulcers, and serious infections such as HIV, the virus that causes AIDS. You have to take these claims with a grain of salt. Researchers are studying internal uses for aloe vera, but nothing is conclusive yet. One thing is certain: Aloe vera is one of the best skin remedies you'll ever use.

Powerful Skin Healer

Scientists aren't entirely sure how aloe vera works, but they have identified many of its active components. The gel contains gummy substances that are nature's soothing emollients. It's rich in anti-inflammatory compounds as well as bradykininase, a chemical that acts as a topical painkiller. The magnesium lactate in aloe vera quells itching, and the gel contains substances that promote healing by dilating blood vessels and increasing blood flow to injured areas.

Aloe vera is helpful for a variety of skin conditions, including:

➤ **Minor burns.** A quick application of aloe vera gel reduces pain, moistens the skin, and keeps germs and air out. It soothes the pain of sunburn as well. To relieve the pain of an all-over sunburn, add a cup or two of aloe vera juice to a tub of lukewarm water and take a soothing soak.

➤ **Cuts and scrapes.** Aloe vera gel dries to form a natural bandage over skin and speed healing. However, it's not a good choice for serious wounds. Researchers at a Los Angeles hospital found that the gel actually increased the time it took such wounds to heal.

 Psoriasis. The gel quells inflammation and softens the itchy skin scales that characterize this chronic skin condition. A four-week study found an 83 percent rate of skin clearing in those who used aloe vera, compared to only 6 percent of those using an inactive cream.

 Acne. Apply aloe vera when you have a painful outbreak. One study found that 90 percent of skin sores were completely healed with aloe vera within five days—nearly twice the success rate of those using standard medical creams.

 Shingles. Painful sores caused by the herpes virus heal more quickly when aloe vera is applied to the skin. The gel appears to have some antiviral effects. And aloe vera dilates tiny blood vessels called capillaries, allowing more blood to reach the area and thereby speeding healing.

The Inside Story

Doctors are unanimous that aloe vera gel is helpful for minor skin ailments, but what about taking the gel or juice internally? Nothing is certain yet, but a number of studies suggest some intriguing possibilities.

For example, a scientific study found that volunteers who took aloe vera juice twice daily for up to 42 days had significant reductions in blood sugar, suggesting that it's potentially helpful for treating diabetes.

Japanese researchers report that the active ingredients in aloe vera inhibit stomach secretions and sores, giving credence to aloe vera's reputation as an ulcer remedy. In fact, two of the active chemical compounds in aloe vera appear to inhibit or destroy *H. pylori,* the bacterium that causes most ulcers.

Finally, a chemical compound called acemannan, found in the outer skin of aloe vera, has potent antiviral activity. It was the preliminary results from clinical studies of acemannan that made researchers wonder whether it can cause a significant reduction in AIDS symptoms. But much more work must be done before they determine whether it helps prevent some declines in immune function.

Too Strong for Comfort

Aloe is a very effective—too effective, really—laxative. Aloe latex, which is extracted from the leaf's rind, is classified as a stimulant laxative. It stimulates intestinal contractions that promote bowel movements. As with other stimulant laxatives, however, doctors rarely recommend it. It can cause severe cramping or diarrhea, along with fluid loss and reductions of vital electrolytes, minerals that play critical roles in the body.

How to Use Aloe Vera

You can buy skin-care products with aloe vera at supermarkets and pharmacies, but it's not entirely clear that the "stabilized" form of aloe vera in these products has the same beneficial effects as the natural gel. If you do buy prepared creams or lotions, make sure that aloe vera is listed near the top of the ingredient list. For internal use, buy juices that contain at least 98% aloe vera.

To get the full benefits of aloe vera, there's no substitute for the real thing. The plant is very easy to grow. Even if you have a brown thumb, aloe vera thrives with little water and can tolerate shade and poor soil.

To soothe sunburn, cuts, and minor burns, clean the area thoroughly with soap and water. Then cut several inches off a large leaf, slice it lengthwise, and squeeze out the gel. Apply a generous coating to the injured area, and repeat the treatment two or three times daily.

Arnica

D on't be fooled by arnica's pretty face. The lovely, daisy-like flowers of this mountain herb can send blood pressure into the stratosphere and cause permanent heart damage. Distilled oils from arnica, or teas made from dried flowers, should never be taken internally. External uses are another story entirely. Arnica is surprisingly effective for treating muscle soreness, bruises, and sprains. In other words, if you've had a little accident or sports injury of just about any sort, arnica is the herb you'll probably want to turn to for relief.

Banish Bruises, Eliminate Aches

Arnica has received the stamp of approval from Germany's Commission E—seen as the world's leading authority on the safety and effectiveness of herbs—as an external treatment for bruises as well as muscle aches and pains. (Never use arnica internally; it's toxic.)

You can buy arnica in gel, cream, ointment, and tincture forms. It's also found frequently in homeopathic preparations. You can also make an arnica compress. First brew up a strong tea using 2 teaspoons of arnica flowers per cup of boiling water. Let the tea cool, then soak a clean cloth in it and apply. Arnica is most effective for:

 Banishing bruises. Arnica erases bruises by helping the body reabsorb the blood that has seeped into the tissues. A cream or ointment containing 5% to 25% arnica extract, applied several times daily, reduces pain and swelling—along with that ugly eggplant color. If you prefer to use the tincture form, mix 1 part tincture with 3 to 10 parts water, soak a clean cloth in the liquid, and apply to the bruise. Two of the chemicals in arnica, helenalin and dihydrohelenalin, have painkilling and anti-inflammatory properties when absorbed through the skin. You can also take one or two tablets of the homeopathic remedy Arnica 30C as soon as possible after you've bumped yourself to minimize bruising. Follow the dosage instructions on the label.

What's it
good for?

- Bruises
- Bursitis and Tendinitis
- Carpal Tunnel Syndrome
- Foot Pain

❧ **Soothing sprains and strains.** Because it curbs inflammation, arnica is perfect for treating mild sprains. It may also improve circulation, increasing the flow of healing nutrients into sore muscles while removing pain-causing injury by-products such as lactic acid. It also helps relieve pain. Because arnica can be toxic when taken internally, don't use it on broken skin.

❧ **Tending tender tootsies.** Feet hurt at the end of the day? Soak them in a warm-water footbath spiked with 15 milliliters of arnica tincture. The improved blood flow almost instantly results in less pain.

Watch Out for Rashes

Most people can enjoy the benefits of arnica without any side effects. Not so if you're one of the unlucky ones allergic to helenalin, one of the active chemicals in arnica. Regular use of the herb can result in contact dermatitis, a harmless but potentially itchy skin rash. This usually occurs in people who use the herb often or apply a too-strong tincture to the skin.

If you're allergic to ragweed, you'll definitely want to avoid arnica. They're both members of the aster family, a common allergy culprit.

Baking Soda

Entire books have been written about baking soda, and for good reason: It's among the most versatile products ever made. It's renowned as a household cleanser. It's also a leavening agent in baking, because it reacts with acidic ingredients and produces the carbon dioxide bubbles that give breads, muffins, and pastries their "lift." But best of all, it has a long history of healing.

Baking soda, also known as sodium bicarbonate, is among the fastest-acting antacids. It stops itching from insect bites and stings. It helps remove dental plaque and neutralizes tooth-damaging acids. It eases symptoms of bladder infections. Doctors even use it to reduce blood acids during dialysis for kidney disease. So don't take that yellow box in the back of the refrigerator for granted.

Nature's Neutralizer

All chemicals can be rated according to their pH, a measure of acidity and alkalinity. Chemicals with pH values of 6 and lower are acids. Those with a pH of 8 or above are alkaline. (Water, which comes in at 7, is neutral.) With a pH of 9, baking soda is mildly alkaline and takes the edge off potentially harsh acids.

Consider heartburn. It usually occurs when the highly corrosive hydrochloric acid in the stomach splashes upward into the esophagus, causing a temporary chemical burn. You can get relief by taking a sodium bicarbonate tablet or a teaspoon of baking soda, with a few drops of lemon juice, mixed in a glass of water. When you down this fizzy stuff, it neutralizes hydrochloric acid by converting it to harmless sodium chloride and carbon dioxide. The effects last only about 30 minutes, but they occur almost instantly. (Don't use this remedy too often, however, because baking soda contains a lot of sodium, which may raise your blood pressure. Lemon juice helps dispel some of the gas baking soda can form when it combines with stomach acid.)

What's it good for?

- Anal Itching
- Athlete's Foot
- Body Odor
- Canker Sores
- Chicken Pox
- Dry Mouth
- Foot Odor
- Gum Problems
- Heartburn
- Heat Rash
- Hives
- Insect and Spider Bites
- Indigestion
- Sore Throat
- Splinters
- Sunburn
- Urinary Tract Infections

There are many other ways to take advantage of baking soda. For example, with baking soda on hand you can:

Reduce tooth-damaging acids. Acids produced by bacteria in the mouth gnaw away at tooth enamel. You can neutralize them by swishing your mouth with a baking soda solution several times a day. Or moisten your toothbrush with water, dip it in baking soda, and brush. Baking soda is slightly abrasive, so it polishes teeth without damaging the enamel.

Make feet smell sweet. Added to a footbath, it neutralizes bacterial acids that cause foot odor. You can also pit it against underarm smells.

Take the bite out of stings. Don't scratch yourself raw when mosquitoes or other insects have made you the day's buffet. Instead, mix a little water with baking soda and apply the paste to the itchy areas. A baking soda paste can also help ease the itching of poison ivy and chicken pox.

Soothe tender tushies. Infants with diaper rash feel better after a baking-soda soak. It decreases itching and helps irritated skin heal more quickly.

Ease bladder infections. Bacteria thrive in the slightly acidic environment inside the bladder. When you have an infection, a cocktail of baking soda and water is the perfect after-dinner drink.

Soothe sunburns. Added to a warm bath, baking soda "softens" the water and makes a soothing soak.

Ease a sore throat. Add a half-teaspoon of baking soda to a glass of water and gargle every four hours to reduce pain-causing acids. Swishing the solution around your mouth will ease mouths sores, as well.

Fight bad breath. When combined with hydrogen peroxide, baking soda has a powerful oxidizing effect that destroys odor-causing bacteria. Combine 1 tablespoon baking soda with 1 cup hydrogen peroxide (2% to 3%) and use as a gargle.

Chamomile

With its agreeable taste and apple-like aroma, chamomile makes a pleasant tea for sipping. The very thought of drinking a cup of chamomile tea at night is almost enough to soothe frazzled nerves and summon sleep. But chamomile's benefits don't end there. Scientists have identified more than a dozen active chemical compounds within the herb's daisy-like flowers that not only take the edge off stress but also soothe stomach upset almost as fast as you can say Pepto-Bismol.

A chemical in chamomile called apigenin calms the central nervous system and makes it easier to fall asleep at night. All wound up with tension? Enjoy a cup of chamomile tea, or lounge in a warm bath spiked with several cups of chamomile tea, 10 drops of chamomile oil, or a handful or two of chamomile flowers. The essential oil penetrates the skin and take the edge off anxiety and stress.

What's it
good for?
- Belching
- Boils
- Conjunctivitis
- Foot Pain
- Gum
  Problems
- Hives
- Indigestion
- Inflammatory
  Bowel
  Disease
- Menstrual
  Problems
- Psoriasis
- Rosacea
- Stress
- Teething
- Ulcers

More Uses Inside and Out

Chamomile isn't just for helping you relax. Several of its chemical compounds, especially bisabolol, act as antispasmodics: They relax the smooth muscles that line the digestive tract and uterus, easing after-meal stomach discomfort and soothing menstrual cramps. A cup or two of chamomile tea daily might reduce the stomach-gnawing effects of aspirin and related drugs—good news for people with arthritis or other painful conditions who depend on such painkillers for daily relief.

Because of its anti-inflammatory and antiseptic powers, chamomile is also very useful for a number of other minor health complaints.

Rashes and burns. Chamomile can do good things for your skin as well as your intestinal tract. When chamomile is applied externally in the form of chamomile cream or a compress made with strong chamomile tea, it helps cuts, burns, and rashes heal more quickly. If you have a sunburn, try chamomile oil (sold in health-food stores) mixed with equal parts almond oil or another neutral oil to reduce the inflammation that causes itching.

🍂 **Skin irritations.** In Germany, where herbs are standard treatments in the medical mainstream, doctors often recommend a chamomile-based cream, called Kamillosan, for wounds or inflammation caused by eczema, contact allergies, and post-radiation skin damage. Chamomile oil can be applied in small amounts to treat skin ailments such as boils.

🍂 **Infections.** A wash of chamomile kills some of the bacteria and fungi that cause eye or skin infections. Chamomile tea can be used as a mouthwash to soothe inflamed gums, help fight gum disease, and speed the healing of mouth sores.

Buying and Using Chamomile

You can buy chamomile tea bags or look for the dried flowers in health-food stores. Some people have successfully grown chamomile in their garden by simply sprinkling the contents of a bag of chamomile tea on the soil. Note that there are two different chamomile plants: Roman chamomile *(Chamaemelum nobile)* and German chamomile *(Matricaria recutita),* also known as Hungarian chamomile. While the two plants look almost identical, German chamomile is more popular and is thought to have greater healing powers.

You might find chamomile cream in health-food stores, but it's just as easy, and less expensive, to make your own skin-healing brew. Pour a cup of boiling water over a heaping tablespoonful of chamomile flowers. Let it steep 10 minutes, wait until it cools to room temperature, then soak a cloth in the tea and apply it to a cut, rash, or burn for about five minutes.

A media uproar followed a report in the *Journal of Allergy and Clinical Immunology* that chamomile tea might cause a potentially fatal allergic reaction in people allergic to ragweed. But when scientists looked at the available data, they were only able to identify a handful of reactions (none of them fatal) to German chamomile, the variety commonly used in North America. Though some red flags have been raised about allergic reactions, these appear to be so rare that most people needn't worry. The only people who should avoid it are those who have already had a severe reaction to ragweed.

Epsom Salt

You wouldn't think that a common mineral could do so much. Magnesium sulfate, better known as Epsom salt, is popular in stress-reducing, skin-softening, and ache-relieving soaks. Outside of the remedy arena, gardeners swear by it because it helps roses thrive. And raccoons, for some reason, hate it: Epsom salt drives them away!

Epsom salt is found anywhere mineral or seawater evaporates. It takes its name from a mineral spring in Epsom, England. Not long ago, Epsom salt was given as part of the spring round of purgatives to cleanse the body of "toxins" that supposedly built up over the winter. One reason was probably its laxative effect. Until a few decades ago, when commercial laxatives began to line pharmacy shelves, Epsom salt was a popular shortcut to regularity. The active ingredient in milk of magnesia, Epsom salt is a saline-type laxative: The magnesium pulls fluids from the blood into the intestine, making stools softer while triggering intestinal contractions that stimulate bowel movements.

Occasionally, people still take one or two teaspoons of Epsom salt in a glass of water to ease constipation. The problem with this remedy is that it's often too powerful, causing diarrhea or abdominal cramps. And it can interfere with the body's absorption of nutrients. So it's not recommended unless you're under a doctor's care.

What's it good for?
- Acne
- Calluses and Corns
- Dry Skin
- Foot Odor
- Hemorrhoids
- Muscle Cramps
- Poison Ivy
- Ringworm
- Shingles

Soaks and Softeners

External uses of Epsom salt, on the other hand, are entirely safe—and incredibly handy. Among other things, Epsom salt can be used to:

🖝 **Draw out splinters and stingers.** Epsom salt draws toxins from insect stings and pulls splinters to the skin's surface. If you add water to Epsom salt to make a paste and apply it to the affected area, it will usually go to work in about 10 minutes.

Soothing Foot Soak

This recipe for "fabulous feet" comes from the Epsom Salt Industry Council.

Mix the following ingredients in a foot basin or large pot:

2 cups Epsom salt
1 cup Dead Sea salt
1 tablespoon olive oil
½ teaspoon peppermint oil
¼ cup plain oatmeal (non-instant)
Approximately 15 liters warm-to-hot water

Soak your feet until the water turns cold, then, using a pumice stone, buff all the rough areas of skin. Rinse your feet in cold water and dry thoroughly. Then slather petroleum jelly on your skin and slip into thick socks. (Don't try to walk around until you put on the socks. Petroleum jelly will make your feet very slippery.) Keep socks on overnight for best results. Repeat as often as needed.

You can also soak in an Epsom salt bath to soften the skin and help draw out the splinter.

◄ **Deep-clean pores.** Add a teaspoon Epsom salt to a quarter-cup warm water, and rub your skin with the mixture to dislodge blackheads, open pores, and freshen skin.

◄ **Ease muscle aches.** Epsom salt draws fluid out of the body and helps shrink swollen tissues. As it draws fluid through the skin, it also draws out lactic acid, the buildup of which can contribute to muscle aches. Add a cup or two of the salt to a hot bath and enjoy a relaxing soak.

◄ **Sprains and bruises.** Epsom salt will reduce the swelling of sprains and bruises. Add 2 cups Epsom salt to a warm bath, and soak.

◄ **Help hemorrhoids.** Because it shrinks swollen tissues, Epsom salt makes an excellent sitz bath for hemorrhoids.

◄ **Soften skin.** Massage handfuls of Epsom salt over your skin while bathing. The massaging action will exfoliate the skin—that is, slough off dead skin cells—leaving your skin looking smoother and refreshed.

Garlic

Garlic's therapeutic benefits have been so exaggerated by enthusiasts that it's a challenge to separate scientific fact from hopeful fancy. The history of this pungent herb certainly suggests its wide-ranging potential. The Egyptians rationed it to the pyramid builders to boost their strength and prevent dysentery. Europeans ate it to protect themselves during the plague. Battlefield physicians in both world wars used it to disinfect wounds. It's been used to treat athlete's foot, tuberculosis, and high blood pressure, not to mention colds and coughs. It's even been said to stimulate sexual desire. All told, medical historians have logged more than 100 non-culinary uses for "the stinking rose."

In the last few decades, research has caught up with folklore. Garlic is the subject of more than 1,200 pharmacological studies. Most of them have focused on garlic's role in cardiovascular disease and cancer, along with its antibacterial and antioxidant powers. It's abundantly clear that garlic is a medicinal herb to be reckoned with—one that, in some cases, can rival the effects of prescription drugs.

Help for the Heart

Garlic contains more than 100 chemically active compounds. One of the most important is alliin, a sulfur compound that's transformed into allicin when the bulbs are crushed or chewed. Scientists think that allicin is responsible for garlic's antibiotic properties as well as many of its heart benefits. What's certain is that in countries where people consume liberal amounts of garlic, there seem to be unusually low rates of heart disease.

Consider garlic's effects on platelets, cell-like structures in blood that tend to stick together and form clots in the coronary arteries. One study found that the rate of platelet aggregation, or clumping, in men given the equivalent of six cloves of fresh garlic dropped anywhere from 10 to 58 percent.

What's it **good for?**

- Colds and Flu
- Coughs
- Cuts and Scrapes
- Diarrhea
- Earache
- High Blood Pressure
- High Cholesterol
- Insect and Spider Bites
- Sinusitis
- Sore Throat
- Sties
- Swimmer's Ear
- Urinary Tract Infections
- Yeast Infections

Certain chemicals in garlic may be as effective as aspirin at inhibiting the formation of blood clots.

Garlic appears to function somewhat like prescription drugs that inhibit the liver's production of cholesterol, the fatty stuff that contributes to plaque formation and increases the risk of heart disease. Reviews of dozens of scientific studies suggest that eating garlic daily can lower cholesterol 9 to 12 percent.

Garlic improves blood flow throughout the body, not just in the coronary arteries. It's a vasodilator, which means it causes blood vessels to expand and blood pressure to drop. It also appears to improve the flexibility of arteries.

A Cancer Fighter

Dozens of studies suggest that garlic blocks cell changes that can lead to cancer—and may destroy cancer cells that have already formed. In one study, eating less than a clove a day was shown to cut the risk of prostate cancer in half. A study of women in Iowa found that those who ate garlic weekly were about a third less likely to get colon cancer than those who never ate it. Chinese studies suggest that garlic can reduce the incidence of stomach cancer by a factor of 12. And there is laboratory evidence that garlic can shrink cancers of the breast, skin, and lungs. The diallyl trisulfide in garlic is thought to be as effective at killing cancer cells as 5-fluorouracil, a chemotherapy drug.

How does garlic act against cancer? No one is certain. Allicin and other compounds it contains seem to work directly against tumors. Garlic may also block the formation of cancer-causing compounds. It neutralizes dangerous molecules called free radicals, by-products of the oxidation process that contribute to cell aging and also damage DNA and initiate carcinogenic cell changes. It inhibits the formation of nitrites, chemicals involved in triggering stomach cancer. And it boosts the immune system.

An Edible Antibiotic

Raw garlic that's crushed and applied to wounds kills a variety of infection-causing organisms, including the fungi that cause athlete's foot, vaginal yeast infections, and many cases of ear infection. It kills many different types of bacteria, including the one that causes tuberculosis, and the dreaded *E. coli,* the cause of many urinary tract infections. It may even kill some germs that are resistant to standard antibiotics.

Garlic destroys germs on the outside and the inside of your body. Eating it may help protect the lining of your stomach from *H. pylori,* the bug that causes most ulcers. And since garlic's essential oil is excreted through the lungs, it's particularly useful when you have a respiratory ailment.

How Much to Take

One to two cloves of raw or lightly cooked garlic daily are probably enough to get most of the healing benefits. Raw garlic packs more healing punch, since cooking inhibits the formation of allicin and eliminates some other healing chemicals. You should bruise, chop, or chew the clove to make sure the alliin is converted to allicin.

The problem with fresh garlic, of course, is the overwhelming (for some people) smell and taste. Enteric-coated garlic supplements won't give you garlic breath because they pass through the stomach undigested, and they probably work as well as fresh garlic, although this is the subject of some debate. Doctors advise taking 400 to 600 milligrams of garlic daily—more if you're fighting a cold or flu. Look for a supplement standardized to contain 4,000 micrograms of "allicin potential."

Ginger

Ginger, that gnarled root with the pleasantly pungent flavor, is among the most used and best studied of all "kitchen cures." Closely related to the spices turmeric and cardamom, it has been used medicinally and as a seasoning for at least 5,000 years. Ginger is used worldwide to ease nausea, vomiting, morning sickness, and other digestive complaints—conditions that aren't always helped by modern drugs. And in the last few decades, the potential uses for ginger have expanded far beyond the stomach.

What's it good for?

- Arthritis
- Belching
- Bursitis and Tendinitis
- Colds and Flu
- Coughs
- Flatulence
- Headache
- Heartburn
- High Cholesterol
- Hives
- Indigestion
- Irritable Bowel Syndrome
- Jock Itch
- Menstrual Problems
- Migraines
- Morning Sickness
- Nausea
- Toothache
- Ulcers

Whether you have chills and a cold or an upset stomach, ginger can help. You can take it in tea, capsule, or candy form. Of course, you can also add it to your food. Many healing herbs have to be taken in whopping amounts to provide health benefits. Ginger is different, because the amount you'd add to a curry or stir-fry can easily equal or exceed the amount used in supplements. This means you can enjoy good flavors along with good health.

Stomach Soother

Ginger is among the most potent remedies for motion sickness as well as garden-variety stomach upset. In fact, studies have shown that it works just as well as Dramamine (dimenhydrinate) and other nausea-stopping drugs. In one famous study, scientists strapped volunteers in rotating chairs and took them for a ride. Those given dimenhydrinate lasted only about 4½ minutes before begging to stop. Half of the people given ginger, on the other hand, lasted six minutes, with less nausea than the dimenhydrinate group.

The chemical compounds that give ginger its zesty taste—mainly gingerol and shogaol—appear to reduce intestinal contractions, neutralize digestive acids, and inhibit the "vomiting center" in the brain. Doctors often recommend ginger to prevent nausea because it doesn't cause grogginess the way anti-nausea drugs can. It has even been used to lessen chemotherapy-induced nausea and postoperative nausea.

Ginger is better at preventing nausea than stopping it. If you're susceptible to motion sickness, for instance, the time to take ginger is before you get in the car or climb aboard a seafaring yacht. Take about a quarter-teaspoon powdered ginger, 1 gram of ginger in capsule form, or a one-centimeter (half-inch) slice of fresh gingerroot at least 20 minutes before leaving.

Whole-Body Protection

Ginger is most popular for nausea and stomach upset, but there is strong evidence that its benefits go much further. For example, it's been shown to:

Short-circuit migraines. Danish researchers report that a third of a teaspoon of fresh or powdered ginger, taken at the first sign of migraine, may reduce symptoms by blocking prostaglandins, chemicals that cause inflammation in blood vessels in the brain. Unlike aspirin and related drugs, ginger blocks only the types of prostaglandins that cause inflammation, not the ones that have beneficial roles, such as strengthening the stomach lining.

Ease arthritis pain. The same prostaglandins that contribute to migraine pain also cause joint swelling in people with rheumatoid arthritis or osteoarthritis. A study of 56 people found that ginger eased symptoms in 55 percent of people with osteoarthritis and 74 percent of those with rheumatoid arthritis. Repeatedly applying crushed gingerroot to the skin may provide additional relief by depleting stores of substance P, a neurotransmitter that carries pain signals to the spinal cord and, ultimately, the brain.

Reduce blood clots. Doctors often advise patients to take aspirin every other day because it "thins" the blood by interfering with the action of platelets, cell-like structures that cause blood clots and increase the risk of heart attack. Ginger has similar effects, but without the stomach upset often caused by aspirin (unless, of course, your stomach is sensitive to ginger or you eat too much of it).

Take the stuffiness out of colds. Ginger blocks the body's production of substances that contribute to bronchial constriction as well as fever. The gingerols in ginger also act as natural cough suppressants.

Lower cholesterol. Laboratory studies suggest that ginger reduces the absorption of cholesterol by the body and also promotes its excretion. Ginger also appears to help lower blood pressure.

Relieve menstrual cramps. The chemical compounds in ginger act as antispasmodics. They inhibit painful contractions not only of the smooth muscles of the digestive tract but also of the uterus.

Condiments, Candies, and Capsules

The active ingredients in ginger retain their potency when they're processed into almost every form of supplement. Many people prefer ginger capsules because they're easy to take and provide a concentrated (and predictable) source of ginger's chemical compounds. The usual dose is 100 to 200 milligrams, taken up to four times daily.

Here are healing amounts of other forms of ginger:

A one-centimeter (half-inch) slice of gingerroot. Grating the ginger will release more of the active ingredients than slicing or chopping. It's also important to buy ginger when it's fresh. Avoid gingerroot that has soft spots or moldy, wrinkled skin.

One teaspoon of powdered ginger.

One or two pieces of crystallized, candied ginger.

One cup of ginger tea, made with a ginger tea bag or a half-teaspoon grated gingerroot. Steep in a cup of hot water.

A 350-milliliter glass of natural ginger ale. But check the label to make sure it contains real ginger, not ginger flavoring.

Goldenseal

If you're dubious that herbs can heal as well as drugs, consider this: In studies, goldenseal proved more effective against certain infections, such as the bugs that cause infectious diarrhea and certain eye infections, than prescription medications. One of its compounds, berberine—which gives the root its rich yellow color—prevents streptococci bacteria from gaining a foothold in the body. Goldenseal is so effective, in fact, that some 11 countries recognize the herb as medicine.

Traditionally used to fight sore throat, infections of the digestive tract, and as an eyewash, goldenseal gets its name from the small scars that dot the vibrant yellow root—markings that resemble the wax seals once used to close envelopes. It's no wonder the herb is a favorite among herbalists and naturopaths: It directly fights bacteria, viruses, and fungi—and it boosts the immune system too. Goldenseal works especially well on mucous membranes, making it useful against canker sores, cold sores, stomach complaints, urinary tract infections, and eye infections. It also stimulates digestive secretions.

Herbal Antibiotic

Berberine and another of goldenseal's compounds, called hydrastine, give the herb its infection-fighting powers. They kill a variety of bacteria as well as some strains of yeast (such as *Candida*) and parasites (such as *Giardia*). They also enhance the activity of virus-fighting white blood cells. Among goldenseal's healing benefits:

 Staves off colds and flu. Taken at the first sign of symptoms, goldenseal can actually prevent cold or flu viruses from fully taking hold in the body, thereby easing the severity of symptoms. It also reduces the risk of secondary bacterial infections. Some herbalists recommend combining it with echinacea for best results.

 Battles urinary tract infections. All antibiotics, herbal as well as synthetic, concentrate in the urine. This makes gold-

What's it **good for?**

- Canker Sores
- Colds and Flu
- Conjunctivitis
- Dandruff
- Diarrhea
- Earache
- Jock Itch
- Urinary Tract Infections
- Warts

enseal an excellent choice for treating minor infections in the bladder or urethra.

Fights infectious diarrhea. The berberine in goldenseal helps prevent diarrhea-causing organisms such as *Vibrio cholerae* and *E. coli* from clinging to the lining of the intestine.

Destroys warts. A diluted goldenseal tincture applied to the skin fights the human papilloma virus, the organism that causes warts.

Soothes the eyes. Goldenseal is too bitter to enjoy as a tea (unless you add a lot of honey), but you can strain the beverage, let it cool, and use it as an eyewash to speed the healing of eye infections such as conjunctivitis (pinkeye). Prepare a fresh batch every day, and store it in a sterile container. Berberine kills staph and strep bacteria, common causes of pinkeye. It also constricts the blood vessels, helping eyes look less bloodshot. (It's the main ingredient in at least one brand of eye drops.)

Dosages and Warnings

For colds and other infections, take 125 milligrams goldenseal (preferably in combination with 200 milligrams echinacea) five times daily for a few days. For treating canker sores and warts, an undiluted goldenseal tincture can be applied directly to the skin or mouth.

Goldenseal is a member of the daisy family, so you won't want to take it if you know you're allergic to plants such as chamomile or marigold. Also, doctors advise that goldenseal should not be used for more than a week for any condition. Taken longer, it can decrease the absorption of vitamin B_{12}. (*Off-limits* . . . for people who have hypoglycemia [low blood sugar], high blood pressure, weak digestion, or an autoimmune disease like multiple sclerosis or lupus.)

Honey

Sweet foods are hardly in short supply these days, but there's still something special about honey. After all, honey is the unique creation of swarms of bees that cover a 10-kilometer radius in nectar collection. Anything that takes so much work to make has to be good! Honey is sweeter than sugar, with 65 calories per tablespoon, compared to white sugar's 48. And of course, it offers health benefits that are all its own.

Honey is not a nutritional powerhouse. It does contain trace amounts of B vitamins, amino acids, and minerals, but it's really no more nutritious than plain sugar. If honey gets attention from doctors, it's for other reasons. Its thick, syrupy texture makes it a natural for easing sore throat pain, especially when it's added to hot lemonade or a soothing tea such as chamomile.

But honey does much more. It kills bacteria and helps cuts and wounds heal faster. It's a natural laxative. It appears to reduce ulcer pain. And it's a fast-acting energy source that can reinvigorate tired muscles faster than you can say "Gatorade." Scientists have actually found that athletes perform better when they eat a little honey.

What's it **good for?**
- Acne
- Age Spots
- Allergies
- Coughs
- Insomnia
- Laryngitis
- Sore Throat
- Ulcers

A Sweet Antiseptic

Infection was the greatest health threat in the days before antibiotics. Even small cuts or scrapes could turn deadly, which is why doctors often carried a little honey in their black bags. Honey contains hydrogen peroxide and propolis, a compound in nectar that kills bacteria. Even today, now that triple-antibiotic creams are in every medicine chest, some doctors believe that honey might be a superior wound dressing in some cases. It works so well that a number of manufacturers sell honey-impregnated dressings for hard-to-heal wounds.

The high sugar content of honey pulls moisture from wounds and denies bacteria the moisture they need to survive. It also locks out harmful external contaminants. And because

Where Honey Comes From

Bees sip a little bit of nectar when they make their flowery rounds, but they carry most of it back to the hive and stash it into hexagonal wax cells of the honeycomb to nourish young bees. The liquid nectar turns into honey when moisture evaporates. The finished product is mainly sugars—fructose and dextrose—with a little bit of pollen, wax, proteins, vitamins, and minerals. The clover honey that hogs most of the shelves in supermarkets is the blandest variety. More flavorful honeys come from buckwheat, citrus blossoms, and raspberry flowers.

honey is inexpensive, it can be an optimal choice in countries without access to modern wound creams.

As far back as the 1970s, surgeons reported that women who had gynecological surgery had shorter hospital stays and showed no signs of infection when incisions were coated with honey. Studies in India show that burns dressed with honey heal more quickly and with less pain and scarring than burns slathered with silver sulfadiazine, a conventional burn treatment.

Honey even shows promise for eye disorders, including conjunctivitis and chemical burns. In a study of more than 100 patients with eye disorders that didn't respond to conventional treatments, doctors tested a honey ointment. It brought improvement in 85 percent of cases. Applying honey to the eyes (don't do it without a doctor's supervision) may cause a brief stinging sensation and some redness, but is unlikely to cause other side effects.

Sweet Digestion

Traditional healers used honey to treat a variety of gastrointestinal complaints. Now there's good evidence that it works. For example:

◆ **It soothes ulcers.** Honey may reduce ulcer symptoms and speed the healing time. Honey appears to reduce inflammation, stimulate blood flow, and enhance the growth of epithelial cells, the ones exposed along the interior of the stomach or intestine. Studies have also shown that honey kills *H. pylori,* the bacterium responsible for most ulcers. Raw honey is probably the best choice. The high-heat processing used to create pasteurized honey may neutralize some of the active compounds. A form of honey called Active Manuka Honey, produced in New Zealand from the manuka tree and available in health-food stores, appears to be more effective than other types.

 It promotes regularity. Honey's high concentration of fructose makes it just the thing for occasional constipation. Undigested fructose provides nourishment for normal intestinal bacteria. The resulting fermentation brings water into the large intestine and has a laxative effect.

A Warning

Never give honey to children under the age of one, since it may contain a small number of spores called *Clostridium botulinum*, the organism that causes botulism. The spores don't thrive in the intestines of adults and older children. But in infants, the spores are able to grow, possibly causing a serious form of food poisoning known as infant botulism.

Lavender

Who would have thought that medicine could smell so sweet? The oils in lavender, long prized for making perfumes, soaps, and sachets, also aid digestion, ease anxiety, and put insomnia to bed. There's even scientific evidence that one of the oils in lavender, perillyl alcohol, may someday play a role in treating cancer.

What's it good for?
- Anxiety
- Athlete's Foot
- Body Odor
- Dandruff
- Flatulence
- Foot Odor
- Head Lice
- Headache
- Insect Bites
- Insomnia
- Oily Skin
- Swimmer's Ear

A perennial shrub with spikes of purple or light blue flowers, lavender has a long history of healing. The dried flowers can be sewn in a pouch and placed under the pillow to restore restful sleep. The lavender aroma comes from airborne molecules of linalyl esters, oils that stimulate the olfactory nerve in the brain and calm the central nervous system. The mere smell of lavender may be as effective for setting the stage for peaceful rest as more powerful (and potentially habit-forming) sleep drugs.

Lavender is also an herb you want when you're feeling anxious or keyed-up. Researchers have discovered that lavender increases the type of brain waves associated with relaxation. Add some lavender oil to a diffuser to disperse the scent throughout a room. If you don't have a diffuser, add three drops of lavender oil to a pint of steaming water and inhale the steam. When you have the luxury of time, add lavender bath oil or a handful of dried lavender flowers to bathwater for a stress-busting soak.

It's no coincidence that massage oils are often infused with lavender. The essential oils in lavender are readily absorbed through the skin. Their sedative effects on the central nervous system can help you feel relaxed. The full-strength oil, sold in health-food stores, is too strong to apply more than a drop or two directly to the skin. Mix it with a "carrier" oil such as olive or vegetable oil. Other uses for lavender:

⤙ **Headache medicine.** Dab a bit of the oil onto each temple when you have a headache and massage it in for remarkable relief.

 Tummy tamer. German physicians often recommend lavender tea as a digestive aid. The oils relax the smooth muscles of the digestive tract and soothe after-meal cramps in the stomach and intestine. Lavender also helps ease intestinal gas. To make an infusion, use 1 or 2 heaping teaspoons of lavender flowers and steep for 10 minutes in a cup of boiling water.

 Infection fighter. The tannins in lavender kill bacteria and help prevent minor cuts and scrapes from becoming infected. Soak a clean cloth in a lavender infusion and apply the compress to the wound.

 Ear soother. The same chemical compound in lavender that fights skin infection will knock out the itch and irritation of swimmer's ear.

 Pain reliever. Lavender oil has minor painkilling properties. It appears to reduce the transmission of nerve impulses that carry pain signals. Mix a few drops of the oil in a tablespoon of carrier oil and rub it in. Lavender also relieves itching, thanks to its anti–inflammatory action. It's the perfect remedy for insect bites and stings.

A Cure for Cancer?

Cancer specialists have noticed that a class of chemical compounds in lavender called monterpenes inhibit the development of cancerous cells and may prevent them from multiplying. Early laboratory research suggests that monterpenes such as perillyl alcohol inhibit soft-tissue cancers, such as those in the liver, breast, and prostate gland. They've even been shown to slow the growth of colon and liver tumors.

It's too soon to say for sure that lavender has beneficial effects on cancer. But the early results are so promising that the essential oils are being tested in clinical studies for their anti-cancer potential.

Lemon

You get more than a tart blast when you suck on a lemon slice or sip lemonade. Lemons are an extraordinarily rich source of healing chemical compounds that improve immunity, strengthen blood vessels, help skin heal, and block cell changes that can lead to cancer. A quick rub of lemon on the underarms helps combat unwanted odors. A squeeze of lemon added to hot water and honey is the perfect sore-throat elixir. And lemon is an indispensable ingredient when it comes to making homemade cough syrup.

What's it good for?

- Acne
- Age Spots
- Body Odor
- Calluses and Corns
- Cold Sores
- Colds and Flu
- Coughs
- Dry Mouth
- Head Lice
- Heartburn
- Hiccups
- Kidney Stones
- Laryngitis
- Morning Sickness
- Oily Hair
- Oily Skin
- Pregnancy Complaints
- Sore Throat
- Varicose Veins
- Warts

Centuries ago, British sailors ate lemons by the boatload to prevent scurvy, a deadly disease caused by vitamin C deficiency. A single lemon packs 39 milligrams of vitamin C, more than half the Daily Value. We don't have to worry about scurvy anymore, because there are so many sources of vitamin C in our diet. But lemons provide a host of other tangy benefits.

Pucker Power

Never underestimate the power of vitamin C—or the time-tested advice to drink lemon-flavored tea when you have a cold. The vitamin C in lemons lowers levels of histamine, the chemical that contributes to stuffy noses and runny eyes. The vitamin is a powerful antioxidant that also reduces levels of unstable cell-damaging molecules known as free radicals, and helps guard against heart disease. (Several studies have shown that low levels of vitamin C increase the risk for heart attacks. When cholesterol becomes oxidized—attacked by free radicals—it's more likely to turn into artery-clogging plaque.) The body uses vitamin C to boost the activity of immune cells and manufacture collagen, the tissue-building substance that assists in wound healing.

Here are more reasons to enjoy the zesty pleasure of lemons:

Fewer kidney stones. Lemons are loaded with citric acid, a chemical that reduces calcium excretion and helps prevent the formation of these painful little stones. Two liters of lemonade made with fresh lemon juice daily (sweetened with as little sugar as possible) are as effective as citrate medications.

➤ **Stronger veins.** Lemon zest is rich in a bioflavonoid (a group of antioxidant plant chemicals) called rutin, which strengthens the walls of the veins and capillaries and reduces the pain—and even the occurrence—of varicose veins.

➤ **Breast protection.** Another chemical, found in the lemon peel and the white membrane underneath it, is limonene. Scientists have discovered that limonene has significant anti-tumor activity. It is now being studied for its ability to treat and even prevent cancer, especially breast cancer. Scientists tested the substance against human breast cancer cells and found that it inhibits their growth. Limonene also causes estrogen to break down into a weaker form in the body, which is important because higher levels of estrogen are linked with a higher risk of breast cancer. Limonene also boosts the liver's ability to remove potential carcinogens from the blood.

➤ **Beauty benefits.** If applied often enough to age spots, lemon juice will eventually fade these marks of maturity. You can also dab it on acne for faster healing.

➤ **Stave off skin cancer.** A study on 450 people found that adding some grated lemon peel to your morning tea could potentially reduce the risk of some skin cancers by as much as 70 percent. (Black tea alone brought reductions of up to 40 percent.) Lemon works possibly by stepping up the activity of an enzyme, called glutathione S-transferase, that detoxifies cancer-causing compounds.

Mustard

S cientists have known for a long time that mustard's pungent heat thins mucus and makes it easier to breathe when you have a cold or flu. But this versatile kitchen condiment has turned out to be more than a feel-good remedy. A close relative of broccoli, cabbage, and other cruciferous vegetables, mustard contains a variety of chemical compounds with impressive healing credentials.

What's it good for?

- Athlete's Foot
- Back Pain
- Colds and Flu
- Fever
- Headache

Start with its role as an expectorant. When your nose is so stuffy you can hardly breathe, a dollop of mustard—on a hot dog, for example—delivers a hefty dose of myrosin and sinigrin, chemicals that make mucus watery and easier to expel from the body.

A traditional congestion remedy is to apply a mustard plaster—made by crushing a few tablespoonfuls of mustard seeds and adding them to a cup of flour or cornmeal along with a little water to make a paste—to your chest. The aroma unclogs nasal stuffiness, while the "heat" increases blood circulation in the chest and makes it easier to breathe. Just don't leave the plaster on too long (usually no more than 15 minutes) or it will burn the skin. You can protect the skin before you put the plaster on by applying a coating of petroleum jelly. Be sure to wash your hands thoroughly after handling a mustard plaster and before touching your eyes, nose, or mouth.

Another way to reap mustard's congestion-busting magic is to add a bit of ground mustard seed to your bath.

That's just the beginning of mustard's magic. It's also used for:

◦ **Rubbing out Raynaud's disease.** For people who periodically suffer the painfully cold fingers that characterize this circulatory problem, a mustard compress has been found to help. Mustard is a counterirritant: It irritates the skin, increases blood circulation, and causes a warm, tingling sensation—a perfect antidote when fingers are frigid.

◦ **Stimulating appetite.** Adding mustard to your food increases the flow of saliva and digestive juices—natural ways to stimulate appetite when you've been under the weather and aren't eating as well as you should.

❧ **Kicking athlete's foot.** A bit of mustard powder added to a footbath can help kill athlete's foot fungus.

❧ **Bucking back and joint pain.** Herbalists call mustard a rubefacient, which means that it stimulates soothing warmth when applied to the skin. Like cayenne pepper, it also appears to deplete nerve cells of substance P, a chemical that transmits pain signals from the back to the brain. In fact, mustard oil is the main ingredient in at least one brand-name arthritis liniment. To use mustard for pain, either mix up a mustard plaster or soak a cloth in strong mustard tea and apply the compress to the sore spot. One arthritis sufferer suggested massaging a mixture of warm mustard oil and camphor into aching joints—but mustard oil is simply too strong to use on the skin, so we don't recommend this approach.

❧ **Easing headache, fever, and congestion.** Soaking your feet in hot water with a little mustard powder added can accomplish a number of goals. It can unblock a stuffed head, help ease fever, and soothe a headache—all by drawing blood to the feet. This eases the pressure on the blood vessels in your head, helps disperse congestion, and increases circulation.

There are several varieties of mustard, including black, brown, and white (also called yellow). White mustard seeds aren't quite as hot as other varieties. If you take mustard seeds internally, beware: They have a laxative effect if you eat enough of them. Mustard powder is also used to induce vomiting. Don't ingest more than a teaspoonful unless you desire this effect.

Omega-3 Fatty Acids

You might think that fat is bad for you. But there's one kind of fat, namely, omega-3 fatty acids, that you should make every effort to get more of. Found mainly in fish, omega-3s—a collective name for a group of polyunsaturated fats that include eicosapentaenoic acid, docosahexaenoic acid, and alpha-linolenic acid—play a key role in many vital body processes, from controlling blood clotting and blood pressure to reducing inflammation.

What's it good for?

- Arthritis
- Asthma
- Bursitis and Tendinitis
- Depression
- Dry Skin
- Eczema
- Gout
- High Blood Pressure
- High Cholesterol
- Hives
- Inflammatory Bowel Disease
- Memory Problems
- Menstrual Problems
- Nail Problems
- Palpitations
- Prostate Enlargement
- Psoriasis
- Wrinkles

Scientists first began looking at omega-3s when they noticed that the Inuit seldom suffered from rheumatoid arthritis or heart disease, even though their diet was a veritable slick of fish, seal, and whale oils. All of these seafoods, as it happens, are high in omega-3s, so it didn't take doctors long to realize that this class of fats is essential for good health.

Swim Away from Heart Disease

Heart disease is the number-one killer of Canadian adults. Most heart attacks occur when blood clots form in the arteries and block the flow of blood and oxygen to the heart. Study after study has shown that a diet rich in omega-3 fatty acids can reduce the risk of heart attack and also stroke. How do omega-3s help?

They lower blood pressure by inhibiting the body's production of prostaglandins, leukotrienes, and thromboxane, substances in the body that cause blood vessels to narrow.

They make cell-like structures in blood called platelets less likely to clump together and form clots.

They reduce levels of triglycerides, blood fats related to cholesterol that have been linked to heart disease.

They reduce inflammation in the arteries and also appear to strengthen the heart's pumping rhythm.

The omega-3s clearly play an important role in prevention. There's also good evidence that they provide a valuable treatment option for people who already have heart disease. When taken in large amounts, they help prevent restenosis, the reblockage of arteries that often occurs after a person has undergone angioplasty to open up a blocked blood vessel.

If you already have heart disease, or want to make sure you never get it, doctors advise having at least two—and preferably three or four—servings of fish a week. Fatty, cold-water fish such as salmon, mackerel, and tuna provide the most omega-3s. Ground flaxseeds are another excellent source. Or you can take a fish-oil supplement daily.

Oil Away Bone and Joint Pain

You can think of omega-3s as WD-40 for the joints. Because they inhibit the effects of inflammatory chemicals such as prostaglandins, they're a natural choice for people who suffer joint pain and stiffness from rheumatoid arthritis. They work so well, in fact, that people who depend on aspirin or other anti-inflammatory pain-fighting medications are often able to lower the dose once they start taking fish-oil supplements.

What's good for the joints also seems to be good for the bones, especially in postmenopausal women who either have osteoporosis or are at risk of getting this bone-depleting condition. A study of 65 women found that those given omega-3 fatty acids for 18 months had denser bones and fewer fractures than women who didn't get omega-3s.

An Ocean of Other Uses

The more scientists study omega-3s, the more conditions they discover that seem to be helped by these fishy fats. Research results show that omega-3s help to:

↝ **Reduce gut pain.** A year-long study of people with Crohn's disease, a painful type of inflammatory bowel disease, found that 69 percent of those who took fish-oil supplements stayed symptom-free, compared with just 28 percent of those who didn't get the oil.

↝ **Improve mental health.** Some scientists suspect that the increasing incidence of depression in North America is due in part to declining levels of fish consumption. Low levels of omega-3s may weaken cell membranes and the production of certain neurotransmitters in the brain. When scientists looked at 44 people with bipolar disorder, a severe form of depression, they found that nearly two out of three improved if they were given fish oil.

🐟 **Manage lupus.** This serious autoimmune disease appears to improve somewhat in those who take fish-oil supplements, probably because omega-3s reduce inflammation and also modulate the effects of the immune system.

🐟 **Ease menstrual pain.** Women who take omega-3s generally experience less cramping during their periods, probably because the supplements lower levels of prostaglandins, chemicals that increase cramps and discomfort.

🐟 **Possibly prevent cancer.** There is some preliminary evidence that fish oils may help prevent breast and colon cancers.

Some Schooling in Fish Oil

Doctors who recommend fish-oil supplements usually advise people to take anywhere from 3,000 to 5,000 milligrams daily. Side effects—mainly belching, flatulence, diarrhea, or a slightly fishy body odor—are common. Dividing the dose into two or three smaller doses and taking them throughout the day can reduce discomfort. Or try freezing the pills before you take them, and taking them with meals. In some cases, just switching brands will minimize side effects.

Always store fish-oil supplements in the refrigerator to keep them from going rancid. Also, don't use cod-liver oil as a replacement for omega-3 supplements. It's very high in vitamins A and D, which can be toxic in large amounts.

Large amounts of fish oil can interfere with blood clotting, so doctors recommend that you don't take more than 6,000 milligrams a day. And get a doctor's advice if you are taking a blood thinner such as aspirin, coumadin, or heparin, or if you have diabetes. (*Off-limits*...Don't take fish-oil supplements if you have a bleeding disorder, uncontrolled high blood pressure, or an allergy to any kind of fish.)

Peppermint

There's good reason your favorite diner has a bowl of cellophane-wrapped, pink-striped peppermints next to the cash register: They're a minty, sweet, fresh-tasting treat, and great breath fresheners. Peppermint, in the right form, also counters indigestion and reduces gas and bloating. Yes, peppermint makes a dandy candy—and its healing powers are more powerful than you may know.

Intestine Protection

Peppermint is among the best herbs for digestive problems and intestinal pain. The oils it contains, especially menthol and menthone, relax the smooth muscles that line the intestinal tract, helping to relieve cramping. British gastroenterologists who sprayed diluted peppermint oil on endoscopes—the tubelike instruments used in colonoscopy—found that it stopped painful spasms in less than 30 seconds. The herb's antispasmodic properties make it a natural choice for easing irritable bowel syndrome (IBS), a condition that causes unpredictable cramping, indigestion, and alternating bouts of constipation and diarrhea.

In a study conducted at Taichung Veterans General Hospital in Taiwan, IBS patients given peppermint-oil capsules 15 to 30 minutes before meals had a significant reduction in bloating, stomach rumbling, and gas. Abdominal pain was reduced or disappeared entirely in some cases.

Doctors with an interest in herbal medicine now recommend peppermint for a variety of digestive complaints:

🍃 **Gas.** Because it aids digestion, peppermint can help you avoid flatulence.

🍃 **Gallstones.** Preliminary evidence suggests that peppermint helps dissolve gallstones and could potentially reduce the need for surgery.

🍃 **Nausea.** Peppermint slightly anesthetizes the stomach lining and reduces mild nausea.

🍃 **Ulcers.** Peppermint can help relieve the pain and help you heal.

What's it
good for?
- Body Odor
- Flatulence
- Foot Pain
- Headache
- Indigestion
- Inflammatory Bowel Disease
- Insect and Spider Bites
- Irritable Bowel Syndrome
- Morning Sickness
- Nausea
- Oily Skin
- Snoring
- Sunburn
- Toothache
- Ulcers

One note of caution: Don't use peppermint if you have frequent heartburn. In some people peppermint relaxes the esophageal sphincter, the ringlike muscle that prevents harsh stomach acids from splashing upward into the esophagus.

Less Congestion and Pain

Peppermint—drinking the tea or merely sniffing the aromatic vapors—is an effective decongestant that thins mucus and reduces nasal inflammation. Peppermint may even reduce bronchial constriction and the tightening of the airways that accompanies asthma attacks.

Do you get frequent headaches? Dab a little diluted peppermint oil on your forehead and temples. A small study of 32 headache patients found that the oil was an effective painkiller. The menthol in peppermint has significant painkilling powers. Whether you're an athlete or a weekend warrior, keep some peppermint oil (or a menthol-containing ointment) in your medicine chest to rub on sore muscles. Since it's too powerful to use undiluted, mix a few drops in a tablespoonful of a neutral, "carrier" oil, such as canola or olive oil. Because of its numbing properties, peppermint is also useful against toothache.

Like many essential oils, peppermint also kills certain viruses and bacteria. Add a few drops of peppermint oil to a cup of water to make a minty, germ-killing mouthwash. Or, to freshen your breath, place a drop or two of the oil on your tongue. Otherwise, though, don't take the pure oil internally; it's too strong and may upset the stomach. (Peppermint capsules are enteric-coated so they pass through the stomach and are broken down in the intestines instead.)

Teatime

Nearly everyone likes the taste of peppermint tea. Drink a cup or two a day to ease or prevent digestive discomfort. You can also take enteric-coated capsules between meals, following the directions on the label. Or add 10 to 20 drops of peppermint tincture (which is less potent than the oil) to a glass of water and drink it as needed.

Curiously enough, the peppermint candies served by restaurants don't have the digestion-aiding power of the herb itself. They contain only a minuscule amount of flavoring.

Petroleum Jelly

Petroleum jelly, better known by the brand name Vaseline, is the pharmacy equivalent of WD-40—you can use it for just about everything. It's a superb moisturizer. It takes the sting out of chapped lips. It eases skin disorders such as eczema. And if that's not enough, you can coat your car battery terminals to prevent corrosion.

As you can tell from the name, petroleum jelly is made from petroleum, the same basic stuff that lubricates your car engine and goes in the gas tank. The reason that petroleum jelly smears instead of pours is that it's made from heavier petroleum products, including mineral oils and paraffin wax. It makes an excellent base for salves and ointments, and is also useful all by itself.

Doctors often recommend petroleum jelly as a winter moisturizer because it's heavier and traps more moisture than standard lotions. It's perfect for dry hands and feet, especially when you put on an extra-thick coating and cover up with gloves or socks before going to bed. To get the best skin protection, apply petroleum jelly after showers or baths. It traps moisture next to the skin where it's needed. At the same time, the oils seep into the skin and make it supple and soft.

What else is petroleum jelly good for? Plenty. For instance, you can use it to:

Prevent windburn. Petroleum jelly makes an excellent protective barrier between your skin and the wind.

Get relief from psoriasis. Apply petroleum jelly to dry skin patches caused by this chronic skin disorder. It lubricates and helps remove hard, itchy scales.

Eliminate lice. Pesky head lice that are resistant to over-the-counter lice shampoos might succumb to a thick layer of petroleum jelly, applied to the scalp. When you remove it with baby or mineral oil, you get rid of lice at the same time. Some mothers think the remedy is more trouble than it's worth, since the petroleum jelly can be difficult to remove. If mineral oil

What's it
good for?
- Allergies
- Blisters
- Chapped Lips
- Cold Sores
- Cuts and Scrapes
- Dry Skin
- Eczema
- Head Lice
- Hemorrhoids
- Nosebleeds
- Psoriasis

doesn't work, try the trick one mother uses: Apply a runny paste made from dishwashing liquid and cornstarch. Allow it to harden, then wash it out with shampoo.

﹎ **Soothe a chapped kisser.** Rub petroleum jelly on the lips, and it gets in the way of rapid evaporation, which has a drying effect. It's an ideal moisturizer—and makes a nice lip gloss too.

﹎ **Protect cuts and scrapes.** A layer of petroleum jelly keeps moisture in and air and bacteria out.

﹎ **Moisturize burns.** You don't want to apply petroleum jelly right away when you have a burn, because it will trap heat and increase skin damage. After the burn has "cooled," however, coating it with petroleum jelly will reduce dryness and promote better healing.

﹎ **Trap pollen.** Dab a little petroleum jelly under your nose to trap pollen spores that are wafting around before they land in your nostrils.

﹎ **Prevent nosebleeds.** If you want to avoid nosebleeds, keep your mucous membranes moist by dabbing the insides of your nostrils with petroleum jelly.

All-Purpose Goop

Savvy homeowners keep petroleum jelly in the toolbox as well as the medicine chest. When you're painting, apply a coating to door handles and hinges to prevent paint from sticking. Mechanics sometimes coat their hands with petroleum jelly to seal the skin and keep oil and grease out. You can even use petroleum jelly to slip stuck gum from hair, slide off too-tight rings, and remove makeup in a jiffy.

Tea

It's the most popular hot beverage in the world. With half as much caffeine as coffee, it provides a pleasant pick-me-up without giving you the jitters. But drinking tea is far more than just a civilized habit; it could actually be a lifesaving one. That's because tea drinkers may have a lower risk of heart disease, stroke, cancer, and even tooth decay.

In the early 1990s, researchers noted that Japanese women who practiced the art of chanoyu, the traditional tea ceremony, had much lower mortality rates than other women. It didn't take scientists long to realize that the chemical compounds in tea—mainly polyphenols, which make up nearly 30 percent of tea's dry weight—are among the most potent antioxidants ever discovered. Antioxidants are chemicals that block the effects of free radicals, rogue oxygen molecules that damage cells throughout the body and increase the risk of serious diseases such as cancer.

Incidentally, don't confuse herbal teas such as chamomile with "real" tea that comes from *Camellia sinensis,* the tea plant. The green tea popular in Asian countries is simply the steamed and dried leaves of this plant. Black teas undergo a process of fermentation that gives them stronger flavors and darker colors—and perhaps lower levels of health-protective chemical compounds.

What's it **good for?**

- Anal Itching
- Athlete's Foot
- Canker Sores
- Diarrhea
- Fever
- Foot Odor
- Gum Problems
- Headache
- Hemorrhoids
- Sunburn
- Toothache

Brew Some Cancer Prevention

Studies confirm that drinking tea is among the most effective lifestyle approaches to preventing cancer. One study found that people who drank green tea as seldom as once a week had lower rates of pancreatic, rectal, and possibly colon cancers. In fact, women who drink tea regularly run about half the risk of getting rectal and pancreatic cancers, in comparison to women who rarely or never drink it.

Tea contains a chemical compound with the tongue-twisting name epigallocatechin-gallate (EGCG). It's an extremely potent antioxidant—100 times more powerful than vitamin C—that protects the DNA in cells from cancer-inducing changes. What's more, it increases the body's production of enzymes that naturally protect against free-radical damage. EGCG also appears to block the synthesis of cancer-causing compounds from heterocyclic amines, chemicals that form on the surfaces of fried foods.

In skin-cancer studies, laboratory animals that were given tea developed one-tenth as many tumors as animals that were given water instead. When it comes to preventing skin cancer, tea seems to be equally effective whether it's sipped from a cup or applied to the skin. Many cosmetics manufacturers have started adding green tea to skin-care products because its antioxidant effects may reduce wrinkles or other kinds of skin damage.

While tea is mainly valued for its cancer-preventing powers, there's some evidence that it many help people who already have cancer. The EGCG in green tea inhibits the production of urokinase, an enzyme that cancer cells need in order to grow. It also seems to stimulate the process of programmed cell death, or apoptosis, in cancer cells. In a seven-year study of breast cancer patients, women who drank five cups of tea daily were less likely to have their cancers spread to lymph nodes than women who drank less.

Heart Health and More

Because tea's polyphenols are such potent antioxidants, they play a protective role anywhere free radicals wreak havoc in the body, including the arteries. Tea also has antibacterial effects that promote dental health. What tea may offer:

Less heart disease. The chemicals in tea help prevent cholesterol from oxidizing. Oxidation occurs when cholesterol is bombarded by free radicals. The process makes the cholesterol more likely to stick to artery walls, a step on the road to heart disease. Dutch researchers reported that men who consumed the most flavonoids—a chemical family that includes tea's polyphenols—had a 58 percent lower risk of dying from heart disease compared to men who got the least. The healthiest men in the study drank about four cups of tea daily.

Tea

↝ **Reduced stroke risk.** Women who drink tea frequently appear to have lower rates of stroke than those who drink less, probably because the polyphenols in tea reduce damage to vulnerable blood vessels in the brain.

↝ **Stronger teeth.** Tea contains a modest amount of fluoride, the mineral that strengthens teeth and reduces tooth decay. Moreover, the tannins and polyphenols in tea inhibit bacteria that damage the teeth. There's even evidence that tea improves the ability of tooth enamel to resist the onslaught of oral acids.

↝ **Soothe sunburns and more.** Because tea contains astringents that help reduce inflammation, a wet tea bag can offer soothing relief for sunburned skin and well as hemorrhoids and canker sores. (Tea is alkaline, so it neutralizes acids that eat into the tissue in the canker sore.)

Drink to Your Health

Two to three cups of tea a day is probably enough to provide most of the health benefits. Green tea supplements, sold in health-food stores, also appear to be effective. The usual dose is 250 to 400 milligrams taken once daily.

One caveat: If you usually take your tea with milk, you might be missing out on some of the health protection. Proteins in milk may bind to tea's polyphenols and block their beneficial effects.

Vinegar

As tart-tasting as an unripe apple, vinegar is the bane of bacteria, the foe of fungi, the solution to jellyfish stings, and the soother of sunburns. Used right, it can settle your stomach, stave off swimmer's ear, make hair more lustrous and skin softer. Some people swear that vinegar mixed with honey and warm water can take the pain out of leg cramps. Others use vinegar to dry up cold sores. And should someone faint, vinegar is a handy alternative to smelling salts. How can such a sourpuss do so much good work?

What's it good for?

- Acne
- Body Odor
- Bruises
- Dandruff
- Diaper Rash
- Dry Mouth
- Foot Odor
- Head Lice
- Headache
- Hiccups
- Hives
- Indigestion
- Insect and Spider Bites
- Oily Hair
- Poison Ivy
- Psoriasis
- Sunburn
- Swimmer's Ear
- Warts

Put a drop of it on your tongue, and you'll know immediately what gives the tangy liquid its sour reputation. Vinegar is acidic, thanks to a high concentration of acetic acid, formed when bacteria feast on a fermented liquid. Acetic acid may be kind to your body, but it's an industrial-strength product. Millions of tons of it go into the making of photographic films and artificial fibers like rayon. The combination of acetic acid and salicylic acid also creates a very familiar pharmaceutical product: aspirin.

The Power of Acid

Vinegar does a number on bacteria. The infectious invaders have been wiped out and swiped out again and again with vinegar cures. In World War I, the wounds of soldiers were bathed in vinegar, and even today, if you can stand the sting, it's an adequate disinfectant if you have a scratch or sore. With fungi it's equally malevolent. Most kinds beat a retreat before a wave of vinegar.

Vinegar is also good for the hair and skin. As an acid, vinegar reacts with chemical bases to produce neutral H_2O (water!), along with some salt. When spread on skin or used as a hair rinse, it can spirit off soap, shampoo, or conditioner residue. Rinsing the hair with vinegar may also help ease dandruff and scalp itch.

Among vinegar's other prominent uses:

~ **Stomach settler.** If you're suffering from indigestion because of a lack of stomach acid, a teaspoon of vinegar after meals may be just the ticket. (Of course, if your problem is *too much* stomach acid, vinegar isn't any help and will probably make things worse.)

~ **Gentle coolant.** Spread on skin, it evaporates quickly, providing a friendly chill that can quell a sunburn. Vinegar also helps counter the inflammation that causes sunburns to itch.

~ **Bacteria slayer and fungus fighter.** When bacteria or fungi flourish in the warm, moist hollows of an ear canal, the condition is called swimmer's ear. Vinegar does double duty—fighting both kinds of invaders—which is why, when mixed in equal parts with rubbing alcohol and dropped into the ear, it can help cure the condition. And speaking of fungus, soaking your feet in vinegar is an effective treatment for athlete's foot.

~ **Odor eater.** The high acid content gives it a nice, sharp scent that can override less lovely odors. A vinegar rinse will banish the smell of cigar smoke from clothing, freshen a baby's diapers—or expurgate ugly scents from the armpits or feet.

~ **Sting stopper.** Jellyfish stings and mosquitoes have more in common than painful memories. Both can be relieved with vinegar, which neutralizes pain-causing substances that get in the skin. Slightly watered down and dabbed on the skin with a cotton ball, vinegar can also relieve the itching of hives.

~ **Headache tamer.** Vinegar is one of the all-time most popular folk remedies for headache. The traditional approach was to soak brown paper with cider vinegar and apply it to the forehead. You can also soak a clean cloth in vinegar and tie it tightly around your head. We're not sure why vinegar works for headaches, but many people swear by it.

~ **Throat soother.** Vinegar is also a trusted folk remedy for sore throats. Some people recommend gargling with 1 table-spoon of vinegar in a glass of warm water. Others make a homemade cough syrup by combining equal amounts of honey and cider vinegar and stirring or shaking until dissolved.

More Than Sour Grapes

If you travel the world in search of vinegar's many varieties, you'll find the kinds made from sugarcane in the Philippines, coconut in Thailand, malt in the British Isles, and, in China, the red, white, and black rice wine vinegars that have flavored stir-fries for over 5,000 years. Elsewhere you may run across vinegars yielded by honey, potatoes, dates, nuts, and berries. But if you shop near home, the most common kinds you'll find are wine vinegar (made from grapes), cider vinegar (from apples), or plain, distilled white vinegar that's the product of grain.

Among today's promoters of good health, apple cider vinegar is often favored above all others. There are reasons. Fermented apples are rich in pectin, a type of fiber that's excellent for digestion. Apples also contain malic acid, which combines with magnesium in your body to help fight aches and pains.

Should you care to make your own vinegar, it's easy enough, but sterile conditions are called for. Starting with cider or wine, the fermentation is speeded up by addition of a "mother"—that is, a dollop of vinegar that initiates the process. Jars and utensils have to be carefully sterilized to avoid contamination with unwanted bacteria. As vinegar-making skills become honed, the home brewer learns to recognize the moment when the brew is "done." Once bottled, capped, and stored, homemade vinegar stays good for many months.

But for home remedies, any store-bought vinegar will do.

Witch Hazel

Along with aspirin and Band-Aids, witch hazel is a medicine-cabinet staple. A liquid extract made from an American plant *(Hamamelis virginiana)*, it is used externally to ease itching, take the sting out of hemorrhoids, and freshen the skin. It has nothing to do with witches, incidentally, although "witchers" used the forked branches to locate underground water and gold. (The branches are still valued by dowsers today.) The herb's name comes from the Middle English word *wych*, which means pliable. The wood is so springy that Native Americans once used it to make bows.

The active ingredient in traditional witch hazel is tannin, a chemical compound with astringent properties: It tightens skin pores much as skin toners do. Tannin also shrinks blood vessels and can reduce bleeding from shaving cuts or other minor wounds. Because of its tannins, witch hazel was once taken internally to counter diarrhea.

Modern witch hazel, however, is a different remedy altogether. In the late 1800s manufacturers abandoned the traditional steeping method and switched to a steam distillation process. The new technique was more efficient, but the high heat involved in the steaming left the finished product virtually devoid of tannins. The astringent action from today's witch hazel comes from its alcohol content (most commercial witch hazel contains about 14% alcohol).

What's it good for?

- Anal Itching
- Body Odor
- Bruises
- Hemorrhoids
- Hives
- Oily Skin
- Poison Ivy
- Pregnancy Complaints
- Razor Burn

What Good's the Witch?

Even though today's witch hazel has little in common with the traditional remedy, the alcohol content (about the same as table wine) makes it a safe and effective astringen useful for:

Hemorrhoid relief. Pour witch hazel on a cotton ball and apply it to the tender spots. The liquid evaporates quickly, which provides a soothing, cooling sensation. Witch hazel is an ingredient in Tucks, Preparation H Cleansing Pads, and other over-the-counter hemorrhoid treatments.

• **Poison ivy rashes.** Splash the skin with witch hazel after an unkind encounter of the ivy kind to temporarily ease the itch. The alcohol in witch hazel also helps dry the oozy poison ivy rash.

• **Shaving cuts.** Dab on a little witch hazel to disinfect the cut and possibly slow the bleeding. (Don't use witch hazel on serious cuts, however. The alcohol may increase skin damage.) Even if you don't cut yourself shaving, witch hazel will leave your skin feeling softer and soothed when you use it as an aftershave.

• **Fresher skin.** Soak a gauze pad or cotton ball in witch hazel and dab your face to remove surface oils, tighten pores, and tone the skin. Witch hazel is an ingredient in a number of skin-care products.

As a mild astringent, witch hazel is also useful for sunburn, skin inflammation, and insect bites. In the summer, keep witch hazel in the refrigerator so it's cold—and all the more soothing—when you apply it to sunburned skin.

Yogurt

Did you know that there are more bacteria in your body than there are human cells? About 500 species of bacteria inhabit the digestive tract alone. Don't shudder. The vast majority of intestinal organisms—all 1.5 kilograms (3 pounds) of them—are beneficial. They strengthen immunity, digest milk sugars (lactose), assist in the absorption of nutrients, and generally maintain digestive health. But some intestinal bacteria, along with organisms in the vagina and urinary tract, cause all sorts of problems. That's why you should always keep your refrigerator well stocked with yogurt.

Yogurt is milk to which cultures of bacteria are added. The bacteria consume the sugar in the milk for energy and excrete lactic acid (the same acid that builds up in muscles during exercise), which curdles the milk. Yogurt that contains "active cultures"—meaning live bacteria—is the kind that's brimming with health benefits. That's because organisms such as *Lactobacillus acidophilus, Streptococcus thermophilus,* and *Lactobacillus bulgaricus*—collectively known as probiotics—protect your body from harmful bacteria by using up resources that those bacteria need in order to thrive. And some bacteria in yogurt produce acids that kill other bacteria, including the germs that cause botulism, among other ailments.

What's it
good for?
• Athlete's Foot
• Canker Sores
• Cold Sores
• Diarrhea
• Flatulence
• Inflammatory Bowel Disease
• Irritable Bowel Syndrome
• Urinary Tract Infections
• Yeast Infections

Spoon Up Some Digestive Health

When you're healthy, about 85 percent of bacteria in the large intestine are *Lactobacillus* organisms. The other 15 percent consist largely of other beneficial strains. But if you're taking antibiotics, the drugs wipe out the "good" bugs along with the "bad" ones causing your infection. This can lead to diarrhea, cramps, gas, yeast infections, or diminished absorption of nutrients.

Yogurt can turn things around. University of Pittsburgh researchers found that patients who ate two 240-milliliter servings of yogurt daily had only half the rate of antibiotic-associated diarrhea compared to non-yogurt eaters.

Other studies show that the beneficial bacteria in yogurt (or probiotic supplements) reduce infant diarrhea, suppress symptoms of inflammatory bowel disease and irritable bowel syndrome, and ease some types of food poisoning. There's even evidence that yogurt's healthful organisms, in combination with a high-fiber diet, can prevent diverticulosis, a painful and potentially serious condition in which small pouches form on the colon wall.

Can't Live Without 'Em

Yogurt has been used as a multi-purpose healer for centuries, but it's only within the last decade or so that scientists have discovered just how beneficial yogurt really is. Some of the things it can do:

Knock out yeast infections. The fungus that normally inhabits the vagina is usually kept in check by other organisms. It's only when it multiplies that it causes the miserable itching and burning. A study at Long Island Jewish Medical Center found that the rate of infections dropped considerably in women who ate 240 milliliters of live culture yogurt daily. Eating yogurt—or using acidophilus supplements in suppository form—can treat infections that are already under way. Just make sure it's really a yeast infection; treating a bacterial infection with yogurt will make the problem worse.

Protect the bladder. Yogurt can make a real difference if you're one of the millions of women plagued by recurrent urinary tract infections. Finnish researchers report that women who eat at least three servings of yogurt and cheese weekly are almost 80 percent less likely to have urinary tract infections than women who eat these foods less than once a week.

Strengthen immunity. A study at the University of California at Davis School of Medicine found that eating two cups of yogurt daily can quadruple levels of gamma interferon, a protein produced by white blood cells that assists the immune system in fighting off germs.

Combat cancer. The acidophilus in yogurt isn't a cancer cure, but it has been shown to help prevent recurrences of tumors in patients treated for bladder cancer. It's thought that the beneficial bacteria may prevent harmful bacteria from creating cancer-causing substances in the body when the bacteria react with foods.

⇘ **Build strong bones.** Millions of North Americans avoid milk—and the bone-strengthening calcium it provides—because they lack the enzyme needed to digest lactose, a sugar in milk. Yogurt is an easy-to-digest alternative because the live organisms it contains digest the lactose before you spoon it up. This means that people with lactose intolerance can eat all the yogurt they want without suffering from gas or other uncomfortable symptoms. Yogurt is even higher in calcium than milk, with more than 400 milligrams in a one-cup serving.

What to Look For

Don't assume that all yogurt products in the supermarket contain beneficial bacteria. Look for products with the words "live cultures" or "active cultures" on the label. And to ensure that you get as many live organisms as possible, buy a yogurt that's nowhere near its expiration date.

Even if you're not a yogurt fan, you can get most of the benefits by taking probiotic supplements. Optimal doses haven't been determined, but researchers suspect you need about 10 billion organisms daily. That sounds like a lot, but it's just a capsule or two. Be sure to keep supplements in the refrigerator, since probiotics are living organisms. Don't put them in the freezer, though; freezing temperatures (along with high heat) can easily kill the cultures.

Zinc

Zinc

Zinc isn't a home remedy in the usual sense. It's an essential mineral that plays a critical role in hundreds of body functions, from cell growth to maintaining a healthy immune system. Yet scientists have learned that zinc does more than keep the cellular machinery running. It can also be taken in therapeutic doses to ward off colds. It clears the skin of acne and improves night vision. It can boost the functioning of the thyroid gland. And there's some evidence it may help alleviate tinnitus, an annoying ringing in the ears.

What's it good for?
- Acne
- Arthritis
- Canker Sores
- Cold Sores
- Colds and Flu
- Dandruff
- Dry Skin
- Eczema
- Infertility
- Nail Problems
- Rosacea
- Sore Throat

Zinc and Colds

On the one hand, there's no cure for the common cold. On the other hand, a study of 100 people in the initial stages of a cold found that those who sucked on zinc lozenges every few hours recovered three days earlier than those given placebos.

Zinc lozenges are thought to work by releasing zinc ions into the mucous membranes. The ions bind to the cold virus, preventing it from binding to "docking points" on the surface of nasal cells. Zicam, a nasal gel spray that contains zinc, may be even more effective than zinc lozenges at controlling colds. A recent study at the Cleveland Clinic showed that Zicam significantly reduced cold symptoms and the duration of colds, even when treatment was started as late as the second day after the onset of illness.

Even if you do nothing more than get the normal amount of zinc in your diet—the RDA is 12 milligrams for women and 15 milligrams for men—there's a good chance you'll get sick less often because your immune system will be working at full steam. This is probably why nursing home residents given zinc supplements (along with selenium) over a two-year period got sick less often than residents given placebos.

Zinc is readily available in foods, yet many of us don't get enough. This is partly because, in a well-intentioned effort to cut back on dietary fat, we are eating less meat, one of the best sources of zinc. Whole grains, nuts, and yogurt are other sources.

A Mighty Mineral

More than 300 enzymes in the body require zinc to function properly. Given zinc's importance, it's good idea to take a multivitamin/mineral supplement that contains zinc. What can zinc do for you? Among its main uses:

~ **Banishing blemishes.** People with acne tend to have lower-than-normal zinc levels. Zinc supplements won't necessarily cure acne, but they do produce visible improvement in about a third of people who take it. Since the amount of zinc required is high—between 200 and 600 milligrams daily—use it only under a doctor's supervision.

~ **Improving wound healing.** Zinc helps cells divide, or replicate, rapidly, which is why it's so important for wound healing. You need zinc to produce collagen, the connective tissue that helps cuts and scrapes heal.

~ **Preventing cold sores.** In test-tubes, zinc blocks the replication of the virus that causes cold sores. Zinc also fortifies the surface tissue on your lips and on the inside of your mouth, making it difficult for the virus to take hold.

~ **Reducing arthritis risk.** The Iowa Women's Health Study looked at nearly 30,000 women and found that women who took zinc supplements had a lower risk of developing rheumatoid arthritis, an autoimmune condition.

~ **Improving fertility in men.** The mineral boosts levels of testosterone, increases sperm count, and gives sperm a little extra oomph. Zinc may also boost a sagging libido. In fact, it may be the reason why oysters, which are extremely rich in zinc, are traditionally said to be an aphrodisiac

Using Zinc Safely

While getting too little zinc is a bad idea, so is getting too much. Taking 100 milligrams or more daily can actually lower your immunity. Taking take more than 30 milligrams daily may raise your levels of "bad" LDL cholesterol and lower your levels of "good" HDL cholesterol, increasing your risk of heart disease. Zinc supplements can interfere with copper absorption. If you're taking them, your doctor will probably advise taking copper as well. The recommended ratio is 1 milligram of copper for every 10 milligrams of zinc. Since zinc supplements may cause stomach upset, it's advisable to take them with food.

Cautions and Side Effects

Supplements are helpful for scores of health problems, but just as with drugs, you need to use care when taking them. Yes, even herbs and other harmless-seeming substances can have unwanted side effects if you use them inappropriately. Before you take an herb or a supplement recommended in this book, check the information below to learn about cautions to keep in mind. If you experience any side effects while taking a supplement, stop taking it and contact your doctor right away.

ACIDOPHILUS May increase gassiness. Amounts exceeding 10 billion viable organisms daily may cause mild intestinal problems. If taking antibiotics, wait at least two hours before taking a supplement.

ANISE Do not take anise during pregnancy.

ARGININE Take only under the guidance of a knowledgeable medical doctor. High doses may cause nausea and diarrhea. Do not take if you have genital herpes. Long-term effects are unknown. Do not take arginine and lysine at the same time. Take amino acid supplements at least 1½ hours before or after meals.

ARNICA Do not apply to broken or bleeding skin. Not to be used during pregnancy. Can cause an allergic rash in sensitive people or with prolonged use.

ASTRAGALUS Not recommended if a health condition is causing fever or swelling.

B COMPLEX Do not exceed the dosage recommended on the label.

BETA-CAROTENE Avoid single supplements in excess of 25 milligrams daily. Larger amounts have no benefit, and may cause harm. Avoid if you have hypothyroidism; your body may not be able to convert beta-carotene to vitamin A.

BLACK COHOSH Not to be taken by pregnant or nursing women. If you're taking estrogen therapy, consult a doctor before taking. Do not use for more than 6 months. Do not take if you have heart disease or you're on medication for high blood pressure. May cause diarrhea, abdominal pain, headache, lowered heart rate, and elevated blood pressure. Large doses may cause headache, nausea, impaired vision, and impaired circulation.

BROMELAIN May cause nausea, vomiting, diarrhea, skin rash, and heavy menstrual bleeding. May increase the risk of bleeding in people taking aspirin or blood thinners. Do not take bromelain if you are allergic to pineapple.

CALCIUM Do not exceed 2,500 milligrams daily except under a doctor's supervision. Some natural sources of calcium, such as oyster shells, bone meal, and dolomite, may be contaminated with lead; check to make sure it comes from "refined" or "purified" sources. High doses may cause constipation. If you have had calcium oxalate kidney stones, check with your doctor before taking.

CARNITINE Take the "L" form only (L-carnitine), and only with consent of a health-care professional. The "D" form may displace the active form of carnitine in tissues and lead to muscle weakness. Doses above 2 grams may cause mild diarrhea. Use of individual amino acids in Canada is strictly regulated. Mixtures are allowed but these do not contain enough of any single amino acid to take advantage of its therapeutic potential. Certain amino acids can be dispensed by a pharmacist behind the counter without a prescription. All are available from reputable U.S. Internet vendors.

CASCARA Don't take if you're pregnant or in a weakened condition. Do not take for more than 8 days, except with a doctor's guidance. Do not use if you have intestinal inflammation, intestinal obstruction, or abdominal pain, as it may cause laxative dependency and diarrhea.

CASTOR OIL Do not use internally if you have intestinal obstruction or abdominal pain. Do not use for more than 8 days. Not to be used during pregnancy.

CATNIP Not to be used during pregnancy.

CAT'S CLAW Do not use if you have hemophilia or are pregnant. Side effects may include headache, stomachache, or difficulty breathing. This herb also has contraceptive properties.

CELERY SEED Not to be used during pregnancy. Use with caution if you have a kidney disorder. Avoid overexposure to direct sunlight when using this herb: It may make your skin more sensitive.

CHAMOMILE Taken internally, this herb can cause severe allergic reactions. Drink the tea with caution, especially if you are allergic to closely related plants, such as aster and chrysanthemum. Chamomile contains coumarin, an anticoagulant. Use with caution if you have blood-clotting disorders or take anticoagulant medications.

CHASTEBERRY May counteract the effectiveness of birth-control pills. May contain licorice or Siberian ginseng, which can elevate blood pressure. Read product labels carefully if you have high blood pressure.

CINNAMON Do not take large amounts during pregnancy.

COENZYME Q$_{10}$ Get medical advice if you take this supplement for more than 20 days at daily doses exceeding 120 milligrams. Rare side effects may include heartburn, nausea, and stomachache. (These can be prevented by taking the supplement with a meal.) May decrease the effectiveness of the blood-thinning medication warfarin (Coumadin).

COPPER Do not exceed 2 milligrams daily on a regular basis. The recommended form is copper sulfate, since copper oxide (cupric oxide) is not absorbed by the body.

CURCUMIN May cause heartburn in some people.

DANDELION Use with caution if you have gastric acidity, digestive ulcers, gallstones, blockage of the bile ducts, acute gallbladder inflammation, or intestinal blockage. If you have gallbladder disease, do not use root preparations. Do not use as a diet aid.

DEGLYCYRRHIZINATED LICORICE (DGL) Not to be used during pregnancy. If you have high blood pressure, be sure to take only the DGL form of licorice, never straight licorice. Use caution if you have high blood pressure; heart rhythm abnormalities; cardiovascular, liver or kidney disorders; or low potassium levels. Do not use DGL more than three times a week for more than 4 to 6 weeks. Overuse may lead to water retention, high blood pressure due to potassium loss, or impaired heart and kidney function. Do not take with blood pressure, diuretic, corticosteroid, antiarrhythmic, or antihistamine medications.

DIGESTIVE ENZYMES Alpha-galactosidase supplements alter the way you process sugar: Don't use without a doctor's consent if you have diabetes. Do not use if you have galactosemia, a rare condition that causes an adverse reaction to all foods containing the sugar galactose. Do not take if you are sensitive to mold or penicillin. (Digestive enzyme supplements are often made from a type of mold.)

ECHINACEA Should not be taken if you have a chronic immune or autoimmune disease such as tuberculosis, lupus, multiple sclerosis, or rheumatoid arthritis. Avoid using in conjunction with drugs that are toxic to the liver, such as anabolic steroids, amiodarone, methotrexate, and ketoconazole, as it may worsen liver damage. Do not take echinacea if you are allergic to closely related plants, such as ragweed, asters, chrysanthemums, chamomile, and marigold. Do not use for more than 8 weeks.

ELDER, ELDERBERRY Seeds, bark, leaves, and unripe fruit may cause vomiting or severe diarrhea.

FALSE UNICORN Not to be used during pregnancy. Do not take if you are emaciated or experiencing acute inflammation. May cause gastrointestinal irritation.

FENNEL Do not use medicinally for more than 6 weeks.

FENUGREEK Not to be used during pregnancy.

FISH OIL Do not take more than 6,000 milligrams of fish oil a day, since too much can interfere with normal blood clotting. If you are taking blood thinners, such as Coumadin or heparin, or you take aspirin regularly, do not take fish-oil supplements unless advised by your physician. Not to be taken if you have a bleeding disorder, uncontrolled high blood pressure, or an allergy to any kind of fish. If you have diabetes, check with your doctor before taking fish oil because of its high fat content. Fish oil increases bleeding time, possibly resulting in nosebleeds and easy bruising, and may cause upset stomach. Don't take cod-liver oil; it is high in vitamins A and D, which can be toxic in high amounts.

FLAXSEED Do not use if you have bowel obstruction or thyroid problems. Always take with water. May decrease the absorption of medications. Heating or cooking flaxseed oil will destroy the omega-3 fatty acids in it and also cause the formation of harmful free radical oxidants. Best if taken with a meal that contains some fat.

FOLIC ACID Do not take doses above 1,000 micrograms a day without medical supervision. Excess folic acid can cause progressive nerve damage if you have a vitamin B$_{12}$ deficiency. Levels exceeding 400 micrograms can mask vitamin B$_{12}$ deficiencies.

GAMMA LINOLENIC ACID (GLA) Do not use supplements without the supervision of a physician if you are taking aspirin or anticoagulants (blood thinners) regularly, have a seizure disorder, or are taking epilepsy medication such as phenothiazines. Do not take borage oil (containing GLA) if you are pregnant or nursing. May cause headaches, indigestion, nausea, and softening of stools.

GINGER If you have gallstones, do not use the dried root or powder, which may increase bile secretion. Do not use if you are pregnant.

GINKGO BILOBA Rarely, gingko may cause headache, stomachache, or other allergic reactions, as well as restlessness or irritability (these side effects usually subside). Do not use with antidepressant MAO inhibitor drugs such as phenelzine sulfate (Nardil) or tranylcypromine (Parnate); aspirin or other non-steroidal anti-inflammatory medications; or blood-thinning medications such as warfarin (Coumadin). May cause rash, diarrhea, and vomiting in doses exceeding 240 milligrams of concentrated extract.

GINSENG If you have a heart condition, high blood pressure, or an anxiety disorder, consult your doctor before taking ginseng. May cause insomnia, nervousness, diarrhea, headaches, and high blood pressure. Has been reported to cause menstrual bleeding in post-menopausal women. Korean, Chinese or American ginseng should not be used if you have acute illness, fever, or swelling. Don't take Siberian ginseng if you have high blood pressure or high fever. Do not take a ginseng product combined with another herbal stimulant, particularly ma huang (ephedra). When taking ginseng, restrict your intake of caffeinated beverages.

GLUCOSAMINE Glucosamine may cause nausea or heartburn. This can usually be alleviated by taking it with meals.

GLUTAMINE Do not take if you have end-stage liver failure or kidney failure.

GOLDENSEAL Should not be used for more than one week because it decreases the absorption of vitamin B_{12}, thereby leading to deficiency. Do not take if you are pregnant or have high blood pressure, hypoglycemia (low blood sugar), or weak digestion. Do not use if you have an autoimmune disease such as multiple sclerosis or lupus, or if you are allergic to plants in the daisy family such as chamomile and marigold.

GOTU KOLA Do not take if you are pregnant or nursing. Do not use with medications for diabetes or high blood pressure. Talk to your doctor if you are thinking of taking it for an extended period of time. Rarely, may cause rash or headache.

5-HYDROXYTRYPTOPHAN (5-HTP) Pregnant women should not take 5-HTP. It is experimental, and supplements are also reported to cause gastrointestinal distress, muscle pain, lethargy, and headaches. Some brands contain a contaminant called peak X, which may cause serious symptoms associated with eosinophilic myalgia syndrome (EMS). In Canada, 5-HTP is a drug, and it has not been approved for sale, though Canadians may import it into the country for personal use (defined as a 3-month supply).

HAWTHORN If you have a cardiovascular condition, do not take regularly for more than a few weeks. Do not use if you have low blood pressure caused by heart valve problems. For long-term use, consult with a doctor, as it may cause problems at very high doses.

HOPS Do not take if prone to depression. Handle fresh or dried hops carefully, as they occasionally cause skin rashes.

HOREHOUND Not to be used during pregnancy.

HORSE CHESTNUT May interfere with the action of other drugs, especially blood-thinning medications such as warfarin (Coumadin). May irritate the gastrointestinal tract.

HORSERADISH Not to be taken if you have intestinal inflammation or kidney disorder. Not to be used by children under four years old.

LYSINE Experimental, and long-term effects are unknown. Use only under the supervision of a knowledgeable medical doctor. Do not take lysine and arginine at the same time, as they may cancel each other out.

MAGNESIUM Do not take if you have heart disease, arrhythmia, impaired kidney function, high blood pressure, or migraine headaches, or if you are taking diuretics. May cause diarrhea. Do not take doses exceeding 350 milligrams a day.

MANGANESE Do not exceed 10 milligrams daily.

MARSHMALLOW May slow the absorption of medications taken at the same time.

N-ACETYLCYSTEINE (NAC) Do not use if you have peptic ulcers or use drugs known to cause gastric lesions.

NETTLE Not to be taken during pregnancy Some people might experience mild stomach upset or a skin reaction.

PAPAYA ENZYMES May influence blood sugar levels. Do not use if you have diabetes.

PARSLEY Do not use large amounts (several cups a day) if you have kidney disease; it may increase urine flow. Not to be used during pregnancy.

PEPPERMINT May relax the muscle at the lower end of the esophagus, increasing the likelihood of heartburn. Use the herb cautiously if you are prone to acid reflux.

POTASSIUM Do not get more than 5,000 milligrams a day from food and supplements. Large doses of supplements are available only by prescription. Excessive potassium can upset the balance of other minerals in the body and cause potentially fatal heart and kidney problems.

PROBIOTICS May increase gassiness or bloating at first, which is a sign that the good bacteria are fermenting. Within a week or two, your body will adjust to the change.

PSYLLIUM Talk to your doctor before taking this fiber supplement, especially if you have difficulty swallowing or have serious intestinal disorders such as diverticulitis, ulcerative colitis, Crohn's disease, bowel obstruction, or if you are taking insulin (for diabetes) or any other medications. Psyllium should always be taken with water. May cause bloating or constipation.

PYGEUM AFRICANUM Consult your doctor if you're using this supplement to treat an enlarged prostate.

ROSEMARY May cause excessive menstrual bleeding in large amounts. Not to be taken during pregnancy.

S-ADENOSYL-L-METHIONE (SAM-E) May increase blood levels of homocysteine, a significant risk factor for cardiovascular disease.

ST. JOHN'S WORT May take several weeks to become effective. Can cause skin to be light-sensitive. Be sure to wear sunscreen and avoid spending extended time in direct sunlight. Do not use when pregnant. Avoid taking with alcohol, with over-the-counter cold medications, or with prescribed antidepressants. May cause high blood pressure when taken with ephedra compounds. Do not attempt to use this herb as a treatment for clinical depression. Serious depression requires proper medical care.

SAW PALMETTO If you have prostate problems, see your doctor for a diagnosis before using this supplement. Rare cases of stomach problems have been recorded.

SELENIUM Don't take more than 200 micrograms daily. Higher doses may cause fragile, thickened nails; stomach pain; diarrhea; nausea; a garlic odor on the breath and skin; a metallic taste in the mouth; a loss of sensation in the hands and feet; fatigue; and irritability. Doses of about 800 micrograms have been known to cause tissue damage. Works best with vitamin E.

SENNA Don't use for more than 8 to 10 days. Take 1 hour after other drugs, and always with water. Not to be taken during pregnancy. Do not use if you have abdominal pain, diarrhea, hemorrhoids, intestinal obstruction, or any inflammatory condition of the intestines. Not to be used by children younger than 12. Discontinue use if you have diarrhea or watery stools.

TAURINE May increase stomach acid. Do not take if you have diabetes.

VALERIAN Do not use with prescription medications such as diazepam or amitriptyline (Elavil). Valerian should not be combined with alcoholic beverages. May intensify the effects of sleep-enhancing or mood-regulating medications. Discontinue valerian if you experience heart palpitations or nervousness, excitability, headaches, or insomnia.

VITAMIN A Do not exceed 10,000 IU per day. Possible side effects include weight loss, skin problems, bone pain, bleeding, vomiting, diarrhea, fatigue, dizziness, blurred vision, hair loss, joint pain, and enlargement of the liver and spleen. Do not take more than 5,000 IU if you are pregnant or trying to conceive.

VITAMIN B$_6$ Do not take more than 100 milligrams per day. Too much B$_6$ can cause (reversible) nerve damage. Possible side effects include a tingling sensation in the fingers and toes, pain, numbness, and weakness in the limbs, depression, and fatigue.

VITAMIN C Daily doses exceeding 1,000 milligrams may cause diarrhea. Pregnant women should never take more than 5,000 milligrams of vitamin C per day. If you have chronic renal failure or are on hemodialysis, consult a healthcare practitioner before supplementing with vitamin C. Always cut back to 100 milligrams daily at least

3 days before a medical exam, as high amounts can interfere with some tests, particularly for blood in the stool and sugar in the urine. Large doses may also interfere with anticoagulant medications. Supplements made from a corn base may cause a reaction in people allergic to corn.

VITAMIN E The vitamin acts as a blood thinner. Consult your doctor before beginning supplementation in any amount if you're already taking aspirin or a blood-thinning medication such as warfarin (Coumadin). Use only with medical supervision if you are also taking ginkgo or fish-oil supplements; if you take aspirin regularly to help prevent heart disease; if you have high blood pressure, heart disease, or cancer; if you smoke; if you have had a stroke; or if you are at high risk for stroke. Although vitamin E is commonly sold in doses of 400 IU, one small study showed a possible increase in stroke risk in doses over 200 IU. Daily doses of more than 400 IU may cause headache, nausea, diarrhea, and fainting.

WILLOW BARK Do not use if you are allergic to aspirin or if you are taking a blood-thinning medication such as warfarin (Coumadin). May trigger asthma or allergies or cause gastrointestinal bleeding, liver dysfunction, blood-clotting disorders, kidney damage, or anaphylactic reactions. Willow bark may interact with barbiturates or sedatives such as aprobarbital or alprazolam, and it can cause stomach irritation when consumed with alcohol.

YARROW Rarely, handling flowers can cause a skin rash. Do not use during pregnancy.

ZINC Do not exceed 30 milligrams daily. Zinc may interfere with copper absorption. Possible side effects include suppression of the immune system, with increased susceptibility to infections. Daily doses of more than 30 milligrams may cause nausea and vomiting.

Index

Lice, 199-200, 419-20
Licorice, 19
    for canker sores, 105
    cautions and side effects, 435
    for cough, 141
    for eczema, 172
    for heartburn, 206
    for indigestion, 236-37, 237
    for inflammatory bowel
        disease, 245
    for jock itch, 261
    for ulcers, 364
Lipoic acid, for bronchitis, 91-92
Lips, chapped, 114-15
Lovage, for urinary tract infection,
    368
Lupus, 416
Lycopene, for prostate
    enlargement, 20-21, 311-12
Lyme disease, 322
Lysine
    for canker sores, 106
    cautions and side effects, 436
    for cold sores, 120, 122
    for shingles, 330

M

Maca, for impotence, 229-30
Magnesium
    for arthritis, 45
    for asthma, 51
    for carpal tunnel syndrome,
        112
    cautions and side effects, 436
    for depression, 149-50
    for fatigue, 180
    for high blood pressure, 221
    for kidney stones, 264
    for menstrual problems, 277
    for migraine, 203
    for muscle cramps, 282
    for palpitations, 300-301
    for premenstrual syndrome,
        310
    for restless legs syndrome, 319
    for teeth grinding, 354
    for temporomandibular joint
        dysfunction, 358-59
Mag phos, for menstrual problems,
    275

Manganese
    for bursitis and tendinitis, 100
    cautions and side effects, 436
Mango, for oily skin, 299
Marigold, for hemorrhoids, 213
Marshmallow
    cautions and side effects, 436
    for cough, 131
    for heartburn, 205-6
    for inflammatory bowel
        disease, 245
    for sore throat, 341
Mayonnaise
    for dry hair, 158
    for head lice, 199
Meat tenderizer, for insect stings,
    250
Meditation, 25-26
    for high blood pressure, 220
Melissa, for cold sores, 120
Memory problems, 268-71, 415-16
Menopause problems, 272-74, 339
Menstrual problems, 275-77,
    309-10, 377-78, 402, 416
Menthol
    for cough, 141
    for insect bites, 252
Methyl salicylate, for back pain, 60
Migraine, 203, 401
Milk
    for anxiety, 42
    for dry skin, 163
    for insomnia, 254
    for poison ivy, 304
    for sunburn, 350
    for wrinkles, 379
Milk thistle, for menopause
    problems, 273
Mind-body connection, 25-26
Mineral oil, for earwax, 169
Mold allergies, 37, 208
Morning sickness, 278-80
Mosquito bites, 252-53
Motion sickness, 288, 400-401
Mud mask, for oily skin, 298
Mullein
    for bronchitis, 91
    for laryngitis, 266
Muscle cramps, 281-83, 396
Mustard, 412-13
    for arthritis, 413

    for back pain, 61, 413
    for colds and flu, 127, 412
    for cough, 141-42
    for fever, 183, 413
    for headache, 413
    for Raynaud's disease, 412
Myrrh
    for cold sores, 121
    for cuts and scrapes, 143
    for laryngitis, 109
    for toothache, 360-61

N

N-acetylcysteine (NAC)
    for bronchitis, 91
    cautions and side effects, 436
    for colds and flu, 124
    for inflammatory bowel
        disease, 244
Nail problems, 248-49, 284-85
Nausea, 286-87, 339, 400-401, 417
    in pregnancy, 278-80
Neck pain, 290-92
Neck stiffness, 127
Neroli essential oil, for oily skin,
    298
Neti pot, 331-32
Nettle, 339
    for allergies, 34
    for brittle nails, 285
    cautions and side effects, 436
    for gout, 193
    for prostate enlargement, 311,
        339
    for snoring, 336
    for urinary tract infection, 368
    for water retention, 377
Niacin, for high cholesterol, 224
Nipple soreness, 88-89
Nontoxic cleaners, 208-9
Nori, 76, 77
Nosebleed, 293-94, 420
Nursing problems, 86-89
Nutmeg, for acne, 31
Nutritional supplements, 20-22
Nuts
    for heartburn, 307
    omega-3 fatty acids in. *See*
        Omega-3 fatty acids